7304:
INTERNATIONAL RELATIONS ON THE PLANET EARTH

7304: INTERNATIONAL RELATIONS ON THE PLANET EARTH

Finlay, David J.

DAVID J. FINLAY & THOMAS HOVET, JR.

UNIVERSITY OF OREGON ◪ HARPER & ROW. PUBLISHERS. NEW YORK. EVANSTON. SAN FRANCISCO. LONDON

To Belva and Erica

Picture credits: Moon, NASA; p. 1, WHO; p. 13, From the MGM release *2001: A Space Odyssey* © 1968 Metro-Goldwyn-Mayer Inc.; p. 59, Wide World; p. 97, Gerry Cranham, Rapho Guillumette; p. 155, NASA; p. 207, UN; p. 267, UN; p. 323, Exxon; p. 347, Lester Bergman & Associates.

Sponsoring Editor: Ronald K. Taylor
Project Editor: H. Detgen
Designer: Michel Craig
Production Supervisor: Bernice L. Krawczyk
Picture Editor: Myra Schachne

7304: International Relations on the Planet Earth

Library of Congress Cataloging in Publication Data
Finlay, David J
    7304, international relations on the planet Earth.

    Includes index.
    1. International relations. I. Hovet, Thomas, joint author. II. Title.
JX1395.F48   327   74-14107
ISBN 0-06-042067-7

Contents

Preface

A "loving fear," Gunder Anders has written, is "not fear of the danger ahead but for generations to come." This spirit underlies our assessment of international relations—the panorama of interrelated transactions among governments, organizations, and individuals across national boundaries, which continually determine the future shape and form of life on the planet earth. The future, we believe, is a sacred trust held by present generations.

The only known future is uncertainty, despite expectations of catastrophe or beliefs that events to come will vary only in degree from past continuities and discontinuities. Yet the future is not an abstract concept. It is assuredly determined by the recognized and unrecognized implications of the decisions and actions of governments, organizations, and individuals in their separate but inclusive international relations. Each day in a multitude of ways we make decisions that contribute to the construction of the future. But are they choices that will build a world environment people want? Or are they "good" by some other standard?

We believe that the study of international relations should be concerned with the multiplicity of choices and decision-options that governments and individuals face in interrelated national and international problems. At the very least, we should become clear about which futures we do not want, for example, extinction as a species through nuclear radiation or starvation. Beyond that process of elimination, however, we must begin to design preferable futures. Present generations must ask what prescriptive measures are necessary now if mankind is to meet current, basic needs and thrust forward toward a fuller and richer life than past generations have known. The past may be rich and instructive, but preoccupation with history can obscure the task of constructing the future.

We do not have absolute answers to questions such as: Where are we now? How are we relating on a shrinking planet? What alternatives for the future are currently being proposed? What is the status of international relations now, and how will it affect the future? What might be the state of international relations twenty years (7304 days) from now? We focus on these and other unanswered questions not with solutions or prescriptions but with an underlying faith that life with freedom and dignity can prevail. Grounding in reality is our first task as persons and students. Whether we will be able to create beyond that reality still remains questionable, but it is crucial if we are to civilize politics on the planet earth.

We would like to extend our appreciation to Earl L. Backman, Yassin El-Ayouty, John Miller, John R. Raser, Douglas W. Simon, and Vickie Slover for their advice and/or assistance at various stages in the development of the manuscript. We would also like to acknowledge the many students in our international relations classes at the University of Oregon who provided stimulus for the concepts in this study.

D.F.
T.H.

INTRODUCTION: GLOBAL IMPERATIVES

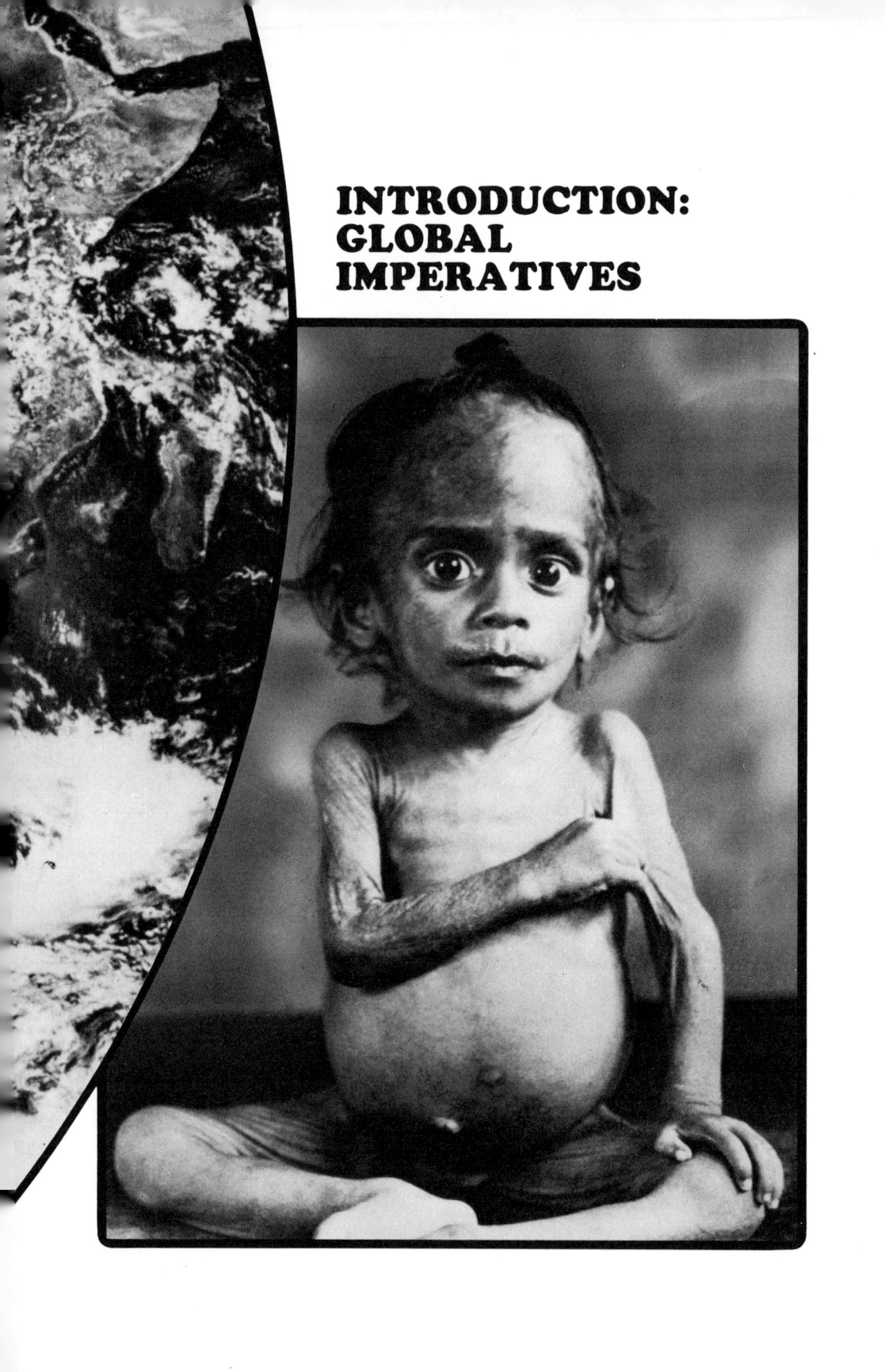

I do not wish to seem overdramatic, but I can only
conclude from the information that is available
to me as Secretary General that members of the
United Nations have perhaps ten years left in which
to subordinate their ancient quarrels and launch a
global partnership to curb the arms race, to improve
the human environment, to defuse the population
explosion, and to supply the required momentum to
world development efforts. If such a global partnership is not forged within the next decade, then I
very much fear that the problems I have mentioned
will have reached such staggering proportions that
they will be beyond our capacity to control.

U Thant
July 1969

This book concerns our global future. In this century no individual, group, or nation on earth lives in isolation. Today there are 4.0 billion people on this planet, 138 member states in the United Nations, some 45 other states and dependent territories, over 2000 public and private international organizations, multinational corporations of gigantic proportions, and hundreds of thousands of group and individual transnational activities. The world-encompassing web of twentieth-century politics, economics, communications, and science and technology weaves each of these entities in a collective destiny. Our purpose in writing this book is to illustrate as clearly and dramatically as we can the interrelatedness of the world's most troublesome problems. The welfare of all peoples and the prospects for world peace, stability, and development are all tied to our recognition and fulfillment of global interdependence. Indeed, we believe that *unless* we quickly acquire a global perspective and construct international means for finding solutions to war, environmental destruction, population increase, and other world problems, we shall be overwhelmed by their consequences and become powerless to deal with them.

We maintain that whatever the psychological, scientific, or ideological

interpretations in which they are clothed, there are certain undeniable realities in our national and international environments that impinge upon and threaten our lives and our futures. At the core of our present difficulties is the failure of national and international bodies, in the face of such realities, to replace obsolete and counterproductive notions of national isolation, antagonism, and competition with more appropriate concepts of interdependence, mutual assistance, and cooperation.

QUANTITATIVE REALITIES

One global reality is militarism or aggressive preparedness. The current amount of nuclear warhead tonnage in the world is approximately 50,000 megatons, which is equivalent to 15 to 20 tons of dynamite for every person on earth and about 60 tons per person in the North Atlantic Treaty Organization and Warsaw Pact nations taken together. In 1972 the United States had approximately 2.3 million men in its armed forces, and annual military expenditures per man were over $25,000. Approximately 556,000 military personnel were stationed overseas in 192 major and 1,221 minor military installations in over 30 countries. The United States and the Soviet Union currently have operational about 2,672 intercontinental ballistic missiles and 1,300 submarine launched ballistic missiles, increasingly deployed with multiple, independently targeted re-entry vehicles (MIRV). With the new MIRV warheads the United States strategic missiles and heavy bombers will carry 5,900 warheads; the Soviet missiles and heavy bombers an estimated 2,200 warheads. Militarism, of course, has not been promoted by the superpowers alone. Military budgets have first claim on government resources in most countries, generally overshadowing civilian programs such as health and education. Of some 93 developing nations almost one-half have more than doubled their military expenditures since 1961.

Another reality is world-wide destruction of our natural environment. In the United States alone environmental pollutants each year include the production of 200 million tons of waste products released into the air, 7 million junked automobiles, 20 million tons of waste paper, 48,000 million discarded cans, 26,000 million used bottles and jars, 3,000 million tons of waste rock and mill trailings, and 50 trillion gallons of hot water. The world has lost an estimated 500 million hectares of arable land through erosion and salinization, and two-thirds of the world's forest area has been lost to production. One hundred fifty species of birds and animals have become extinct through human agency.

The population explosion is another fact of our existence. A population

growth of just 1 percent—the average is 1.9 percent—would double the world's population in just sixty-nine years. If by the year 2000 the developed countries reach the point at which their populations merely replace themselves and if developing countries reach the same rate of population growth by 2050, the world's present population of 4.0 billion would not become stationary before the year 2150, and it would stand at 15 billion.[1] As of 1970 some 48 governments—such as those in Brazil and Paraguay, where the populations are expected to double in twenty-five and twenty-one years respectively—had no population planning policy and provided no assistance to family planning programs.

Another fact is hunger. The Food and Agriculture Organization (FAO) of the United Nations estimates that at least one-third to one-half of the world's population suffers from hunger or nutritional deprivation. The average person in a high-standard area consumes four pounds of food a day, as compared with an average pound and one-quarter in a low-standard area.

Still another reality is the economic disparities among and within nations. In India 12 percent of the rural families control more than half the cultivated land. In Brazil less than 10 percent of the families control 75 percent of the land. Between 1960 and 1970 the per capita gross national product (GNP) of developed countries increased from $1382 to $2701, while that in developing countries rose from $118 to $208. The external public debt of developing countries has increased fivefold since the mid-1950s, and debt service payments have grown at a rate of 14 percent annually, while foreign exchange receipts from exports have risen only 6 percent a year.

The expansion of technology and science is another reality. For example, estimates suggest that all of the information in the world's libraries amounts to 10^{15} bits and doubles every fifteen to twenty years. Advanced computers currently have a memory capacity of 10^{12} and are being improved each year. A unique computer memory that will make it possible for a million bits of data to be written, stored, read out repeatedly, or erased by laser light is being built for the National Aeronautics and Space Administration (NASA). The experimental, telescope-shaped device could be the forerunner of a whole new series of mass memories that are equal in storage to the largest disc memory systems now in use but 1000 times faster. Likewise a small crystal that stores hologram images as atomic patterns to be read out one by one by slow rotation in a laser beam, like photographic slides in a projector, has been developed. This advance may lead to a storage system in which files of statistics, architectural drawings, computer data, photos, maps, and other graphic materials could be stored permanently in crystals the size of sugar cubes. Theoretically, as many as a trillion bits of information could be stored in each crystal. It appears certain that by means of such devices the world's knowledge will soon be at our command.

QUALITATIVE REALITIES

Other realities, which are qualitative rather than quantitative conditions of our existence, include nationalism, chauvinism, ethnocentrism, racism—and above all, *national self-interest*. At best, self-interest may bring security and prosperity to a nation; at worst, it represents a psychotic attachment to views that have no relation to the world situation. All these realities may be explained differently by competing ideologies, but they cannot be explained away.

Having acknowledged these realities, we must also appreciate their interrelatedness. For example, industrial technology has produced environmental deterioration. Racial antagonisms are closely associated with disparities in wealth and resources. And the total world expenditure of over $200 billion each year for armaments and military establishments uses up resources that could be spent, among other things, on programs to save our environment, increase food supplies and distribution, and attack the diseases and pestilence in much of the world.

World problems are also related in another important way. They are truly *world* problems. The fallout from past atomic testing is measured all over the earth's surface, not merely within the national boundaries of perpetrators of these tests. Pollution of seas and sky also ignores governmental and national boundaries. Famine in India is ultimately related to uncertainties in the world supply of food. Simple arithmetic suggests that if world food production maintains its present relative position vis-à-vis population growth, the numbers of people suffering from nutritional deprivation and hunger will double by the end of this century, thus further widening the gap and increasing the bitterness between the "haves" and the "have-nots."

PROSPECTS FOR THE FUTURE

To deal constructively with world problems a global strategy is necessary. Such a strategy must attempt the seemingly impossible: *to establish a sense of common cause among the vastly disparate and competing nations of the world.* It requires that nations move beyond self-interest defined in terms of power and concentrate on common interests defined in terms of realizing man's fullest potentialities. One example of a successful international attempt to apply a strategy of global cooperation to deal with common problems was the International Geophysical Year (I.G.Y.).

Between July 1, 1957, and December 31, 1959, the International Council of Scientific Unions (ICSU) coordinated an International Geophysical Year. Involving more than 70 nations, some 30,000 scientists and observers,

and more than 2,500 scientific stations, the purposes of the I.G.Y. were to coordinate a systematic, scientific study of the earth and her environments, to understand and control nature, and to gain insight into the cosmos. In addition to the study of space some 11 fields of geophysics, including glaciology and meteorology, received emphasis. From the beginning it was clear that such studies required a global perspective and approach and that all nations would gain from the newly acquired knowledge of the earth's physical properties. Among the many significant results of the I.G.Y. were: the creation of international weather maps, revised estimates (up 40 percent) of the amount of snow and ice on the earth's surface, the discovery of new ocean resources and of the Van Allen radiation belts in space. Other results were less dramatic, but no less important for future scientific cooperation. Data were exchanged, scientists in various nations working on similar problems were put in communication with one another, and permanent international scientific organizations were created under the auspices of the ICSU. Finally, I.G.Y. ended a political dispute over the status of the Antarctic. On December 1, 1959, 12 nations signed the Antarctic Treaty, which consecrated the polar region to peaceful, scientific uses. The treaty is the first instance in which a portion of the earth has been set aside for such purposes.

The I.G.Y. illustrates the tremendous benefits to be derived from international cooperation. On the other hand, international rivalries and antagonisms create untold misery as just one example, the military conflict in Southeast Asia, makes clear. In 1945 the communist leader Ho Chi Minh and his troops took control of Hanoi and declared the Democratic Republic of Vietnam independent from France, its former colonial master. Unwilling to accept Vietnamese independence, the French fought Ho Chi Minh until May 1954, when General Giap decisively defeated the French at Dien Bien Phu. The resulting peace settlement signed at Geneva, temporarily divided Vietnam into two areas, separated by a demilitarized zone, with Ho Chi Minh firmly established in the north. When the independent future of noncommunist South Vietnam was threatened by the incapacity of its rulers and the establishment in the south of the communist National Liberation Front (Vietcong), the United States sent additional military advisers to aid the South Vietnamese army. After several years of intermittent fighting between communist and noncommunist factions in South Vietnam, President Lyndon Johnson actively involved U.S. troops in the conflict in 1964, after the North Vietnamese allegedly attacked two American destroyers in the Gulf of Tonkin. At the peak of U.S. involvement 550,000 American troops were stationed in Vietnam. Although peace talks began in 1968, a cease-fire was not concluded until January 1973. By that time over 56,000 Americans were dead and more than 300,000 were wounded. South Vietnamese casualties were over 188,000 dead and 430,000 wounded. An estimated 920,000 North Vietnamese and Vietcong were killed. Between 1965 and 1973 the United States

spent at least $135 billion on the war. Vietnam itself was ravaged by more bombs than were dropped in World War II and the Korean War combined —some 15 million tons of explosives, or more than 500 pounds per acre and 1,333 pounds per Vietnamese.

The Vietnam War killed and maimed millions of people, left both North and South Vietnam in ruins, and tore at the political fabric of the United States. It accomplished very little. North and South Vietnam remained divided, their ideological differences unsettled. Southeast Asia remains in political turmoil.

Of course, international politics is not composed solely of the simple alternatives of cooperation exemplified by the I.G.Y. or lethal conflict as in Vietnam. The complexities of our twentieth-century world seldom result in such obvious or mutually exclusive choices. The tension between national interests and international necessities will not be easily resolved. Complex local conflicts, such as those between the Arabs and Israelis, the border disputes between the Soviet Union and the People's Republic of China (P.R.C.), between Ethiopia and Somalia, and wars of national liberation in Asia and Southern Africa are not easily resolved. Moreover, we face the prospect of a hostile division of the world into haves and have-nots if we do not mobilize our will and resources to cope with global problems of poverty, unemployment, hunger, and overcrowding. As the late Nobel Peace Prize holder, Lester Pearson warned, "a planet cannot, anymore than a country, survive half-slave, half-free, half-engulfed in misery, half-careening along toward the supposed joys of almost unlimited consumption."[2]

It requires energy and creativity to think about and plan for the future. It is far easier to concentrate on the past. Our ideas about the past are rich and complex, but many of our views of the future are meager and empty. Our difficulties are further compounded by the fact that we have few measures and even fewer standards to help us evaluate social change, to tell us whether we are improving the quality of life, or whether international tensions are deepening or easing. In his book *Future Shock* Alvin Toffler has suggested what seems to be a sensible way to begin imagining and shaping the future.

> *Every society faces not merely a succession of probable futures, but an array of possible futures, and a conflict over preferable futures. The management of change is the effort to convert certain possibles into probables, in pursuit of agreed on preferables. Determining the probable calls for a science of futurism. Delineating the possible calls for an art of futurism. Defining the preferable calls for a politics of futurism.*[3]

Such an approach requires efforts far beyond the scope of our current endeavors to deal with the future, which are generally wedded to the status quo and seem to fluctuate wildly between despair and optimism.

One pessimistic view of the future is presented by a group of scientists organized as the Club of Rome Project on the Predicament of Mankind.[4] According to their report, when economic development, population growth, pollution, resource depletion, and food production are correlated and projected, it appears likely that even the developed nations will experience a marked decline in their standards of living within the next three or four decades. A sixty-hour workweek will not prevent hunger in the most automated and industrialized countries their report warns. The possibility of such conditions coupled with the continual threat of nuclear accident or war deepen our despair, create anxiety and depression, and lower our interest in the future.

On the other hand, optimistic futurologists such as Burnham P. Beckwith contend that economic and social progress will continue.[5] He sees no reason why technology will fail to develop new and cheaper substitutes for nearly all scarce materials and believes we can radically reduce the demand for most scarce or irreplaceable minerals by redesigning consumer goods and changing social habits. We can, for example, standardize automobile and appliance designs so that they are built for permanence rather than obsolescence and can be repaired with easily replaceable parts. The revolution in food production will continue to grow according to the optimistic view; industry will stop polluting when it realizes how pollution threatens economic progress and profits, and all countries will encourage adequate birth control. Optimists are encouraged by their observation that man's belief in himself is growing stronger and his sense of guilt becoming archaic, thus diminishing his passive acceptance of suffering. Moreover, says the optimist, we are beginning to acquire a historical, global, and interstellar perspective. One spokesman for this point of view, F. M. Esfandiary, puts it this way:

> This is a beautiful moment in human evolution. It is the stage at which the human species has broken away from its confinement to this planet. . . . We are transcending our world, breaking the umbilical cord that had tied and confined us to a speck of space. . . . This extension into the universe is more than simply a scientific accomplishment or a physical fact. We are transcending basic conditions inherent in all organisms of this planet. We are reversing the most fundamental premises of human life, altering the very nature of nature, redefining concepts of evolution and our situation in the universe. No philosophy, theology, or ideology of the past touches on our new situation in the universe.[6]

Whatever the merits of optimistic or pessimistic scenarios, conceptualizing the *probable, possible,* and *preferable* is at the heart of gaining control

over the future. Adapting ourselves for the future requires that social thinking match and surpass scientific and technological knowledge. National policies might then better reflect ends and values based upon a realistic appreciation of our immediate and long-range human problems and needs.

Lack of direction severely compounds global dilemmas. Often we approach the future as if it were an accident, or we assume that it will take care of itself. The long-range consequences of such fatalism are appalling. For example, knowing the incredible longevity of radioactive particles, in 1958 the U.S. military blithely scattered radioactive plutonium over 250 square miles of Nevada during tests to make certain that the crash of a bomber would not trigger a nuclear explosion. Consequently, the entire area must now remain sealed off for the next 24,000 years.[7] What are future generations to think of us and the "security" achieved by such tests? Our limited perspective and ill-considered sense of the future are captured in former Secretary of State Dean Rusk's summation of a primary accomplishment of his tenure: Nuclear war did not destroy the world. This negative accomplishment is somewhat like gloating over the fact that only the other fellow's end of the ship is sinking. What *did* in fact happen in the years of Rusk's tenure is enough to give us pause.

Patchwork on the status quo, while better than nothing, will not halt the deterioration of world conditions. Our current haphazard approach to problems has only minimal effect. We have perfected our missile warning systems to alert us to danger within a mere ten to fifteen minutes, but we move at a snail's pace in dealing with other dangers just as real and, in the long run perhaps, even more imminent. Even if we were to act now—and we are not—it would still be years before American shellfish beds began to reach production levels of the 1930s, years before population growth leveled off, years before endangered species would recover, years before land could be reclaimed from the toxic substances put there by man. We simply cannot afford the time lapse that now occurs between our recognition of a problem and our doing something about it. In most cases the lag is not the result of scientific ignorance. The majority of our great social problems are political problems requiring political decisions. Only when the political issues have been confronted or resolved can the technical solutions be applied.

The future we would like to anticipate is a peaceful world. Peace is usually defined merely as the absence of war, but this is not the full meaning of the peace we hope to see. The condition traditionally called peace has been nothing more than the interludes between battles when the seeds of destructive conflict are merely dormant rather than active. Many believe "the condition thus seems unavoidable that war is an unalterable feature of human life, part of the very fabric of society, and that therefore hope of eliminating it is a pipe dream. After all, one cannot change human nature."[8] But

we do not believe human beings are nearly so rigid as this thought suggests or that the convertible energy of creative processes has been lost to modern man.

The peace we envision is a condition in which conflict and confrontation lead not to violence, but to renewal, actualization and creativity, trust, and mutual concern. Peace is a condition of reconciliation and compassion. Peace is caring for the human community. Such a peace depends upon our moral development. We must learn to evaluate what we do by the extent to which our actions support or improve a just and humane existence. Men and nations must change their outlook on the world from one that is too often narrow and chauvinistic to one that is universal and then translate this outlook into public policy and choice. To bring about such a revolution in consciousness and conscience is the most exacting problem of the future: It hits us squarely in the middle of our resistance to change and risk taking. If we can conceive a new moral imperative to apply at the world level—that same moral responsibility, that same sharing of wealth, that same standard of justice and compassion without which our most advanced societies would surely fall apart–then we will have made a beginning. Equity and justice are prerequisites for peace at any level of polity. If we want peace, it is not mere sentimentality to suggest:

> *No man will be free until all men have sufficient food, water, and shelter.*
> *No man will be free until all men are free from threat from the environment and from other men.*
> *No man will be free until all men organize their ways of living on the basis of mutual respect for one another and the willingness to settle conflicts through regularized and peaceful agencies.*
> *No man will be free until all men have the opportunity to realize their actual and potential selves.*

These assumptions about the prerequisites for peace and freedom lead directly to several basic imperatives for the international community. First, the armaments race and weapons game must be halted and national defense systems gradually lowered through reciprocal agreements. Second, the international community must set and work toward a morally acceptable standard of existence (e.g., daily caloric intake, literacy) and commit the necessary resources to bring about such conditions. Third, national economic priorities must be recalculated to include assistance to peoples and nations that do not enjoy the basic standards. Fourth, superordinate goals and means for resolving differences must be strengthened as a substitute for the traditional, exclusive goals and alliances of power politics.

While the initial motivation behind such steps might well be nothing more than a clear case of enlightened self-interest, we believe that such commitments would break down long-existing habits of distrust in international politics. Costs will be high, but there is little in the way of alternatives to such common action. If U Thant is correct, what *we* do in the next ten or (if we are luckier than he expects) twenty years (7304 days) will determine the quality of life, if not the continued existence of man, on earth.

In the chapters that follow we seek to highlight a few of what we consider the world's most pressing problems. We start with a brief review of past international politics and the intellectual difficulties of conceptualizing relations among nations. We then move to decision makers, the process of decision making, and the constraints upon future choices. We then look at the physical capacities and limitations of the ecosystem within which nations exist and at the problems posed by the disparities among nations in their ability to meet their essential needs. In the next chapter we consider how nations attempt to maintain maximum freedom of choice by military means. Lastly, we consider the ways in which nations attempt to relate to each other as they deal with economic problems, the environment, the proliferation of weapons, and collective decision making. We cannot provide answers to the many problems we pose, particularly the linking of ends and means. But we do hope to provide some understanding of the choices that will determine the future of international relations and our individual futures as well.

NOTES

[1] World Bank, *Address to the Board of Governors by Robert S. McNamara, President, World Bank Group,* Copenhagen: World Bank, 1970, p. 13.

[2] Quoted in *Ibid.,* p. 21.

[3] Alvin Toffler, *Future Shock,* London: Pan Books, 1970, p. 415. Used by permission of The Bodley Head and Random House, Inc.

[4] Donella H. Meadows, Dennis L. Meadows, Jorgen Randers, and William W. Behrema III, *The Limits of Growth,* New York: Universe Books, 1972.

[5] Burnham P. Beckwith, *The Next 500 Years,* Jericho, N.Y.: Exposition Press, 1968. Also his "The Predicament of Mankind? A Reply," *Futurist,* 6, no. 2 (April 1972), 62–66.

[6] F. M. Esfandiary, *Optimism One,* New York: Norton, 1970, p. 201.

[7] *Eugene Register-Guard,* August 20, 1970, p. 3A.

[8] Jerome D. Frank, *Sanity and Survival: Psychological Aspects of War and Peace,* New York: Vintage Books, 1967, pp. 36–37.

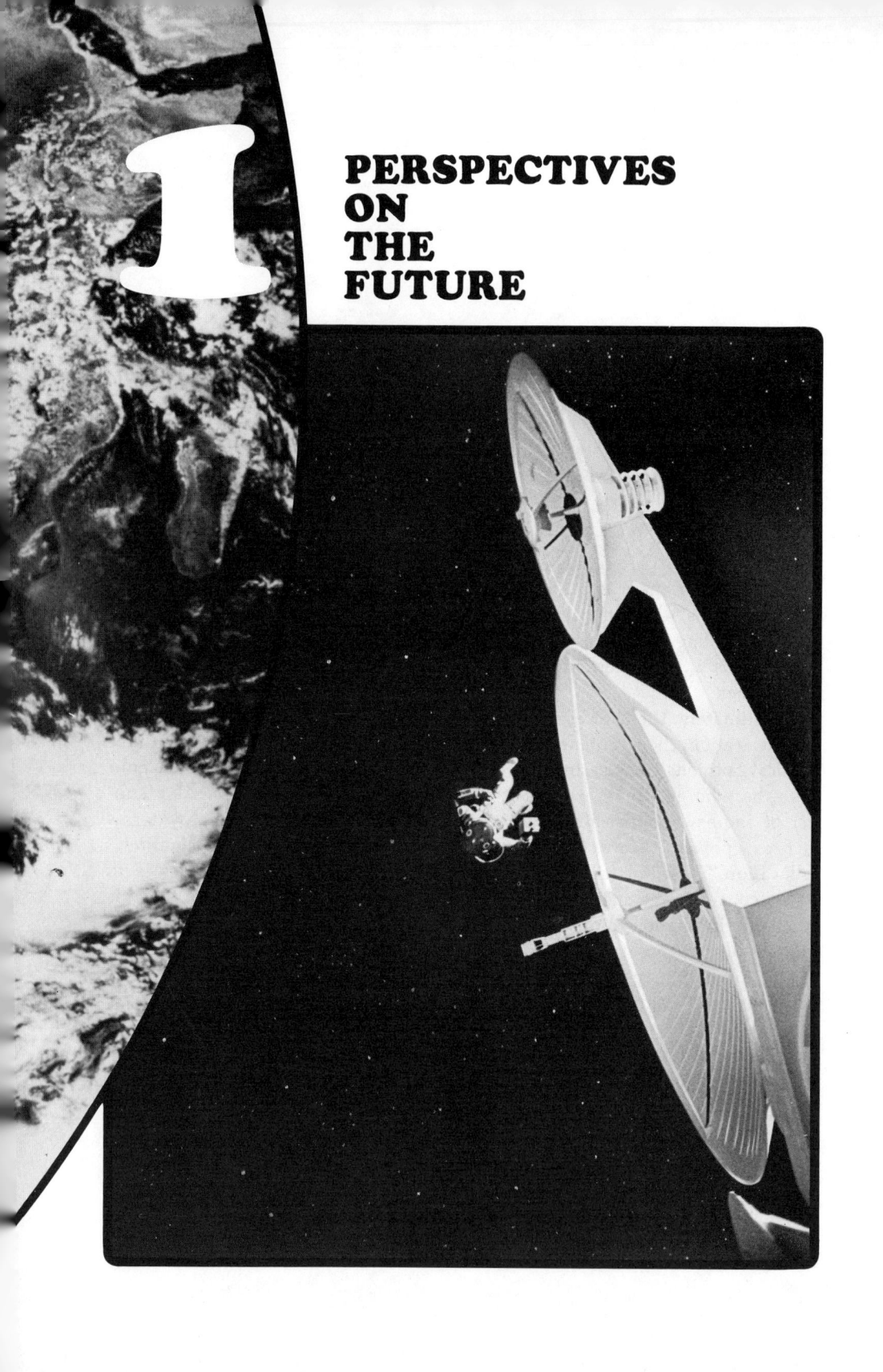

1 PERSPECTIVES ON THE FUTURE

Concern is being proclaimed for the heritage
of our past, yet at the same time we must stretch
our minds into the future. . . .

U Thant
1972

What will be the nature of the world and international relations 7304 days from today? One fact is certain—change is perhaps the only predictable element. And if there is a single, underlying purpose in analyzing international relations, it lies in attempting to understand the choices that have to be made in dealing with world change. The choices we make, consciously and unconsciously, will determine the future. The stakes for mankind have never been higher.

Ultimately, the choices we make about the future are *political* decisions, and ideas about their content vary according to whom you speak. We all have political opinions because in one way or another we are all involved in politics—the who gets what, the why, when, how, and where of life. As a subject of inquiry, politics has many definitions. Most of them employ terms such as "power," "force," "influence," "authority," "control," obligation," "allocation," and "distribution." One simple way of defining politics is to say it concerns the methods by which man, as a social being, orders his public life in relation to others. The art and science of governing and government involve purposeful activity around the formation, execution, and evaluation of public policy. According to such a definition, political behavior does not have strict boundaries by which analysts can state with certainty that a particular act is "political" whereas another is not.[1] Yet the definition would probably lead most of us to agree that while the decisions that determine the type and quantities of food produced and the means of distributing and purchasing food are at least partly political decisions, the simple act of eating generally is not political (although the decision to boycott certain foods or to refuse food altogether has been used as a political tactic).

International politics involves relations among collective entities called nation-states. Here again terminology is elusive. Legally, a *state* is considered a body of people occupying a definite territory and politically organized un-

der one government independent of other governments. Yet some years ago C. H. Titus counted 145 separate definitions of "state," indicating that although we all seem to know, more or less, what constitutes a state, the concept lacks one precise definition.[2] In the broadest sense, international *relations* are the entire panoply of contacts across national frontiers by governments, groups, and individuals. But most often the study of international politics (or relations) concentrates on the intercourse among *governments* as they work out their mutual and exclusive national interests. Although many analysts prefer to make sharp distinctions between international *politics* and international *relations*, we use the terms synonomously because of their imprecision and the increasingly blurred lines concerning what is or is not political or public and private.

All in all, the language of politics and political science is probably more literary than scientific, and this seems appropriate when we consider that, as fields of study, political science and international politics are concerned with questions and problems that for the most part do not have reliable, consensual, or absolute answers. What is the "good" life? What constitutes good government? What is the moral basis of authority? Why does man behave politically the way he does? Why do nation-states behave as they do? These are a few of the questions that concern students of politics, and scholars begin searching for possible answers in many different places.[3] Most believe that the proper starting point is the study of man himself. Heinz Eulau points out:

> Small units like the individual or the small group, and large units like the organization of the nation-states, can be treated not as polar but as continuous variables . . . all units small or large, should be subject to ordering on a single continuum . . . from whatever point on the macro-micro continuum one proceeds, the task of research is to build, by patiently linking one unit with another, the total chain of interrelations that link individual to individual, individual to group, group to group, group to organization, organization to organization, and so on, until one gives the entire network continuous order.[4]

Nevertheless, in this book we do not assume that international politics is simply interpersonal relations writ large. Nation-states are different from persons. The two entities have similarities, but they also have many important differences. Wars among nations may begin in the minds of individual men, but they are fought quite differently from personal feuds among emotionally aroused individuals, especially in an age of impersonal nuclear weapons. Students of international relations can learn a great deal from the study

of interpersonal behavior as an analog to international behavior, but we must keep the two types of interaction distinct.

Other scholars examine the past to discover regularities in the behavior of states as they interact with each other, then look for underlying cultural, economic, political, and social factors that explain this behavior. But unless we want simply to understand the past without considering the present and the future, we must not be content to dwell solely on the previous behavior of nation-states. It is essential to relate our historical knowledge to the current world if we wish to have a measure of control over our future.

INTERNATIONAL RELATIONS—
AN OVERVIEW OF THE PAST

"When several villages are united in a single community," Aristotle wrote some 2000 years ago, ". . . the state comes into existence, originating in the bare needs of life, and continuing in existence for the sake of the good life." Therefore "it is evident that the state is a creation of nature, and that man is by nature a political animal."[5] By such criteria we must conclude that interstate relations are as old as organized society. International relations were conducted in the ancient world of the Pharaohs as well as by the earliest dynasties of China. In Thucydides' *History of the Peloponnesian War*, written 400 years before the time of Christ, we have a monumental record of state relations between Athens and Sparta and an analysis of war that is still instructive. Thus an adequate review of past international relations would probably be a history of civilization itself.

THE WESTERN STATE SYSTEM
Although the scope of international relations encompasses the entire human community and its history, the modern international system has been dominated by European or Western politics. Indeed, many analysts tend to consider the Western state system as though it were synonymous with international relations as a whole, and therefore they tend to ignore the majority of mankind.

Modern European hegemony in international politics dates from the end of the Thirty Years' War and the Peace of Westphalia in 1648, when the division of Europe into fairly well-defined states was completed. The Protestant Reformation had a profound effect on European politics by abetting the separation of the political system from the Roman Catholic Church. Economic feudalism was replaced by mercantilism and the notion that the economic interests of the nation transcend individual or group interests. National political authority was presented as a social contract rather than as a conse-

quence of divine order, and nationalism, the doctrine of supreme loyalty to the state, grew stronger.

From 1648 to the beginning of the nineteenth century international politics in the West was characterized by shifting coalitions among European states. Weak states were either dominated by or in alliance with the dominant powers of Great Britain, Spain, France, Germany, and Austria. Up to the beginning of the Seven Years' War in 1756, no single state was capable of dominating Europe.[6] Under Napoleon France made such an attempt, but with his defeat the 1815 Congress of Vienna reestablished the balance among the European powers.

From 1815 until the outbreak of World War I in 1914, the international political system underwent several important changes. The creation of independent nations out of European colonies in North and South America and the expansion of European colonialism into Africa and Asia broadened the scope and increased the complexity of international affairs. Toward the latter part of the nineteenth century, pressures for national independence among colonial subjects erupted, this time in the Balkans, and new states were created in the Middle East as the Ottoman Empire crumbled. Also during this period the ancient Manchu Dynasty in China was fast disintegrating, and Japan was beginning to emerge from feudalism. The consequences of most of these developments, however, were not fully realized until the twentieth century.

World War I. Meanwhile, world politics continued to be dominated by rivalries among the major European nations, whose conflicting imperialistic ambitions in Africa and Asia and nationalistic dreams of increased power and security in Europe finally resulted in the creation of two hostile camps: Germany, Austria, and Italy formed the Triple Entente while England, France, and Russia combined in the Triple Alliance. Ultimately, the fervent nationalism of the Balkans provided the spark that ignited World War I in August 1914. After the European powers had spent nearly three years of inconclusive fighting, the United States entered the war on the side of Britain and France (Russia withdrew in December 1917, after the Bolsheviks came to power) and tipped the military scales in favor of the Alliance. Peace was concluded in 1918.

World War I marked the end of an era. Even before 1914, the old order, dominated by traditional and aloof elites, was threatened by revolutionary movements espousing democratic notions of responsive government. The overthrow of the czar in Russia during the war is one of the most dramatic examples of this burgeoning revolutionary spirit, even though, in Russia, it finally led to the Bolshevik victory and a new tyranny. The new spirit found one of its most eloquent spokesmen in President Woodrow Wilson, who firmly believed that the old methods of secret diplomacy and secret pacts

among the leaders of the major powers had been largely responsible for World War I. Accordingly, he presented to the peace conference in Paris in 1919 his plans for a League of Nations wherein all states would openly and honorably resolve their differences and aggressors would be dealt with by all League members acting in concert. The League of Nations became Part I of the Treaty of Versailles, which officially ended World War I and went into force in January 1920. Although the United States never became a member, the League operated as the world's first general international organization with about 60 member states from 1920 until 1946, when the United Nations took over most of its functions.

World War II. Despite the efforts of the League and the highly idealistic Kellogg-Briand Pact of 1928, which outlawed war as an instrument of national policy, the seeds of war fell on fertile ground during the twenties and thirties. World War I left behind a legacy of economic chaos in most of Europe and in particular bitterness in Germany, who felt she had been treated unfairly by the Treaty of Versailles. Wounded national pride coupled with economic difficulties led to the rise of Fascism in Italy, Nazism in Germany, and militarism in Japan. Wishing to establish what they considered their "rightful" place in the international order by whatever means necessary, these three states contemptuously ignored the principles of the League and the Kellogg-Briand Pact.

In 1931 Japan invaded Manchuria without declaring war, calling the invasion an act of "self-defense." While the League ponderously debated what constituted aggression in the absence of a formal declaration of war, Japan consolidated her gains. In dealing with a challenge from a major power, the League labored under many disabilities; the two most obvious were the requirement of unanimous agreement in the League Council to make decisions and, once these decisions were made, the lack of methods and machinery to enforce them. When the League eventually did condemn Japan's actions, that nation simply left the world organization. As it became clear that the League was not able to enforce the guidelines for international behavior laid down by the League Covenant, the way was open for other regimes to attempt to force their will upon the international community. Under Mussolini, Italy continued the aggression she had initiated toward Ethiopia in 1923, and in Germany, Hitler went ahead with his plans for the conquest of Europe.

After years of uncertainty and indecision as to what their policy toward fascist aggression should be, Britain and France finally declared war on Germany in September 1939, after her attack on Poland. Alienated by the previous efforts of Britain and France to appease Hitler, Russia had already negotiated a nonaggression pact with Germany that gave the Soviet Union a large piece of Polish territory. By the summer of 1940 Norway, Denmark, the

Lowlands, and France had all succumbed to German military might, and England was subjected to massive air attacks. In the spring of 1941 the Nazi armies moved into the Balkans and North Africa, and their ultimate victory seemed practically inevitable. Then two historic events changed the course of the war. In June 1941 Germany attacked the Soviet Union, her former ally, and in December of the same year Japan attacked the United States at Pearl Harbor in Hawaii. As a result, both major powers that had been attacked were brought into the war against the so-called Axis of Germany, Italy, and Japan. Although early German successes in the Soviet Union and Japan's rapid infiltration of Southeast Asia initially threatened the Allied cause, the tide of battle began to turn in favor of the Allies by late 1942.

Even before the end of the war it was apparent to the Allies that future peace would depend upon the willingness of the major powers to cooperate in maintaining peace through some new type of international organization. At various conferences during the war[7] some or all of the Allies discussed the possibility of establishing a postwar peace-keeping body. These discussions laid the groundwork for the establishment of the United Nations at the San Francisco Conference in 1945. The United Nations Charter was based upon the realization that if the five major powers (United Kingdom, France, China, the Soviet Union, and the United States) were able to agree on matters of international concern, a United Nations might be effective in promoting peace. If they disagreed, the organization would be limited in its ability to prevent aggression. Thus the burning question at the end of World War II was whether the Grand Alliance of five major powers forged because of wartime necessity could continue to work for peace after the war.

THE COLD WAR

Unfortunately, the distrust and rivalry between the United States and the Soviet Union that had been barely kept in check by the necessities of wartime cooperation grew quickly once peace was concluded. The new status of the United States as the world's dominant military and economic power in 1945 and the Soviet Union's ideological goal of consolidating its own revolution and encouraging similar revolutionary changes in the rest of the world created deep tensions between the two nations. The United States considered Soviet influence over communist regimes in Eastern Europe to be a threat to the integrity of Western Europe, especially since the war had weakened the political and economic leadership of Britain and France. In the ensuing cold war between the United States and Russia, two features were prominent: (1) a fantastic escalation of nuclear weapons systems as one armament development led to another, and (2) the building of military and political alliances with other states in the attempt to increase national security.

Although American development of the atomic bomb toward the end

of the war gave the United States the potential for militarily dominating the globe, the American atomic monopoly came to an end in 1949, when the Soviet Union succeeded in developing its own atomic weapons. The following list is a time scale of the development of nuclear (A-bomb) and thermonuclear (H-bomb) capability.

1945   United States—first successful nuclear test—16 July 1945

1949   Soviet Union—first successful nuclear test—19 September 1949

1952   United Kingdom—first successful nuclear test—3 October 1952
       United States—first successful thermonuclear test—1 November 1952

1953   Soviet Union—first successful thermonuclear test—12 August 1953

1957   United Kingdom—first successful thermonuclear test—15 May 1957

1960   France—first successful nuclear test—3 February 1960

1964   China—first successful nuclear test—16 October 1964

1967   China—first successful thermonuclear test—17 June 1967

1968   France—first successful thermonuclear test—24 August 1968

1974   India—first successful nuclear test—18 May 1974

Unable to rely wholly upon American weapons superiority for security, the United States and its Western allies formed the North Atlantic Treaty Organization (NATO) in 1949, combining their military forces against a potential threat from Russia and agreeing that an attack on any member would be considered an attack on all. Predictably, the Soviets responded with the Warsaw Treaty Organization in 1955, a similar alliance of Eastern European states in which communist parties had assumed control. By 1969 the United States had concluded defense treaties with 42 nations and defense pledges and agreements with over 30 other states. The following list enumerates the collective defense treaties that evolved out of the East-West cold war.

UNITED STATES COLLECTIVE DEFENSE TREATIES (THE WESTERN CAMP):

1. Inter-American Treaty of Reciprocal Assistance (Rio Pact 1947)

United States	Dominican Republic	Nicaragua
Argentina	Ecuador	Panama
Bolivia	El Salvador	Paraguay
Brazil	Guatemala	Peru
Chile	Haiti	Trinidad-Tobago†
Costa Rica	Honduras	Uruguay
Colombia	Mexico	Venezuela
Cuba*		

*excluded from Rio Pact in 1962
†joined after becoming independent in 1962

2. North Atlantic Treaty (1949)

United States	Italy	Greece (1952)
Belgium	Luxembourg	Turkey (1952)
Canada	Netherlands	Federal Republic of Germany (1955)
Denmark	Norway	
France	Portugal	
Iceland	United Kingdom	

3. Security Treaty between the United States and Australia and New Zealand (ANZUS 1951)

4. Mutual Defense Treaty with the Philippines (1951)

5. Mutual Defense Treaty with South Korea (1954)

6. Mutual Defense Treaty with (Nationalist) China (Taiwan) (1954)

7. Southeast Asia Collective Defense Treaty (SEATO 1954)

United States	Pakistan	(South Vietnam)*
Australia	Philippines	(Cambodia)*
France	Thailand	(Laos)*
New Zealand	United Kingdom	

*South Vietnam, Cambodia, and Laos are not parties to the SEATO Treaty, but by a protocol they are included in the defense provisions of the treaty. Laos has declared it will not accept such alliance protection, and this was confirmed by the 1962 Geneva Agreement on the neutrality of Laos. Cambodia has also rejected the provisions of this protocol.

8. Treaty of Mutual Security and Cooperation with Japan (1960)

9. By executive agreement, congressional resolutions, or executive declarations the United States has extended other "collective defense" arrangements.
   a) Executive agreements extended defense arrangements with Denmark (1951), Iceland (1951), Spain (1953 and 1969), Canada (1958), Liberia (1959), Iran (1959), Turkey (1959), Pakistan (1959), and the Philippines (1959, 1965).
   b) Executive policy declarations have been issued jointly with Latin American states (other than Cuba), regarding Berlin, Iran, India, Jordan, Israel, Thailand, South Vietnam, Nationalist China, and the Philippines.
   c) Congressional resolutions have also extended "defense security commitments," including the following:
      —1955—to protect Formosa and Pescadores Islands against "armed attack"
      —1957—to defend Middle Eastern states "against aggression from any country controlled by international communism"
      —1962—to defend Latin American states against Cuban aggression
      —1964—(so-called Gulf of Tonkin resolution) to defend any SEATO member or protocol state (including Vietnam) requesting assistance
   d) By its bilateral agreements with Iran, Pakistan, and Turkey the United States participates in CENTO.

SOVIET UNION COLLECTIVE DEFENSE TREATIES (THE EASTERN CAMP):

1. Treaty of Friendship, Cooperation and Mutual Assistance (Warsaw Pact, 1955)

Soviet Union	German Democratic Republic
Albania	Hungary

Bulgaria   Poland
Rumania   Czechoslovakia
(The People's Republic of China is "associated" but is not a member)

2. Bilateral treaties of friendship, cooperation, and mutual assistance between the Soviet Union and Poland (1945, 1965), Czechoslovakia (1943, 1963), Hungary (1948), Rumania (1948), Bulgaria (1948), German Democratic Republic (1964). In addition each of these states has bilateral agreements with every other.
3. By essentially executive "declarations" joint arrangements have been made with North Korea, North Vietnam, and the People's Republic of China.

THE SUPERPOWERS

Since 1945 the nature of the international system has been largely determined by the moves and countermoves of the two superpowers. For example, when the Soviets indirectly supported a revolutionary movement in Greece in 1946, the United States countered with the Truman Doctrine in 1947 providing military and economic aid to support the existing regime. Korea and Germany, both divided by occupying armies of the Soviet Union and the United States and its allies, became areas of major confrontation. The most important restraint on these two bitter rivals as they confronted each other around the globe was the full realization of the other's destructive potential, resulting in a belligerent but cautious stand-off.

For years the United Nations was virtually paralyzed by the hostility between the United States and the Soviet Union. Beginning in 1956, however, the two nations found they could work together in the United Nations when an international crisis did not involve them directly or when a development appeared to threaten the interests of both. In the Middle East conflicts of 1956, 1967, and 1973 and in the two wars between India and Pakistan in 1965 and 1971, the United States and the Soviet Union set aside their own differences and asserted their prestige to prevent the military clashes from getting out of hand.

THE DEVELOPING NATIONS

Although there has not been another world war since 1945, the past three decades have been full of military conflict, the most notable being the Korean War from 1950 to 1953 and the continuing Indochina war, beginning in 1945 with the fight for Vietnamese independence from France. In 1958 alone there were 20 identifiable violent conflicts among nations, and between 1958 and 1966 some 150 insurgencies and 15 conventional military conflicts occurred. Much military activity since the end of World War II has grown out of the tensions accompanying the proliferation of newly independent states, for the end of colonialism and the creation of new nations has had a major impact on the postwar international system. Prior to World War II about one-third of the world's population and land area were under some

form of colonial rule in over 80 separate colonial jurisdictions—colonies, protectorates, mandates, territories, and dependencies. Great Britain, the Netherlands, France, Belgium, Portugal, Italy, and Spain having a combined population of about 200 million, controlled some 700 million people in dependent areas. The United States had jurisdiction over 15 million and Japan over about 60 million people.

A significant call for change was the Atlantic Charter of August 14, 1941, a joint declaration by President Franklin Roosevelt and Prime Minister Winston Churchill acknowledging that all people had the right ". . . to choose the form of government under which they will live" and that self-government should be restored to those who have been forcibly deprived of it.[8] In addition, World War II gave impetus to nationalistic movements in the colonial areas. Imperial powers such as the United Kingdom were greatly aided by their colonies in pursuing the war—a war that shattered the myth of the Crown's invincibility. Servicemen returning to the colonies who had fought in defense of European freedom ". . . considered it their right that they should have some share in the government of their own land."[9] Although Britain made some concessions toward colonial autonomy by opening higher administrative posts to indigenous peoples, the concessions were viewed by local political leaders as inadequate. In Asia, moreover, occupation by the Japanese meant not only a change of colonial control but the creation of an armed, militant resistance movement that later gave new vitality to the incipient nationalist movements.[10]

The United Nations Charter itself affirmed the principle of self-determination for all peoples. Although few at the San Francisco Conference in 1945 expected that goal to be totally achieved in the near future, the movement for self-determination continued to gain momentum in the late 1940s and 1950s. India, Pakistan, Burma, and Israel emerged as full-fledged nations independent of Britain in the late 1940s. Eleven colonies achieved independence in the fifties, including the French colonies in Indochina—Cambodia, Laos, and Vietnam—which had to win their freedom through military means. The spirit of self-determination reached its zenith in 1960 with the unanimous adoption by the United Nations General Assembly of a resolution calling for the complete elimination of colonialism. In that same year 16 independent states were newly created, 14 of which had been former colonies. Except for the Portuguese "overseas territories," South-West Africa, and a few island dependencies, almost all former colonies had achieved independent status in the international system by 1975. See Table 1.1.

If international politics from 1945 to 1956 was dominated by the so-called East-West conflict between the Soviet Union and the United States, from 1956 on the newly independent states added a further dimension to the conflict and to international politics as a whole. As the new states sought

TABLE 1.1 STATES THAT ACHIEVED INDEPENDENCE SINCE THE BEGINNING OF WORLD WAR II

Year	State	Former Colonial Status
1943	Lebanon	French mandate
1944	Syria	French mandate
	Iceland	Danish
1946	Jordan	British mandate
	Philippines	United States
1947	India	British dominion
	Pakistan	British dominion
1948	Burma	British
	Sri Lanka (Ceylon)	British—left British Commonwealth in 1972
	Israel	British mandate
	North Korea	Japanese—under Soviet occupation
	South Korea	Japanese—under U.S. occupation
1949	Indonesia	Dutch
1951	Libya	Italian—under British and French occupation
1954	Cambodia	French—Associated State in French Union
	Laos	French—Associated State in French Union
	North Vietnam	French—Associated State in French Union
	South Vietnam	French—Associated State in French Union
1956	Morocco	French and Spanish protectorate
	Tunisia	French protectorate
	Sudan	British-Egyptian condominium
1957	Ghana	British—plus portion of former French Togo
	Malaysia	British
1958	Guinea	French
1960	Cameroon	French Trust Territory
	Central African Republic	French
	Chad	French
	Congo (Brazzaville)	French
	Cyprus	British
	Dahomey	French
	Gabon	French
	Ivory Coast	French
	Malagasy Republic	French
	Mali	French
	Mauritania	French
	Niger	French
	Nigeria	British
	Senegal	French
	Somalia	Italian Trust Territory
	Togo	French Trust Territory
	Upper Volta	French
	Zaire (Congo)	Belgian
1961	Sierra Leone	British
	Tanzania (Tanganyika)	British Trust Territory
	Kuwait	British protectorate

TABLE 1.1 (*Continued*)

Year	State	Former Colonial Status
1962	Algeria	French
	Jamaica	British
	Burundi	Belgian Trust Territory
	Rwanda	Belgian Trust Territory
	Uganda	British
	Trinidad and Tobago	British
	Western Samoa	New Zealand Trust Territory
1963	Kenya	British
	Zanzibar	British—merged with Tanganyika in 1964
1964	Malawi	British protectorate
	Malta	British
	Zambia	British protectorate
1965	Gambia	British
	Maldives	British protectorate
	Singapore	Part of Malaysia
1966	Botswana	British protectorate
	Lesotho	British protectorate
	Barbados	British
	Guyana	British
1967	South Yemen	British protectorate
1968	Equatorial Guinea	Spanish
	Mauritius	British
	Swaziland	British protectorate
	Nauru	Australia–New Zealand–British Trust Territory
1970	Fiji	British
	Tonga	British protectorate
1971	Bangladesh	Part of Pakistan (East Pakistan)
	Bahrain	British protectorate
	Qatar	British protectorate
	United Arab Emirates	British protectorate
1973	Bahamas	British
1974	Grenada	British
	Guinea-Bissau	Portuguese
1975	Mozambique	Portuguese

to assert and sustain their independence, they looked for aid and assistance from the developed states and increased trade with them. Since the United States and the Soviet Union were eager to widen their respective spheres of influence, the new states sometimes found themselves in a good bargaining position between the two antagonists; but at other times they became mere pawns in the cold war struggle.

The developing nations recognized that their ability to sustain themselves might depend to a large degree upon their ability to stick together.

The Bandung Afro-Asian Conference in 1955, the All-African Peoples' Conference in 1958, and the Conference of Non-Aligned Powers in 1961 were three major efforts to create solidarity among the new nations. Subsequent conferences of nonaligned powers were not so successful and included only a portion of the developing states. While most of these nations have poverty and underdevelopment in common, politically they vary considerably, which has proved to be an obstacle to closer cooperation. In Africa, for example, there were various attempts to establish some sort of union of African states. A meeting of independent African states in Ghana in 1958, and two other meetings, in Ethiopia and the Congo in 1960, failed to lead to any permanent pan-African organization. The more "conservative" African states, especially former French territories, coalesced in a loose organization as a result of meetings held in Brazzaville (French Congo) in 1960 and Monrovia (Liberia) in 1961. At the same time the "radical" African states—Ghana, Guinea, Mali, Egypt, Morocco, Libya—formed the so-called Casablanca bloc in January 1961. Eventually, however, all were drawn together in the Organization of African Unity in 1963 when it became apparent that they ran the risk of being played off against each other by the East-West powers unless they stood together. It was not until the United Nations Conference on Trade and Development in Geneva in 1964 that the developing states in Asia, Africa, Latin America, and elsewhere began to mobilize themselves to deal in a body with the developed states. Even though the developing states have gradually realized that the particulars of each country's economic problems vary, they are in substantial agreement on the common goals of achieving development and realizing freedom from undue influence from the major powers.

THE ERA OF THE 1960s

At least four other major developments since 1960 have significantly changed the international system: (1) the rise of the People's Republic of China, (2) the growing economic power of Japan, (3) the integration of Europe as an economic community, and (4) the altered image of the United States.

The Chinese communists progressed from cadres of beleaguered revolutionaries in the 1920s to become the founders of the P.R.C. in 1949, and the new republic developed from a backward, agrarian, isolated nation in 1949 to an economically successful, industrial, and atomic power with membership in the United Nations and widespread diplomatic and economic ties around the world by 1973. The largest nation on earth is now a full participant in international politics and a force to be reckoned with in the future. But for some time already, China has affected the East-West cold war and the split between developed and developing states.

Although the P.R.C. initially aligned itself with the Soviet bloc, a widen-

ing ideological and political split between China and the Soviet Union has been apparent since 1958. China scorned Moscow's ambition to be the communist Rome and vehemently disagreed with Khrushchev's policy of coexistence with the noncommunist world.[11] China argued that the communist movement must not slacken its efforts to spread the revolution against capitalism. And while the Soviets have appeared to be decreasing their direct support to revolutionary movements, since 1970 the P.R.C. has been expanding its assistance to neutralist states such as Tanzania, considered by the Chinese to be entering a crucial revolutionary stage. The P.R.C. has viewed itself as part of the Asian, African, and Latin American Third World (separate from the First World of the United States and its Western Allies and the Second World of the Soviet Union and its Eastern Bloc Allies) approximately since the 1955 Conference of Afro-Asian States in Bandung, Indonesia. In fact, she has argued that the major problem confronting the Third World is American *and Soviet* imperialism and collusion. Consequently, many communist revolutionary movements are now divided into Soviet and Chinese factions. The USSR and the P.R.C. backed different sides during both the 1967–1969 Biafran seccessionist movement in Nigeria and the 1971 Indo-Pakistan war over Bangladesh. The Soviets provided the major material support to North Vietnam during the Vietnamese war, but China competed for Hanoi's allegiance as well. Neither China nor the Soviet Union has viewed the other's moves toward rapprochement with the United States in a very favorable light.

Tensions between China and the Soviet Union are exacerbated by disputes over their common border and by the success of China in becoming a nuclear power. Although China has not begun to approach the nuclear delivery capability of the Soviet Union or the United States, her military potential, especially in conventional warfare, is indisputable and has become a formidable challenge to the Soviet Union with which she shares some 5000 miles of border.

Another major development within the postwar international system has been the recovery of Japan from her defeat in World War II and her emergence as one of the major economic powers in the world. Aided by close cooperation between government and business and minimal expenditures on rearmament, Japan's gross national product has expanded at the unprecedented rate of over 10 percent per year for the past twenty years. Exports have increased by 15 percent per year, more than twice the rate of the expansion of world trade. The only non-Western nation to achieve modern economic growth rivaling, and in many cases surpassing, European nations, Japan is a major source of modern technology, investment, and trade, with considerable power to help as well as to dominate other nations.[12]

Comparable to the economic growth of Japan has been the emergence

of the European Economic Community (EEC), originally composed of France, West Germany, Italy, Belgium, Luxembourg, and the Netherlands and expanded in 1972 to include Great Britain, Denmark, and Ireland. Often called the Common Market, the EEC began its operations on January 1, 1958, with the fifteen-to-twenty-year goal of gradually integrating the separate economies of its member states into one single economic unit. The first step toward establishing a complete customs union took place in 1959 with reductions in tariffs and import quotas among members. Since that time the EEC has worked toward a common agricultural policy, harmonization of indirect tax systems, abolition of restrictions on capital movements among members, the creation of a monetary union, and enhanced political cooperation. The Common Market has been so successful that it is second only to the United States in industrial production, and together with its associated members it constitutes the world's largest trading unit. Through it, European bargaining power in international politics has been greatly enhanced.

The last development, clearly evident since the early 1960s, has been a change in the international image of the United States. As one of the first nations to throw off the colonial yoke in favor of representative government, the United States was long a symbol of freedom for colonial peoples fighting for their right of self-determination. As one of the most democratic and equalitarian societies in the world, the United States historically stood for justice, equality, and fair play in the minds of oppressed people everywhere. At the Paris Peace Conference at the end of World War I the United States argued persuasively for an honorable peace and open diplomacy in the conduct of international affairs. Gradually, however, the image of the United States as the champion of democratic government and equalitarian principle has tarnished. Nonwhite races have wondered whether the United States would have used the bomb against Japan had the Japanese been white. Revolutionary leaders in many nations have charged that American policy of containing Soviet influence has led the United States to support the status quo —which often means totalitarian regimes—rather than encourage the process of political, economic, and social reform. Developing nations have questioned whether the United States is really interested in their welfare or whether it merely views them as sources of economic profit and political advantage vis-à-vis the Soviet Union.

The changing image of the United States is in large part the result of the nation's tremendous growth and the accompanying internal strains and contradictions. Racial inequities and injustices still abound and are loudly publicized in the international press. Many recognize the United States as a microcosm of the larger world, divided between rich and poor, nonwhite and white. With about 6 percent of the world's population, the United States consumed over half the resources of the world by the beginning of this decade.

Nevertheless, the country is still unwilling or unable to find viable ways of eliminating the persistent poverty of nearly 20 percent of its own population. Moreover, many contend that the United States is hypersensitive to real and imagined threats from communism, both internal and external, and has forced its views upon other nations as a condition of aid, friendship, and good relations. All of these doubts about the accuracy of the image of the United States as champion of the underprivileged coalesced when the United States became involved militarily in Vietnam. To critics at home and overseas it appeared that instead of supporting self-determination for the Vietnamese people, the United States was shoring up a corrupt, dictatorial regime for its own selfish purposes while ignoring its own domestic problems. Far from acting as a friend of change, the United States seemed to choose the role of the arrogant, self-interested, and self-appointed policeman to the world.

Our brief survey of international politics has, of necessity, omitted many important historical developments. For example, we have not discussed movements to restructure the international monetary system or the growth and role of the ubiquitous international corporations in world politics. But in the early 1970s international politics is still dominated by the moves and countermoves of the two superpowers. Their rivalry remains of paramount concern not only to themselves but to every other nation as well. At the same time, the potential of their destructive capabilities has promoted caution in their responses to each other and to the world. So far they have stopped short of all-out confrontations and have shown some restraint in their indirect conflicts in trouble spots around the globe. The cold war has changed from belligerency and imminent threats of war to coexistence—a protecting of the status quo while seeking incremental gains. More recently, in the Nixon-Brezhnev summit meetings and in agreements such as the 1972 Strategic Arms Limitation Treaty, we have seen evidence of a détente—a lowering of tensions and the negotiating of agreements in areas of mutual interest and advantage. The next step toward peace would be accommodation where cooperation and reciprocation build trust and promote the possibility for further reducing tensions between the United States and the Soviet Union as well as in other geographical areas where the cold war has fanned the flames of violence. What these and other trends mentioned portend for the next twenty years is difficult to perceive; yet on the basis of this past experience we often attempt to suggest the future behavior of nation-states.

PROBLEMS OF CONCEPTUALIZATION

The task of conceptualizing—that is, of intellectually comprehending and generalizing from particular events—something so complex as interna-

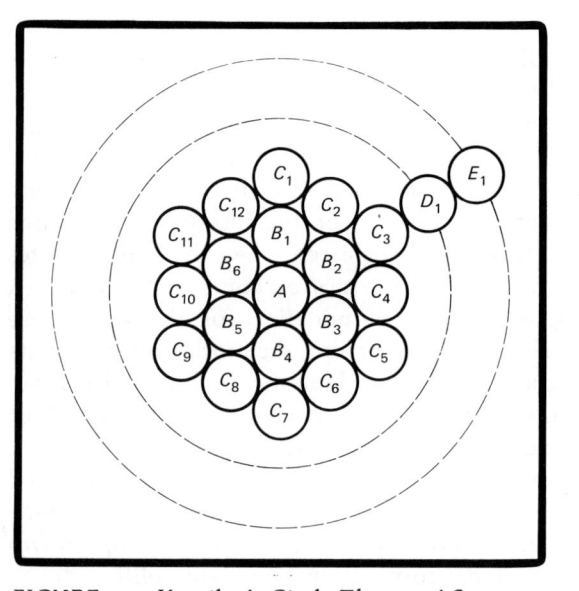

FIGURE 1.1 Kautilya's Circle Theory of States

tional politics is almost as old as political history itself. For example, about 321 B.C. the Indian philosopher Kautilya attempted to explain the process of international relations among the many states occupying the subcontinent of India. He argued in the *Arthasastra* that it was natural for neighboring states to be enemies. Survival for a particular state, therefore, depended upon making alliances with states on your neighbor's border, as Figure 1.1 illustrates.

According to Kautilya, state A is most likely to make alliance treaties with states C. For example, feeling a threat by state $B1$, state A would most likely make alliances with states $C1$, $C2$, and $C12$ against $B1$. State A might make a temporary alliance with $B2$ and $B6$ against $B1$, but they could not be lasting arrangements. Similarly the alliances might therefore involve the A, C, and E circles of states in opposition to the B and D circles of states. Kautilya argues that any state placing itself in the A position can discern its logical allies in the C and E circles of states.[13] In addition to this "circle theory of states" as he called it, Kautilya offered suggestions for conducting interactions among states, including advice on methods of negotiating and on poisons to be used by spies.

Vintage views of politics still have currency. Otto von Bismarck, the first chancellor of the German Empire, held the opinion that the great questions of our day cannot be solved by speeches and majority votes but by blood and iron. Nineteenth-century Austrian diplomat Prince von Metternich

viewed international politics as a juggling act, the maintenance of a balance of power among states being the sole guarantee of international peace and security. American President Woodrow Wilson believed that "a universal dominion of right by . . . a concert of free people . . . shall bring peace and safety to all nations and make the world itself free."

How are we to view international politics today? The intellectual odyssey of one scholar, Professor John H. Herz of City College of New York, illustrates the difficulties and risks involved in theorizing about international relations. In 1957 Herz published an article that persuasively argued that the territorial state was diminishing in importance as a result of new weapons that made its defensibility increasingly impossible.[14] According to his analysis, the era of the atom presaged the end of territoriality and a trend toward international integration. But in 1968 Herz had the intellectual courage to reassess his argument.

> *The theory of "classical" territoriality and the factors threatening its survival stands. But I am no longer sure that something very different is about to take its place. There are indicators pointing in another direction: not to "universalism" but to retrenchment; not to interdependence but to a new self-sufficiency; toward area not losing its impact but regaining it; in short, trends toward a "new territoriality."*[15]

The dilemma Herz faced is the same for all analysts: What are the realities of our world? What are the nature and dynamics of the international political system? What are the current trends? Reality still awaits explanatory theory.

APPROACHES

Conceptualizations of international politics grow according to how international politics is viewed. At least two distinct approaches exist in academic studies. Many scholars prefer to view international politics as a *system* and assess patterns of action and interaction among the units (normally states) over a period of time. Richard Rosecrance, for example, identified nine distinct international systems that existed with varying degrees of stability and for varying lengths of time between 1740 and 1960.[16] According to K. J. Holsti, historical systems such as those Rosecrance describes can be distinguished by (1) the boundaries of the system or whatever separates the area of interaction among members of the system from the larger environment, (2) the main characteristics of the political units involved in the system, (3) the structure or configuration of power and influence within the system, (4) the common forms of interaction (e.g., diplomacy, trade, war), and (5) rules, customs, and values.[17] Thus the systems approach emphasizes interactions within the world system or within its subsystems such as the Western

European allies in, say, the North Atlantic Treaty Organization. This approach stresses patterns of behavior within the system rather than the actions of individual states.

A second emphasis within the study of international politics is *foreign policy*—the actions (decisions, policies, programs) of individual states toward the external environment or, more simply put, toward other states. This way of looking at international politics focuses on the *conditions* (such as characteristics of decision-making bodies) that lead particular states to behave the way they do toward other states. Past studies within this context vary theoretically according to the relative potency they assign to variables or determinants of state action such as geography, resources, development, military capacity, population, technology, type of government, quality of leadership, ideology, and the like.

James N. Rosenau has developed a framework for the *comparative* study of foreign policy that goes beyond the assessment of individual nations.[18] States are classified by size (geography and physical resources), the state of the economy (developed, underdeveloped), and the nature of the polity (open or closed). Within the appropriate classification, influences on foreign policy are (1) systemic variables (e.g., the nature of the international system), (2) individual variables (e.g., personality, perceptions), (3) role variables (e.g., position and duties in an organization, career patterns and expectations, decisional latitude), (4) governmental variables (e.g., nature of the regime, degree of bureaucratization), and (5) societal variables (e.g., economic capabilities, social cohesion, values). The relative potency or ordering of these variables changes for each nation. Ultimately, Rosenau's approach would facilitate the conceptual *linking* of national and international politics in terms of how and why states seek to maximize their physical preservation, political independence, social stability, and economic viability. Theoretically and practically this is an essential task. Events in the Middle East, Southeast Asia, and elsewhere continue to blur old distinctions between national and international systems. However, the transnational activities of huge conglomerates and corporations as well as regional and international organizations bring into question any approach that considers nation-states as the only actors in international politics.

Conceptualizing international politics is marked by more disagreement than agreement among scholars over what is the most suitable or appropriate focus and method of study. The field is marked by "pockets of theory" or partial theories (with descriptive, explanatory, and predictive components) in areas such as decision making, conflict, deterrence, integration, and communications. We even have studies that suggest a majority of war cycles are significantly correlated with planetary positions.[19] The point is that without adequate conceptualization and theory, explanation, understanding, and con-

trol suffer; all "facts" appear to be equally valid, and we are without guidance both in increasing our knowledge and in applying it to contemporary problems.

AN ECOLOGICAL PERSPECTIVE

The normative perspective and approach of this book were presented in the Introduction. Our analytical orientation follows Harold and Margaret Sprout's "ecological perspective." To quote them, ". . . the ecological way of seeing and comprehending envisages international politics as a *system* of *relationships* among *interdependent, earth related* communities that share with one another an *increasingly crowded planet* that offers *finite* and exhaustible quantities of *basic essentials* of human well-being and existence."[20] Our focus, however, is more limited than their thorough framework for analysis. Within the ecological perspective we seek to elaborate upon major international *problems*, the course of which will largely determine both the nature of the international system and the degree to which national and international politics become compatible and complementary. Identifying problems is a first step in attaining desired goals or in developing a series of alternative strategies for defining new goals. Where our analysis stops short is the built-in limitation of most social science theories and methodologies—the capability to demonstrate adequately the interrelatedness of world problems in a way that crystallizes the range of alternatives and spells out relations between means and ends. Such policy positions are determined by the way problems are defined as well as by the assessment of priorities and trade-offs involving opposing values, costs, and benefits. The policy implications of an ecological perspective involve both certainties and uncertainties concerning what is probable, possible, and preferable as we face global and national problems of population, pollution, resource shortages, war, race conflict, political breakdowns, and change. We must assess the seriousness of these problems toward the goal of attaining operational knowledge to improve public policies. The ecological perspective builds forward rather than backward, and ultimately, in our view, seeks a greater degree of isomorphism between national and international interests based on an authentic value of equitable resolution of problems. Whether such a value is *acceptable* to decision makers and their constituencies and is *feasible* in terms of implementation remain the key question of the planet earth as a "congenial habitat."[21]

From our point of view the primary conceptual problem in the study of international relations is *not*, as many writers contend, the analysis of power. Power involves the ability or capability of individuals or societies to prevail in conflict situations and to attain their goals. Behavior is predicated on interest defined in terms of power. Accordingly, international politics, like all politics, is, to use Hans J. Morgenthau's phrase, "a struggle for power."[22] We do not deprecate power as a central concept in international politics,

though we consider any view of man as *primarily* power oriented to be inadequate psychology and questionable as "fact." In any case, what is in question is the *use* of power, or more pointedly, the way in which individuals and societies do or do not *adapt, set and attain goals, and integrate in political communities in light of problems common to their separate and competing habitats in the shrinking world in which they must coexist.* The difference between an International Geophysical Year and the Vietnam War illustrates the point. This conception of politics is not a fully developed scheme for organizing information, but it does encourage us to focus on salient questions in international politics.

CONTENDING DESCRIPTIONS, MODELS, AND THEORIES OF THE INTERNATIONAL POLITICAL SYSTEM

MIGHT MAKES RIGHT

Some social scientists view international politics as basically *anarchical*, or lacking in authority, order, regulation, consensus, and rules that would control the forces leading to intermittent warfare and perpetual hostility. According to this argument, we are not far removed from a "state of nature" without government. In a somewhat similar vein, Roger D. Masters has characterized international politics as "primitive."

> . . . *Four elements common to politics in a number of primitive societies and international relations deserve mention: first, the absence of a formal government with power to judge and punish violations of law; second, the use of violence and "self-help" by members of the system to achieve their obligations; third, the derivation of law and moral obligations either from custom or from explicit, particular bargaining relationships (i.e., the absence of a formal legislative body operating on the basis of—and making—general rules); and fourth, a predominant organizational principle which establishes political units serving many functions in the overall social system.*[23]

In many ways this description of international politics is accurate. Consider the vocabulary of world politics. We speak of power, national self-interest, territoriality, sovereignty, cold war, deterrence, protective-reaction raids, first and second strike lines of defense, first and second strike capabilities, protectionism, "our way of life," patriotism, loyalty, subversion, counterintelligence, espionage, guerrilla warfare, pacification, and the like. A political system based upon "us" versus "them" is indeed "primitive" and close to anarchical. Critically viewed, our international organizations have

seldom been more than very weak attempts at collective decision making. Might still makes right in the international community.

THE BALANCE OF POWER

A majority of writers still follow Metternich's example and consider international politics as a process of *balancing power*.[24] Like the previous model, this conceptualization is based on the theory that states look first to their own survival and national self-interest; but in this model, self-interest and coexistence go hand in hand. Since excessive concentrations of power threaten the existence of weaker states, equilibrium is sought through alliances, coalitions, pacts, and shifting relations among individual states. According to Morton A. Kaplan, the balance of power is a system of interdependent rules: States will (1) strive to increase their own capabilities but will negotiate for them rather than fight; (2) fight rather than fail to increase capabilities; (3) stop fighting rather than eliminate a member of the system; (4) oppose any coalition or single actor who tends to aggregate power and assume a position of predominance in the system; (5) constrain states that subscribe to supranational organizational principles; and (6) permit defeated or constrained states to reenter the system as acceptable partners.[25]

The rules that Kaplan abstracts from the balance-of-power system as it operated in nineteenth-century Europe assume there are five or six more or less equally powerful states in the system. As he and others have contended, this is not a very accurate description of the international community today when power is concentrated primarily in the United States and the Soviet Union while other states such as the United Kingdom, France, and China play subsidiary roles. In our opinion, the inordinate power of the United States and the Soviet Union since World War II require a shift in conceptual perspective.

A BIPOLAR AND MULTIPOLAR WORLD

We find that the description of international politics since 1945 as *bipolar* reflects the emergence of the two superpowers, whose competition, rivalry, and hostility led to the opposing alliances of the North Atlantic Treaty Organization and the Warsaw Pact. In the bipolar model, international politics is characterized by confrontation between the two principal actors with minor states attempting to remain neutral or lining up on one side or the other. Stability depends upon the commitment of the two superpowers to the view that the status quo (or incremental gains) is preferable to the dangers inherent in seeking major gains over the other. Kenneth N. Waltz has said that

> . . . bipolarity is expressed as the reciprocal control of the two strongest states by each other out of their mutual antagonism. What is unpre-

*dictable in such a two-party competition is whether one party will try
to eliminate the other. . . . Fear of major war induces caution all around;
the Soviet Union and the United States wield the means of inducing
that caution.*[26]

The recent emergence of Japan, China, and the European Common
Market is beginning to challenge the notion of a world dominated by two
superpowers. In the event that these and possibly other political entities continue to grow stronger, a *multipolar* system may develop, particularly if some
or all of the new power centers obtain nuclear weapons and delivery systems.
The consequences for the international system of such a change would undoubtedly be great, since instead of concentrating power as the bipolar system does, the multipolar system diffuses it. The dynamics of a multipolar
model reflect many of the elements of a balance-of-power system. In the former, however, there are a greater number of possible interactions with some
150 states in the international system, and gains by one state are not necessarily made at the cost of another. Alternatively, there is the possibility that
individual states will coalesce into blocs operating as units in international
politics—for instance, a Far Eastern bloc dominated by China and Japan, a
Soviet bloc ruled by the Soviet Union, a European bloc growing out of the
European Economic Community, an African Union of States, an American-
controlled bloc in the Western Hemisphere, and so on. The bloc arrangement
might resemble an unstable balance-of-power system.

Another conceptualization of present and future international politics
is Rosecrance's view of the system as one of *bi-multipolarity*.[27] He argues
essentially that the concentration of power in blocs led by the United States
and the Soviet Union will continue, but they will be influenced or conditioned by the presence and activity of other states. Thus relations between
the United States and USSR, while marked by competition, might also be
characterized by an increase in cooperation to stabilize each state's power
and to prevent multipolar conflicts that threaten the stability of the international system. In turn, the so-called multipolar states would act as mediators
or buffers in conflicts between the bipolar states. When Rosecrance published these views in 1966, he did not feel they were an accurate description
of the existing international system. American and Soviet moves toward rapprochement since 1966, however, give Rosecrance's theory practical rather
than abstract currency. Although both blocs still emphasized formal alliances
in 1966, the importance of those treaty organizations has since appeared to
recede. Rosecrance's assessment that nonaligned states would be treated less
favorably in a bipolar-multipolar world seems to be borne out by recent trade-
and-aid figures (see Chapter 4). In our opinion the bipolar-multipolar conception points to the fact that the international system is in flux and, as in the
past, we are still uncertain of the rules, if any, that govern such change.

A NEW BIPOLARITY

Another generalization about the international political system, as yet not theoretically developed, is that world politics is and will be increasingly dominated by a *new bipolarity*—a split between the developed and less-developed states (sometimes referred to as the North-South struggle in contrast to the cold war East-West conflict). According to this view, a major issue in future world politics will be competition growing out of the economic goals of the two groups of states. The developed countries will seek resources and markets (which will produce competition and rivalry among them); the developing countries will want to increase capital, trade, and technology. Paradoxically, the less-developed states may have the potential to reverse their historical treatment and treat developed nations as "hostages" (even though remaining, at the same time, dependent). The Middle East war of 1973 and the oil embargo to Israel's supporters imposed by the Arab nations is an example of the new ability of the Third World to wield potent sanctions against the developed nations. If conflicts between developed and less-developed states accumulate and shift from political to economic to racial lines, and if each "camp" finds some common solidarity in the face of such tension or threats, the potential for a new bipolarity will increase.

Alternatively, if individual states—developed or less developed—acquire nuclear capabilities, they may seek to use them as a *veto* involving threats or blackmail against other states. Certainly the costs of a small nuclear force (one 20-kiloton warhead a year) are modest enough—approximately $11 million a year or $110 million over a ten-year development period. With some sacrifices at least 15 or so nonnuclear powers could develop such capability. But let us not restrict ourselves to states—corporations, too, could do it, and so could organized crime syndicates. Despite strict government supervision, quantities of plutonium have "mysteriously" disappeared in the past. One thing is certain—the uncertainty of future international politics if such scenarios should be even partially acted out.

Few scholars are satisfied with the adequacy of the various views of the nature and dynamics of the international political system. The task of theory building continues. Interestingly, one of the more recent and novel conceptualizations has come from Timothy W. Stanley, executive vice-president of the International Economic Policy Association. Testifying before the House of Representatives Subcommittee on Europe, Dr. Stanley stated:

> . . . *earlier this year, I attended a conference of political scientists who debated at length how best to describe the changes in the world power structure. The shift from a bipolar to a multipolar world has become a cliché; so the choice was between triangles, squares and even pentagons. I found none of these fully satisfactory; and so I suggested a three dimensional model. . . . Let us imagine a pyramid on a square*

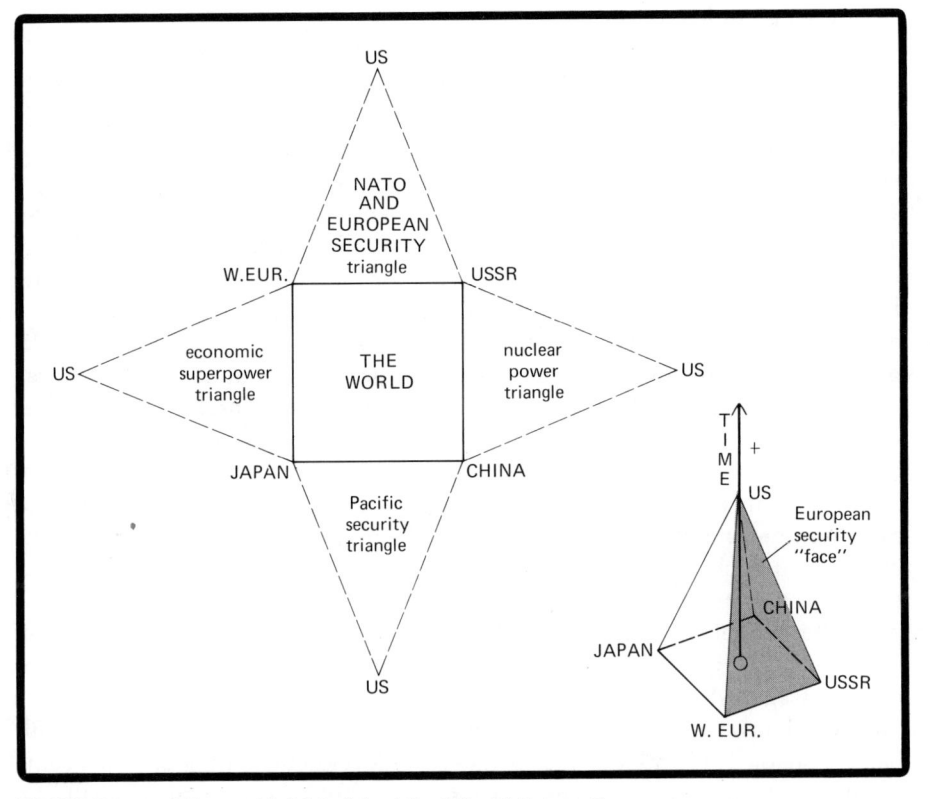

FIGURE 1.2 *A Pyramidal Model of the World Power Structure*

Source: U.S. House of Representatives, Committee on Foreign Affairs, Subcommittee on Europe, *Hearings—Conference on European Security*, April 25, May 10, 17, September 7, 27, 1972, 92d Cong., 2d sess., 1972, p. 112.

base. *The United States is at the apex—not out of chauvinism but because that is necessarily the perspective from which we view ourselves in relation to the rest of the world. At the four base corners, as illustrated on the accompanying diagram [Figure 1.2] starting in the upper right and moving clockwise, we can place the Soviet Union, China, Japan, and Western Europe. The base might be called "the world," since all other countries are also involved.*

This pyramid, then, has four faces: One, linking the United States, the U.S.S.R., and China might be called the potential nuclear super triangle. The next linking the United States, Japan, and China is the Pacific security triangle. The third, linking the United States, Japan and Europe is an "economic power" triangle, while the

fourth involving the United States, Europe and the Soviet Union represents NATO and European security. . . . This model is a simplistic way of illustrating the changes that are taking place in the world. The third dimension of the triangle, that is, its perpendicular height, represents time; so that as the pyramid grows in height, its four faces lean closer together and are, therefore, more interdependent. One can see movement clearly depicted, for example, in the historic visit now taking place of the Japanese Prime Minister to Communist China; and the possible geometric stresses on the rest of the model are obvious.

What conclusions can we draw from the model? First the economic face is leaning ever more heavily on the other. The trade, investment, and financial relationships among the United States, Japan, and Europe are of increasing importance and complexity in their own right as well as in political terms. Second, the United States has created an "opening" towards Communist China with the Soviet Union which has been a factor in the successful conclusion of the first SALT agreement with the Soviet Union, even as the "U.S.-U.S.S.R." line is also assuming an economic dimension. The "U.S.S.R.-E.U.R." base of the "European security" triangle has a dimension of Ostpolitik, détente diplomacy, and East-West trade overlaying the traditional ideological and political conflicts and potential military confrontation. The line connecting the United States and Europe is represented by NATO, as far as defense is concerned. Although the alliance was created in order to bring U.S. power to bear against the tendency for Soviet power to creep westward and thus influence, if not dominate, Western Europe, NATO has been trying for several years to cope with the implications of détente diplomacy. To this has now been added a U.S.-U.S.S.R. détente, or at least a shift from confrontation to negotiation.[28]

POLITICAL UNCERTAINTIES

Everyone interested in international affairs has his own idea about which of these conceptualizations (and others) is most appropriate, most descriptive, most useful. It is undoubtedly true that our varying concepts reflect the flux in international politics as a result of the demise of colonialism, changing weapons systems, and the growth of regional and international organizations. More important for the future than the debate over these models are the *questions* we now ask. In 1960 Karl W. Deutsch posed a group of questions that still remain largely unanswered.

We know that much in the world of relations among nations has changed and is still changing, but what is the nature of the change? Is the world becoming more international? Is it turning into one world

in which even the United States and the Soviet Union are influencing
each other ever more, or at least into two worlds of two rival and
ever more tightly integrated Communist and non-Communist blocs?
Is the nation-state being superseded by the rise of new continent-wide
or ocean-wide treaty organizations or federations? And what is
happening within most of the old and new nation-states, as they enter
upon these new arrangements? Are their governments becoming more
stable or less? Are their political and administrative capabilities rising
or declining? Are power and prestige within these states shifting toward
the elites or toward the masses of their populations? Are political
controls of economic life in the long-run growing or receding? Are we
moving toward a world of "garrison states," or toward a world of
"open societies," or is the world moving in uncharted directions for
which not even images have yet been found?[29]

In addition to our uncertainties about what the international system
actually looks like at present, analysts of international affairs face the further
difficulty of making even tentative judgments concerning which type of international system is most desirable—most stable, most likely to promote international well-being, and least likely to lead to war. These are normative
and value-laden questions, yet even if we could agree on answers, we are left
with the problem of discovering how we might constructively intervene in
the meandering processes of the international system so as to shape it to conform with the model we have chosen.

These are hard questions and problems, but they must be addressed by
academicians, policy makers, and citizens alike. The study of international
relations can be the pursuit of knowledge for its own sake, but its purpose is
also that of aiding public policy making and collective choice.[30] Academicians
and policy makers do have a common ground. While the policy maker shapes
reality as he copes with day-to-day events, the academician attempts to ren-
der reality into intelligible forms. Persons in both professions face the problem of creating order in a seemingly unordered world. If the gap between
them is large—as it often is—the tasks of each suffer: The academician gets
lost in excessive abstraction, and the policy maker loses the benefits of a
perspective larger than his own.

FUTUROLOGY

If we are to engage in anticipatory or prescriptive action, we must give
serious thought to the future. A few decades ago, the majority of social scientists would have most likely insisted that predicting the future be left to
astrologers and clairvoyants. But in recent years as change threatens to run

away with us, most scholars have come to appreciate the importance of using our knowledge about the past and present to help us anticipate and prepare for the future. Growing interest in futurology, the study of the future, is reflected in social science publications such as the *Futurist*, a journal published by the World Future Society since 1966. In the summer of 1967 an entire issue of *Daedalus*, entitled "Toward the Year 2000: Work in Progress," was devoted to the publication of articles prepared for, and the working discussions of, the American Academy of Arts and Sciences' Commission on the Year 2000. Likewise, the *International Social Science Journal* devoted an issue to "Futurology" in 1969. Most of these publications and other writings such as Herman Kahn and Anthony J. Wiener's *The Year 2000* have included discussions of the problems surrounding the forecasting of the future, attempts to project current trends in technological, social, economic, and political change into the future, and even outright predictions of future developments.[31] Although largely ignored by the social sciences, science-fiction literature also presents a wealth of thought-provoking scenarios of the future. In recent years futurist publications have increased in numbers and quality, particularly with regard to environmental concerns. Also new are materials relating the future to specific academic disciplines such as the recent book of readings edited by Albert Somit entitled *Political Science and the Study of the Future*.[32] Researching the future, as Franklin Tugwell has pointed out, has also become a significant transnational activity involving scholars in numerous countries.[33]

LIMITS OF FUTUROLOGY
Before we go further it may be wise to acknowledge some of the limitations of futurology. G. K. Chesterton humorously makes the point clear.

> *When we see a pig in a litter larger than other pigs, we know by an unalterable law of the Inscrutable it will be larger than an elephant,— just as we know, when we see weeds and dandelions growing more and more thickly in a garden, that they must, in spite of all our efforts, grow taller than our chimney-pots and swallow the house from sight, so we know and reverently acknowledge, that when any power in human politics has shown for any period of time any considerable activity, it will go on until it reaches the sky.[34]*

There are limits to the accuracy of generalizations we can make from trends and exponential growth rates. For example, in predicting population growth from past and current trends, we must remember that there is a maximum level of population after which population levels off as a result of conscious controls, wars, pollution, famine, and so on. We cannot assume that curves

of growth continue into infinity. Most predictions have an *if* statement attached: We face serious problems of overcrowding *if* we do nothing to alter
the current trends of population growth. Moreover, such statements often
contain within them the contingencies by which an undesirable state of affairs
might be alleviated or avoided. For example, one study has pointed out that:

> *The U.S. demand for primary minerals in the nonfuel category is
> expected to increase an estimated 400 percent by the year 2000 if efforts
> are not made to reuse processed materials. Based on present trends, the
> nation's self-sufficiency in primary nonfuel minerals would drop
> from 69 percent in 1968 to less than 30 percent by 2000. This failure of
> domestic production to keep pace with demand is the result of dwindling
> reserves of rich domestic ores; increased exploration, mining, and
> processing costs; an expanding population; and increased per capita
> utilization. Adequate technology has not been developed to recycle used
> materials, to find concealed ore deposits efficiently, nor to allow
> economic extraction and processing of lower grade ores.*[35]

"Ifs" and "contingencies" are in turn dependent upon the values we hold, the
priorities we establish, and the decisions we make.

Political trends are more difficult to ascertain than rates of mineral depletion and the like. We cannot, with any precision, predict man's behavior
except by holding past conditions constant, that is, assuming that future behavior will follow the pattern of past behavior, as in voting; but this assumption itself may lead us into error. As Gardner Murphy has stated:

> *Considering the rate at which scientific discovery and technological
> engineering, medical and other skills are growing, there is every reason
> to believe that within twenty, thirty, or forty years the extrapolation
> technique will be the most unrealistic of all; i.e., that statement that
> there will be just so much more of what we already have will be the
> least of all the possibilities that can be imagined. . . . Then someone
> comes along and says that human nature is always the same. Well, I
> don't know, maybe he means some hypothetical human nature that we
> can't ever observe. Very likely he does; or he may mean something
> rather trivial, such as that people get their feelings hurt because of pride
> or vanity or power-needs. You can see these things operating in your
> dog. You can see them operating in the zoo or in most higher animals.
> They exhibit ease in taking offense, and so forth. If that is all they mean
> by human nature, let them have their little quip. But when the expression
> is typically and seriously used to confine man to the traditional con-
> ception that he has to be essentially as he has been, it is the most*

unrealistic of all the concepts that this view of human nature could give us.[36]

SEVERAL FUTURE RESEARCH APPROACHES

However, the study of the future is not restricted to extrapolations, trends, and growth rates or necessarily to some specific assumptions concerning human nature. The predictions, projections, and forecasts addressing possibilities and alternatives for the future are quite varied. Daniel Bell has described twelve modes of prediction to illustrate the range of approaches in the art of conjecture.[37] A brief sample of some futures research approaches and techniques illustrates the point.

1. *Delphi Forecasting.* One goal of Delphi projects is to establish probable dates for potential scientific and technological developments through questionnaires filled in by experts. The end product is a derived consensus as will be illustrated below.

2. *Cross-Impact Analysis.* This involves the attempt to evaluate average likelihoods of occurrences (or nonoccurrences) among a set of interrelated events (e.g., the economic, social, and political conditions in the United States). The relationship between events and developments are called cross-impact and result in probabilistic statements.

3. *Simulations.* The technique of simulation involves approximating complex systems by dynamic models. The models are analogs of, say, mechanical or human systems such as a wind tunnel or an economy. Simulation *gaming* is often an exercise in role playing with either simple or very elaborate rules and scoring techniques.

4. *Scenario Construction.* These are generally descriptions of some future state of affairs dependent in their construction upon the genius of the author, intuition, and (perhaps) luck.

5. *Social Physics.* A loose description for future research that is patterned on social or historical "laws" illustrated, for example, by Karl Marx's theorems concerning the inevitable decline of capitalism or the notion that communism grows out of socialism as its direct continuation.

Whatever the technique and however loose or precise the methodology, judgments are involved in basic assumptions and interpretations. Future research is not an exact science, but it does bring some order to topics that are not always amenable to systematic or scientific inquiry. Nevertheless, it is hard to determine what conclusions are accurate. Predictions once were made that flying was a physical impossibility, and some scientists today believe that an antigravity machine or technique is theoretically and practically im-

possible. Table 1.2 illustrates a range of predictions in physical and biological techniques made by experts in 1964 and 1969 utilizing Delphi Forecasting. The opinion of experts indicates relative consistency in the forecasts. What the table does not consider are the *impacts* of such technologies or the interplay between technology and public policy. For example, an *economic* desalination process would seem a possible and necessary future development. However, such an innovation will be costly in dollars and in the use of energy to operate such plants. If distillation and freezing methods are used, the energy drain increases. Do we, then, start a crash program of building nuclear reactors to produce the necessary power (with all of the mixed blessings such energy sources represent)? If so, what will be the cost to other programs? By what criteria are such value trade-offs decided? Perhaps by the year 2000 the need for pure and abundant water will exceed the importance of all other material problems and will force a drastic revision of priorities in public policy if not in life styles as well. Changes in one sector of an economy or environment usually produce concomitant changes elsewhere, some of which may be foreseen while many others may not.

Cautions and other caveats aside, we wish to reaffirm our belief that the social sciences and decision makers must become much more future oriented if we wish to avoid being overwhelmed by the forces of change. We must ascertain what it is we want to know about the future, what are our normative concerns, and how we formulate and translate such values into public policy. Most of us take for granted the utility of forecasting the weather. It aids us in planning vacations, planting crops, determining military possibilities, space adventures, and so on. Social and political forecasting is just as useful in alerting us to the consequences of our current behavior. The first step in creating a future we can look forward to is sensitizing ourselves to the possible futures that await us.

POSSIBLE SCENARIOS OF FUTURE INTERNATIONAL DEVELOPMENTS

Obviously, there are many ways to conjecture about international politics of the future. We see two fundamentally different ways in which the international system may develop during the next twenty years. One cluster of scenarios represents an "evolutionary" development of conditions already present or emerging in the international system (continuity). The other cluster of possible scenarios constitutes a radical break from past patterns resulting from traumatic or unique catastrophic events (discontinuity).

Within both clusters of scenarios there are five general types of possible developments. One type is characterized by the dominance of certain states

TABLE 1.2 COMPARISON OF FORECASTS, 1964 AND 1969 DEVELOPMENTS

1964	1969	Possible Bias from Phrasing	1964			1969			Correlation
			LQ	Median	UQ	LQ	Median	UQ	
Availability of a machine which comprehends standard IQ tests and scores above 150 (where comprehend is to be understood as the ability to respond to questions printed in English and possibly accompanied by diagrams)	Availability of a computer which comprehends standard IQ tests and scores above 150 (where comprehend is to be understood as the ability to respond to questions printed in English and possibly accompanied by diagrams)	none	1984	1990	1996	1980	1992	2012	about the same; later upper quartile
Permanent base established on the moon (ten men, indefinite stay)	Establishment of a permanent base on the moon (say ten men, indefinite stay)	none	1981	1982	1983	1992	1992	1992	later, a less optimistic forecast
Widespread use of robot services for refuse collection, as household slaves, sewer inspectors, etc.	Availability of complex robots which are programmable and self-adaptive and capable of performing most household chores, such as independently preparing meals and cleaning or otherwise disposing of dishes	none	1980	1987	1996	1992	1992	2000	later, a less optimistic forecast
Economic feasibility of commercial manufacture of many chemical elements from subatomic building blocks	Economic feasibility of commercial manufacture of many chemical elements from subatomic building blocks	none	2007	2100	never	1992	2012	2012	earlier, a more optimistic forecast

TABLE 1.2 (Continued)

1964	1969	Possible Bias from Phrasing	1964 LQ	1964 Median	1964 UQ	1969 LQ	1969 Median	1969 UQ	Correlation
Two-way communication with extra-terrestrials	Discovery of information that proves the existence of intelligent beings beyond the Earth	earlier, since discovery could come without communication	2000	2075	never	1985	2025	later	earlier as expected
Commercial global ballistic transport (including boost-glide techniques)	Routine use of re-usable ballistic sub-orbital transports for military or commercial passenger and cargo transportation	none	1985	2000	never	1992	2030	later	later, though more likely in the long run
Control of gravity through some form of modification of the gravitational field	Revision of gravitational theories leading to the possibility of new modes of space travel	revision of theories could come before control	2035	2050	never	1985	later	never	earlier possibility, more optimistic forecast
Non-rocket space drive: anti-gravity			2050	2400	never				later
Reliable weather forecasts	Demonstration of regular and reliable weather forecasts 14 days in advance for areas as small as 260 km² (100 sq miles)	more limiting definition should bring later forecast	1972	1975	1988	1980	1980	2012	later
Controlled thermo-nuclear power	Laboratory demonstration of continuously controlled thermo-nuclear power	none	1980	1986	2000	1980	1985	1992	about the same; quartile range narrowed
Economically useful exploitation of the ocean bottom through mining (other than offshore petroleum drilling)	Invention of devices to permit economically useful exploitation of the ocean bottom through mining (other than offshore drilling)	none	1980	1989	2000	1980	1992	2000	same

First formulation	Second formulation		Year forecasts						Comment
Economically useful exploitation of ocean through farming, with the effect of producing at least 20% of the world's food	Availability of techniques that permit useful exploitation of ocean through aquaculture farming (including expanded fishing and ocean fishing cultivation) with the effect of producing at least 20% of the world's calories	none	2000	2000	2017	1985	1992	2000	earlier, a more optimistic forecast
Feasibility of limited weather control, in the sense of substantially affecting regional weather at acceptable cost	Feasibility of limited weather control, in the sense of predictably affecting regional weather at acceptable cost	second formulation is more demanding	1987	1990	2000	1980	1992	2012	as expected
Earth weather control, in the sense of having the highly reliable capability of causing precipitation from certain types of clouds			1978	1982	2002				
Economically useful desalination of sea water	Demonstration of large-scale desalination plants capable of economically producing useful water for agricultural purposes (5.3 cents/1000 l (20 cents per 1000 US galls))	more specific, hence perhaps later	1964	1970	1980	1973	1980	1985	later, as suggested
Operation of a central data storage facility with wide access, for general or specialized information retrieval	Establishment of a central data storage facility for several regional or disciplinary facilities) with wide public access (perhaps in the home), for general or specialized information retrieval primarily in the areas of library, medical, and legal data	none	1971	1980	1991				
Automated libraries looking up and reproducing copy			1971	1976	1982				
Automated looking up of legal information			1971	1978	1998				

TABLE 1.2 (Continued)

1964	1969	Possible Bias from Phrasing	1964			1969			Correlation
			LQ	Median	UQ	LQ	Median	UQ	
Development of new synthetic materials for ultra-light construction	A large number of new materials (for example, filament-re-inforced composites) for ultra-light construction (density of aluminum, strength and toughness of steel) commercially available for private use at competitive prices	later, since question ponders commercial availability of development	1970	1971	1978	1975	1980	1992	later, as suggested
Automated language translators	Laboratory operation of automated language translators capable of coping with idiomatic syntactical complexities	later	1968	1972	1976	1980	1980	2012	later
Automated language translators—correct grammar			1971	1978	1996				
Widespread use of sophisticated teaching machines	Development of sophisticated teaching machines utilising adaptive programmes which respond not only to the students' answers but also to certain physiological responses of the students, for example tension	more specific, hence perhaps later, likely the same	1975	1975	1990	1980	1980	1992	slightly later
Manned scientific orbital space station—ten men	Launch of continuously manned scientific Earth orbital space station, say ten men with 90-day crew rotation	probably none	1970	1970	1975	1980	1980	1992	later, more distant forecast

First formulation	Second formulation	Relation							Note
Creation of a primitive form of artificial life (at least in the form of self-replicating molecules)	Laboratory creation of a primitive form of artificial life (at least in the form of self-replicating molecules)	none	1979	1989	2000	1980	1980	1980	earlier, with precise consensus
Economic feasibility of commercial generation of synthetic protein for food	Laboratory demonstration of artificial generation of protein for food through in vitro cellular processes	earlier, since only laboratory development is described	1985	1990	2003	1980	1980	1980	earlier, as called for
New organs through transplanting or prosthesis	Laboratory demonstration of biochemical processes which stimulate growth of new organs and limbs	none	1979	1989	2000	1980	1980	1980	earlier, with precise consensus
Biochemicals to stimulate growth of new organs and limbs			1995	2007	2040				earlier, precise consensus
Implantable artificial organs made of plastic and electronic components	Demonstration of implantable artificial hearts with very long-duration power source	second formulation is narrower	1975	1982	1988	1980	1980	1992	
Feasibility (not necessarily acceptance) of chemical control over some human hereditary defects by modification on genes through molecular engineering		none	1984	2012	2050	1980	2000	2012	
Feasibility of using drugs to raise intelligence level (other than as dietary supplements and not in the sense of only temporarily raising the level of apperception)	Feasibility of raising the level of intelligence in some persons (other than as dietary supplements and not in the sense of only temporarily raising the level of apperception) allowing adults to solve problems previously unsolvable	none	1984	2012	2050	1980	2000	2012	earlier, a more optimistic forecast

TABLE 1.2 (Continued)

1964	1969	Possible Bias from Phrasing	1964 LQ	1964 Median	1964 UQ	1969 LQ	1969 Median	1969 UQ	Correlation
Chemical control of the ageing process, permitting extension of the life span by 50 years	Demonstration of chemical control of the human ageing process, permitting extension of the life span by 50 years with commensurate increase in years of vigour	possibly later because of qualification	1995	2075	2075	1980	2012	later	substantially earlier, a more optimistic forecast
Use of telepathy and ESP in communications	Laboratory demonstration of electronically amplified or augmented communication between brains (controlled ESP). Reliable use of ESP (such as telepathy in communications)	none	2040	never	never	later / 2025	later / later	never / never	no substantial change, median from never to later
Effective widespread fertility control by oral contraceptive or other simple and inexpensive means	Development of economical mass-administered contraceptive agents	none	1970	1970	1983	1973	1980	1985	later, a less optimistic forecast
Widespread and socially widely accepted use of non-narcotic drugs (other than alcohol) for the purpose of producing specific changes in personality characteristics	Availability of cheap, non-narcotic drugs (other than alcohol) for the purpose of producing specific changes in personality characteristics, such as euphoria, anti-anxiety, anti-aggression, in-	second formulation is more specific	1980	1983	2000	1973	1980	1980	later for changes in life style and attitude, earlier for temporary changes

1964 event	1969 event	Change in definition	1964 forecast			1969 forecast			Comparison
creased perception and increased attention Public availability of cheap, non-narcotic drugs (other than alcohol) for the purpose of producing specific changes in personality characteristics such as alterations in attitudes and life styles						1992	2012	2025	
Biochemical general immunisation against bacterial and viral diseases	Development of immunising agent which can protect against most bacterial and viral diseases	more limiting definition	1983	1994	2000	1973	1980	1985	earlier, as was slightly expected
Long-duration coma to permit a form of time travel	Demonstration of long-duration coma or hibernation to permit a form of time travel	none	2006	never	never	1985	2012	later	much earlier, a more optimistic forecast
Man-machine symbiosis, enabling man to extend his intelligence by direct electro-mechanical interaction between his brain and a computing machine	Demonstration of man-machine symbiosis, enabling man to extend his intelligence by direct electro-mechanical interaction between his brain and a computing machine	none	1990	2020	never	2012	2012	later	about the same
Feasibility of education by direct information recording on the brain	Feasibility of education by direct information recording on the brain	none	1997	2600	never	2012	later	never	same

Source: Robert H. Ament, "Comparison of Delphi Forecasting Studies in 1964 and 1969," *Futures* (March 1970), pp. 38–42.

(more than likely the already powerful) resulting in some form of bipolarity or multipolarity or a combination of the two. A second general type is a new polarization of the system between developed and developing states. A third type is a situation in which the overwhelming destructive capability of certain states allows them to exercise a veto within the international system. A fourth possibility is the creation of universalism, in which the political divisions of the world are minimized or eliminated. Lastly, there are scenarios that lead to the total destruction of the international system.

I. Evolutionary Scenarios
    A. Dominant Systems
        1. The United States and the Soviet Union continue to dominate the international system by virtue of their tremendous capabilities for mobilizing resources. The economic growth of the United States and the Soviet Union continues but at the expense of the welfare of less-developed states. As the competition for resources increases, both states exert military pressure to obtain their needs.
        2. China continues to develop her potential, and she, together with the United States and the Soviet Union, dominate the international system. As in the first scenario, there comes a time when the dominant powers cannot grow economically without exerting military pressure to get the resources they require. Their ability to exert pressure depends increasingly upon threats and the use of force.
        3. China develops her potential to such a degree that the United States and the Soviet Union form a coalition to balance China in a 1990 version of the cold war. China's development to a level approximating that of the United States or the Soviet Union requires the United States and the USSR to form an opposing coalition in order to maintain their dominant positions.
        4. Japan and China form an alliance to confront the coalition of the United States and the Soviet Union. (Japan and China together might well dominate the international system unless offset by a coalition of the Soviet Union and the United States.)
        5. The Soviet Union and China reach a rapprochement and confront a coalition of the United States, Japan, and the European Economic Community. (Here we assume the possibility of an ideological unification of the two socialist countries that could potentially dominate the globe unless balanced by a coalition of the other major economic powers.)
        6. China, the Soviet Union, the United States, Japan, and the European Economic Community choose mutual coexistence rather than try to assert dominance over each other, and they choose to cooperate among themselves in order to dominate the rest of the world.

7. The competition among China, the Soviet Union, and the United States leads to costly and debilitating conflict, and Japan and the European Economic Community, by remaining aloof, emerge as the dominant forces.

8. The European Economic Community gradually expands to include Eastern Europe and the Soviet Union, while the United States, China, and Japan build upon their common interests and form a coalition to balance the European bloc.

9. The United Arab Republic, India, Indonesia, Nigeria, and Brazil all achieve a level of economic development to accord them major-power status along with China, Japan, the Soviet Union, the United States, and a unified Western Europe emerging from the European Economic Community. (This scenario might come about only if the other major economic powers relinquish or lose some of their dominance.)

10. A group of less-developed states possessing crucial energy resources —the Arab oil-producing states, for example—unify to achieve dominance over such oil-dependent states as the EEC and Japan, and thus acquire a position in world politics comparable to that of the Soviet Union, the United States, and China and would coexist with the latter states. (This assumes that energy-dependent states would acquiesce to "colonial" status vis-à-vis the oil-rich states in order to sustain their economic growth. It also assumes that the other dominant states would tolerate this situation and would not attempt to exert control over the energy resources.)

B. New Polarizations

1. The developing states acquire a common awareness of their potential powers and unify in order to bargain with their respective natural resources and manpower for a more dominant position in world affairs. The result is the coexistence of two coalitions—one composed of developed nations, the other composed of less-developed states.

2. The developing states put aside their cultural and ideological differences and align themselves with China for the purpose of working toward a common goal of preserving their integrity in the face of constant political and economic encroachments on the part of the developed nations.

C. Vetos Within the International System

Nations that have the potential for developing nuclear weapons— Canada, West Germany, Japan, Italy, Sweden, Australia, Belgium, Brazil, Czechoslovakia, East Germany, Israel, the Netherlands, Poland, Switzerland, and the United Arab Republic—do develop them and coexist in a state of tension with the six existing nuclear powers (China, the United States, the Soviet Union, France, the United Kingdom and

India). Because the new nuclear powers may remain second-rate economic powers, their exertion of dominance may involve nuclear threats
and blackmail.

  D. Universalism
     1. Nations agree to cooperate internationally in the use and develop-
        ment of the sea bed and the ocean floor. The mutual trust and con-
        fidence that grows out of an international ocean authority—a land-
        mark precedent in international affairs—is transferred to other
        relations among nations resulting in the gradual development of
        new procedures for peacefully resolving international conflicts.
     2. Conflict in the international system becomes so devastating that the
        survivors form a new United Nations invested with enough author-
        ity to effectively maintain peace and security. In this case universal-
        ism is achieved only when it is perceived as a last grasp at survival
        in the wake of nuclear warfare.
     3. All states come to realize that the largest threat to their survival is
        the disparity between developed and developing nations and join
        in an effort to reduce international tension by providing for an
        equitable sharing of global resources. This scenario assumes a high
        degree of rationality on the part of individuals and their govern-
        ments as well as the recognition of the limited ability of the bio-
        sphere to support life. It would involve the working out of a new
        balance among production, distribution, and consumption on a
        world-wide scale.

  E. Destruction of the System
    International conflict destroys mankind altogether. (This possibility
    may be viewed as the inevitable result of the unchecked evolution of
    forces currently at work in the international system.)

II. Radical Scenarios
  A. Dominant Systems
     1. China alone dominates the world. At a level of economic develop-
        ment equivalent or superior to the United States, China may have
        to dominate the rest of the world in order to acquire the resources
        she would need to sustain her growth, especially if her population
        continued to grow. She may achieve dominance through ideological
        conquest of the Third World. Politically and economically isolated,
        the United States, Europe, and the Soviet Union would then be
        unable to acquire the resources necessary to their continued eco-
        nomic expansion.
     2. The United States dominates the world as conflict between the So-
        viet Union and China eliminates the influence of both these states.
        (As a result of their proximity and ideological differences, nuclear
        conflict may occur between China and the Soviet Union; it will

severely weaken both nations and will leave the United States the most powerful of the three, provided, of course, that the United States is not drawn into the Sino-Soviet conflict.)

3. New and more destructive weapons systems are developed, and the state that creates them—probably the United States, the Soviet Union, or China—decides to use its military advantage to dominate the globe by threatening to use the new weapons.

B. New Polarizations

1. Major powers in the Third World such as India, Brazil, Indonesia, Pakistan, or Nigeria decide that their economic plight is so acute that they have no alternative but to concentrate on the development of nuclear weapons with which to blackmail the developed states for a more equitable share of the world's resources, or, out of desperation, they may actually use these weapons. (This scenario assumes that evolutionary adjustment of problems appears impossible to the Third World, which comes to believe that radical action alone will create change.)

2. The plight of the developing states becomes so acute that, even without nuclear weapons, these states choose conflict with the developed nations as their only viable means of wresting a fair share of the world's limited resources away from the developed nations.

3. Conflict breaks out between the black African states and the racist regimes of South Africa and Rhodesia and grows into a race war between the white and nonwhite states of the world. (This scenario is based upon the assumption that any conflict among nation-states based primarily on racial grounds will spread world-wide and will polarize nation-states according to whether their population is white or nonwhite.)

C. Veto Within the System

In desperation over its economic situation, one of the developing states opts to develop, threatens to use, or actually uses chemical or bacteriological weapons against the developed states. (Since chemical or bacteriological weapons are relatively cheap to produce, they are capable of being acquired by virtually every state, even underdeveloped nations. These weapons are therefore potential weapons of blackmail for every state, regardless of economic development.)

D. Universalism

1. A regional nuclear conflict develops in the international system—perhaps between the Soviet Union and China or between Israel and the Arab states—and the devastation is so shocking that the other nations unify and disarm to prevent such horrors in the future. (We assume here that nuclear conflict can be localized.)

2. The environmental crisis becomes so acute that the survival of man-

kind is possible only through the establishment of a universal authority to control and police population growth, pollution, and the use of the limited natural resources.

3. The environmental crisis increases international tensions among states to the point that solutions are impossible. Each state nationalistically attempts to assert its own solutions, resulting in interstate conflicts of all varieties. Many nations cease to exist. In desperation, the surviving states establish a world system to prevent new conflicts from destroying them all.

4. Nations and their leaders decide that the greatest threat to their survival is the existence of separate political units, and they develop some form of global government.

E. Destruction of the System

International conflict destroys mankind altogether. (This is comparable to the last scenario in the evolutionary cluster and can also be conceived as a radical development. Any of the scenarios of desperation in this cluster may lead to the ultimate destruction of life on this planet.)

These scenarios for the future are not intended to be exhaustive. Obviously, many other scenarios might be conceived as well as many variations on the themes we have suggested. We believe, however, that these are all within the realm of possibility. Whether they are *probable* scenarios, and which are most probable, will be a subject of debate among different individuals. Regardless of which scenarios an individual may believe are most probable and why, the problem of deciding which are *preferable* and how they might be brought into existence still exists. The decisions made by nations and their leaders based upon their awareness of the nature and problems of the international system will determine which scenarios will be realized. We devoutly hope it is the scenario of peaceful universalism.

NOTES

[1] See, for example, Seymour L. Halleck, *The Politics of Therapy*, New York: Harper & Row, 1972, which suggests that psychiatric treatment affects the distribution of power within the social systems in which the patient lives.

[2] C. H. Titus, "A Nomenclature in Political Science," *American Political Science Review*, 25, no. 1 (1931), 45.

[3] See James N. Rosenau, *The Drama of Politics: An Introduction to the Joys of Inquiry*, Boston, Mass.: Little, Brown, 1973; James N. Rosenau (ed.), *International Politics and Foreign Policy*, rev. ed., New York: Free Press, 1969.

[4] Heinz Eulau, *The Behaviorial Persuasion in Politics*, New York: Random House, 1963, pp. 3, 126.

[5]Aristotle, *Politics*, in Richard McKeon (ed.), *Introduction to Aristotle*, New York: Modern Library, 1947, pp. 555–556.

[6]See Richard N. Rosecrance, *Action and Reaction in World Politics*, Boston, Mass.: Little, Brown, 1963, for an analysis of the shifting coalitions in the international system from 1740 to the 1960s.

[7]Conferences were held at Moscow in 1943, Dumbarton Oaks in 1944, and Yalta in 1945.

[8]Text contained in James T. Watkins IV and J. William Robinson (eds.), *General International Organization*, Princeton, N.J.: D. Van Nostrand, 1956, pp. 163–164.

[9]Great Britain, Colonial Office, *Gold Coast: Report to His Excellency the Governor by the Committee on Constitutional Reform*, London: His Majesty's Stationery Office, 1949, pp. 7–8.

[10]See K. M. Panikkar, *The Future of South-East Asia*, New York: Macmillan, 1943, who predicted that the net effect of Japanese occupation would be the inability of the colonial powers to recover their control after the defeat of Japan.

[11]Edward Crankshaw, *The New Cold War: Moscow v. Peking*, Baltimore, Md.: Penguin, 1963, p. 22.

[12]See Herman Kahn, *The Emerging Japanese Superstate: Challenge and Response*, Englewood Cliffs, N.J.: Prentice-Hall, 1970.

[13]See Kautilya's *Arthasastra*, 3rd ed., R. Shamasastry (tr.), Mysore: Wesleyan Mission Press, 1929, pp. 344–349.

[14]John H. Herz, "The Rise and Demise of the Territorial State," *World Politics*, 9 (1957), 473–493.

[15]John H. Herz, "The Territorial State Revisited: Reflections on the Future of the Nation-State," *Polity*, 1, no. 1 (1968), 13.

[16]Richard Rosecrance, *Action and Reaction in World Politics*, Boston, Mass.: Little, Brown, 1963.

[17]K. J. Holsti, *International Politics: A Framework for Analysis*, Englewood Cliffs, N.J.: Prentice-Hall, 1967.

[18]James N. Rosenau, *The Scientific Study of Foreign Policy*, New York: Free Press, 1971.

[19]Norman Z. Alcock, "War Cycles and Planetary Positions," *Peace Research*, 5, no. 12 (December 1973), 88–94.

[20]Harold and Margaret Sprout, *Toward a Politics of the Planet Earth*, New York: Van Nostrand Reinhold, 1971, p. 14.

[21]*Ibid.*, p. 15.

[22]Hans J. Morgenthau, *Politics Among Nations: The Struggle for Power and Peace*, 5th ed., New York: Knopf, 1973.

[23]Roger D. Masters, "World Politics as a Primitive Political System," *World Politics*, 16, no. 4 (1964), 597.

[24]Morgenthau, *loc. cit.*

[25]Morton A. Kaplan, *System and Process in International Politics*, New York: Wiley, 1957, p. 23.

[26]Kenneth N. Waltz, "International Structure, National Force, and the Balance of World Order," *Journal of International Affairs*, 21, no. 2 (1967), 230. Copyright by the Trustees of Columbia University in the City of New York. Permission to reprint from the *Journal of International Affairs* is gratefully acknowledged to the Editors of the *Journal*.

[27]Richard Rosecrance, "Bipolarity, Multipolarity, and the Future," *Journal of Conflict Resolution*, 10, no. 3 (September 1966), 314–327.

[28]U.S., House of Representatives, Committee on Foreign Affairs, Subcommittee on Europe, *Hearings: Conference of European Security, April 25, May 10, August 10, 17, September 7, 27, 1972*, 92d Cong., 2d sess., 1972, pp. 111–113.

[29]Karl W. Deutsch, "Toward an Inventory of Basic Trends and Patterns in Comparative and International Politics," *American Political Science Review*, 44, no. 1 (1960), 34.

[30]Robert S. Lynd, *Knowledge for What?* Princeton, N.J.: Princeton University Press, 1939.

[31]Herman Kahn and Anthony J. Wiener, *The Year 2000: A Framework for Speculation on the Next Thirty-three Years*, New York: Macmillan, 1967.

[32]Albert Somit (ed.), *Political Science and the Study of the Future*, New York: Holt, Rinehart & Winston, 1974.

[33]Franklin Tugwell (ed.), *Search for Alternatives: Public Policy and the Study of the Future*, Cambridge, Mass.: Winthrop Publishers, 1973, p. vi.

[34]G. K. Chesterton, *The Napoleon of Notting Hill*, London: John Lane, 1904, p. 19, quoted in Bruce M. Russett, "The Ecology of Future International Politics," *International Studies Quarterly*, 11, no. 1 (1967), 17–18.

[35]U.S., Department of State, *National Report on the Human Environment*, Prepared for the United Nations Conference on Human Environment, June 1972, Stockholm, Sweden, Department of State Publication 8588 (1971), pp. 16–17.

[36]Gardner Murphy, "Where Is the Human Race Going?" in Richard E. Farson (ed.), *Science and Human Affairs*, Palo Alto, Calif.: Science and Behavior Books, 1965, pp. 9, 14.

[37]Daniel Bell, "Twelve Modes of Predictions" in Somit, op. cit., pp. 40–67.

2

MAN
AND
HIS
DECISIONS

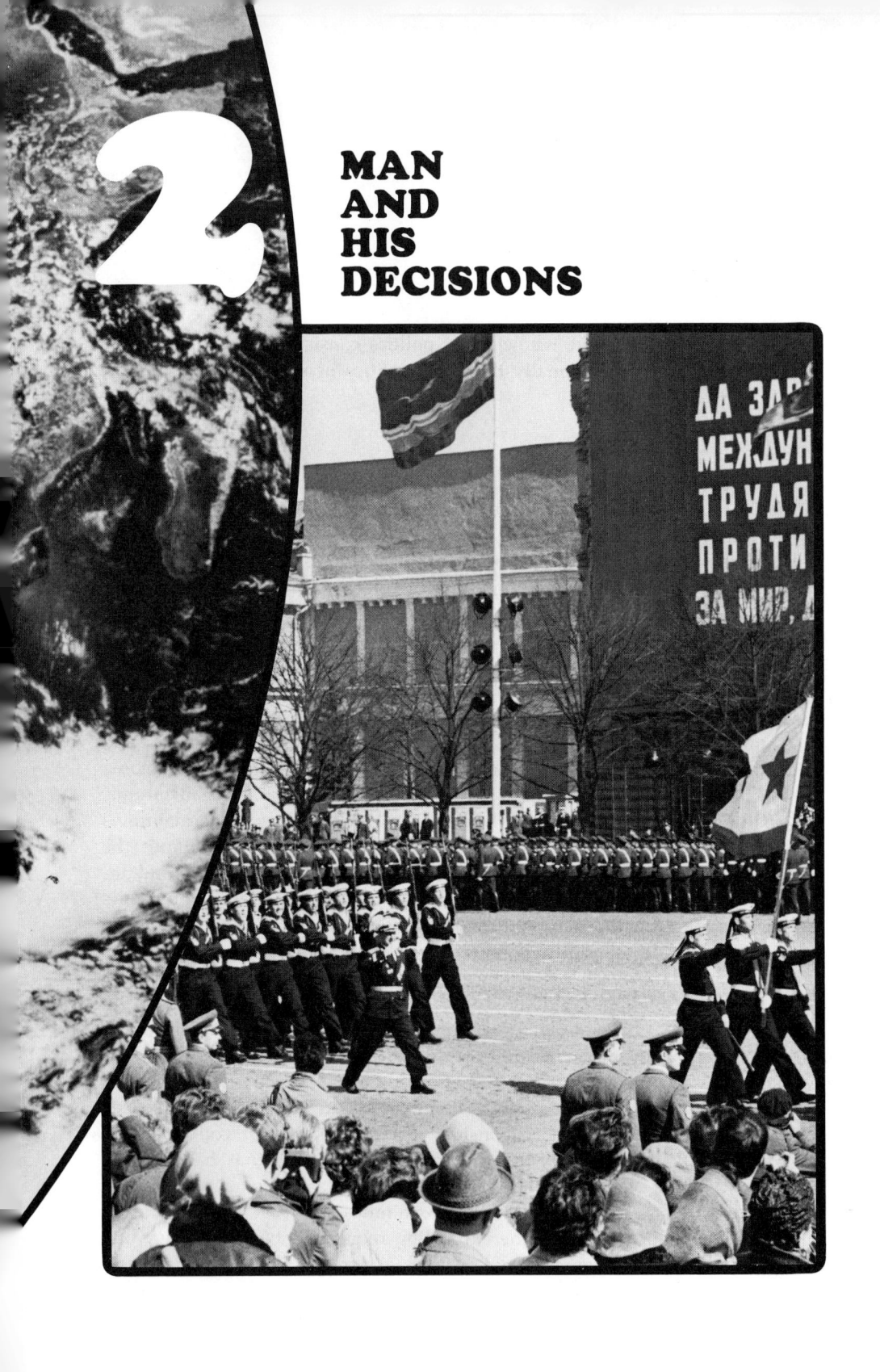

The whole art of politics consists in directing
rationally the irrationalities of men.
                                    Reinhold Niebuhr

The decision-making process is at the heart of dealing with our global future. In fact, we believe it is more critical than world dilemmas themselves, for only through correct decisions can we build a sane and humane world, fulfilling the hopes and alleviating the fears of peoples everywhere. Yet decision making has grown increasingly difficult as a result of expanding requirements on policy, a shortening of the time allowed for responses, and the growing complexity of issues.

As President, George Washington had only three departments to administer and only infrequently found it necessary to communicate with ministers in foreign capitals. He was able to draw from his own knowledge and experience most of the facts he needed to make most decisions.[1] By contrast, world leaders today must deal with an arena of 150 independent nation-states, some 33 dependent territories, over 400 international and regional organizations, and countless private international bodies. The United States alone maintains almost 300 embassies, consular posts, and special missions throughout the world. Approximately 10,000 reports, messages, policy statements, and instructions are exchanged daily between the United States government and its foreign missions. Of those 10,000, more than 2,000 are telegrams requiring attention and action. In addition, American delegates attend nearly 600 international conferences each year. During his first three-and-a-half years in office, Secretary of State William Rogers traveled 270,000 miles, visited 40 countries, held 485 private meetings with chiefs of state and foreign ministers. Hour after hour, day after day, world leaders make decisions that affect not only their own people but have repercussions for the rest of the world as well. And whereas world decision makers once had the luxury of weeks, sometimes months, in which to consider alternatives, weigh consequences, make judgments, and write brilliant reports on situations that had entirely altered by the time their dispatches arrived, they now at times have only days, hours, or even, in the case of military alerts, minutes.

Another manifestation of the expanding requirements upon policy and decision makers is the increasingly complex nature of the decisions them-

selves. When European leaders committed their nations to war in the nineteenth century, for example, they had rather clear ideas of the costs and risks involved. Of course, they never knew when their enemies would spring upon them a new weapon or military tactic, but even those unforeseen events changed only the magnitude, not the nature of the risks, taken by the warring nations. Today the smallest military engagement between states carries with it some potential risk of total warfare, the consequences of which are of an entirely different nature from those we have known in the past.

It is clear that modern decision makers make more decisions and more decisions having great consequences in less time than ever before. But some scholars have questioned whether we understand a great deal more about *inter*national—compared to *intra*national—decisions than we did some years ago. James A. Robinson and Richard C. Snyder have commented: "To discuss decision-making in international politics is to engage in an essentially prescientific exercise, one that involves analogy, extrapolation, projection, and reduction from decisional studies of other units and levels of analysis to the international political system."[2] Beyond these analytical problems is the question of whether or not the decisions being made are in the best interests of the world as a whole. Irving L. Janis reminds us that: "Improving the quality of decision-making by eliminating certain sources of error that prevent a group from achieving its goals can be expected to have good social consequences for policy-making groups that have good goals; otherwise not."[3]

In this chapter we present some basic ideas about the decision-making process, what goes into it, what impedes it, what influences it, and how we might modify it to make it work more constructively so that, to paraphrase Henry A. Kissinger, the demands of the present do not overwhelm the future.[4]

DECISION MAKING

ENDS AND MEANS

Decision making may be defined as the selection of a course of action intended to bring about a desired state of affairs. In a decision-making process there are two paramount factors: the *end* to be accomplished (goals, policy conditions, aims, purposes) and the *means* to be used (methods, instrumentalities). Both means and ends may be matters of considerable debate among policy makers. In 1946 during the debate in the U.S. Senate concerning American participation in the International Court of Justice, two distinctly different views of the goal emerged. Supporters of world order through world law believed that the jurisdiction of the Court should be compulsory; that is, it should be possible for any state to bring action against any other state without the latter's consent. But many political leaders, including Senator

Tom Connally, supporting the paramountcy of national sovereignty were unwilling to commit the United States to the principle of compulsory jurisdiction without some safeguards. They feared that the Court might use its power to interfere with domestic policy on immigration, tariffs, civil rights, and the administration of the Panama Canal. In the end Senator Connally's views prevailed. The Senate gave its "advice and consent" to the charter and thus accepted compulsory jurisdiction; but it included the proviso that the United States be free to determine for itself what matters were of an essentially domestic nature and therefore outside the jurisdiction of the Court.

During the Cuban missile crisis in 1962, members of the Executive Committee of the National Security Council generally agreed on ends: The introduction of intermediate-range missiles in Cuba by the Soviet Union was intolerable to the United States and must be removed. But they disagreed upon the means the United States should take to accomplish its goal. Some argued for immediate military intervention in Cuba; others, who wished to keep several options open, advocated a naval blockade as a first step in convincing the Russians to remove the missiles.

The distinction between means and ends is often purely arbitrary; it may be a matter of definition and timing. The same airplane is a goal for its builder and a means for its pilot, so its definition depends upon a particular context. The eventual decision to establish a naval blockade in the missile crisis was a means toward the ultimate goal of getting the missiles removed. But once the blockade was decided upon, it then became a goal in itself, the realization of which made necessary many further decisions concerning implementation.

Theoretically, the steps in the decision-making process involving both means and ends are the following:

1. Definition of the situation
2. Definition (or redefinition) of interests
3. Calculation and evaluation of alternatives
4. Selection of a course of action
5. Implementation of choice
6. Assessment of effect and redefinition of the situation.

RATIONAL AND NONRATIONAL DECISION MAKING

At each stage of this process three considerations implicitly or explicitly influence the decisions: what is desired, what can be done, and what must be done.

What these steps describe is a model of rational decision making. According to Sidney Verba:

> *Rational models of individual decision-making are those in which the individual responding to an international event bases his response upon a cool and clearheaded means-ends calculation. He uses the best information available and chooses from the universe of possible responses that alternative most likely to maximize his goals. The rational decision-maker may, for instance, respond aggressively to an international event, but the aggressive response will have its source in calculations based upon the nature of the international situation. It will be directed against the real enemy—the nation threatening or inflicting damage to one's interests—and the decision-maker will have some reasonable expectation of achieving his ends through the aggressive response. Furthermore, the decision will either have no psychological side-effects on the decision-maker (he will not experience tension release or guilt because of it), or, if there are psychological side-effects, they will be irrelevant as far as the nature of the decision is concerned.[5]*

Models of rational decision making tend to minimize factors that contaminate orderly and clear processes. Decision making appears logical and rational when its components are presented theoretically. Yet in real life any number of contingencies may muddy the waters. Most obvious, of course, is the fact that policy makers differ in their assessments of nearly every situation. Conflict in decision making is heightened according to the degree to which the participants stress:

1. *Different facts*
2. *Different inferences from the same facts*
3. *Different values*
4. *Different entailments of the same values*
5. *Different processes or conclusions when values and facts are joined in a definition of the situation*
6. *Different roles or different perceptions of the same roles.[6]*

Part of the controversy over Vietnam, for example, was a result of disagreements over what, exactly, was happening there—civil war, revolution, or external aggression and subversion—whether American interests were sufficiently involved to warrant intervention and, if so, what type of intervention and toward what ends. Lurking in the background were still broader controversies over the general posture of the United States toward national liberation movements, the Third World as a whole, and competition with major and minor communist powers.

But differences among policy leaders are only one difficulty to be dealt with in making decisions. Anthony Downs lists six more:

1. *Each decision-maker can devote only a limited amount of time to decision-making.*
2. *Each decision-maker can mentally weigh and consider only a limited amount of information at one time.*
3. *The functions of most officials require them to become involved in more activities than they can consider simultaneously; hence they must normally focus their attention on only part of their major concerns, while the rest remain latent.*
4. *The amount of information initially available to every decision-maker about each problem is only a small fraction of all the information potentially available on the subject.*
5. *Additional information bearing on any particular problem can usually be procured, but the cost of procurement and utilization may rise rapidly as the amount of data increases.*
6. *Important aspects of many problems involve information that cannot be procured at all, especially concerning future events; hence many decisions must be made in the face of some ineradicable uncertainty.*[7]

The image of statesmen objectively and dispassionately analyzing problems, hearing recommendations, and ordering courses of action that are then implemented is more rhetoric than fact. President Harry S. Truman lamented that "I sit here all day trying to persuade people to do things they ought to have sense enough to do without my persuading them. . . . That's all the powers of the President amount to."[8] John F. Kennedy, after promising to take certain measures during a press conference, is said to have remarked: "Today I actually made a little policy."[9]

There is an opposite argument suggesting that the decision-making process is nonrational, illogical, and wholly dependent upon personal idiosyncracies.

> *Non-rational models assume that when an individual is faced with a choice situation in relation to an international event . . . he responds in terms of what we shall call non-logical pressures or influences. These are pressures or influences unconnected with the event in question.*
> *A gross case occurs when an individual responds aggressively to an international event because of internal psychological pressures toward aggression, having their root in childhood experiences. A non-logical influence is any influence acting upon the decision-maker of which he is unaware and which he would not consider a legitimate influence upon his decision if he were aware of it.*[10]

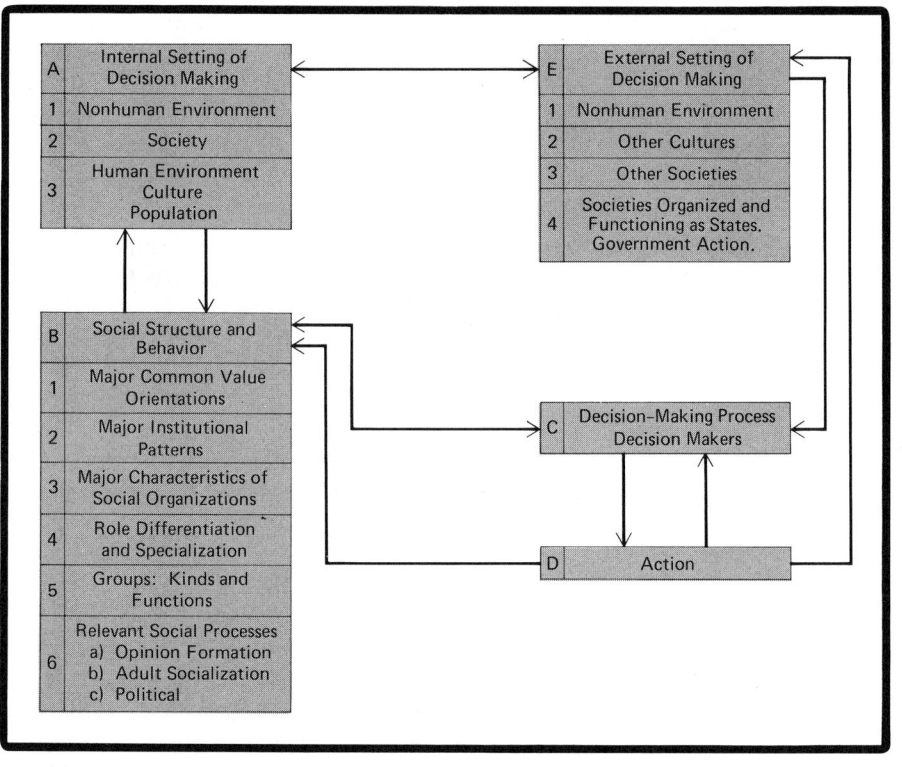

FIGURE 2.1 State "X" as Actor in a Situation

Note: Situation is comprised of a combination of selectively relevant factors in the external and internal setting as interpreted by the decision makers.

Source: Richard C. Snyder, H. W. Bruck, and Burton Sapin (eds.), *Foreign Policy Decision Making*, New York: Free Press, 1962, p. 72. Copyright © by The Free Press, a division of The Macmillan Publishing Co., Inc.

According to this argument the question in decision making is not "What is reality?" but "Whose image of reality will prevail?"[11]

Both rational and nonrational assumptions about decision making are useful in understanding the complexity of factors involved. Often, however, they ignore the larger context of elements that impinge upon and influence decision making. Figure 2.1 attempts to list and untangle some of the encyclopedic factors related to the actions, reactions, and interactions in international politics and the way decision makers perceive situations and make choices.

While the figure alerts us to many salient factors and relationships in decision making, it does not suggest the relative importance of each category. Yet we cannot assume that each factor carries equal weight. Neither does

such a model tell us what combination of situations and conditions might be expected to produce what types of decisions and with what consequences.

Our theoretical knowledge about how we make decisions is still embryonic. Decision making is not analogous to a factory assembly line that produces a standardized product from standard parts according to an established timetable with assigned costs and benefits. If decision making were like this, we might find it easier to alter the process in order to thread our way more clearly through the conundrums of international politics in the twentieth century. Nor is decision making a random process devoid of order. Most decisions are only slight modifications of existing policy. The challenge in decision making is whether we can adjust and deal with so many immediate issues. To do so demands that we ask the right questions about processes, preferences, and purposes.

DECISION MAKERS

THE RESPONSIBILITY FOR DECISIONS

In theory, decision makers are persons who occupy positions of responsibility for formulating and executing policy. According to the United States Constitution, for example, the President is the ultimate decision maker in the realm of foreign policy. As President Truman put it, "the buck ends here." Yet it is too simplistic to view foreign policy as either made or executed by the President himself, except in its broadest outlines. Congress, presidential advisers, the Secretaries of State and Defense, the Director of the Central Intelligence Agency (CIA), the Joint Chiefs of Staff, various private interest groups, and a host of other individuals and institutions are all responsible in some degree for the shape of American foreign policy. Policy decisions in almost every other field are likewise the result of the converging of many persons and groups, official and unofficial.

Situations in which it is immediately obvious who are the primary decision makers and what motivates them to make a particular decision are rare indeed. When President Truman removed General Douglas MacArthur from his position as Commander of U.N. Forces during the Korean War there was no doubt that the President himself made the decision largely because of policy differences with the general. But we cannot so easily say who was responsible for the decisions that brought about the My Lai massacre of more than 400 Vietnamese civilians. Was it Lieutenant Calley, who was charged with the crime? or his immediate military superiors? or General William Westmoreland and Creighton Abrams? or then Secretary of Defense Robert McNamara?

Even when we can attribute a certain policy to a particular decision

maker or group as a function of their position or reputation, it is important to remember that policy is often altered in the process of implementation. Administrators and bureaucrats who translate words into action have some opportunity to imprint policy with their own individual interpretations. This appears to have been the case with the bombing attacks against North Vietnam ordered by General John Lavalle, Commander of U.S. Air Force units in Southeast Asia in the early months of 1972. General Lavalle was relieved as commander, demoted, and retired after ordering repeated and unauthorized attacks against military targets in North Vietnam during a period when such bombing was prohibited by the White House. According to a high-ranking military source close to the incident, Lavalle was known to have received no written orders authorizing the attacks, but the general "thought it was implied in the instructions that were given him." Lavalle believed, said the source, that he had the authority as a battlefield commander "to make a determination of how far you can stretch rules before going up through the chain of command."[12] Officials in the Pentagon seemed to have a different view of how far rules could be stretched.

On the other hand, General Lavalle claimed to have believed that his superiors in Saigon were aware of his bombing attacks and tacitly condoned them. If that was true, who then was responsible for allowing the attacks to continue? The difficulty of clearly identifying those responsible for any particular decision contributes to scapegoating, and many of General Lavalle's supporters claim that he became the scapegoat for his superiors when the unauthorized bombing unexpectedly came to light.

More often, it is the President who is blamed when foreign affairs go badly, for he is not only the most visible policy maker but, according to the Constitution, the final authority over foreign policy. Certainly Lyndon Johnson and Richard Nixon were villified for the Vietnam War, but the Congress of the United States was the agency appropriating the monies for its conduct. Other favorite scapegoats in the United States are the amorphous "power elites," "the Establishment," and the "military-industrial complex." The actual existence of a power elite that exercises inordinate influence over decision making in the United States has long been a matter of debate. Richard J. Barnet points out that most of the top 400 presidential appointments since 1945 could be located in ten city blocks in five of America's largest cities.[13] We believe that the elite groups that influence, and perhaps determine, policy shift in composition depending upon the issue and are not a unified, homogeneous, and stable group of persons.

In authoritarian and centralized societies it seems somewhat easier to identify decision makers. Kremlinologists maintain that members of the Soviet Politburo are the most important policy makers in the Soviet Union. Even so,

when Nikita Khrushchev and Nikolai Bulganin "shared" power, it took the experts some time to sort out exactly which man was dominant. The same was true when Leonid Brezhnev and Alexis Kosygin took over Soviet leadership. When the Strategic Arms Limitation agreements were signed in 1972, it was the General Secretary of the Communist party, Brezhnev, rather than the titular leader of the government, who signed for the Soviet Union.

Through laborious case studies of specific decisions scholars ferret out their components. Roberta Wohlstetter untangled the Pearl Harbor disaster of December 7, 1941, and showed which key officials were responsible for the decision that Pearl Harbor could not be attacked by the Japanese, even though warnings of impending aggression had been communicated to Washington.[14] Glenn D. Paige unraveled the decision to intervene in Korea, tracing both the various decisions between June 24 and June 30, 1950, and the "decisional units," that is, the persons involved, and suggested that in crisis situations the principal decision-making group consists of 12 to 15 officials.[15] One study of American involvement in Vietnam attempted to sort out the individuals responsible for various phases of American involvement and by naming the officials countered the oft-repeated opinion that the war was merely a result of the workings of a faceless system or inexorable bureaucratic processes.[16] By focusing upon policy statements, communication, and actions among preselected key officials, Ole R. Holsti found that in the five-week period immediately preceding the outbreak of World War I, key decision makers in Britain, France, Russia, Germany, and Austria-Hungary all perceived time as crucial and their options as limited. As stress mounted, the volume of communication among the parties greatly increased, as did the proportion of stereotyped information, particularly among allies. The intense and protracted strain eroded the ability of decision makers to sift information accurately. As their perceptions became more distorted, they narrowed their range of options and moved closer to war.[17]

Of course, these studies are *post hoc*. They are fascinating recapitulations of former decisions and the source of many useful hypotheses.[18] As a whole, however, they have low predictive power. But we can learn broader lessons from such case studies: Hindsight should lead to foresight regarding the dynamics of decision making. As Paige has suggested:

> . . . *somewhat more precise guides may now be suggested for the analysis of the "givens" that precede an occasion for decision; i.e., (1) specification of major policies in force; (2) understandings about the main features of the internal and external settings; (3) major values evoked and salient; (4) principal constraints upon and pressures for action; (5) outstanding interpretations given to past learning experiences; (6) principal anticipated future states of affairs; and*

*(7) objective capabilities for implementing actual or potential courses
of action. The* a priori *analysis of "givens" may thus be accomplished
with or without reference to a specific occasion for decision and for a
wide range of analytically defined decisional units from individuals to
whole governments.*[19]

Furthermore, by employing a multiplicity of approaches in assessing decisions
and decision making we move closer to developing both conceptual and substantive understanding. Graham T. Allison demonstrates such an analytical
process in his assessment of the Cuban missile crisis.[20] Utilizing three different models, he shows how the assumptions of each influence understanding
of the same event and, at the same time, produce explanations of quite different occurrences. The different models refract reality into different shapes.

Yet once we have discovered what we can about how a decision has been
made and by whom, we are still left with the problem of evaluating the decision. While it is possible to become so engrossed with the process that we
lose sight of the result, it is the result that shapes national policies and world
realities.

CONSTRAINTS ON
DECISION MAKING AND POLICY

Secretary of State Henry A. Kissinger posed one of the most difficult
questions we face in meeting global problems: "The question is whether or
not it is possible in the modern bureaucratic state to develop a sense of long-
range purpose and to inquire into the meaning of activity."[21] To understand
why it is so difficult to change our individual and national approaches to
problem solving, we must look behind present policies into the political, sociological, and psychological factors that motivate men to behave as they do.

The remaining pages of this book could be filled with lists of factors
that one way or another influence or impinge upon policy decisions, and we
still would not have included them all. We have selected for discussion a
number of constraints on policy and decision making that we believe to be
among the most salient. They are constraints that appear to operate in almost
all nations: the negative influences of national traditions and interests, bureaucratic imperatives, and man's psychological behavior. Most of these constraints originate and operate at the individual, group, and national levels
rather than at the international level. They contribute to the well springs of
foreign policy rather than constitute distinct features of international politics
per se. But politics concerns men. It is persons acting in the name of the state
who make decisions, persons who get disembowled in war, persons who suf-

fer from hunger. It is man who must confront and adapt to what Alvin Toffler calls "future shock," the state of paralysis increasingly manifest in
modern technological societies.[22]

NATIONAL INTERESTS

As we have already noted, the competing and exclusive interests of
states are a primary characteristic of international politics. True, there are
identical, complementary, and shared interests among nations, but national
self-interest is almost always paramount. While national interests may have
some foundation in human nature, more often than not they are products of
custom, habit, tradition, cultural mores, and values. History acts as a condi-
tioning process, creating a political culture with customary ways of viewing
and dealing with the world. Consider the Monroe Doctrine. Although the
doctrine was promulgated as long ago as 1823 and has since acquired several
corollaries, the United States still views interference in or penetration of the
Western Hemisphere by an outside nation as a violation of American national
interest. Czarist and Soviet regimes alike maintained as a prime objective of
foreign policy the obtaining of ice-free ports. In the nineteenth- and early
twentieth-century efforts to maintain European order, the United Kingdom
played "perfidious Albion," shifting policies and allies in order to maintain
what it defined as its primary interest: an independent position as the balancing power in Europe.

If the wellsprings of policy are history, tradition, and national myths
rationalized as national interests, we can expect decision makers to respond
to new situations in historical and ethnocentric terms. New realities in international politics are often very difficult for both national leaders and their
constituencies to accept. One of the reasons European statesmen were so slow
to recognize the threat posed by Napoleon was that history told them such
men only wanted to modify the existing European political system, not overthrow it. They repeated the same mistake with Hitler. More recently, when
criticism was voiced in the United Nations concerning impending nuclear
tests by France in the South Pacific in 1973, French Defense Minister, Michel
Debre, responded that to renounce France's independent nuclear force would
be unthinkable. "It would mean losing our place as a Great Power. . . ."[23]
Debre may be correct about the status of France as a great power (although
one has only to read J. J. Servan-Schreiber's *The American Challenge*[24] to
realize that the "independent" France of yesteryear is not the France of today), but it appears that France has not yet adjusted the great-power notion
to the realities of the twentieth century. The free-wheeling, independent foreign policies of the past are no longer the unquestioned prerogatives of the
individual nation, particularly where thermonuclear testing is concerned. Yet
almost all national leaders follow the time-worn credos of national interest

as if they were wearing blinders, and few governments are willing to admit that the policies they pursue may not be the best possible policies for themselves or for the world. Perhaps to break the status quo dictated by national styles and interests, leaders who have learned from the past must also imagine history as beginning today.

BUREAUCRATIC IMPERATIVES

By the sheer force of their personalities, men such as Churchill, Roosevelt, Stalin, and Gandhi changed the course of national and world events. Historian Sidney Hook once tried to imagine "A World Without Lenin," to demonstrate the historical importance of the "event-making man."[25] Nevertheless, in the modern state it is the bureaucracy that keeps the government running. Presidents and parliaments, charismatic leaders, and popular movements may come and go, but the bureaucracy remains, performing essentially the same tasks year in, year out. Kissinger points out, "Policy-making in our society confronts the difficulty that revolutionary changes have to be encompassed and dealt with by an increasingly rigid administrative structure."[26] To make change still more difficult, rigidity of the administrative structure is coupled with complexity. When Nixon began his second term as President, there were no fewer than 800 interagency coordinating committees on top of the already bewildering maze of federal departments, bureaus, and agencies.

Self-Perpetuating Systems. Bureaucracies are inherently conservative. They value order, stability, and routine far more than they value change, creativity, and experimentation. The State Department, for example, has only recently begun to utilize long-available computerized storage and retrieval systems for processing information.[27] The basic bureaucratic imperative is self-perpetuation—to go on doing things more or less as they have always been done, to acquire power and maintain or achieve status, and to protect the bureaucracy from outside forces. Toward these ends bureaucracies engage in lobbying, logrolling, propagandizing, and the wooing of power away from other agencies.

The bureaucratic goal of self-perpetuation also leads to the kind of defensive management that caused the Pentagon, in 1969, to refuse to send to Congress the text of a military-aid agreement the Defense Department had reportedly made with Thailand. If the congressmen wished to see the document, said the Pentagon, they could come to the Pentagon. Auditors from the Bureau of the Budget received the same treatment: When they wished to inspect Defense Department records, they, too, were obliged to go to the Pentagon.

Defensive management protects the bureaucratic organization against criticism, creativity, and nonconformity on the part of its own members,

elected officials, and the general public. Principles of defensive management include low trust, data distortion, and high control maintained through procedures and rules such as:

—Keeping a close check on people
—Requiring frequent reports
—Maintaining a tight security system
—Making many inspection trips
—Checking closely all expense vouchers
—Making inconsistent policies
—Issuing frequent orders with explanations
—Having strict rules
—Withholding information from subordinates
—Insisting that people stay in "channels"
—Classifying information as secret
—Evaluating employees regularly.[28]

All told, defensive management is policy making in which the interests of the bureaucracy are paramount. It led President Truman to declare: "Those fellows in the State Department, who stay there no matter what happens in elections, can't be trusted to carry out a President's policies."[29]

Other Bureaucratic Weaknesses. Bureaucratic organizations can become aberrant, irrational, and singleminded advocates of a very particular point of view as a result of what Roger Hilsman has termed a "strain for consensus."[30] Hilsman applied the concept to the State Department, but it is appropriate for any organization characterized by a low degree of trust and a high degree of control over its employees. In such an atmosphere decision makers avoid conflict and debate. Options are narrowly defined and seldom deviate far from existing policy. The 1961 Bay of Pigs incident is a classic example of the sometimes tragic consequences of the strain for consensus. After the Cubans failed to rise against Castro in support of the attempted American invasion of the Bay of Pigs, President Kennedy discovered that the interpretation of intelligence data and the resulting evaluation of the entire project was distorted. The advice he had received concerning the invasion had been influenced more by what his advisers wanted to believe and what they thought he wanted to hear than by reality. As Janis points out: *"The more amiability and ésprit de corps among the members of a policy-making in-group, the greater is the danger that independent thinking will be replaced by groupthink, which is likely to result in irrational and dehumanizing actions directed against out-groups."*[31]

When an individual becomes a member of a bureaucratic organization,

he occupies a highly structured position. His responsibilities and his professional behavior are defined by administrative regulations and by well-established custom. In separate surveys of junior and senior United States foreign-service officers taken in the mid-1960s, both groups stressed the importance of role demands in the performance of their duties: (1) supporting and complying with policy decisions even when personally disagreeing with them, (2) maintaining proper dress and manners, (3) placing the "good of the service" above the good of the individual, and (4) being ready and available to comply with orders to serve anywhere in any job. One foreign-service officer commented: "Once decisions are reached, conformity is not only a virtue, but an imperative. It is not the proper role of the foreign service in implementing our foreign policy to undercut the political decisions which have been made." He does distinguish, however, between implementation and formulation of policy by warning that ". . . *the conformity that is appropriate in policy implementation can be suicidal in policy formulation.*"[32]

The Struggle for Individualism. The startling effects of submission or obedience to authority are illustrated in the Milgram experiments.[33] It was demonstrated, for example, that subjects will obey instructions to the point of thinking they have inflicted intense electrical shock on another person, often regardless of the distress it causes themselves (and those shocked) simply because someone in authority (the experimenter) told them to do so. Particularly when we need an infusion of new ideas, obedience to ritual and submission to authority are counterproductive. Bureaucratic tyrannies and dictatorships are built with persons who conform, comply, and do not question. But there are other dangers as well. Although military alert systems and arming of nuclear weapons are controlled by a "fail-safe" system—that is, a means for recalling bombers and separate keys for arming and firing missiles—no system is foolproof. Even if a system is 99 percent reliable, there is always the possibility that someone may overcome the obstacles, order the weapons used, and find that subordinates obey their orders. Political and social rationality presupposes individual rationality.

Of course, there are always individuals who are not content to allow their private concepts of their roles to be determined by anything so uninspired as a routine administrative code. This can be either a plus or a minus depending on whether the exercise of power is used well or abused. John Foster Dulles, American Secretary of State between 1953 and 1959, was one such unique personality. He was, in the words of one associate, "a man of supreme confidence within himself. . . ." As a consequence, "he simply did not pay any attention to staff or to experts or anything else." Dulles' conception of himself and his job led Undersecretary of State Christian Herter to describe himself as "No. 2 man in a one-man show."[34]

Whether Secretary of State or low-level administrative assistant, all decision makers in a bureaucracy must balance a number of roles. The diplomat, for example, is both a national agent representing his government and a member of the diplomatic community. The result is competing loyalties. Describing British diplomats of the nineteenth century, Harold Nicolson says the diplomat

> . . . owes his loyalties to his own sovereign, government, minister, and foreign office; he owes loyalty to his own staff; he owes a form of loyalty to the diplomatic body in the capital where he resides; he owes loyalty to the local British colony and its commercial interests; and then he owes another form of loyalty to the government to which he is accredited and to the minister with whom he negotiates.[35]

To continue the example of the diplomat, he is also a private citizen, with many personal needs, roles, and obligations to fulfill. We are not certain how all these competing demands and nonrational influences affect policy decisions. But to the extent that bureaucracies ignore or deny human loyalties and the conflicts they generate, decision making will remain a haphazard and poorly understood process. We do know, however, that the bureaucratic imperative, which discourages creativity and promotes conformity, defensive management, the strain for consensus, and the dissonance created by competing role demands—all these to some degree impair the ability of both organizations and individuals to respond to world and national problems with fresh approaches and expanded options.

MAN'S PSYCHOLOGY

In opening hearings on psychological aspects of foreign policy before the Senate Committee of Foreign Relations, J. W. Fulbright remarked, "an examination of the human mind in order to understand our own political behavior has not heretofore appealed to either the public or to political leaders. It may be we are frightened by the possibilities that might be revealed by some self-examination."[36]

Most of us are inclined to assume that governmental and international affairs are conducted by persons whose values, critical faculties, and mental health are above suspicion. In the odd event they are not, we trust the bureaucratic process or the good judgment of other officials or the influence of countervailing groups to provide the necessary antidotes. History belies our trust. In the nineteenth century, European immigrants to Tasmania systematically exterminated the entire aboriginal population. The assessment by most of the German people, and by the rest of the world, that Hitler was of the same species as they, sealed the fate of millions of Jews and brought home

the truths of human depravity on a gigantic scale. And over 1 million Viet-namese were deprived of their right to life in the name of preserving their freedom of political choice.

We know considerably more about how atoms behave than we know about man's psychological behavior. We have some evidence and many con-tending theories concerning the psychological roots of human behavior, but we cannot state with any degree of certainty what motivates decision makers to behave as they do. It is still difficult if not impossible, for example, to reconcile the conscious individual aversion to war and the collective prepared-ness to wage war.

In the following pages we highlight a few of the basic features of man's psychology that we believe have direct bearing upon the kinds of decisions he makes. First we consider the process of perception and how it is that in-dividual perceptions differ so greatly from person to person. Then we examine approach-avoidance conflicts and the effects of stress upon decision making. Finally, we describe some experimental efforts to effect change in human be-havior and consider how they might be applied to international relations.

1. Perception. Perception is the process by which persons select, evalu-ate, and organize information (stimuli) from the environment. It is also the process by which the nature of an object is recognized through memory asso-ciations. Our perceptions are partially shaped by our feelings—our desires, fears, aspirations, and prejudices. We interpret what we perceive to fit our needs, and at the same time, our needs determine what we perceive. Psy-chologist Jerome Frank describes how culture, prejudice, and past experience condition our perceptions. We call the result *selective* perception.

> *We are not aware that our expectations are constantly shaping our picture of the world because the process goes on outside our conscious-ness. To take a simple example, a psychologist had Mexican and American school teachers look into a device that showed a different picture to each eye at the same time. A picture of a baseball player was presented to one eye and a picture of a bullfighter to the other. An overwhelming proportion of the Mexicans "saw" the bullfighter; and overwhelming proportion of the Americans "saw" the baseball player. What they saw was largely determined by whether they were Mexicans or Americans. A person's group membership also influences what he hears and remembers. Back in 1941 some Republicans and Democrats were asked to listen to a speech containing equal numbers of statements for and against the New Deal. A little later they were asked what it contained. The Republicans said it was a speech denouncing the New Deal and remembered quotations supporting their position. The*

Democrats said it favored the New Deal and recalled quotations
supporting this view.[37]

These experiments illustrate how two groups of people who have different stakes in the same social or political event and who start out with different assumptions and predispositions selectively perceive information that
supports their own position and, in effect, experience different "realities."
When Princeton students viewed a film of an unusually rough football game
between Dartmouth and Princeton a few years ago, almost nine-tenths of the
Princeton students surveyed accused the other side of starting the rough play.
They attributed to Dartmouth players over twice as many infractions of the
rules as the Dartmouth students themselves acknowledged.[38]

We can become so selective in our perceptions that we are simply blind
to certain aspects of particular issues or events. To many loyal Nazis, for
example, the gassing of Jews was not a heinous crime, but a "laudable and
necessary act." As one Nazi Major General put it:

> . . . *if after us such a cowardly and rotten generation should arise that
> it does not understand our work which is so good and necessary, then,
> gentlemen, all National Socialism will have been for nothing. On the
> contrary, bronze plaques should be put up with the inscription that it
> was we, we who had the courage to achieve this gigantic task.*[39]

All these examples make it clear that perceptual material is easily as-
similated if it is congruent with our existing attitudes, goals, and standards.
If it differs, we have several ways of reducing the dissonance. We can be
selective in our perceptions, or we can reinterpret what we perceive so that
it better fits our expectations, or we can deny the information altogether. The
abortive American invasion of the Bay of Pigs in 1961 was either based upon
a serious misinterpretation of available information about the mood of the
Cuban people or upon denial of its accuracy. According to Joseph de Rivera:

> *In May of 1960, a carefully conducted poll of 1,000 Cubans showed
> that a strong growth in optimism followed the revolution. Eighty-six
> percent of the people were in favor of the Castro regime, and it seemed
> clear, in the light of these data, that there was no hope of stimulating
> the Cuban people to take action against Castro. A report of this poll
> was widely distributed in the American government but seems to have
> not been attended to.*[40]

One of the most blatant recorded cases of a decision maker simply denying information that did not coincide with his predispositions was Nazi
Reichsmarschall Herman Goering's response when he was informed that sev-

eral American fighter planes had been shot down over Aachen, Germany. Refusing to believe that American planes could penetrate that far into Germany, Goering is reported to have said: "I herewith give you an official order that they weren't there! Do you understand? The American fighters were not there! Get that! I intend to report that to the Fuehrer."[41]

Another method of dealing with perceptions that are incongruent with our existing attitudes is to *displace* our feelings about the particular situation. When we do this, we avoid contact with the original stimulus, or source of discomfort, and direct our attention to a less-threatening or more convenient target. It is easier to kick the dog than to express our anger toward a wife or parent. At the same time, we often project onto others the feelings we ourselves have, then blame them for what are in fact feelings we wish to avoid dealing with in ourselves.

One famous historical example of displacement behavior is the "stab-in-the-back" myth that undermined the Weimar Republic in Germany after World War I. Opponents of the Republic, particularly the military leadership, insisted that the German army had not been defeated but had been stabbed in the back by the "republicans, socialists, and Jews" who capitulated to the Allies in 1918 and signed what most Germans considered an unjust peace settlement in 1919. Although the leaders of the Republic could not justly be held responsible for Germany's defeat or her treatment at the hands of the victorious allies, many Germans preferred to find scapegoats in the so-called "November criminals" rather than accept the painful reality of Germany's military defeat.

> *Whenever the causes of frustration in a large organization or a nation remain somewhat ambiguous, as in periods of economic depression and prolonged military stalemates and defeats, the stage is set for selecting a minority group . . . as scapegoat. Once people have begun to displace their aggression to an out-group target, they become inclined to rationalize and justifying their hostility . . . [and] any single act of scapegoating can lead to an escalation of intergroup hostility, which strongly reinforces the initial negative stereotypes.*[42]

The more accurately we perceive a person or state, the more likely we are to have a satisfactory relationship with him or it. Yet stereotypical thinking can exercise great influence over our perceptions of others. The stereotypes of union leaders formed by business executives, for example, are quite different from the stereotyped notions union leaders have of themselves. Likewise, stereotypes of one's own country are usually flattering, while stereotypes of an enemy nation are invariable negatives. In fact, the proportion of complimentary and derogatory terms of one nation's stereotype of another is a good index of the friendliness or hostility between two states. Thus if

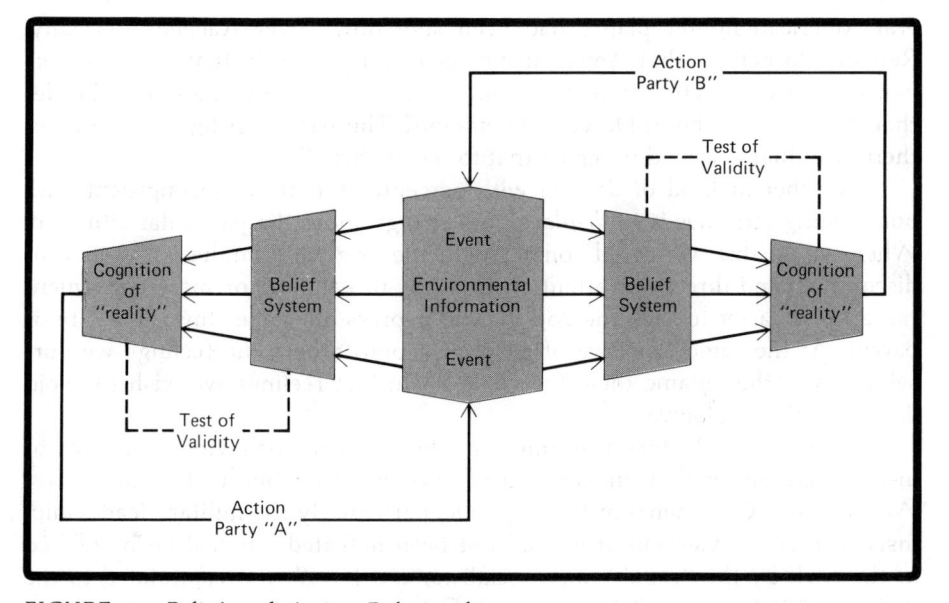

FIGURE 2.2 Belief and Action Relationship

Source: Joe Cochran Ray, "The Indirect Relationship Between Belief and Action in Soviet-American Interaction," Stanford University, unpublished manuscript, 1961, p. 21.

we wish to alter our interactions with others, we must examine our perceptions and images. We must also keep in mind, however, that our perceptions are influenced by our own actions. There is experimental evidence that persons who behave violently also tend more readily to perceive violence in others than do relatively nonviolent persons.[43] Aggressor states usually accuse the other side of being the provocateur. We perceive and act in light of our own values.[44]

The social sciences cannot yet state with certainty that particular attitudes and beliefs predict a specific political or social behavior, or vice versa. But we do know that belief and behavior form an interactive process in which the belief system functions as a filter lens for viewing the environment. One scholar has illustrated the relationship between beliefs and actions as in Figure 2.2.

To return for a moment to the Dartmouth-Princeton football game, the two opposite interpretations of the same game formed a "mirror image" in which each adversary perceived the same negative conduct in the other that his opponent attributed to him. The same reverse images have been characteristic of American-Soviet relations since World War II. Ralph K. White has found both sides mirroring statements such as "their rulers are bad," "they are imperialistic," "they are against democracy," and "they distort the

truth."[45] As a result of these images, the United States and the Soviet Union each quickly constructed rigidly hostile and defensive foreign policies toward the other that remained intact and largely unquestioned for over two decades. Yet the world's fate depends upon the degree to which such states accurately perceive the intentions and actions of each other.

2. Motivation. The interests and values that guide man's behavior are myriad. There exists no theoretical or empirical statement that adequately explains why man behaves as he does. We expect him to seek consistency between his beliefs and behavior, either by shaping behavior to fit beliefs or by modifying beliefs to harmonize with behavior. Our interest, however, is in the ways in which man responds to problems and conflicts, not necessarily the consistency of his values and actions.

Conflict occurs in human relations whenever we perceive, accurately or inaccurately, that one or more of our goals, interests, purposes, or preferences is being jeopardized or threatened.[46] Most conflicts probably have their origins in the anticipation of threat from another rather than in a specific hostile act. One useful view of responses is the approach/avoidance paradigm developed by Irving Janis and others. According to their formulation, we may be motivated to approach a goal and at the same time avoid doing so because we fear undesirable consequences. Consider the man who wishes to ask a woman for a date but fears she may reject him. His desire to approach is stymied by his defenses against rejection and hurt. How does he break out of this inner conflict? He may engage in a type of reaction-formation, rationalize that "she is not really attractive," and thereby achieve resolution. He may approach her in conversation simply to see how she responds to him but still stop short of his goal. Or he may take a risk, overcome his fears, approach her, and ask her for a date.[47] But this interaction increases the possibilities of a new conflict. She may say yes, no, or maybe; she may laugh, ignore the suggestion, insult him, or accept. The process continues until trust develops between them or they cease to interact. Diagrammatically, the approach-avoidance conflict is illustrated in Figure 2.3.

There are variations of approach and avoidance that illustrate other forms of conflicts and decisions. In approach-approach conflicts we are motivated to approach two desirable but mutually exclusive goals (e.g., two attractive toys). In avoidance-avoidance conflicts we may be prompted to avoid two goals or courses of action (the voter who dislikes both Republican and Democratic candidates in an election).[48]

Analogous processes operate in international politics. Recent relations between the United States and the Soviet Union are full of approach and avoidance conflicts. In fact, President Nixon characterized Soviet-American relations in just such terms: ". . . our two nations have substantial mutual incentives to find ways of working together. We are realistic enough

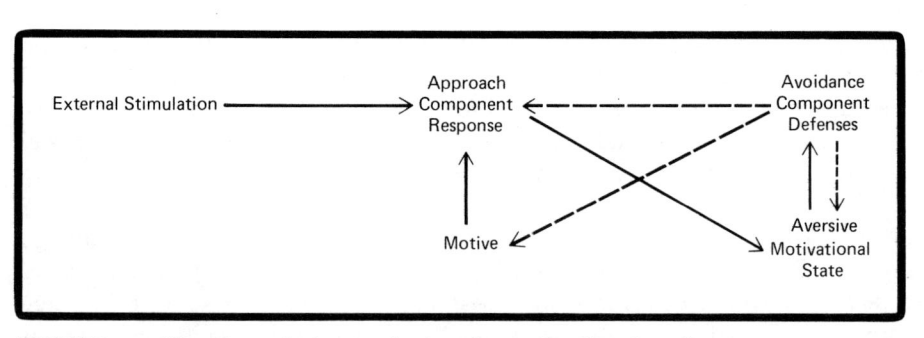

FIGURE 2.3 *The General Approach-Avoidance Conflict Paradigm*

Note: An external stimulus or an approach motive or, more often, a combination of the two instigates an approach response. In turn, the approach response evokes distressing emotions, which are usually some kind of anxiety—anticipatory fear, shame, or guilt. The distressing emotion motivates defenses, which have the effect of ending or preventing the painful emotion. Some defenses interfere with the approach motive or drive; some interfere with the approach response; and some are oriented directly against the unpleasant emotion.

Source: Irving L. Janis, George F. Mahl, Jerome Kagan, and Robert R. Holt, *Personality*, New York: Harcourt Brace Jovanovich, 1969, p. 237.

to recognize, however, that we also have very real differences that can continue to divide us."[49] The Strategic Arms Limitation Talks are an example. Both parties have approached the negotiations with a compatible goal—reducing the spiraling arms race. Nevertheless, their mutual distrust makes them both suspicious of the other's motives and intentions. Such negotiations must confront the dual possibilities of heightening tensions as well as reducing them. Given the dynamics of the approach-avoidance syndrome, the positive results are likely to be very limited. For when a group or an individual must choose alternatives of equal but opposite value, the result may be a form of paralysis that is often rationalized as a "wait-and-see" response. Ultimately, turning problem solving and conflict management into a creative and nurturing process will depend upon lowering levels of threat and increasing positive reinforcements of trust. We must develop the motivation to take the risks of approaching our problems rather than avoiding them.

3. Stress. We have already noted that today's decision makers are bombarded with more information and have more complex decisions to make in less time than ever before. There is increasing evidence that long-term stress such as national and international leaders experience as an integral part of their jobs takes a high toll in both physical and psychological functioning. When individuals must continually adapt to situations involving change, uncertainty, and conflict, the hormone system speeds up body metabolism, raises blood pressure, and begins turning fat and protein into extra supplies

of energy. Scientists are now beginning to suspect that repeated and sustained stimulation of this adaptive reaction to stress produces excessive "wear and tear" on the body and is permanently damaging.

The psychological reactions to prolonged stress are even more apparent. They generally follow a pattern: (1) confusion, distortion of reality or disorientation; (2) fatigue, anxiety, or extreme irritability; (3) apathy and emotional withdrawal. We have countless examples of the bizarre, nonrational behavior of individuals under extreme stress. In a study of the responses to tornadoes in Texas, H. E. Moore recounted the incident of a girl in Waco who "climbed into a music store through a broken window, calmly purchased a record, and walked out again, even though the plate glass front of the building had blown out and articles were flying through the air inside the building."[50] During World War II, it became so common for English guerrilla soldiers who had penetrated behind Japanese lines in Burma to simply fall asleep while machine-gun fire raged around them that British physicians gave the phenomenon a name: Long Range Penetration Strain. After about a year in office, the first American Secretary of Defense, James Forrestal, began showing signs of strain: loss of weight, insomnia, absent-mindedness and, finally, paranoiac delusions of being followed by communist and Zionist agents. Although his colleagues attributed his strange behavior to exhaustion, no one realized how fatal it would be. In May of 1949, he committed suicide by jumping from the second floor of a hospital building.[51]

The job of a policy maker is to gather, absorb, retain, manipulate, and evaluate information. Current research is making it clear, however, that there are built-in limits to our ability to process information. The results of experiments designed to measure the speed and accuracy of human information processing show that whatever the task, there is a speed beyond which it cannot mentally be performed. Dr. James Miller, director of the Mental Health Research Institute at the University of Michigan states that "Glutting a person with more information than he can process may . . . lead to disturbance."[52] The disturbed behavior often resembles some forms of mental illness, particularly schizophrenia, in which the process of association is impaired.

Experiments also show that the greater number of alternative actions available to a person, the longer it takes him to make a decision and execute it. Yet the rate of social and technological change demands that both the private citizen and the policy maker spend less time with each decision if they wish to avoid losing control over their destinies altogether.

Author Alvin Toffler believes that large masses of persons in the technologically advanced societies are suffering from what he calls "decision stress."[53] He distinguishes between programmed decisions—those that have become habit and require almost no thought—and nonprogrammed decisions

in which psychic energy is expended to meet a new situation. Life is a mixture of both kinds of decisions. When most decisions are programmed, life is dull. When the proportion of nonprogrammed decisions increases, challenge and excitement pick up, but so do tension and stress. Individual tolerance for novelty differs, but for each there is a limit, and when it is reached, the anxiety becomes so painful that the individual attempts to alleviate his discomfort by retreating to what is familiar and predictable. Toffler suggests four responses to decision stress. First is denial. The individual simply refuses to take in any more new information and rationalizes his behavior with notions such as "The more things change, the more they stay the same." A second reaction is specialism, in which the person attempts to keep up to date in one or two fields but refuses to acknowledge that change is also taking place elsewhere. A third response is obsessive reversion to previously successful behavior that has since become irrelevant and inappropriate. Instead of adapting to the new, he automatically applies old solutions, growing more and more divorced from reality as he does so. Simplification is the fourth method of adapting to overwhelming stress produced by change. The individual searches for a single, explanatory idea that will make his environment once again manageable: the communist conspiracy, the profit motive, astrology, the theories of Herbert Marcuse. All of these methods of coping with decision stress distort reality and result in behavior that is incapable of bringing about the changes the individual wishes to effect. Under stress conditions critical questions are most necessary and least likely to be forthcoming.

International conflict—cold or hot—may place entire societies under stress conditions and lead to irrational behavior, inaccurate perceptions, avoidance, panic, and distrust. For example, at the beginning of the cold war, the sense of threat in the United States produced strong reflective fears and a climate of indiscriminate vigilance in which scare rumors, exaggerated fantasies, and a loss of perspective infected a large part of the country. The anxiety made many unresponsive to new information, and the blocking and distorting of information prevented reality testing and the correction of false images. Hence it took considerable time after the death of Stalin for Americans to begin to accept the fact that the most perverted forms of Stalinism in the Soviet Union no longer existed and then to begin working toward a détente in areas of mutual interest.

It is ironic and even tragic that under conditions of mental and emotional stress, when we most need to think clearly, be open to new information, evaluate alternatives, and make competent and realistic decisions—that these are the conditions in which we are least likely to be able to do so. This alone is a supremely powerful argument for doing everything possible in the international field to alleviate threat, tension, and uncertainty among nations. We shall clearly have more than enough stress in the coming decades trying

to manage social and technological change without unnecessarily compounding it with international bitterness and rivalries.

Former Secretary of State Dean Acheson once remarked that decisions could not be completely understood or analyzed without the use of psychoanalytic techniques.[54] He was probably not seriously suggesting to us that Chairman Mao, Secretary Brezhnev, President Ford, and other world leaders agree to sessions on the couch with a public-interest analyst, but the idea has certain appeal. From time to time there have in fact been serious suggestions that politicians be psychologically tested before they assume responsible public positions. Kenneth Clark, past president of the American Psychological Association, believes that the paramount transgression of political leaders is the abuse of power. He therefore proposes that a drug that inhibits aggression, cruelty, and destructive behavior be administered to all key decision makers who make life-and-death decisions for the rest of us.[55]

As far-fetched as Clark's proposals may appear at first blush, they do point out the growing sense of our common vulnerability to the consequences of decisions made by others whose values, judgment, and mental health are largely unknown to us. We are beginning to feel some urgency about reducing the margins of human error in decision making without, at the same time, losing our humanity to machine processing of "inputs" and "outputs." But unless we are able to develop criteria with which to evaluate public policy, we will not have a standard against which we can measure specific decisions. We have learned a great deal about individual mental health, but what constitutes mental health in the global community?

MODIFYING BEHAVIOR

It would be easy to give in to fatalism and decide that nothing can be done to reverse the present gloomy trends. Yet unmitigated pessimism is as delusive as eternal optimism. Although the constraints upon developing a new global perspective are great indeed, history has proved human resilience and adaptability over the long run. As Toffler observes, "Most of the problems besieging us . . . stem not from inplacable natural forces but from man-made processes that are at least potentially subject to our control."[56]

We believe that nations can begin to control the international environment for more positive ends by focusing their efforts in four areas. First is expanding the process of information sharing among nations and encouraging the consideration of new alternatives to old and unfruitful policies. The second grows out of the first but will also require programs of political socialization not yet beyond the experimental stage. It is the development of a consciousness of the interrelatedness of national and international interests.

Third is taking policy risks to develop trust among nations so that circular conflicts such as the arms race may be broken. Finally, and most important, superordinate goals must be developed to move us from the tensions and stalemate of ideological, economic, and military competition toward international cooperation.

A superordinate goal induces an individual, group, or nation to subordinate a specific interest to a common task or interest because the "payoff" is greater than the factors that separate them. In the absence of superordinate goals, conflicts may be endless and may even increase. In one experiment, for example, Muzafer Sherif divided a group of eleven-year-old boys into two subgroups, the "Eagles" and the "Rattlers."[57] They were kept apart until each group developed its own internal styles and customs and saw the other as an "outgroup." Then they were brought together in competitive activities such as softball, in which victory for one meant defeat for the other. These activities produced conflict between the two groups, each praising its own attributes and castigating the other in ways reminiscent of the mirror-image phenomenon in American-Soviet relations. As hostility mounted, the "other" became defined as the "enemy," and the leadership structure in each group changed, with those advocating more peaceful relations being replaced by the physically stronger and more belligerent. From this point on, bringing the groups together for social activities actually increased hostility between them instead of restoring peace. Finally, the experimenters created problems for the two groups that made collaboration between them a necessity. The crises included a shortage of water and the breakdown of a truck bringing food supplies. Once cooperation began out of concern for solving a mutual problem, hostility between the groups diminished and group boundaries became relatively insignificant.

In Chapter 3 we cite the controversy over territorial rights to halibut in the North Pacific as an example of denial behavior. Yet the political conflict was greatly alleviated when the dispute was viewed, not as a political matter, but as a biological problem of overfishing affecting all parties concerned. Most of the work of the specialized agencies of the United Nations grows out of attempts to realize supranational goals. In the nineteenth century the unification of the Italian city-states into the modern state of Italy and the unification of Germany under Bismarck also marked the subordination of local interests to a larger cause. Yet the lesson of the effectiveness of uniting behind a common cause is generally ignored. At the Stockholm Conference on the Environment in 1972 political considerations generally overshadowed the superordinate goal of alleviating threats to the natural environment.

The United Nations Institute for Training and Research (UNITAR) is itself searching for methods to encourage trust and cooperation among international leaders. In one UNITAR program, government officials from various

countries were brought together for a kind of high-level sensitivity training session. The participants were urged to share the perceptions, motivations, and the goals they pursued in the course of their work as well as their views about the internal political situations in their own nations. Another UNITAR experiment provided a two-week workshop in which 18 representatives from the African countries of Ethiopia, Kenya, and Somalia were invited to examine the border disputes among the three nations in light of four objectives: (1) to exchange relevant information and express attitudes and ideas regarding the disputes in question, (2) to move closer to a resolution of the differences among the countries, (3) to establish personal bonds among the participants of the three countries, and (4) to inform national policy makers regarding the workshop discussions.[58]

In both programs investigators reported favorable results: development of feelings of group solidarity, growth of mutual trust, and increased willingness to search for positive resolutions to national differences. These were experimental efforts, but they are examples of techniques that might be refined and built upon to broaden the time-worn methods of conducting international relations. Yet even such mild innovations run the risk of being rejected out of hand, as Marshall R. Singer has noted:

> The largest business firms in both Europe and America have for years now spent large sums of money training their top management (including their chief executive officers) in the art of being more open and receptive to ideas, values, attitudes, and feelings of others. This so-called "sensitivity training" utilized by big industrial corporations is aimed precisely at making their executives more sensitive to the needs of others. It has "paid off" for big business to such an extent that sensitivity training in the United States has itself become big business today. Yet the American government generally remains hostile to the entire notion. One American congressman summed up this hostility when he said, in answer to a suggestion that Agency for International Development personnel be selected on the basis of their psychological sensitivity to different ideas and different cultures, "If those people want our help it's up to them to become sensitive to us. We're not going to decide who to send overseas and who not to send, just to suit them."[59]

It is a discouraging fact that a good many national and international leaders, though they are people of good will, are trapped in conventional approaches to international relations. For the sake of international survival, however, we need to support and encourage those who are willing to look for new ways to build a sense of interrelatedness among nations and to work for superordinate goals and international cooperation.

Another method of modifying behavior at the international level has been proposed by Charles E. Osgood and is entitled "graduated and reciprocated initiatives in tension reduction," or simply GRIT.[60] In essence, it is a strategy to reverse tension generated as a result of, say, the arms race, through small increments in mutual understanding, respect, and trust. Osgood suggests that a nation begin with a public announcement of intended policy changes ("We intend to scrap our B-52s") with adequate time lag between announcement and execution to give the opponent opportunity to respond. The initiator does what is possible to prove its sincerity and invites the other to reciprocate. Even if the other responds with nothing more than token reciprocation, such moves begin establishing a pattern that can lead to more significant actions. If there is no response, very little is lost. Essentially this approach uses positive motivators, or "carrots," to bring about change, rather than the negative motivation, "sticks," which are so predominant in strategies of deterrence and coercive diplomacy. Psychologists who have studied behavior modification have found that people learn most easily when they receive positive, rather than negative, reinforcement. Former Secretary of War Henry L. Stimson found that this is also true in politics. "The chief lesson I have learned in a long life is that the only way you can make a man trustworthy is to trust him; and the surest way to make him untrustworthy is to distrust him and show your distrust."[61]

Superordinate goals and strategies can be techniques for modifying behavior, for reducing the potential of lethal conflict, for realizing the fullness of interdependence. Alternatives for the future are feasible if man is purposive. Change can be built and can induce us to work toward policies and programs overcoming deprivation and realizing actualization.

GOALS AND PURPOSIVE BEHAVIOR

As we perceive and act we shape the world around us. If that world is to be substantially different in the future, we must come to terms with our fallibilities, including our resistance to change. As analysts of international relations we cannot rely upon the comfortable assumption that a greater comprehension of why international politics and foreign policy unfold as they do will facilitate actions designed to influence how they ought to unfold any more than our leaders can rely upon man's inherent capacity to adapt as a solution to world problems.[62] For students and leaders alike, the perceptions and priorities of the past are in question. A perspective on the future must link how we do behave with how we ought to behave, particularly in regard

to foreign policy. But we must keep in mind that the world does not stand still while any nation shapes and then sets in motion its foreign policy. A policy of reacting to events lacks purpose, a sense of mission, a positive conception of where and how matters should develop, a conscious effort to create conditions of a durable peace.

Foreign policy consists of the *goals* and *actions* of a state in relation to other states or external agencies. As complex as national policies are today, distinctions between domestic and foreign policy are somewhat meaningless. Polaris missiles and gigantic corporations obliterate traditional conceptions of national boundaries, just as American domestic monetary policy set by the Federal Reserve Board not only affects this country's external financial standing but the monetary policies of other nations as well.

Most states have similar domestic and foreign policy goals: (1) to protect their national autonomy, preserve the integrity of their national political culture, and promote national social values, (2) to defend themselves successfully against external aggression, (3) to foster economic independence through favorable international trade balance, and (4) to create an international climate favorable to their own national interests. The first three aims probably receive more emphasis than the fourth, which implicitly requires some acknowledgment of the mutual interdependence of all nations. In the most general sense all states seek peace, prosperity, and security.

Between May 1968 and June 1970 the Canadian government of Pierre Elliot Trudeau undertook an extensive and instructive review of its external relations. The resulting report lists six general issue areas that constitute challenges, threats, opportunities, and constraints upon foreign policy. The issue areas are (1) sovereignty and independence, (2) peace and security, (3) social justice, (4) quality of life, (5) harmonious natural environment, and (6) economic growth.[63] These six factors are all distinctive and, at the same time, overlapping with supportive and competitive impacts upon one another. Since not all things are possible, public choice must determine which areas are to be given priority with what kinds of temporal and material commitments. Here values and influence are determinants of which choices are made and in what order. Many value trade-offs are involved. For example, the Canadian study suggested the following:

—— *In striving to raise national income through economic growth, policies may be pursued which adversely affect the natural environment by increasing the hazards of pollution or by depleting resources too rapidly. Such policies might also cause infringement of social justice (because of inflation, for example) and impair the quality of life for individual Canadians.*

―――― *In seeking social justice for developing nations, through trade policies which offer them concessions or preferences, the Government's policy may adversely affect the domestic market opportunities for certain Canadian industries, or it might involve parallel policies to curtail or reorient their production.*

―――― *Similarly, if international development assistance programmes require a substantial increase in Canadian resources allocated, the trade-off may be some reduction of resources allocated to other governmental activity, like the extension of Canadian welfare programmes or the attack on domestic pollution.*

―――― *Reductions in military expenditure may lead to results difficult to gauge as regards Canada's capacity to ensure its security, to safeguard its sovereignty and independence, and to make a useful contribution to the maintenance of peace; though resources might thereby be freed for other activities.*

―――― *The most difficult choices of the future may result from seeking to recapture and maintain a harmonious natural environment. Such policies may be essential to enhance the quality of life (if not ensure human survival) but they may well require some curtailment of economic growth and freedom of enterprise and a heavy allocation of resources from both public and private sources.*[64]

The Canadian government gave priority to economic growth, social justice, and improving the quality of life. Diagrammatically, the conceptualization of the matrix of issue areas is illustrated in Figure 2.4.

Assuming the representation is a fair description of foreign-policy issue areas, a speculative question arises: What happens if we substitute *international* for basic *national* aims? Most of the basic issue areas remain applicable. What is unclear is the degree of isomorphism between national and international perspectives that might exist as the content of each issue area is worked out. Yet even a speculative unfolding of such a scheme from an international point of view might help us more clearly define realms where agreements are possible as well as isolate obstacles and differences between national and international perspectives. Such a shift in conceptual focus might facilitate a transcending of traditional means of viewing, defining, and implementing foreign policy. It would not require some sort of "world government" as a prerequisite. As matters now stand, however, the world is tied to traditional, reactive, and ad hoc foreign policies with their exclusive definitions of national interest. Within such a system conflicts are bound to occur as nations implement their foreign policy goals and compete to promote their national welfare. Indeed, conflict seems endemic to the politics of who gets what, when, and how, particularly with an international arena defined as a contest involving fights, games, and debates.

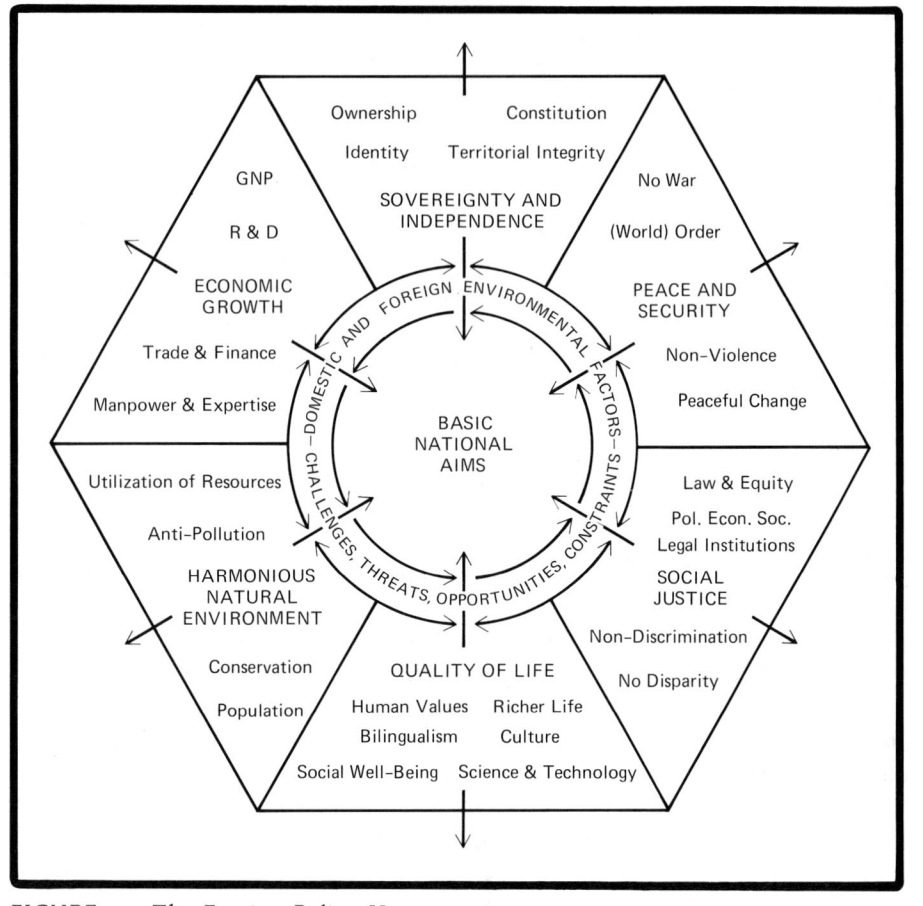

FIGURE 2.4 The Foreign Policy Hexagon

Note: (1) In each segment the "key words" in small print indicate the kind of policy questions that may arise, though not always under the same theme necessarily. (2) The straight arrows indicate the relationship between basic national aims and external functions. The one-way arrows in the inner circle indicate the ever-changing environmental factors; the two-way arrows in the outer circle signify the interrelationships among the policy themes.

Source: Canada, House of Commons, The Standing Committee on External Affairs and National Defense, *Fourth Report Respecting "Foreign Policy for Canadians,"* June 1971, p. 48.

Traditionally states have responded to conflict with other states through: (1) the quick and decisive use of military power, (2) the posturing of military might as a threat or deterrent, (3) coercive diplomacy (i.e., actions to get another party to undo what they have done or to stop short of their goals), and (4) testing each others' capabilities through activities such as espionage

and subversion, which normally do not involve threats of escalation.[65] The eminence of force in international politics is uncontested. Between 1480 and 1941 a new war broke out among nations on the average of once every two years (and these wars do not include revolutions, punitive expeditions, pacifications, and explorations).[66]

Short of force, nations have used diplomacy, that is, bargaining, negotiating, persuading, and compromising, to achieve their objectives. International politics is a continuous process of diplomatic activity, sometimes between two nations, other times among several nations, sometimes secret, other times in full view of the international community. Diplomacy is a method of achieving national interests, and not an end in itself. Agencies such as the United Nations are, in one sense, little more than permanent forums for the conduct of diplomacy.

EVALUATING POLICY

How do we evaluate the foreign and domestic policies of a state?[67] Pragmatic criteria suggest that if the policies work—that is, if they accomplish what they are designed to do—then they are successful. According to instrumental criteria, policies can be considered successful if they contribute to short- or long-range objectives to maximize self-interest. Adversary criteria tell us policies are successful if a state is able to maximize its gains and minimize its losses vis-à-vis its competitors or enemies.

Let us assume that a particular state is able to accomplish its policy goals, attain most of its short- and long-range objectives and therefore maximizes its gains and minimizes its losses. Conventional wisdom would say that such a state is successful. But—by what criteria do we evaluate what it has actually done? How do we judge whether a state is "good" or "bad," "right" or "wrong"? To some these may be irrelevant *moral* questions, too laden with value preferences and too normative for the scientist of international relations. Yet without a moral and normative framework that concerns itself with ultimate ends and consequences, we are left with the notion that what succeeds is most desirable. We believe that such an attitude spells disaster for our contemporary world. Power is not a moral force.

We are convinced that any policy should be judged according to whether it meets the basic human need of biological survival, reduces the level of threat from the natural environment or from man, facilitates the settling of conflicts through regularized and peaceful agencies, and promotes opportunities for improving the quality of life. As we stated in the Introduction, these criteria dictate (1) a reduction of the emphasis upon military means to achieve national objectives, since military force is inherently destructive, (2) the international acceptance and promotion of a morally acceptable standard of living for all peoples, (3) a recalculation of national economic priorities toward re-

ducing disparities among peoples and nations, and, finally, (4) the promotion of goals and means that transcend the narrow self-interest generated by traditional, exclusive relations among nations.

These are *moral* imperatives in that they are designed to motivate behavior in directions that are dictated by certain values. Without a sense of common moral imperatives for evaluating and judging national policies, we run the risk of indulging our selfish interest in the short run only to discover later that we have jeopardized our own future interests. Even the most atrocious and irrational behavior can be justified by national interest, the profit motive, prestige, and security. Yet it is difficult to ask individuals and nations to sacrifice what appears to be in their immediate self-interest in favor of a more illusive and complex goal, say the elimination of world hunger or the promotion of international trust, unless they can see some relatively concrete and immediate advantage to themselves for making such a "sacrifice." Moral norms seem to be persuasive only when they happen to include immediate and tangible positive reinforcement. We do not recognize many potentially powerful reinforcements as such simply because they are conditions that, until very recently, we have taken entirely for granted or have not valued highly: clean air, clean water, a viable natural environment, sufficient space, sufficient food, healthy bodies, and a peaceful world.

We need to expand our choices in international politics so that we have greater latitude in arriving at solutions to our difficulties. Even though such expansion contains the danger of further complicating decision making, it may well be that relatively slight shifts in the assessment of available choices will bring about considerable changes in behavior. The Strategic Arms Limitation Talks, for example, open up the possibilities of defusing the arms race between the United States and the Soviet Union. Since 1945 the United States and the Soviet Union combined have spent some $2.5 trillion on defense. If both countries continue to grow as projected and if they spend the same proportion of their wealth on defense, another $5 trillion or so will be expended in the name of "national security" before the end of this century.[68] Both states are now so "secure" that neither side can start a nuclear war without triggering its own destruction as well as destroying the rest of the world. The two nations ". . . have lived in the pawn of each other's whim— or calculation—for the past twenty years."[69] And what has their rigid enmity accomplished? Perhaps if as much attention had been given to policies of "attractiveness" as has been given to "coerciveness," the world would be a better place in which to live. With the end of American military involvement in Vietnam and recent cautious moves to open up trade between the United States and the Soviet Union, it is conceivable that the two superpowers and others could begin to explore the infinite possibilities associated with accommodation instead of hostility. Any number of imaginative changes in inter-

national politics are feasible provided decision makers and their constituencies are willing to take the risk of breaking from the security of past behavior. We shall refer to questions of "means" in each chapter but more so in our conclusion.

NOTES

[1]President Washington did seek advice, however. At a time when the executive branch of government seems paramount in the conduct of foreign policy, the following request from Washington to the Senate in 1792 may seem ironic: "Gentlemen of the Senate: If the President of the United States should conclude a convention or treaty with the Government of Algiers for the ransom of the thirteen Americans in captivity there for a sum not exceeding $40,000, all expenses included, will the Senate approve the same? Or is there any, and what, greater or lesser sum which they would fix on as a limit beyond which they would not approve the ransom?" U.S. Congress, Joint Committee on Printing, *A Compilation of the Messages and Papers of the President*, 52d Cong., 1897, vol. 1, p. 115.

[2]James A. Robinson and Richard C. Snyder, "Decision-Making in International Politics," in Herbert C. Kelman (ed.), *International Behavior*, New York: Holt, Rinehart & Winston, 1965, p. 435.

[3]Irving L. Janis, *Victims of Groupthink: A Psychological Study of Foreign-Policy Decisions and Fiascoes*, Boston: Houghton Mifflin, 1972, p. 222.

[4]Henry A. Kissinger, "Conditions of World Order," *Daedalus*, 95 (Spring 1966), 529.

[5]Sidney Verba, "Assumptions of Rationality and Non-Rationality in Models of the International System," in Klaus Knorr and Sidney Verba (eds.), *The International System: Theoretical Essays*, Princeton, N.J.: Princeton University Press, 1961, p. 95. Reprinted by permission of Princeton University Press.

[6]Richard Snyder, "Introduction," in Glenn D. Paige, *The Korean Decision, June 24–30*, New York: Free Press, 1968, p. xxiii.

[7]Anthony Downs, *Inside Bureaucracy*, Boston, Mass.: Little, Brown, 1967, p. 75.

[8]Richard E. Neustadt, *Presidential Power*, New York: Wiley, 1960, pp. 9–10.

[9]Quoted in Roger Hilsman, *To Move a Nation*, New York: Delta Books, 1967, p. 6.

[10]Verba, *op. cit.*, p. 94.

[11]Norman J. Padelford and George A. Lincoln, *The Dynamics of International Politics*, New York: Macmillan, 1962, p. 231.

[12]*The New York Times*, June 11, 1972, p. 1.

[13]Ralph Stavins, Richard J. Barnet, and Marcus G. Raskin, *Washington Plans an Aggressive War*, New York: Vintage Books, 1971, p. 202. See also G. William Domhoff, *The Higher Circles*, New York: Vintage Books, 1971.

[14]Roberta Wohlstetter, *Pearl Harbor: Warning and Decision*, Stanford, Calif.: Stanford University Press, 1962.

[15]Glenn D. Paige, *The Korean Decision, June 24–30, 1950*, New York: Free Press, 1968. Copyright © The Free Press, a division of The Macmillan Publishing Co., Inc.

[16]Stavins, Barnet, and Raskin, *op. cit.*

[17]Ole R. Holsti, "The 1914 Case," *American Political Science Review*, 59, no. 2 (June 1965), 365–378.

[18]Propositions from Paige's study of the Korean decision are illustrative:
1.1   Crisis decisions tend to be reached by ad hoc decisional units.
1.2   Crisis decisions tend to be made by decisional units that vary within narrow limits of size and composition.
1.21 The more costly the commitment anticipated, the larger the unit up to a psychologically and physically acceptable limit.
1.3   The greater the crisis, the greater the felt need for face-to-face proximity among decision-makers.

1.5 The greater the crisis, the greater the acceptance of responsibility for action by the leader and the more the follower expectation and acceptance of the leader's responsibility.

2.3 The greater the crisis, the greater the reliance upon the central themes in previously existing information.

2.31 The greater the confidence in existing information, the greater the amount of contrary evidence and the greater the authority of the sources required to bring about a change in interpretation.

Examples are from Paige, *op. cit.*, pp. 281–295.

[19]Paige, *op. cit.*, p. 8.

[20]Graham T. Allison, *Essence of Decision: Explaining the Cuban Missile Crisis*, Boston, Mass.: Little, Brown, 1971.

[21]François Duchêne (ed.), *The Endless Crisis*, New York: Clarion Books, 1970, p. 289.

[22]Alvin Toffler, *Future Shock*, London: Pan Books, 1970.

[23]*New Zealand Herald*, December 12, 1972, p. 1.

[24]J. J. Servan-Schreiber, *The American Challenge*, New York: Avon Books, 1968.

[25]Sidney Hook, *The Hero in History*, Boston: Beacon, 1955, Ch. 10.

[26]Duchêne, *op. cit.*

[27]The State Department is not alone in slowness to modernize. According to E. Drexel Godfrey, Jr., the *Cour des Comptes*, the organization of the French bureaucracy responsible for the review of all official accounting reports and procedures, did not discover the existence of the typewriter and calculating machine until after World War II. At the end of the war they were still using quill pens and ledgers. *The Government of France*, 2d ed., New York: T. Y. Crowell, 1963, pp. 103–104.

[28]Adapted from Jack R. Gibb, "Fear and Façade: Defensive Management," in Richard E. Farson (ed.), *Science and Human Affairs*, Palo Alto, Calif.: Science and Behavior Books, 1965, pp. 197–214.

[29]Quoted in Robert Murphy, *Diplomat Among Warriors*, Garden City, N.Y.: Doubleday, 1964, p. 456.

[30]Roger Hilsman, *The Politics of Policy Making in Defense and Foreign Affairs*, New York: Harper & Row, 1971.

[31]Janis, *op. cit.*, p. 13.

[32]Edward S. Walker, Jr., "Profile in Conformity," *Foreign Service Journal* (September 1969), p. 19. (Emphasis added.) Likewise another report states: "The intense competition for promotion which continues all through a Foreign Service officer's career may in some cases tend to instill excessive caution and conformity which has a stultifying effect on creativity." U.S. Department of State, *United States Foreign Policy 1971: A Report of the Secretary of State*, Department of State Publication 8634 (March 1972), p. 392.

[33]Stanley Milgram, "Behavioral Study of Obedience," *Journal of Abnormal and Social Psychology*, 67 (1963), 371–378. Also his "Liberating Effects of Group Pressure," *Journal of Personality and Social Phychology*, 1 (1965), 127–134. For one man's agonizing reappraisal of his own submission see Albert Speer, *Inside the Third Reich*, New York: Avon Books, 1971.

[34]David J. Finlay, Ole R. Holsti, and Richard R. Fagen, *Enemies in Politics*, Skokie, Ill.: Rand McNally, 1967, p. 45.

[35]Harold Nicolson, *Diplomacy*, 3rd ed., London: Oxford University Press, 1963, pp. 122–123.

[36]U.S. Senate, Committee on Foreign Relations, *Hearings, Psychological Aspects of International Relations*, 89th Cong., 2d sess., 1966, p. 1.

[37]*Ibid.*, p. 10.

[38]Albert H. Hasdorf and Hadley Cantril, "They Saw a Game: A Case Study," in Hans Toch and Clay Smith (eds.), *Social Perception*, Princeton, N.J.: D. Van Nostrand, 1968, pp. 63–72.

[39]Ellie A. Cohen, *Human Behavior in the Concentration Camp*, New York: Norton, 1953, p. 229.

[40]Joseph de Rivera, *The Psychological Dimension of Foreign Policy*, Columbus, Ohio:

Merrill, 1968, pp. 41–42. After the Bay of Pigs fiasco Arthur Schlesinger, Jr., then serving as special assistant to President John F. Kennedy, wrote to the Institute for International Social Research, "I read with interest your Cuban report–and only wish that a copy had come to my attention earlier." Albert H. Cantril and Charles W. Roll, Jr., *Hopes and Fears of the American People*, New York: Universe Books, 1971, pp. 26–27n.

[41]Speer, *op. cit.*, p. 378.

[42]Irving L. Janis, George F. Mahl, Jerome Kagen, Robert R. Holt, *Personality*, New York: Hartcourt Brace Jovanovich, 1969, pp. 166–167.

[43]Ernest L. V. Shelley and Hans H. Toch, "The Perception of Violence as an Indicator of Adjustment in Institutionalized Offenders," in Toch and Smith, *op. cit.*, pp. 198–208.

[44]This is particularly important as we make judgments and interpret the actions and motives of others. A great deal of latitude exists as in intelligence estimates. As former Secretary of Defense Melvin Laird has testified:

> There are two categories of judgment encompassed in the intelligence estimate. The first has to do with the interpretation of the existing and near-state of affairs, based on the interpretation of the information which is collected. The second has to do with the anticipation of probable and possible future events and circumstances. It should be obvious that although our intelligence community does an unbelievably good job of collecting an astounding amount of information, we do not collect all of the information that exists. Accordingly the conclusions of an intelligence estimate must be stated in terms of what the information we do have in hand proves. In addition, there are usually notations of additional possibilities for which conclusive evidence is not yet available. The information is skillfully collected from many sources, but even so is composed of many bits and pieces, which still require considerable evaluation to arrive at a useful judgment.

U.S. Senate, Committee on Foreign Relations, *Hearings, Intelligence and the ABM*, 91st Cong. 1st sess., June 23, 1969, p. 3.

[45]Ralph K. White, "Images in the Context of International Conflict," in Herbert C. Kelman (ed.), *International Behavior*, New York: Holt, Rinehart & Winston, 1965, pp. 238–276. See also Robert Jervis, *The Logic of Images in International Relations*, Princeton, N.J.: Princeton University Press, 1970.

[46]Robert C. North, Howard E. Koch, Jr., and Dina A. Zinnes, "The Integrative Functions of Conflict," *Journal of Conflict Resolution*, 4 (September 1960), 356.

[47]". . . whenever any form of anxiety is aroused, whether by verbal communication or by direct encounter with signs of danger, the person becomes motivated to get rid of the unpleasant emotional state. If the threat cues that arouse the distressing state do not promptly disappear as a result of environmental changes, the emotionally aroused person will exert his own efforts toward coping with them or will try to escape either physically . . . or psychologically. . . ." Irving L. Janis et al., *op. cit.*, p. 111.

[48]*Ibid.*, p. 219.

[49]Richard M. Nixon, *U.S. Foreign Policy for the 1970s: A Report to the Congress* (February 25, 1971), p. 157. Of course President Nixon has also mentioned another facet of his approach in the following statement:

> . . . where the battle against Communism is concerned, victories are never final so long as the Communists are still able to fight. There is never a time when it is safe to relax or let down. When you have won one battle is the time you should step up your effort to win another–until final victory is achieved.

Richard M. Nixon, *Six Crises*, Garden City, N.Y.: Doubleday, 1962, p. 38.

[50]Toffler, *op. cit.*, pp. 314–315.

[51]Arnold A. Rogow, *James Forrestal*, New York: Macmillan, 1963.

[52]Quoted in Toffler, *op. cit.*, p. 321.

[53]Toffler, *op. cit.*, pp. 323–331.

[54]Paige, *op. cit.*, p. 28.

[55]*The Oregonian*, September 5, 1971, p. 16.

[56]Toffler, *op. cit.*, p. 337.

[57]Muzafer Sherif, O. J. Harvey, B. Jack White, and William R. Hood, *Intergroup*

Conflict and Cooperation: The Robbers' Cave Experiment, Norman, Okla.: University of Oklahoma Press, 1961.

[58]See UNITAR, *Social Psychological Techniques and the Peaceful Settlement of International Disputes*, UNITAR Research Reports No. 1 (1970). Also, J. W. Burton, *Conflict and Communication*, London: Macmillan, 1969; L. W. Doob (ed.), *Resolving Conflict in Africa: The Fermeda Workshop*, New Haven, Conn.: Yale University Press, 1970.

[59]Marshall R. Singer, *Weak States in a World of Power*, New York: Free Press, 1972, p. 412. Copyright © The Free Press.

[60]Charles E. Osgood, *An Alternative to War or Surrender*, Urbana, Ill.: University of Illinois Press, 1962.

[61]Memorandum for the President, 11 September 1945, in Gar Alperovitz, *Atomic Diplomacy: Hiroshima and Potsdam*, New York: Vintage Books, 1965, Appendix III, p. 278.

[62]James N. Rosenau (ed.), *International Politics and Foreign Policy*, New York: Free Press, 1969, p. xix.

[63]The principal ingredients of Canadian foreign policy are contained in the following descriptions of the six policy themes:

—*Fostering Economic Growth* is primarily a matter of developing the Canadian economy, seeking to ensure its sustained and balanced growth. This embraces a wide range of economic, commercial and financial objectives in the foreign field, such as: promotion of exports; management of resources and energies; trade and tariff agreements; loans and investments; currency stabilization and convertibility; improved transportation, communications and technologies generally; manpower and expertise through immigration; tourism. It involves varying degrees of co-operation in a group of international institutions–e.g., the International Monetary Fund (IMF), the General Agreement on Tariffs and Trade (GATT), the Organization for Economic Co-operation and Development (OECD), the Group of Ten—vital to the maintenance of a stable and prosperous economic community in the world.

—*Safeguarding Sovereignty and Independence* is largely a matter of protecting Canada's territorial integrity, its constitutional authority, its national identity and freedom of action. Sovereignty and independence are challenged when foreign fishermen illegally intrude into Canadian territorial waters, when Canadian constitutional arrangements are not fully respected by other governments. They may be affected by external economic and social influences (mainly from the United States); or qualified by international agreement, when Canada in its own interest co-operates internationally in trade (GATT) or financial institutions (IMF), for example. Sovereignty may have to be reaffirmed from time to time, especially when territorial disputes or misunderstandings arise, and should be reinforced by insistence on compliance with Canadian laws and regulations and by employing adequate means of surveillance and control to deal with infringement. Above all, sovereignty should be used to protect vital Canadian interests and promote Canada's aims and objectives.

—*Working for Peace and Security* means seeking to prevent war or at least to contain it. It includes identifying the kind of contribution which Canada can usefully make to the solution of the complex problems of maintaining peace, whether through defence arrangements, arms control, peacekeeping, the relaxation of tensions, international law, or improvement in bilateral relations. In essence, peace and security policies are designed to prevent, minimize or control violence in international relations, while permitting peaceful change.

—*Promoting Social Justice* includes policies of a political, economic and social nature pursued in a broad area of international endeavour and principally today with international groupings (the United Nations, the Commonwealth, la Francophonie). It means, in the contemporary world, focusing attention on two major international issues—race conflict and development assistance. It is also related to international efforts: to develop international law, standards and codes of conduct; and to keep in effective working order a wide variety of international organizations—e.g., the UN Development Programme (UNDP), the UN Conference on Trade and

Development (UNCTAD), the International Development Association (IDA), the Development Assistance Committee (DAC).

—*Enhancing the Quality of Life* implies policies that add dimension to economic growth and social reform so as to produce richer life and human fulfillment for all Canadians. Many of these policies are internal by nature, but in the external field they involve such activities as cultural, technological and scientific exchanges which, while supporting other foreign objectives, are designed to yield a rewarding life for Canadians and to reflect clearly Canada's bilingual and multicultural character. Part of this reward lies in the satisfaction that Canada in its external activities is making a worthwhile contribution to human betterment.

—*Ensuring a Harmonious Natural Environment* is closely linked with quality of life and includes policies to deal not only with the deterioration in the natural environment but with the risks of wasteful utilization of natural resources. Implicit are policies: to rationalize the management of Canada's resources and energies; to promote international scientific co-operation and research on all the problems of environment and modern society; to assist in the development of international measures to combat pollution in particular; to ensure Canadian access to scientific and technological information in other countries.

Foreign Policy for Canadians, published by authority of the Honourable Mitchell Sharp, Secretary of State for External Affairs, Ottawa, Canada, Ottawa: Queen's Printer for Canada, 1970, pp. 14–16. Reproduced by permission of Information Canada.

[64]*Ibid.*, p. 17.

[65]Alexander L. George, David K. Hall, and William R. Simons, *The Limits of Coercive Diplomacy*, Boston, Mass.: Little, Brown, 1971.

[66]Quincy Wright, *A Study of War*, Chicago: University of Chicago Press, 1965.

[67]For an excellent analysis of problems and approaches in public policy see Joyce M. Mitchell and William C. Mitchell, *Political Analysis and Public Policy: An Introduction to Political Science*, Skokie, Ill.: Rand McNally, 1969.

[68]U.S. Department of State, Bureau of Public Affairs, Office of Media Services, news release, August 1, 1972.

[69]Herbert F. York, *Race to Oblivion*, New York: Clarion Books, 1971, p. 229.

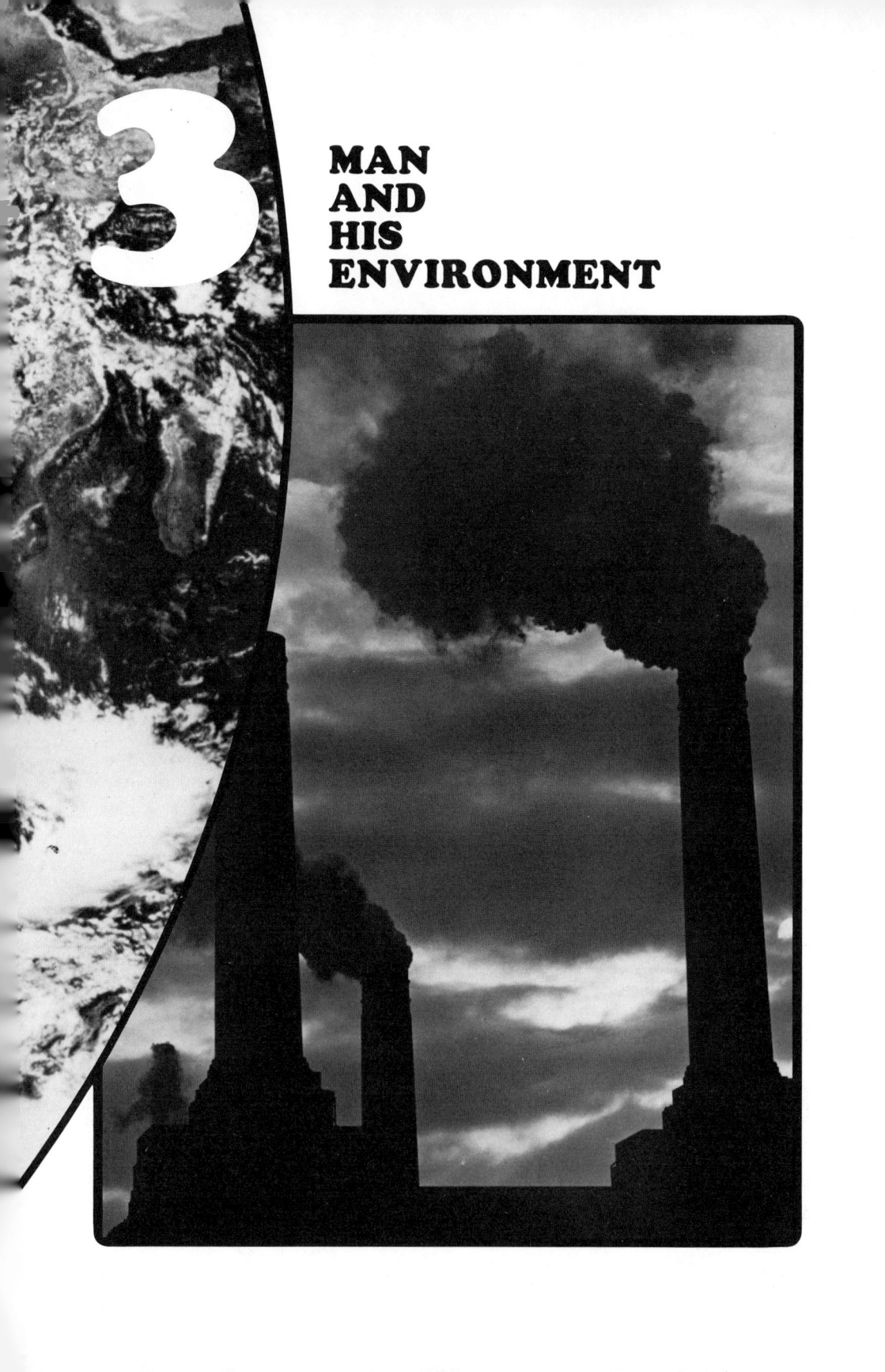

3
MAN
AND
HIS
ENVIRONMENT

Every cloud, even if it consists of smog, may have a silver lining. The crisis of the environment could be the challenge which might show us the way forward to a responsible and just world society. . . .

U Thant
1971

On June 15, 1972, a counterculture group petitioned the 114 states attending the United Nations Conference on the Human Environment in Stockholm, Sweden, to have *Homo sapiens* (mankind) placed on the "endangered species list" as an animal form threatened with extinction. The petition called for a ten-year moratorium on the acts of states and governments that resulted in the killing of man. This plea was a plaintive one by people frustrated with the progress of negotiations among states in trying to deal with the crisis of the human environment.

The Stockholm Conference, some three years in the planning, was convened to try to cope with the trends in the use of the environment of man that were threatening the future of life on earth. Evidence on the waste and depletion of natural resources, questions of pollution, residual effects of chemicals on plant and animal life, and the ecological balance between man and other living things had compelled states to seek means to preserve the environment before it was too late. Yet the urgent necessities that brought about the conference could not be extricated from the desires of each government to maintain its own share of the earth's resources and their development. The people's petition highlighted for the moment, at least, that the threat to mankind was man and the manner in which his organization of society used the environment.

History, and especially the history of international relations, is replete with illustrations of human denial of the reality that mankind lives in a carefully balanced system. Astronauts viewing the earth from the vantage point of outer space see a tiny ball of oceans, continents, and the atmosphere. Its physical aspect is set; it is not expanding or growing. The earth is finite. People, plants, and animals, including microorganisms, live in this physical area in an interconnected web of relationships. These interdependent biological and physical elements are called an ecosystem. While one often char-

acterizes an ecosystem as limited like the cycle relationships of, say, the nitrogen cycle, which is critical to the growth of plants that supply the amino acids necessary to build body proteins, in reality the total ecosystem is a global system of the web of interconnecting relationships among all the biological and physical elements that make up and occupy the planet earth.

The resources of the earth in a broad sense can be divided into renewable and nonrenewable resources. The renewable resources, like water, air, flora, and fauna, are in natural ecosystems that can be thrown, if misused, into imbalance that will threaten the possibility of renewing these renewable resources. The nonrenewable resources, like oil or iron or mercury, have actual limits—once used they are gone forever.

There are limits in the use of the resources of the earth that cannot be exceeded. The survival of mankind depends upon the maximum maintenance of these resources—to ensure that the nonrenewable resources are utilized in a manner to ensure the balances required to preserve the renewable resources. These are the absolutes of the closed system of the earth's environment, the reality that the earth is finite. The actions of man—especially the actions of man through the institution of the state—historically have been to deny the finite character of the environmental system within which he lives.

This paradox of the finite nature of the world and mankind's denial of this reality has assumed a crisis magnitude in the last half of the twentieth century because the population growth in its exponential increases has made undeniable the fact that the finite resources may not be capable of supporting the increasing population in the future. The Stockholm Conference was convened on the assumption that the time to act was immediately because the necessity of resolving the crisis between population growth and limited resources was so critical that mankind's capacity to control the situation may already have been weakened. Yet, while the Stockholm Conference recognized the real dilemma of mankind, the unanimity of this acceptance was not present in the decisions undertaken to cope with the environmental crisis. The political divisions of the earth, which were not discernible to the astronauts viewing the planet, deny the oneness and the finite character of the world.

The approach of the international system of states has been to deny the reality of the physical environment within which it exists. Each group of individuals, each state, in an almost historical inevitabilty has argued against the finiteness of the earth. Each state has singly sought an escape from this closed system of limited resources, each has sought the means to obtain its "just" share of these resources and their use. The dilemmas in the relationships of states and peoples as they relate to the physical environment in the last half of the twentieth century are, in part, the product of certain common behavioral patterns of states in facing the problems posed by the limits of the earth.

While the 1970s is a period in which many individuals are beginning to accept the fact that the earth has a set and limited life-support environment, the momentum to organize the international system of states to assure maintenance of this life-support system is still plagued by behavior patterns of escapism, denial, greed, and optimism. While each of these behavior patterns manifested by nations or states is not mutually exclusive, each does typify ways in which man has tried to deny the finiteness of his environment. The international relations among states provide many examples of these various behavior patterns.

ESCAPISM BEHAVIOR

Faced with an awareness of the limitations of the environment, nations have often pursued policies to escape facing their environmental limits and to avoid mobilizing their societies to maintain themselves in their given environments. The policy answer is often sought in a dream or a venture that will bring the wealth of resources to the particular state.

THE NEW CALEDONIA EXPERIMENT

A classical example of this type of behavior was exhibited by Scotland in the latter part of the seventeenth century. Scotland, in 1690, was a country devastated by political and religious wars, both physically and intellectually, as well as deep in poverty from a period of the English occupation during the Cromwellian Commonwealth. Scotland seemed unable to mobilize her meager resources, and her population and leaders, rather than focusing on how to organize the society with the available resources, became enticed with a dream.

William Patterson, a Scottish merchant who had visited the West Indies (though he never set foot on Central America), conceived the establishment of a colony on the Isthmus of Panama. Filled with stories based on the rumors of seamen about the lush productiveness of the land and the potential of untapped mineral resources, Patterson argued for the establishment of a settlement that would not only be productive in its own right, but by virtue of being located on the Isthmus it would also become a major free-trade area for transferring goods from the West to the East (thus providing a shorter, alternative route to the long trade routes around Africa to Asia). As his dream took hold among Scottish leaders, it developed into an idea to establish a Scottish Trading Company and colony on Darien, as the Isthmus of Panama was then known. Beginning with an act of the Scottish Parliament authorizing formation of companies to seek foreign trade in 1693, Patterson's idea seized the imagination of Scottish merchants.

The Scottish merchants tried first to get approval for the company in London, where money was available, but this effort to obtain English financial support failed, and the Company of Scotland Trading in Africa and the Indies then opened a stock sale in Edinburgh. In a wave of excitement, bordering almost on hysteria, not only merchants but a wide cross section of people sacrificed every available asset to buy shares to finance the venture. The whole country became engulfed in dreams of Darien. Few questions were raised as to the practicality of the idea. No one was sent to see if the dream of the venture was a reality. Boats were purchased in Holland, and by November 1697, five ships took off for the promised land that would solve the problems of Scotland, "the key to the universe" as it was characterized.[1] The ships were outfitted with not only a wide variety of trade goods, but the individuals in the expedition were carefully selected so that the colony would have every skill and talent to maintain a well-balanced settlement.

Plagued by storms, fever, and quarrels among the leaders, the expedition finally arrived at Caledonia Bay on November 2, 1698. Instead of a lush area available for cultivation, and soil filled with gold, they found that New Caledonia was an impenetrable mangrove jungle and swamp in an oppressively hot and humid climate conducive to disease. It was an effort of weeks before sufficient land could be cleared to build a few huts, a task hampered by people sick and dying from fever and the bickering of the disillusioned leaders. In addition, the colonialists discovered that their settlement was in an area claimed by Spain, and rumors of Spanish military interventions added to their dilemmas. While these problems were plaguing the settlers in New Caledonia, additional supply ships from Scotland were either captured by the Spanish or lost at sea. Dispatches requesting help reached Scotland at about the same time that the initial survivors decided to abandon the hopeless venture.

The first-expedition survivors abandoned the New Caledonia settlement in 1699, while a second expedition, unaware of this decision, left Scotland for the promised land in September. The majority of the first-expedition survivors were either lost at sea or captured by the Spanish in their endeavor to reach New York on their return journey. On November 21 one ship of the first expedition arrived back in Scotland with the real story of the abortive attempt at settlement. Just nine days later the second expedition arrived at the site of the abandoned settlement. Within a few months the survivors of the second expedition, also debilitated by the tropical environment, were attacked by Spanish forces, and the colony ceased to exist.

The disillusionment over the failure of the colony had its final episode in recriminations in Scotland; the captain of one of the ships was charged with piracy and publicly hanged in symbolic vengeance for the failure of the lost dream.

The energies expended, the lives lost, and the savings depleted in chasing the dream of the New Caledonia debacle was a policy escape from facing the realities of the Scottish environment. If these energies and organization had been directed instead toward mobilizing Scotland with what she had in her limited resources, Scotland might well have recovered from her state of poverty. But it was easier to escape and dream. Scottish hope for continued independence was shattered by the experience, and the Company of Scotland was dissolved by the Treaty of Union of the two Kingdoms of Scotland and England in May 1707.

If the New Caledonian Experiment had succeeded it would have temporarily relieved the problems in Scotland. Many colonial ventures have served this purpose, but all only delayed the time when the mother country was forced to face its own environmental problems. England in the late 1960s, after the loss of the bulk of her colonies, finally gave major attention to land use planning, preserving its limited resources, and cleaning up pollution.

THE DREAM OF THE AMAZON BASIN

A somewhat comparable dream behavior occurred in the twentieth century as a solution to the world's population problem. It was hoped that the surplus populations of states could be moved to the comparatively unoccupied Amazon Basin Region of South America, without the comparable tragic results of the New Caledonia experiment. Following World War II there was a realization of the very rapid growth of population, especially in many areas of Asia, for example, India. Filled with enthusiasm that the solution to population growth was to find vacant areas of the globe to resettle the excess populations, the idea of resettling this excess in the Amazon Basin was put forward by a number of states at the first session of the General Conference of the United Nations Educational, Scientific, and Cultural Organization (UNESCO) in December 1946. This proposal resulted in the executive board of UNESCO establishing an International Commission on the Hylean Amazon concerned with investigating the possibilities of the development and settlement of the whole Amazon Basin. Unlike the New Caledonia dream, however, further discussions of this hope for a population solution revolved more about the necessity for carefully examining the potential of the Amazon. At a meeting in August 1947 the commission recognized that, while the Amazon Basin was one of the largest underdeveloped areas in the world, extending over portions of six South American countries as well as the colonial area in the Guianas, it was impossible without accurate knowledge of the conditions in the region to see what problems would be involved in the economic development of the area. The eight states at this conference decided that what was needed was an institute that would sponsor and coordinate the studies with

respect to the prospects for human ecology, human welfare, and economic progress in the area. The result was the formulation of an agreement proposing the creation of an International Hylean Amazon Institute[2] to accomplish these goals. The idea collapsed shortly, thereafter, when the countries directly involved were not willing to fund the organization.

This dream of the Amazon Basin as a solution to the world's excess population problem was probably unrealistic in the beginning. Though it captured the popular press of many countries in 1946 and 1947, it, like the New Caledonian scheme, was a policy dream—it was an attempt to solve a very difficult problem by an escapist route. Delegates to UNESCO enthusiastically endorsed the project when it was first proposed, but later discussions focused more on the unknowns in terms of the problems of the Amazon Basin. In the final analysis the states in the region itself were unwilling to commit themselves to the project when they themselves felt little population pressure. (One could sense, however, that in Brazil at least, this dream for development of the Amazon Basin was a germinal concept in the subsequent Brazilian government's effort to develop its interior around Brazilia.) In a sense this dream was an attempt to respond to the environmental dilemma, but it failed because it was entrusted in its realization to those who did not then accept or had not yet experienced acute population pressures.

A SPACE ODYSSEY

Escapism concepts and policies were prevalent when man first ventured into outer space in the 1960s. One argument was that outer space would be a new frontier for man to develop. Excitement during the first Venus and Mars probes was caught up in the possibility of an environment that would support man—again an escapism dream. Paul R. Ehrlich pricked this dream as any immediate possibility (although not denying other positive gains) when he pointed out that assuming a spaceship like the U.S. Apollo spacecraft could hold 100 people and transport them to a planet, it would take 2000 flights a day for a year to transport 70 million people—the approximate yearly increase in the world's population at the current growth rates. The cost of this venture alone would use up the yearly gross national product of the United States in three days.[3]

The whole dream concept of the never-ending frontier—that there is *always a new frontier* as a solution to pressing social problems—which has been prevalent in the environmental behavior of states—is an underlying assumption of escapism behavior.

Whether it is the dream of the new frontier, a New Caledonia, the Hylean Amazon, or outer space, these examples of escapism behavior are all evasions of acceptance of the reality of the finite environment. Escapism dreams even if they are realized are delays or diversions in the efforts of

mankind to cope with the problem of organizing their immediate environment within its absolute limitations.

DENIAL BEHAVIOR

People, nations, and states often ignore the limitations inherent in the total environment setting by denying it has limitations. In a sense this is another type of escapism, but it is an implicit policy behavior characterized by both mental and action denial of the reality that seems inescapable.

The disparity between the consumption of the world's resources by the developed and developing states is an example of denial behavior. The United States and the Soviet Union with about 12 percent of the world's population in 1971 were consuming about 61 percent of the resource production of the world. While these facts are often talked about, these two states continue the consumption process in a manner that constitutes denial of the fact that there are limits to the nonrenewable resources of the earth.

The contrast of the behavior of these states is even more apparent with some comparisons. In 1971 $4 billion was spent on supplies for pets in the United States (dog and cat food, animal toys, cages, clothes, cookies, collars, jewelry, nail polish, and animal coats of arms, etc.). Of the 135 member states in the United Nations in 1973, 84 of these states had a gross national product of less than $4 billion. In fact, $1.5 billion was spent in the United States on just dog and cat food. This was more than the annual gross national product in each of 74 members of the United Nations. Ethiopia with 24.5 million people had a gross national product just about equal to the amount of money spent on dog and cat food in the United States. Haiti in 1971, with a population slightly over 5 million, had a gross national product about equivalent to the $390 million spent in the United States on deodorants.

The consumption of the world's resources by major states, such as the United States, continues with no abatement as if there was no awareness of limits of the earth. The president of the International Bank for Reconstruction and Development (IBRD) pointed out that in 1970 the United States with about 6 percent of the world's population was consuming almost 40 percent of the world's resources, and at its 1970 rate of growth would need to consume about 60 percent of the world's resources by 1979.[4] Thus this illustrates one type of denial behavior: Those states that are more developed consume resources as they are able to command them in a manner that ignores the limited capacity of the total environment—they deny acceptance of this reality as long as the limits do not have to be immediately faced.

HALIBUT FISHERIES

Another type of denial behavior is the situation in which environmental facts are denied by focusing on another issue. An illustration is interstate

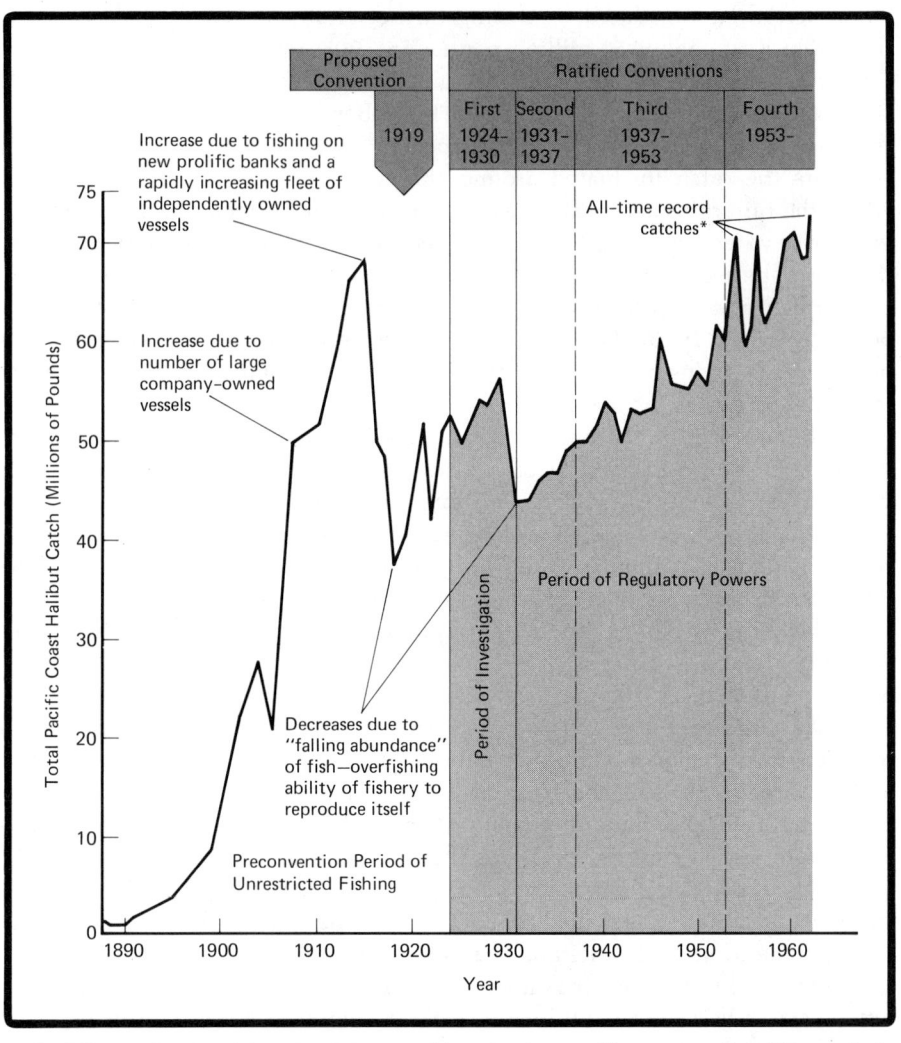

FIGURE 3.1 *Catch of Pacific Coast Halibut by Year: Illustrating the Effect of the Various Halibut Commission Regulations on the Total Catch*

*Seasonal fluctuations like 1955 were due to weather and tide conditions.
Source: Based on the International Pacific Halibut Commission *Reports.*

relations with respect to ocean fisheries. In the North Pacific, for example, fishermen from Canada and the United States first started to exploit the halibut fishery in the 1880s. The halibut catch, as depicted in Figure 3.1, gradually rose from 1 million pounds in 1888 to about 28 million pounds in 1904, when it began to decline, dropping off by 5 million pounds in 1906. Larger

boats were then introduced, venturing farther offshore, and the halibut catch then went up to about 50 million pounds in 1908, when it again tapered off. Then the fishing fleets moved farther into the Gulf of Alaska, and the catch rose to a peak of 69 million pounds by 1915. Between 1915 and 1918, despite these increased efforts, the catch dropped to 38 million pounds. In the next six years the catch fluctuated around this level, dropping in some years in which the failure to get a catch resulted in fewer fishermen and then rising a year or so after when the fishery was recovering. What was happening was that the fishermen from the two countries were overfishing the ability of the halibut fishery to reproduce and maintain itself. As the catch dropped nearly 50 percent from 1915 to 1918, there was increased agitation between the two nation-states to ensure that the fishermen from one state did not invade the territorial waters of the other state.

The problem of the halibut fishery was in reality a biological problem, one of overfishing the ability of the halibut fishery to maintain itself. The problem as the states saw it at the time, however, was really a question of international law—the question of territorial jurisdiction. Charges were made that Canadian fishermen were invading American waters, thus reducing the American fisherman's catch and vice versa. In the particular case of the halibut fishery in the North Pacific, the economic crisis to the fishing industries in the two states became so acute that the states agreed in a treaty in 1924 to the creation of an international commission to study the problem.

Once the problem was recognized as a biological problem and not a question of the violation of international boundaries, the two states were able to agree in 1930 on the creation of a permanent commission to conserve and therefore help build up the halibut fishery. In a steady rate of growth this was accomplished, and by the 1960s the catch was being sustained at around a rate of 60 to 70 million pounds per year. The fishery had declined previously because the states denied the fact that the fishery—a renewable resource —was being overfished in its ability to renew itself.[5]

Even if one assumes that many fisheries were destroyed by competition among states because the problem was seen wholly as a question of invasion of each other's territorial waters, as happened in many places in the world before this study commission in the 1920s on the halibut fishery, it seems self-evident that since that time fishery problems are not boundary problems but biological problems. Since the creation of the Halibut Commission in 1931, there have been a number of other international commissions created to conserve particular fisheries. Yet in the 1970s there still are many examples of attempts to deal with fishery problems by viewing them as boundary problems and not as a question of sustaining nonrenewable resources. Soviet and Japanese fishing vessels are accused of invading American waters in the Pacific Ocean. Pressure is exerted on the federal govern-

ment to extend the limits of American territorial water boundaries. Previously, the territorial limit was 3 miles, but to control fishing it was extended 12 miles. Some states, such as Peru, then claimed a 200- or 300-mile territorial limit. By July 1974 (at the 3rd U.N. Conference on the Law of the Sea held in Caracas, Venezuela), most states, including the United States, advocated a 200-mile fishing zone.

The prevalent practice of states is still to deny that fisheries may be depleted by overfishing; each persistently argues for an extension of its own boundaries. It is almost as if states were denying that fish do not observe international boundaries in the ocean. In a sense this behavior denies the fact that renewable resources may be maintained if they are recognized as renewable resources. More often than not, states are asserting that these are resources that will always be there if only they can control the situation to get their prime share.

NUCLEAR TESTING

A more insidious kind of denial behavior is that in which states pursue actions for a goal of "political" security and deny that these actions are endangering "physical" security—the environment. An illustration of this kind of denial behavior is evidenced in efforts to limit the testing of nuclear weapons. While theoretically the possibility of radioactive fallout was acknowledged in 1945, the first atomic tests did not make the possibility a clear reality. In October 1952 the United States exploded its first thermonuclear device, and the Soviet Union conducted a similar experiment in August 1953. On March 1, 1954, radioactive fallout clearly became a reality when a United States thermonuclear test on Bikini Atoll anticipated to be 7 megatons in magnitude had an unexpected yield of 15 megatons.

The fallout was widespread and particularly affected the crew of a Japanese fishing boat *Fukurya Maru*, about 100 miles from the test site. Until the Japanese boat reached port weeks after the explosion, the United States had kept secret the extent of the fallout and its possible dangers.[6] In 1955 the United States Atomic Energy Commission (AEC) did admit the possibilities of genetic damage from the fallout. While it was several years before people became fully aware of the fact that the radioactive fallout from these thermonuclear tests spread around the globe in the trade winds, the incident of the *Fukurya Maru* indicated that there were sufficient unknowns in these thermonuclear tests to constitute a danger to life.

Responding to the questions raised by the Bikini test, Prime Minister Nehru of India in April 1954 wrote to the Secretary-General of the United Nations urging that the tests be discontinued until the question of fallout danger could be answered. Partly in response to the public doubts about assurances of the United States to minimize the dangers from such tests, the

United States on August 4, 1955, requested the United Nations to consider the "co-ordination of information relating to the effects of atomic radiation upon human health and safety."[7] A few weeks later, India made the point more directly by suggesting that the United Nations consider means to disseminate information "on the effects of atomic radiation and on the effects of experimental explosions of thermo-nuclear bombs."[8]

These two proposals resulted in the creation of a U.N. Scientific Committee on the Effects of Atomic Radiation, which has since made periodic detailed reports on the effects of all varieties of atomic radiation. The committee's initial reports indicated that the world-wide spread of the radioactive fallout from the tests was more pronounced than originally suggested. India persisted during the next few years to urge a cessation of such thermonuclear tests because of the possible damage to man and his environment.

The United States and the Soviet Union on the other hand talked of a suspension of such tests but tied it primarily to disarmament efforts. In see-saw discussions from 1955 to 1963 in the General Assembly and in the Disarmament Commission of the United Nations, and then in the Eighteen Nation Disarmament Talks in Geneva, the issue was debated. The United States argued that there could be a cessation of tests only if there was a verification system to see that no violations of the test ban were made. The Soviets argued publicly for an outright ban, although privately they assumed there would be no ban unless the United States changed its position on verification.[9] The issue was tied in with "gamesmanship" to assure that if there was a test ban, each of these two superpowers would be in the best position in its weapons developments. Public apprehension, as well as public awareness of the danger of fallout led to the development of underground tests, which were said to minimize the fallout danger. In addition there was unilateral discontinuance of the nuclear tests by both the United States and the Soviet Union in efforts to gain world support for their potential positions. Finally in 1963 agreement was reached on a partial nuclear test ban treaty—partial in that it covered tests in the atmosphere, outer space, and underwater, but it still allowed for underground tests. The deadlock between the two positions was broken primarily because technological developments allowed a verification of compliance with the treaty without the necessity of on-the-site inspection teams.

This whole episode in which for the sake of development of weapons the two major powers were proceeding with little attention to the possible dangers to the ecosystem really constituted a public policy of denying the reality of the pollution danger to the environment and man. That there was an impact of this testing on the earth system was clear in the various reports of the U.N. Scientific Committee on the Effects of Atomic Radiation.[10]

Explosions of nuclear weapons in the atmosphere release material (fallout) that is radioactive—that is, they emit ionizing radiations that affect

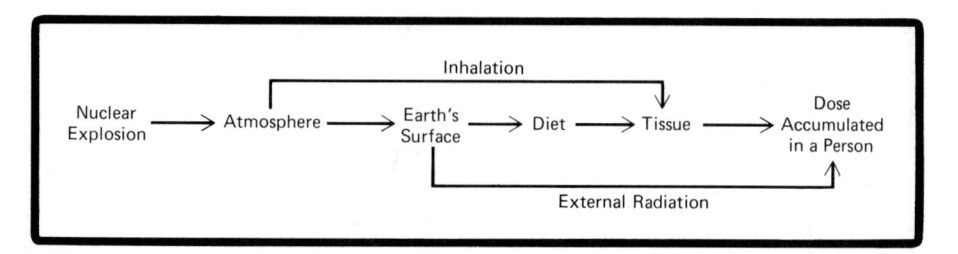

FIGURE 3.2 Radiation Effects of a Nuclear Explosion

living organisms. Apart from the immediate area of destruction in a nuclear explosion there are at least four radioactive by-products that have serious hazards for human health. These are:

1. Iodine-131 (halflife 8.1 days), which may become concentrated largely in the thyroid gland;
2. Strontium-90 (halflife 27.7 years), which becomes concentrated in bone and affects blood-forming cells and bone cells;
3. Caesium-137 (halflife 2616 years), which spreads throughout the body; and
4. Carbon-14 (halflife 5600 years), which accumulates in human tissue.

Figure 3.2 depicts the process of the effects of radiation from nuclear explosions. The studies analyzed by the U.N. Scientific Committee on the Effects of Atomic Radiation—of which Figures 3.3 and 3.4 and Table 3.1 are examples —indicate that while there is a gradual dissipation of the radioactive materials from the atmosphere as they are deposited on the earth's surface in a gradually declining rate, this causes a steady and cumulative deposit of radioactive materials on the globe. Innumerable studies have demonstrated the effects of radiation, particularly on the nervous system and radiation-induced chromosome aberrations in human cells.

While the United States and the Soviet Union (and Great Britain by virtue of discontinuing nuclear tests) have ceased atmospheric nuclear testing, China and France have continued to contaminate the atmosphere—especially France. In the summer of 1973, for example, a new series of French tests were conducted in the South Pacific. Australia and New Zealand along with the governments of Nauru, Tonga, Western Samoa, and Fiji protested this resumption of tests. Despite the fact that Australian and French scientists agreed on the radiation effects of previous French tests, which are shown in Tables 3.2 and 3.3, France conducted tests in 1973 and planned more for 1974–1975. Australia and New Zealand have taken a case to the International Court of Justice to try to prohibit future tests, but France has denied the jurisdiction of the Court.

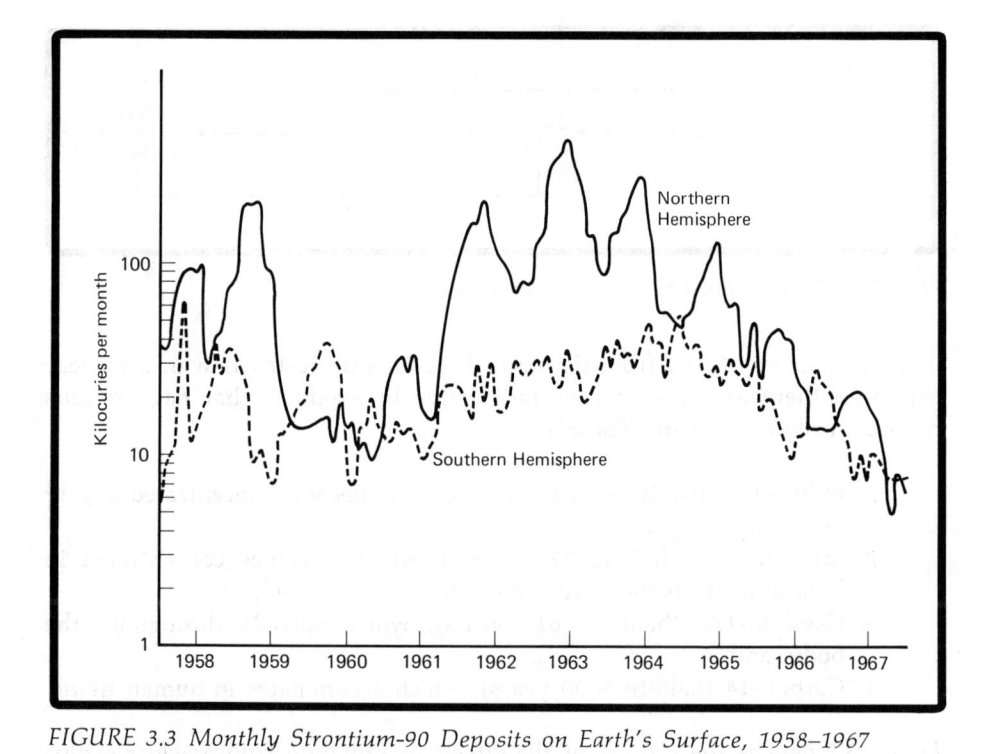

FIGURE 3.3 *Monthly Strontium-90 Deposits on Earth's Surface, 1958–1967*

Source: U.N. General Assembly, XXIV Session, Official Records, Supp. No. 13: *Report of the United Nations Scientific Committee on the Effects of Atomic Radiation, 1969,* p. 16.

France has argued that these atmospheric tests are essential to her national security (as was previously argued by the other nuclear powers). For the sake of military security, or so-called security, the major powers ignored or denied impacts on the environment that might affect the survival (security) of man.

MILITARISM

This denial of environmental facts in the name of military security is manifested in other ways in the contemporary world. For military reasons damage is done to the ecosystem with little concern for the consequences. In the name of the land war in Vietnam, the United States created 20 million craters, engaged in massive land-clearing efforts to level the jungle, and produced instant clearings in the jungle with the BLU-82/B general-purpose high-explosive bomb,[11] and used chemical sprays to defoliate the land.[12] The impact of these military operations for the future use of this land for cultiva-

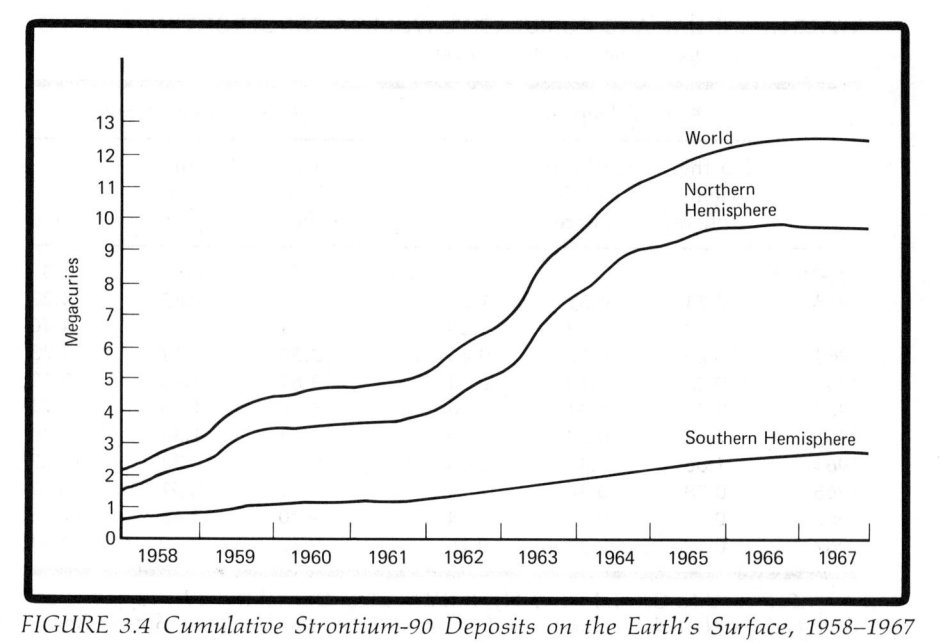

FIGURE 3.4 Cumulative Strontium-90 Deposits on the Earth's Surface, 1958–1967

Source: U.N. General Assembly, XXIV Session, Official Records, Supp. No. 13: *Report of the United Nations Scientific Committee on the Effects of Atomic Radiation,* 1969, p. 17.

tion or logging is unknown. The total impact on the spread of disease carriers reproducing in the water-filled craters is not fully known. The impact of the removal of the enormous water-carrying capacity of the dense forest with implications for erosion and subsequent flood damage is not fully realized.

The implications of these military operations for the future cannot yet be fully appraised, although the scientific evidence suggests they will bring very fundamental and long-lasting changes in the Vietnam environment. In July 1971 it was even confirmed that the American war effort in Vietnam involved "meteorological warfare," in that since 1964 efforts were made to seed clouds and cause rains and possible flooding.[13]

In the name of national security states deny that their international policies have an impact on the environment. They deny almost consciously the finite character of the earth. The "environment which supports us has only a limited capacity for radiation, and that capacity can only be used once."[14] In the development of nuclear weapons, states have used part of this limited capacity for radiation in a denial of the scientific reality.

Denial behavior in which states consciously deny the limitations of the world environment in which they exist is a practice of most states. The devel-

TABLE 3.1 ANNUAL AND CUMULATIVE WORLD-WIDE STRONTIUM-90 DEPO-
SITION (Values in Megacuries)

	Annual Deposition			Cumulative Deposit		
	Northern Hemi-sphere	Southern Hemi-sphere	Total	Northern Hemi-sphere	Southern Hemi-sphere	Total
Pre-1958				1.7	0.6	2.3
1958	0.74	0.31	1.05	2.39	0.83	3.22
1959	1.10	0.19	1.29	3.41	0.99	4.40
1960	0.26	0.17	0.43	3.59	1.14	4.73
1961	0.35	0.19	0.54	3.84	1.28	5.12
1962	1.45	0.31	1.76	5.16	1.55	6.71
1963	2.62	0.33	2.95	7.62	1.84	9.46
1964	1.66	0.44	2.10	9.06	2.21	11.27
1965	0.78	0.36	1.14	9.61	2.51	12.12
1966	0.33	0.21	0.54	9.70	2.65	12.35
1967	0.17	0.11	0.28	9.62	2.69	12.31

Source: U.N. General Assembly, XXIV Session, Official Records, Supp. No. 13:
*Report of the United Nations Scientific Committee on the Effects of Atomic Radia-
tion* (1969), p. 45.

oped states deny reality in the name of development, and the developing
states argue their development should not be precluded because of the environmental dangers already created by the actions of the developed states.

GREED BEHAVIOR

COLONIAL IMPERIALISM

The focus of another type of behavior of states on the environment system of the earth is one in which states consciously seek to maximize their
benefits at the expense of the resources of other states and/or peoples. This
type of behavior is often accompanied by some type of rationalization, which
attempts to justify seizing the resources of another on some high-sounding
grounds other than simple greed. The policy of imperialism followed by states
is a prime example of greed behavior. Rather than either remaining satisfied
with the resources of their own area or focusing on how to maximize the
utilization of their own local environments, states from earliest times have
ventured forth into other areas of the globe to extract resources or to resettle

their populations. Most often imperialism has been rationalized as bringing civilization to the uncivilized.

Even the ancient Greek city-states established colonies in Italy and Sicily, in the Aegean Islands, or on parts of Asia Minor, primarily to accommodate their surplus populations. The period of the imperial age however reached its heights with the movement of the Western European states—primarily Portugal, Spain, France, England, the Netherlands, Belgium, and Germany—into the Americas, Africa, and Asia. Various rationales, from spreading God's work to the concept of the white man's burden, were used as justifications for what was essentially greed behavior to get the resources and lands of other peoples. If there were not sufficient "primitive" people in the area, slaves from one area were moved to another area to maximize the development of renewable resources—crops, and so on.

These policies of imperialism were fundamentally policy decisions to solve the resource limitations of the imperial states by taking resources from others whom they could dominate by force if necessary. Rather than trying to accept the limitations of their particular environment, most of the Western European states pursued this sort of greed behavior to avoid acceptance of the finite character of their particular sections of the earth.

TABLE 3.2 DOSE COMMITMENTS (IN MILLIRADS) IN AUSTRALIA AS A RESULT OF FRENCH ATMOSPHERIC TESTS PRIOR TO JUNE 1973

Element	Thyroid (Young Children)	Thyroid (Older Children and Adults)	Blood-Forming Cells	Bone Cells	Whole Body
Iodine-131	97	9	0	0	0
Short lived	1.5	1.5	1.5	1.5	1.5
Strontium-90	0	0	4.0–6.2	5.6–8.5	0
Caesium-137 (external)	2.0–3.0	2.0–3.0	2.0–3.0	2.0–3.0	2.0–3.0
Caesium-137 (internal)	0.9–1.3	0.9–1.3	0.9–1.3	0.9–1.3	0.9–1.3
Carbon-14	0.2	0.2	0.2	0.3	0.2
Total (in round figures)	102–103	14–15	9–12	10–15	5–6

Source: Parliament of the Commonwealth of Australia, 1973-Parliamentary Paper No. 29: *Biological Effects of Nuclear Explosion Fallout—Report of Meeting Between Australian and the French Scientists*, Canberra, 7–9 May 1973, p. 4.

TABLE 3.3 DOSE COMMITMENTS (IN MILLIRADS) IN AUSTRALIA FOR ALL ATMOSPHERIC NUCLEAR TESTS PRIOR TO JUNE 1973

Element	Thyroid (Young Children)	Thyroid (Older Children and Adults)	Blood-Forming Cells	Bone Cells	Whole Body
French tests	103	15	12	15	6
Tests by other nations	74	54	83	96	52
Total for all tests[a]	177	69	95	111	58

[a]Note the cumulative effects of the previous tests. The French tests are not as dirty in Strontium-137, Caesium-137, and Carbon-14 as previous tests.
Source: Parliament of the Commonwealth of Australia, 1973-Parliamentary Paper No. 29: *Biological Effects of Nuclear Explosion Fallout—Report of Meeting Between Australian and French Scientists,* Canberra, 7–9 May 1973, p. 4.

The methods of this greed behavior are varied. In some instances they involved private trading companies operating under governmental charters. In other instances they were more direct government ventures. Some were based on first-hand "discovery," others on areas "allotted" to the states, as in the instance of the papal bull that "divided" the New World for exploitation between Portugal and Spain or as in the Congress of Berlin in 1885 which "divided" up Africa among the various contending powers. In the case of the United States and czarist Russia the push was not overseas but a gradual continental push against indigenous peoples occupying the interior areas.

In every case, the imperial states were more developed in terms of arms or economic organization than the areas they sought to occupy or control. The justification for these greed behaviors were always couched in high-level rationalizations. For example, as rivalry arose between the efforts of Prince Henry of Portugal and the Kingdom of Castile with respect to their movement toward West Africa, a papal bull of 1455 gave Portugal exclusive right to acquire title to these areas in the name of expanding the bounds of Christendom. The papal bull authorized the Portuguese to "conquer, enslave and Christianize" the peoples and their lands.[15] The religious rationalization was wrapped around many imperial ventures by the European powers.

Inherent in such rationalization was the assumption that the areas occupied or seized were "unoccupied"—that is, unoccupied by the "civilized" states of Western Europe. The international law of the eighteenth and nineteenth centuries assumed lands that were not in European control were *terra*

nullis (territory belonging to no one)—while in fact they were populated by the indigenous inhabitants. Paintings of early European explorers in the New World often show Europeans planting a flag on shore with the "natives" looking on in the background. One of the legal evidences of a claim for title to these territories was whether a flag of the claiming country was planted. Again the assumption, justified by a European version of international law, asserted that these lands were "unoccupied" and thus could be claimed for the imperial states. Whether rationalized on religious grounds or on international law, the facts in every instance involved an assertion of control over an area that before that time was occupied by another group of people.

Venturing abroad with superior weapons, the imperialist powers seized other lands often by imposing "treaties" on the indigenous peoples. Even these treaties were violated, usually by the imperialist states themselves and new treaties were "renegotiated" as the desire for further acquisition of territory increased. The example of American relations with the Nez Perce Indians is typical. Successive treaties with the Nez Perce were violated by the United States, each reducing the territory belonging to the tribe. In each treaty an exclusive area was established for the Nez Perce, but then rumors of gold or other resources in the Indian territory led to pressures on the United States to condone treaty violations to acquire the resources.

This pattern of first forcing treaties and then forcing the renegotiating of them has been as much a pattern in the greed behavior of imperialism as the rationalization of religion or international law. Yet the motivations behind the greed behavior were all tied to acquiring either space for settlement of populations or more generally acquiring resources to supplement the resource-limited environments of the imperial states at the expense of other peoples.

Domination of most of Africa, Asia, and the Americas by successive drives of European powers was at its peak between 1775 and 1900, when as much as two-thirds of the world was in some sort of colonial relationship with the European states. With the independence of the American states increased efforts were pushed by the imperial states into Asia and other parts of Africa. In addition, Russia and the United States pushed their continental expansions. By 1900, and as late as 1939, one-half of the world's area and one-third of the world's population were under colonial domination.

ECONOMIC IMPERIALISM

The period from 1945 to the present, and especially during 1955 to 1965, saw many of these former colonial areas achieve political independence. The membership of the United Nations increased from 50 to 138 states from 1946 to 1974, with most of these new members being former colonial areas. Yet the achievement of political independence has not meant the end of im-

perialistic greed behavior. By economic devices many of the imperialist states continue to dominate the utilization of resources from these former colonial areas. An examination of the trade patterns of these former colonies indicates that the exploitation of their limited share of the finite resources is being diverted to the former imperialist states at an economic disadvantage to the former colonial areas.[16]

This economic imperialism no longer has rationalizations of religion or civilization or international law. Now some imperialistic governments deny that there is economic imperialism by arguing it is just the normal process of nongovernmental or private free enterprise. Others rationalize their economic influences as either fostering "democratic regimes" or "socialist regimes"; some even assert they are solidifying "anti-imperialist regimes."

Whatever form, whatever method, whatever rationalization, greed behavior has been a basic policy of many states to solve their environmental problems at the expenses of other peoples. In a sense, it is a denial of the environmental realities because it directs efforts away from coping with the limitations a given people has within its own area. Greed behavior is acted out only by a more powerful state against a weaker state, and for some 2000 years it has been a prevalent behavior of the more powerful states. One might hypothesize that greed behavior is more likely to be practiced by states in which there is an internal disparity of wealth. The economic leaders of the state have acquired their position at the expense of other individuals in the state, and they may similarly exert an influence to have the state pursue greed behavior in external relations.

ETERNAL OPTIMISM BEHAVIOR

This type of behavior by states and peoples is characterized by a conscious acknowledgment of the environmental problem but includes an assumption that there is a simplistic solution. It is not a denial of reality, but in accepting the finite nature of the biosphere this type of behavior exudes an optimism as to the way in which the problem of a particular portion of the world environment can be resolved.

THE MAORI EMIGRATION

A historical illustration of eternal optimism behavior can be seen in the Maori emigration to New Zealand in the fourteenth century. Prior to this time the Maoris were living primarily in the islands of Central Polynesia. New Zealand had been discovered by a Maori explorer named Kupe about 925 A.D. His navigating instructions were passed from generation to generation by word of mouth on how to reach these large, apparently unoccupied islands. As overpopulation in the central Polynesian Islands became inevita-

ble and as the overpopulation resulted in increasing social discontent, plans were made to have a portion of the population move to Ao Tea Roa (The Land of the Long White Cloud), as Kupe had named New Zealand. The so-called fleet of Maori tradition was a "carefully planned colonizing expedition."[17] Not only were choices made in terms of people by age and skills, but every effort was made to take varieties of plants and seeds and animal life.

In addition, each of the longboats in the fleet were microcosms of the entire expedition, and in landing in New Zealand each boat carefully sought different landing sites so that they would have sufficient living space in settling their new environment.[18]

The Maoris recognized the fact that their original environment was exceeding its capacity to accommodate their population. They were aware of the uninhabited area of Ao Tea Roa in their folklore, and so rather than dealing with the problems in Polynesia, their solution was to move to the vacant area. Their knowledge of the world was limited to this area of the South Pacific—they were very optimistic that all they needed was more space. They seemed to have no realization that this was not an ultimate solution. It was not a dream of unreality, as in the case of New Caledonia or the Hylean Amazon; it was a very pragmatic step carefully taken in the optimistic belief that it was the solution. It was carefully planned and executed. They seemed to have no realization that not only would their population eventually expand in the new setting, but they might also subsequently find themselves in contention over the land with Europeans who four centuries later also emigrated to the islands of New Zealand.

TECHNOLOGY—A PANACEA

There is a correlation between the extent of eternal optimism behavior and technological development. Historically, one can trace the expansion of states in terms of their mastery and utilization of various forms of energy. Newtonian physics states that energy is never lost or gained, that the amount of energy in the universe is constant. Fred Cottrell in his study on *Energy and Society* has pointed out that man by his ability to master various sources of energy most efficiently is able to extend the capacity of a given society. Early societies tied to cultivating fields lost their dominance to those that mastered the energy capacity of rivers.[19] Or for that matter, those basic agricultural societies that domesticated animals as sources of energy surpassed those that did not.

One can sift through history and see that the mastery of wind energy by the sail was an important factor in the development of Phoenicia, Greece, and Rome and that the development of sailing vessels and later steamships contributed significantly to the expansion of the European maritime powers. The ability to achieve a high-energy technology becomes therefore a key element in motivating states to have an optimistic outlook on their ability to

cope with the finite capacity of the earth. They may recognize that their energy-producing capacity is dependent on such fuel sources as coal or petroleum. They may recognize that these sources are finite and may be exhausted, but their awareness of the technological skills that made possible the tapping of these energy sources provides them with an optimism that technology is the key to any problem.

Technology and its development becomes almost a lodestone to the future. The splitting of the atom and the discovery of the possibilities of nuclear energy—an energy source the extent of which is not yet fully comprehended—is seen by many as ultimate proof that the capacity of states to conquer the finite concept of earth is possible. The attitude of most developed societies toward the environmental problem is acceptance; any apprehensions they may have, however, they offset with a belief that technological developments will be able to surmount any problem in the future. This view seems to dominate the view that the development of energy by the manipulation of molecules may have repercussions in the multiplicity of interrelated systems involved in the total biosphere.[20]

Eternal optimism behavior is the behavior evidenced by the most-developed states in the 1970s. Such technologically reliant states assert their dominance by using their technology to attempt to influence other states in the international system. Technological optimism assumes that man's ability to master the earth will offset any problems. It also assumes that man has the insight to overcome environmental problems in a manner that will preserve the biosphere. Yet, as we have indicated by inference, such technological optimism may result in these states also practicing greed behavior. It is almost as if those that pursue eternal optimism behavior do so from an egocentric point of view.

This was true of the Maori emigration, which assumed there was a vacant environment for them, as it is of the technological development of the United States and the Soviet Union, which assumes the resources of the world can be utilized preponderantly by the most technologically developed. The United States and the Soviet Union through their technological mastery of weapons can command the "vacant" resources of the earth for them to utilize in the most "efficient" manner.

COMPARISON OF BEHAVIOR PATTERNS OF STATES TOWARD THE ENVIRONMENT

From an analytical point of view the behavior of states has been categorized into four types. These are not necessarily exclusive categories, but rather they suggest the traditional thrust of the policy attitudes of states and

groups of peoples toward the environment. The first two of these, escapism behavior and denial behavior, have in common the fact that the states have an awareness of the dilemmas of the limitations of their particular environments, but in both instances the focus is away from the problem. The attitude appears to be that if one doesn't look too hard, maybe the problem is not too acute. In escapism behavior the society becomes enamored with focusing on a dream that precludes it from looking at the actual problem. In denial behavior the state actually attempts to ignore the situation and attempts to exist in a blissful ignorance.

The last two types of behavior, greed behavior and eternal optimism behavior, are characterized by a keen awareness of the problem of the limitation of the state's environment, and the state does place its policy focus on how to resolve the problem. In greed behavior the policy attitude is to attempt to solve the limitations of the particular state by taking, by one device or another, either resources or space from other states and peoples. In eternal optimism behavior the problem of the limitations of the environment are carefully recognized by the society; the state or society seeks a solution by itself, separate from other states or societies, to resolve the problems—or at least to appear to resolve the problems for the immediate future.

States, in all of these characteristic behavior attitudes and policies, tend to have an egocentric orientation, to see the problem from their own points of view. Rather than seeing the entire earth as one ecosystem, each state tends to see it only as an ecosystem of its own particular state, regardless of the fact that such attitudes will lead to types of behavior by other states that may frustrate the particular state in its attempt to protect itself.

ENVIRONMENTAL FORCES IN THE INTERNATIONAL SYSTEM

The behavior of states, irrespective of types or a mixture of types, is the product of certain elemental forces within the physical and biological environment within which the international political system operates. There is a continual interplay between the facts that certain resources of the earth are nonrenewable while others are renewable. Consequently, the extent to which the nonrenewable resources are depleted and the extent to which the renewable resources are renewed is dependent upon the size and growth rate of the human population and the efficiency with which the resources are used.

MALTHUSIAN PREDICTIONS
While the Reverend Thomas R. Malthus had suggested in 1824 the inherent dangers in the rate of population growth on food resources, awareness

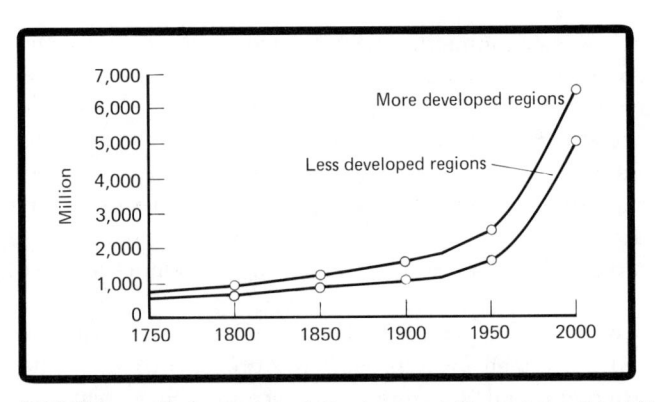

FIGURE 3.5 Estimated and Conjectured Size of the World's Population, 1750–2000, More-Developed and Less-Developed Regions

Source: U.N. Department of Economic and Social Affairs, *The World Population Situation in 1970*, Population Studies, No. 48, 1971, p. 5.

of the delicate nature of the biosphere was not generally apparent until the exponential growth of population reached its current dramatic proportions. This dramatic increase can be visualized when one realizes that it took from the beginning of man until 1600 for the world's population to reach 1 billion. Then by 1900, three hundred years later, the population reached 2 billion, and by 1950, only fifty years later, it reached 3 billion. By 1980, in a thirty-year period, the United Nations estimates that the world population will have surpassed 4 billion, and then in the next ten years at the present rate of growth these estimates add another billion, raising the population to 5 billion. As illustrated in Figure 3.5, at these rates of growth the world's population according to U.N. estimates will be about 6.5 billion by the year 2000.[21] This means that the world's population, which took from the beginning of mankind to 1970 to reach 3.6 billion, will virtually double in the next thirty years. Even if this momentum of population growth is recognized, it cannot be easily stopped. If all the nations of the world adopted policies to control the birth rate to mere replacement, the population would continue to increase, as in Figure 3.6, for several decades before a zero population growth would actually be obtained. The pressures that this fact of population growth poses on the use of non-renewable and renewable resources is almost more than the mind can visualize.

DIMINISHING RESOURCES

United Nations Secretary-General U Thant's warning in July 1969 that the states of the world had perhaps ten years in which to organize themselves to defuse the population explosion was based on an awareness that it is not simply the population that needs to be limited, but the consequences that flow

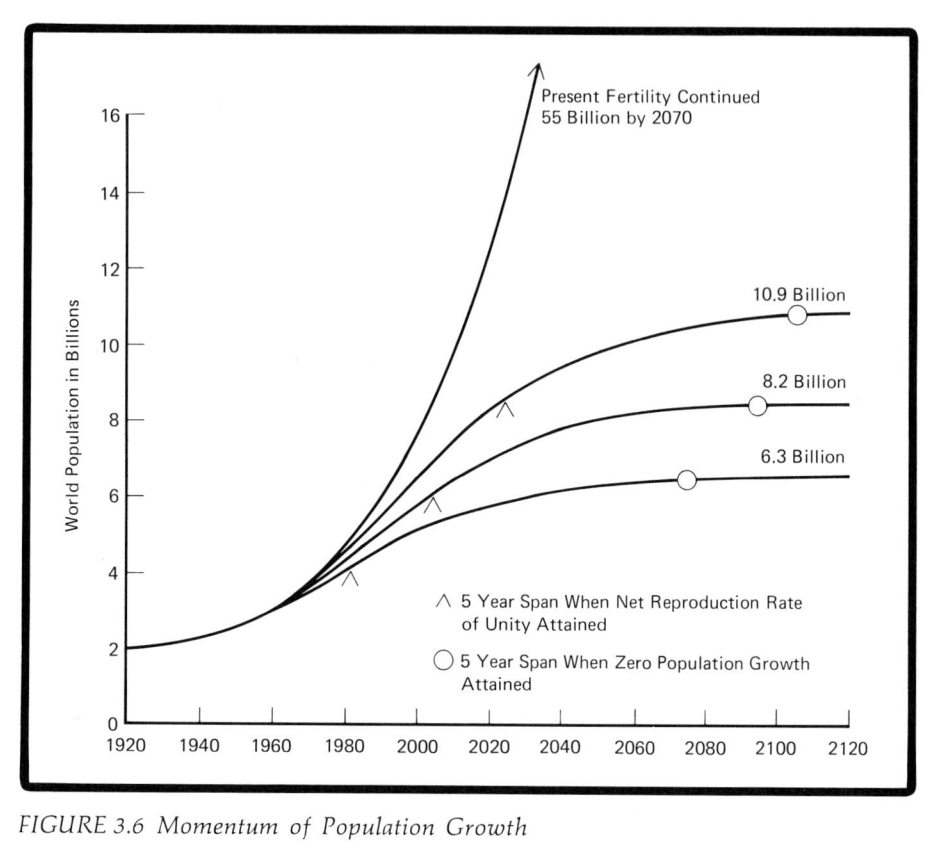

FIGURE 3.6 Momentum of Population Growth

> *Source: United States Foreign Policy 1969–1970—A Report of the Secretary of State,* Washington, D.C.: GPO, 1971, p. 268.

from and are interrelated with the population explosion. If one accepts that the biosphere of the earth is a single ecosystem, this means that every element in the life cycle process is interrelated, and a shift in one element has consequences for other elements. An increase in population requires an increase in food and other necessities; an increase in capital investment for efficiency in the production of goods for the increased population means an increased consumption of nonrenewable resources and increased pollution in the process of consumption and utilizations of these resources. At this stage in the development of knowledge we are not completely aware of all of the elements involved, let alone the total interrelationships of these elements in the global ecosystem.

It is easy to recognize and accept the fact that, for example, minerals (a nonrenewable resource) available in the global ecosystem are finite. The crucial question remains as to where the world stands in the consumption of this

finite amount of minerals on the earth. Meadows et al., taking calculations from a 1970 assessment of global reserves by the U.S. Bureau of Mines, indicate that at the *current* rate of usage the supply of copper, gold, lead, mercury, silver, tin, tungsten, zinc, and petroleum will be exhausted in forty or fewer years.[22] Assuming that there are five times the known reserves but recognizing that the rate of use will not continue at the current rate but will increase exponentially, this same study suggests that copper, gold, mercury, petroleum, silver, and zinc would be exhausted in fifty or fewer years. The steadily increasing rate of consumption of these resources has been supported by a study of the Committee on Resources and Man of the National Academy of Sciences/National Research Council, which pointed out in 1969 that in the previous thirty years the consumption of metals approximated the total amount consumed in all previous times.[23] Yet as this study and others[24] point out, there are a variety of factors that complicate efforts to estimate validly the extent of the finite resources remaining. As scarcity sets in, prices increase, which may in turn make it economically feasible to work less high-grade ores or to seek satisfactory substitutes for the mineral in short supply. For example, an obsolete study on energy resources in Canada, depicted in Figures 3.7 and 3.8, clearly illustrates that the productive capacity of oil in Canada would be greatly increased in a shift of the international price of oil from $4 to $6 a barrel. This price increase would open up the financial feasibility of using oil sands as a source for oil, which is not possible at the $4 price.

Beyond these rather clear responses other reactions might involve development of technological skills either to utilize the mineral resources of the sea and sea bed or to lead to ventures deeper into the earth's crust. Furthermore, increasing certainty of the finiteness of a given mineral or minerals could result in exploitation policies that maximize and extend the period in which these resources could be consumed. Technology and the increase in price may also increase the success of recycling processes as the coming of the finite limit stimulates these developments. On the other hand, such efforts may well have the effect of putting increased pressures on energy sources. The point is that there are not only serious questions in attempting to assess the finite amount of a resource remaining on the globe, but even more important are questions that when answered could provide a clear understanding of the matrix of interconnecting relationships between not only the biological and physical aspects of the environment but also among the political, social, and economic aspects that can affect choices.

MAN'S PREDICAMENT
One of the most interesting attempts into an understanding of the interdependent components of the earth system was initiated in 1968 with a meeting of specialists and businessmen from various fields to consider the

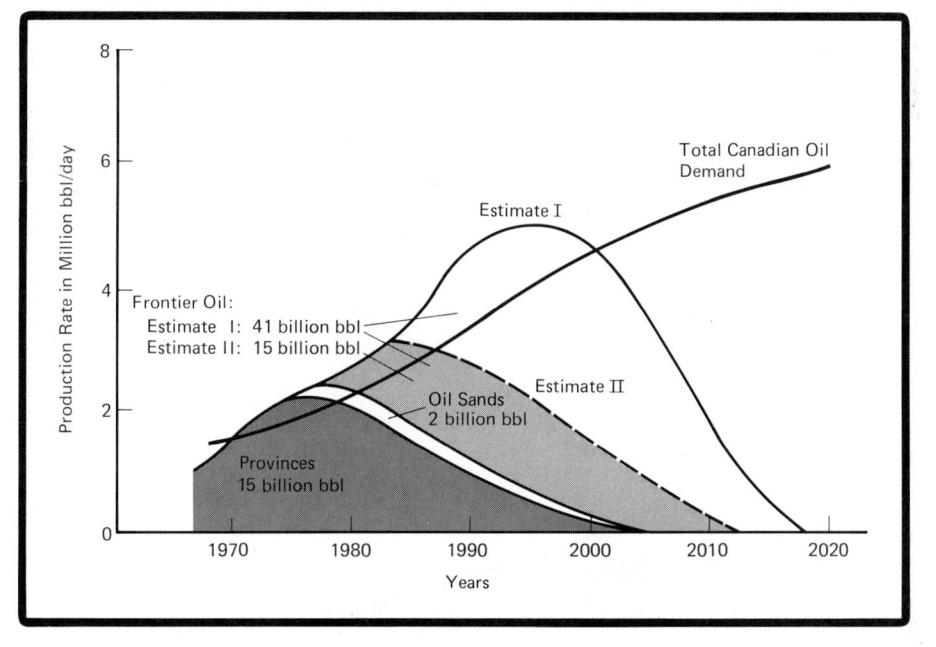

FIGURE 3.7 *Maximum Production Capacity for Oil Based on an International Oil Price of $4 (1972 $) and Resource Estimates I and II*

Source: Canada, The Minister of Energy, Mines, and Resources, *An Energy Policy for Canada—Phase I*, Ottawa: Information Canada, 1973, Vol. I, p. 95. Reproduced by permission of Information Canada.

predicament of man in the present and the future. The outgrowth of this meeting was an informal organization known as the Club of Rome and subsequent decisions to embark on a Project on the Predicament of Mankind. Researchers at the Massachusetts Institute of Technology who were supported by the project published in 1972 the *Limits of Growth*, which is a preliminary attempt to map out the major economic, political, natural, and social components of the world's ecosystem.[25] They looked at the exponential growth increases in population, food production, industrialization, pollution, and the consumption of nonrenewable natural resources. They constructed a preliminary computer model of the elements in the ecosystem that were interrelated to these five elements and then projected them into the future.

Assuming no changes in the current policies of states, their projections showed that even assuming a doubling of the current estimates of nonrenewable resources, food needs, industrial output, and population will continue to grow, as will the pollution level with the increased industrial growth, until the resources are depleted—at which point there will be a sharp decline in industrial growth and then a stop, followed by a marked decline in popula-

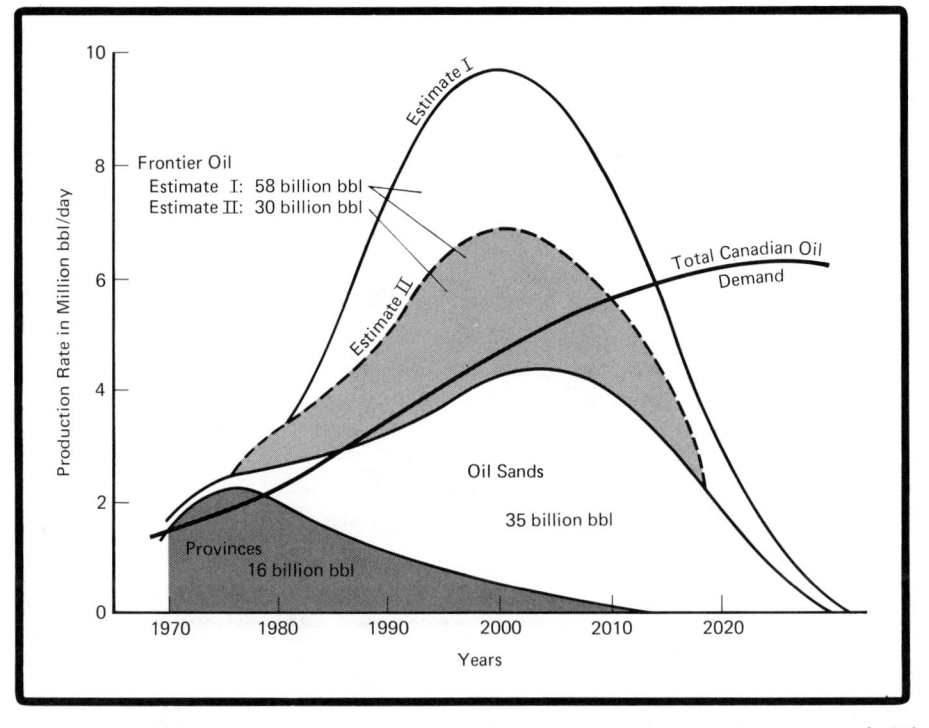

FIGURE 3.8 Maximum Production Capacity for Oil Based on an International Oil Price of $6 (1972 $) and Resource Estimates I and II

Source: Canada, The Minister of Energy, Mines, and Resources, *An Energy Policy for Canada—Phase I*, Ottawa: Information Canada, 1973, Vol. I, p. 96. Reproduced by permission of Information Canada.

tion as the death rate increases from pollution and the decline in food production. Their projection, even with doubling our current assumption as to the amount of remaining nonrenewable resources, indicated that with no changes in current policies the whole interrelated system would collapse by no later than the year 2100.

They then explored the possibilities of technological policies altering the situation. Assuming (1) that resources would be fully developed by technology and that 75 percent of the resources would be recycled, (2) that pollution generation by technological means would be reduced to one-fourth of what it was in 1970, (3) that land yields are doubled, and (4) that all available means of birth control are made available to the world population— they then projected these factors into the future. The computer result again suggested, that even with all of these technological advances, the ultimate collapse of the system would result by 2100 or before. While there would be

a temporary achievement of a constant world population in this situation with a fairly high per capita income, industrial growth would eventually halt with the death rate rising as food production declines, resources become depleted, and pollution accumulates.

Concluding that the application of technology in itself, even if applied to the major areas of population, use of resources, and food supplies would not prevent the eventual collapse of the ecosystem, the Club of Rome Project then explored the possibility of major policy shifts in each of these areas. They concluded by their computer projections that if the birth rate were equated with the death rate by 1975, that the continual exponential growth of industrial output, service, and food production would still result in a sudden depletion of the nonrenewable resources that would collapse the industrial system. Comparable policies with respect to only one of these major areas would not prevent collapses in the system.

They eventually came to the conclusion that if there is a combination of policies in which (1) population is stabilized by making the birth rate equal to the death rate by 1975; (2) industrial capital is stabilized after 1990; (3) the consumption of resources is reduced to one-fourth of 1970 by 1975; (4) economic preferences are shifted from material goods to education and health; (5) pollution is reduced by technological advances by 1975 to one-fourth of what it is in 1970; (6) stress is placed on diverting capital, even if uneconomic to adequate food production for all, including efforts to maintain the soil fertility; and (7) industrial production stresses durability instead of built-in obsolescence—then it might be possible to stabilize the ecosystem so that it could sustain itself without a sudden collapse. Their computer analysis, however, revealed that if the institution of these policies were delayed from 1975 to the year 2000, the possibility of achieving a state of equilibrium in the system is no longer possible.

Thus their analysis suggested that policies taking full advantage of technological advances have to be tied to a stability of the population and industrial capital development if there is any possibility of preventing the inevitable total collapse of the ecosystem in terms of the present growth rate in population, industrialization, food production, pollution, and the consumption of the nonrenewable resources. More significantly they suggest that the initial steps that need to be taken on a total system basis have to start no later than 1975 if there is any expectation of not having the system collapse by its own weight.

This projective analysis in the Club of Rome Project coincides very closely with Secretary-General U Thant's statement based on U.N. studies in July 1969 that the world has at the most ten years to undertake steps to manage itself or the forces of population, pollution, and so forth, will reach a situation beyond the capacity of technology to prevent a disaster. The chief disparity between the Club of Rome's projections and those of U Thant is

that he allowed four more years from 1975 to 1979 before the situation exceeded the possibility of ever getting the system into manageable possibilities. The collapse of the system might not be until the year 2100, if only partial measures are taken, or it might be earlier depending upon which partial measures are invoked.

DILEMMAS FOR THE STATES IN THE INTERNATIONAL SYSTEM

Accepting and understanding the nature of the environmental forces at work in the international system does not solve the problem for the preservation of the world and its human life as we now know it. The exponential growth forces currently at work indicate that the time is immediate in which states have to take unified actions, or the time for such action will shortly pass, beyond which it will be impossible not to reap the inevitable consequences of these forces. These facts pose real dilemmas for the political states that operate within the ecosystem of the earth's biosphere.

DEVELOPED VERSUS DEVELOPING STATES

Assuming that all the states of the world understood and accepted these projections for the future, and the necessity of undertaking the necessary policies possibly by no later than 1975, their willingness to do so is complicated by the already great disparity between the developed and the developing states.

Population trends in birth and death rates as shown in Figure 3.9, indicate that the less-developed states are just coming into their period of greatest population growth, a fact that will increase the population pressure on their economic development. In addition, the economic growth for the major economic powers is projected to continue if not accelerate. This projection is shown in Figure 3.10. The disparity is not simply in terms of economic development but is also in terms of technological and educational development, and even development in terms of organizing society within the states. To the underdeveloped the needed policies may seem to be a method of continuing their economic dependence and/or technological dependence on the most developed states. At the World Population Conference in Bucharest in August 1974, most underdeveloped states opposed any proposal to limit their population growth. They argued that people were their most important resource and the effort of the developed states to control population growth was an additional attempt to keep the underdeveloped states from developing.

Even if industrialization is allowed to continue until 1990, until it is stabilized, questions can be raised as to whether the industrial growth that

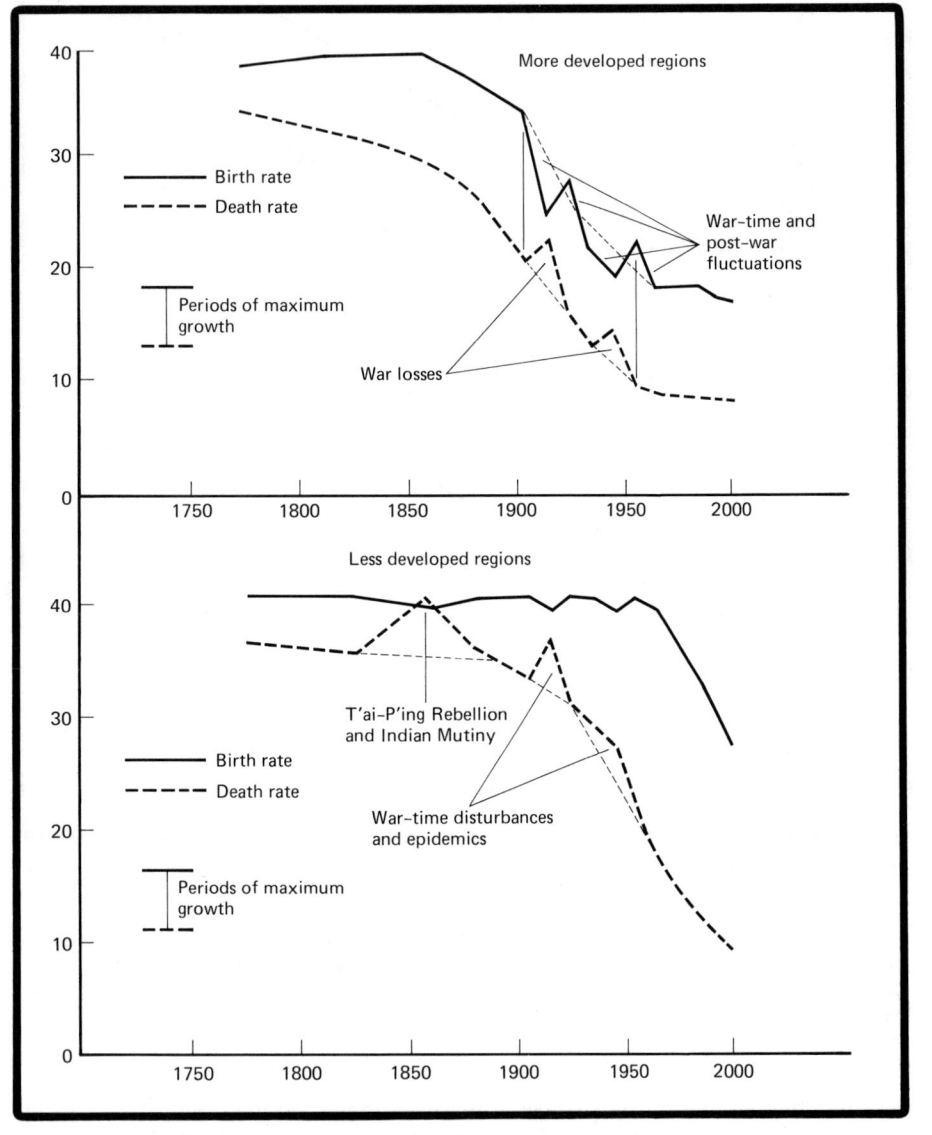

FIGURE 3.9 Estimated and Conjectured Trends in Birth Rate and Death Rate, 1750–2000, More-Developed and Less-Developed Regions

Source: U.N. Department of Economic and Social Affairs, *The World Population Situation in 1970,* Population Studies, No. 48, 1971, p. 4.

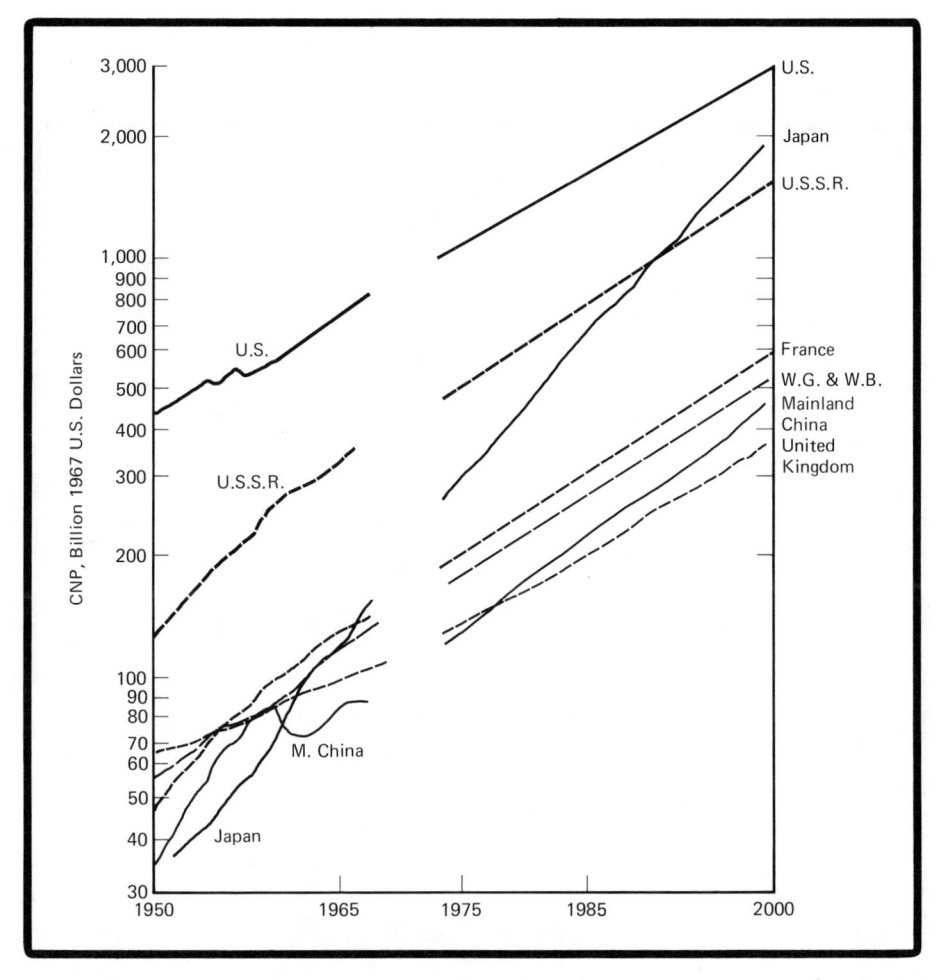

FIGURE 3.10 Postwar Economic Growth and Medium Projection for the Super-
powers and "Large" Powers

   Source: A Look at Business in 1990, A Summary of the White House Conference
on the Industrial World Ahead, Washington, D.C., February 7–9, 1972, Washington, D.C.:
GPO, 1972, p. 17, inserted in an address by Herman Kahn on "A View of the Economic
World of 1990."

is to be allowed should be primarily in the underdeveloped countries so that
they can come out of the starvation mire that they currently find themselves
in. Such a collective decision by states would mean drastic changes in the
developed states, where the material demands for consumer goods from industrialization are acutely cultivated. How can one argue that the more

developed must sacrifice for those further down the economic ladder? To the most developed states, large proportions of their industrialization are already devoted to military items to protect their dominance. If their industrialization is curtailed, how can they be assured the security that they demand?

THE PROBLEM OF SELF-DETERMINATION

If any principle is prevalent in the 1970s in the international system, it is the concept and belief in self-determination—that each group of peoples shall determine its own destiny. It is extended further in the continual expansion and acceptance of the concepts of human rights that assert that each individual should have the highest degree of possible freedom of action. The environmental forces at work in the international system require policy solutions that would virtually eliminate these concepts.

Acknowledging that the ecosystem is a whole implies that the preservation of life depends upon the universal adoption of policies that will stabilize the ecosystem. If such policies are developed, fundamental human rights could be grossly altered. One might well argue that there are no alternatives, that the most fundamental human right is life itself. But to argue this implies that each individual will accept the necessity for steps to be taken in his lifetime that will allow for the survival of generations in the future. It is difficult to assert that policies must be instituted by 1975 when it is apparent that the generation now living will in all probability survive because the suggested collapse of the ecosystem will not occur until the next generation's lifetime. How are states to organize themselves on policies common to all? How are they to do this when historical evidence abounds with the inability of the disparate members of the state system to cooperate?

UNEVEN RESOURCE DISTRIBUTION

A more difficult dilemma is posed by the fact that the availability of nonrenewable resources is unevenly distributed among the states of the world. Some states may appraise the future in terms of the capacity of their own boundaries. How are these states to be convinced that their eventual survival depends upon an acceptance of the fact of the oneness of the biosphere? Certainly the policies pursued by peoples and states, as we have explored earlier, suggests the unlikelihood of their acknowledging this unity of the ecosystem.

FACING THE IMMEDIACY OF THE PROBLEMS

Even these few dilemmas barely indicate the problems facing the states in the international system. And these dilemmas are based on the assumption that all states recognize and accept the facts about the environmental forces that are working within the international system. This may well be a false assumption—the reality is that *not* even the populations of the most-devel-

oped states actually believe or accept the fact that unless policies are instituted between 1975 and 1979, the environmental forces will be beyond control. They may acknowledge with an increasing awareness the environmental problems but not with the immediacy or the totality that the problems demand.

Even assuming that there was an acceptance of these environmental forces, it is a very difficult to design the broad kinds of policies that need to be implemented (possibly by no later than 1975 if one accepts the *Limits of Growth* study). The details of the actual policies pose very difficult problems, which while not insurmountable will involve unprecedented work and cooperation among states.

ATTEMPTS OF STATES TO COPE WITH THE ENVIRONMENTAL FORCES IN THE INTERNATIONAL SYSTEM

There may be no clear answers to the dilemmas posed by the environmental problems in the biosphere, but there have been some attempts by states to begin to take concerted action to face these problems despite the inherent dilemmas.

THE UNITED NATIONS AND THE ENVIRONMENT

While the states of the world have individually, and on occasion collectively concerned themselves with the problems of the ecosystem of the earth, these concerns became focused in the late 1960s in the discussion among states in the United Nations. Their focus was primarily in three general areas: concern for availability of natural resources; concern for resources of the ocean, the sea bed, and the ocean floor; and a broader concern for problems of the degradation of the human environment.

In regard to the availability of natural resources, the studies and discussions of the states have been directed toward support for programs that might help to uncover hereto unknown natural resources (such as mineral deposits) and toward concern for the availability of sources of water supply. In the second area, the states have recognized the ocean and its floor as one of the last remaining large untapped sources for natural resources. Since the ocean is outside the jurisdiction of states, it was recognized as a potential area of conflict among states in regard to attempts made to "seize" these ocean resources. In both of these areas, the states have been delicately vying for advantages in control of the potential resources. In the ocean-floor area there has been more concern with maximizing and in a sense preserving this area of resources.

The broader concern on the human environment is really the first effort of states to face up to the real impending crisis in the ecosystem comparable to the dangers subsequently and provocatively articulated in the M.I.T.-Club of Rome's studies. In December 1968, following discussions prompted by Sweden in the Economic and Social Council of the United Nations, the General Assembly passed a resolution calling for the convening of a conference in 1972 on the human environment. The Secretary-General of the United Nations was directed to submit a report to the General Assembly in 1969 in which he would indicate the main problems facing the developed and developing states and the steps to be taken to bring about an effective concern with these problems at the 1972 conference.

This discussion in the General Assembly was significant in that for the first time the states of the world jointly discussed their common and collective problems about the physical environment in which the political states exist. The discussion emphasized that "for the first time in the history of mankind" the crisis of the human environment was a crisis of world-wide proportions. The discussion stressed that this crisis was evidenced by the

> *explosive growth of human populations, in the poor integration of a powerful and efficient technology with environmental requirements, in the deterioration of agricultural lands, in the unplanned extension of urban areas, in the decrease of available space and the growing danger of extinction of many forms of animal and plant life. It is becoming apparent that if the current trends continue, the future of life on earth could be endangered. It is urgent, therefore, to focus world attention on those problems which threaten humanity in an environment that permits the realization of the highest human aspirations, and on the action necessary to deal with them.*[26]

As one might expect in an international system of states that is historically based on a concept of "sovereign independence" rather than an acceptance of interdependence as one ecosystem, the thrust of the concern was directed more to the deterioration of the human environment rather than on the preservation of the highly interrelated and carefully balanced ecosystem. There was recognition that this deterioration of the human environment has three basic causes: the accelerated population growth, increased urbanization, and a continually expanding technology—all with their associated demands for space, food, and natural resources.

In his report to the United Nations General Assembly in 1969, the Secretary-General looked at these trends in some detail. He pointed out the exponential growth in populations and that the necessities required, such as food, water, minerals, fuel, and so on, were creating pressures that would

TABLE 3.4 URBAN RURAL POPULATION AND PERCENTAGE OF URBAN POPULA-
TION, IN MORE-DEVELOPED AND LESS-DEVELOPED REGIONS, 1950–
2000

	More-Developed Regions			Less-Developed Regions		
	Population (Millions)			Population (Millions)		
Year	Urban	Rural	Percentage Urban	Urban	Rural	Percentage Urban
1950	439	418	51	265	1,363	16
1960	582	394	60	403	1,603	20
1970	717	374	66	635	1,910	25
1980	864	347	71	990	2,267	30
1990	1,021	316	76	1,496	2,623	36
2000	1,174	280	81	2,155	2,906	43

Source: United Nations, Department of Economic and Social Affairs, *The World
Population Situation in 1970*, Population Studies No. 48 (1971), p. 24.

affect all portions of the earth and demand careful planning and management in view of the absolute limit on nonrenewable resources. The U.N.
Secretariat studies indicated that accompanying the population growth was
the spread of urbanization. By 1969, 40 percent of the world's people lived
in urban areas and within the next fifty years, if the trend continued, the
overwhelming majority would live in towns and cities. In the developing
states 100 million were in urban populations, but by the year 2000 it was
estimated there would be a twentyfold increase. Table 3.4 and Figure 3.11
show that by the year 2000, it is also estimated that there will be a four fold
increase in urban populations in the developed countries. Urbanization need
not be a destructive principle to the environment, but it could be so if there
were not proper efforts to manage the trend.

The Secretary-General also pointed out that most governments were
neither prepared for nor able to cope with the movements into the urban centers. Slums were environments detrimental not only to the health and dignity
of people, but urban areas everywhere have the problems of pollution of air,
water, and land, and disease. An added element in urban areas in the developing states is the noise and congestion that contribute to physical and mental problems.

*Accompanying population growth and urbanization is the accelerated
impact of industrialization, and of an advanced technology that is
often poorly integrated with human needs and environmental*

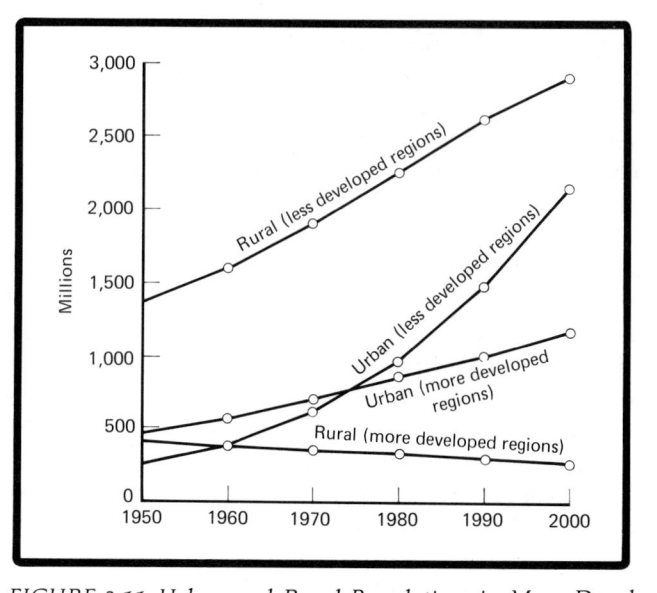

FIGURE 3.11 *Urban and Rural Population, in More-Developed and Less-Developed Regions, 1950–2000*

Source: U.N. Department of Economic and Social Affairs, *The World Population Situation in 1970*, Population Studies, No. 48, 1971, p. 24.

necessities. *The rate of industrial growth can be indicated by various statistics. Thus, the production of crude petroleum was negligible a century ago. By 1966, however, it amounted to 1,641 million metric tons per year. Between 1937 and 1966, the annual rate of production increased six fold. In the same period, the passenger motor vehicle, scarcely known at the start of this century was produced at a rate that grew from five million to 19 million per year. In the most recent decade, the total value of all industrial production had doubled. Virtually all measures of industrialization show an increasing rate. Industrialization is of vital importance to nations which seek to elevate the living standards of their people. Improved technology is necessary if productivity is to increase and the products of industry be provided to growing numbers of people. However, the side effects of poorly planned or uncontrolled industrialization and of the one-sided application of technology have a direct cause of many serious environmental problems. During the discussions of the General Assembly at the twenty-third session, it was pointed out that the reliance of modern technology upon the combustion of fossil fuels has brought a 10 percent increase in atmospheric carbon dioxide over the past century. With*

*increased rates of combustion, this could rise to 25 percent by the year
2000. The consequence of such an increase upon world weather and
climate are uncertain, but it could eventually be catastrophic. The
increased use of modern technology has brought major increases in the
amount of waste products which serve as environmental pollutants.
While technology is adequate to cope with these problems of pollution,
the planning and application of pollution controls lags far behind what
is required, often due to economic considerations.*[27]

The Secretary-General's report then pointed to the disappearance of
open space that results from the expansion of transportation facilities associated with the spread of the urban-industrial network. In the United Kingdom this expansion, if the current rate of increase continues, will mean that
about one-sixth of the farming land will be replaced by transportation facilities within 30 years. This uncontrolled urban sprawl destroys resources as
well as land spaces and living things. Furthermore, the increased population
has placed increased demands on agricultural production, and technology has
and will have to continue to facilitate more efficient production.

*It is of great importance, however, that such gains be not offset by
environmental deterioration. Thus increased food crop yields have
accompanied the increased use of fertilizers and new varieties of
pesticides produced by chemical industries. However, some of these
agricultural chemicals have side effects on the environment that we are
only now beginning to comprehend. Thus the maintenance of both
atmospheric oxygen and the productivity of marine environments
depends upon photosynthesis of marine plants, mostly the floating
algae of microscopic size. Minute amounts of such pesticides as DDT
have been found to inhibit photosynthesis in these algae by 75 percent.
Nevertheless, we have dumped an estimated billion pounds of DDT into
our environment and are adding an estimated 100 million pounds per
year. The total world production of pesticides is estimated at over
1,300 million pounds annually. The United States of America alone
exports over 400 million pounds per year. Apart from their potential
effects upon the productivity of the oceans, many of these have known
effects upon fish, wildlife and human health.*[28]

Finally, the Secretary-General's report pointed out that much of the land
upon which man depends for his sustenance has been damaged by past and
continuing practices.

Following the analysis of the crisis in the human environment, which
was based on the latest scientific studies, the Secretary-General, after con-

sultation with experts in many countries, suggested that there were three main areas of problems in which action is needed to be taken to arrest this crisis in the environment. These three areas were:

1. Human settlements problems—affecting local areas of population concentration for which action is primarily the responsibility of national governments or local authorities;
2. Territorial problems—problems of land areas including nonoceanic and coastal waters—for which action is primarily the responsibility of national governments but may in a region involve several state governments;
3. Global problems—those of world-wide nature that potentially affect all countries and that are soluble only by international agreement and a willingness for states to cooperate.

Many of the environmental problems could be significant at all three of these levels. Water pollution occurs at the local level, the territorial level, and the global level. Twenty-five percent of the oxygen in the environment is produced at the ocean shoreline by plankton, and oil pollution anywhere in the globe that interrupts this oxygen production on the shoreline affects the total oxygen circulating in the atmosphere.

Following this kind of analysis, the Secretary-General then suggested to the states that the Preparatory Commission for the 1972 Conference on the Human Environment should organize the conference to focus on what he called substantive problems and strategic problems. Substantive problems would deal with particular situations in the human environment such as urban planning, national land use, water pollution, and so on. The strategic problems would be those that involved choices of action such as environmental values in economic analysis, fiscal methods of preventing pollution, administration for regional planning or international agreements.

While his proposals did include an awareness of limitations of the ecosystem, the focus was much more directly on dealing with the deterioration of the environment than in assessing the crisis in the terms of the necessity of stabilizing the exponential growth rates of population, industrialization, food production, and pollution before the system collapsed. This was probably a conscious recognition of the deep cleavages among states concerning their degree of willingness to accept the facts as were to be projected later in the Club of Rome Project. However, apart from this official report to the states, as we have indicated, U Thant, in public utterances in the summer of July 1969, pointed to comparable conclusions about the real issues of survival that the Club of Rome Project would arrive at two years later.

That the Secretary-General was correct in moving the way he did in the

proposals he suggested in this May 1969 report to the member states of
the United Nations was confirmed in March 1970 when the Preparatory Committee for the U.N. Conference on the Human Environment held its first
meeting. The debate in this body showed a high degree of consensus on the
characteristics and seriousness of environmental problems in the various
states. At the same time, there was acceptance of the view that there is great
diversity and complexity in environmental problems, varying among regions
of the world and among the separate states.

The states were not fully prepared to acknowledge the unity of the ecosystem but continued to regard many problems as local. They emphasized
the problems of pollution as being of the highest order, but they placed questions such as urban and rural planning, conservation of nature, and management of natural resources on a lower order of priority. They stressed also
that there was a difference between the problems facing the developed and
developing states and that any management of environmental problems
should not arrest the developmental process in the developing states. The
dilemma of how to arrest growth in the whole system without perpetuating
the status of those states on the bottom of the economic level was also emphasized in the discussion.

The significance of the work of the Preparatory Committee and the
actual U.N. Conference on the Human Environment, held in Stockholm in
June 1972, lies in the fact that for the first time, most nations of the world
were prepared to consider the problems of the ecological balances in the
earth's biosphere.[29]

For the first time most states in the international system attempted to
take steps that were consistent with their physical interdependence. The conference focused its attention on problems of human settlements, educational
and social aspects of environmental issues, the problem of development and
environment, natural resources management, pollution, and international organization matters. The conference was preceded by extensive studies on
these problems by experts in each of the states.

Symbolically the conference theme was "Only One Earth." The conference adopted 106 *recommendations* that were to constitute an "Action Plan"
for states. In essence these recommendations fit into three areas of activity:
(1) a global assessment program to identify and measure enivronmental
problems of international importance and to warn against possible crises in
the environment; (2) activities to use what is known or learned about the
environment to help preserve what is desirable and prevent what is undesirable; and (3) supporting measures such as education and training, public
information, and international organizational and financing arrangements to
help carry out these activities. The Stockholm Conference also adopted a
Declaration on the Human Environment indicating the common conviction
of these states on 26 environmental principles.

ASSESSING THE STOCKHOLM CONFERENCE

If one accepts the Secretary-General's assessment that very serious efforts must be evoked by no later than 1979 to offset the exponential growth rates of negative environmental factors, or if one accepts the 1975 deadline of the Club of Rome, one may question whether the steps taken at Stockholm come anywhere near what is needed to stabilize the ecosystem instead of allowing its inevitable collapse. Of course 1975 or 1979 may not be absolute deadlines for beginning effective changes to prevent a collapse of the ecosystem, yet the Club of Rome projections indicated that if steps on stabilizing the birth rate with the death rate and other policy actions were delayed to 1990, the growth rates will have proceeded beyond the possibility of policy shifts altering the eventual system collapse.

How far do the actions of the Stockholm Conference go toward implementing policies that are essential for survival? Without examining all 106 of the recommendations, some conclusions may be suggested. First, it should be noted that the conference did not obligate any states to any action—all of the actions of the conference were recommendations only. Accepting this limitation, an examination of some of the recommendations will illustrate some of the strengths and weaknesses of the "actions" of the conference.

Some of the recommendations were symbolic—for example, one recommendation was to request that governments reach an international agreement to stop the commercial hunting of whales for a ten-year period. Obviously, whales are an endangered species, but within the dimensions of the environmental crisis, they are hardly more than a symbolic gesture. Even here, there was no agreement to stop the killing of whales—rather a plea to governments to reach an agreement to stop their killing. Such a plea is far from an actual agreement.

The conference adopted a recommendation to establish a world-wide network of at least 110 atmospheric monitoring stations to keep a watch on changes in pollution levels that might lead to climatic changes. While this kind of proposal is very useful in providing more information on the dangers to the atmosphere by pollution, it does not prevent the pollution; instead it only provides the basis for stronger arguments on why pollution is a threat to the entire earth's atmosphere.

In a similar sense, the establishment of an International Referral Service that would link institutions or persons in one country who want specific environmental information with those in other countries who could provide the desired data is a necessary step; but it falls short of providing a basis for implementing policies.

The creation by the states of an Environmental Fund on a voluntary-pledge basis (with an initial goal of $100 million) to finance monitoring and data-assessment systems, projects to improve environmental quality, management, public education, and so on, does provide international support for

environmental programs for the first time. But states are not obligated to contribute or to avail themselves of the projects. In addition, $100 million is a small sum to expend for projects around the entire world when it is compared to the fact that New York City alone is investing $2 billion for a ten-year pollution-control program, and the United States is estimated to have already spent $200 billion on water pollution alone at all levels, public and private.[30]

The conference created an Environment Coordination Board to provide a basis of coordination between the United Nations and the specialized agencies and other international organizations on environmental problems. Obviously, such coordinated efforts are desirable. However, one might note that if the governments coordinated their own efforts, there would be little necessity of coordinating the efforts of the various international organizations to which they belong.

These are only a few examples of the recommendations adopted at Stockholm. They are indicative of the fact that while the conference was a landmark in that most of the political states of the world met and discussed the complexity of elements involved in maintaining the survival of the eco-system, these same states were not fully convinced that the environmental crisis was of the magnitude that the Secretary-General suggested. The states may acknowledge that the biosphere is a finite system, but each for varying reasons is still seeking means that will favor itself over the other political states.

The preference for protecting the separate interests of states, rather than the collective global need, is evidenced in the 26 principles adopted in the Declaration on the Human Environment at the Stockholm Conference. Principle 16, for example, states that:

> *Demographic policies, which are without prejudice to basic human*
> *rights and which are deemed appropriate by Governments concerned,*
> *should be applied in those regions where the rate of population growth*
> *or excessive population concentrations are likely to have adverse*
> *effects on the environment or development, or where low population*
> *density may prevent improvement of the human environment and*
> *impede development.*[31]

Under this principle population policies are the province of each state and are to be determined in terms of that particular state. This is contrary to the concept that it is the population growth of the entire earth system that needs to be stabilized. It is understandable, of course, that each state may assess its population dilemma in different terms, especially when many believe

that one of their greatest resources is the human resource. Yet the principle does not even set a goal of equalizing the birth rate with the death rate, an essential element of the Club of Rome projections for stabilizing the system.

In fact, a zero-population policy does not mean that the population growth of a country ceases at that moment, but rather that it will begin to approach a zero growth rate generally in about twenty years. Figure 3.12 illustrates this. On the other hand, it is a very complex problem to devise a population policy that will equate birth and death rates. This involves some very difficult choices for governments. To preclude such a goal, however, is to continue the denial behavior of states in the light of reality of the implications of the exponential growth of populations. Principle 13 states:

> *Resources should be made available to preserve and improve the environment, taking into account the circumstances and particular requirements of developing countries and any costs which may emanate from their development planning and the need for making available to them, upon their request, additional international technical and financial assistance for this purpose.*

This principle seems to imply that each developing country shall make its own development plan and that other states, in order to decrease the likelihood of environmental dangers, will be required to assist the developing state in its plan—but only if the developing state so requests. Again, the emphasis is on the action of the individual state rather than on the common good. This principle seems in contrast with Principles 3 and 5, which state universal goals:

> 3. *The capacity of the earth to produce vital renewable resources must be maintained and wherever practicable restored or improved.*
> 5. *The non-renewable resources of the earth must be employed in such a way as to guard against the danger of their future exhaustion and to ensure that benefits from such employment are shared by all mankind.*

These two goals appear to stress resources for the global good, and their development should benefit the entire system; Principle 13, on the other hand, implies that certain decisions can be made by a single state.

The Declaration on the Human Environment presents the overall goals in the first seven principles and then lists exceptions that revolve around the inherent dilemma that any policies directed toward arresting growth trends

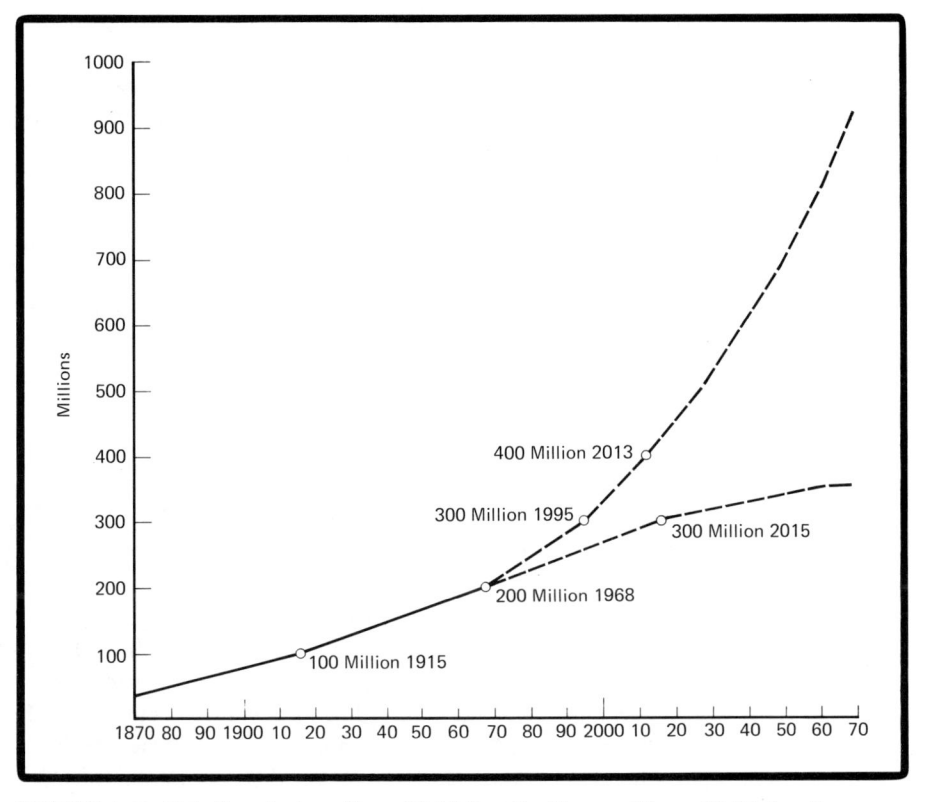

FIGURE 3.12 U.S. Population: Two-Child Family Versus Three-Child Family

Note: The population of the United States passed the 100-million mark in 1915 and reached 200 million in 1968. If families average two children in the future, growth rates will slow, and the population will reach 300 million in the year 2015. At the 3-child rate, the population would reach 300 million in this century and 400 million in the year 2013. (Projections assume small future reductions in mortality, and assume future immigration at present levels.)

Sources: Prior to 1900—U.S. Bureau of the Census. *Historical Statistics of the United States, Colonial Times to 1957, 1961.* 1900 to 2020—U.S. Bureau of the Census Current Population Reports, Series P-25. 2021 to 2050—unpublished Census Bureau projections. Beyond 2050—extrapolation. From *Population and the American Future*, The Report of the Commission on Population Growth and the American Future, Washington, D.C.: GPO, 1972, p. 23.

should not be undertaken if they perpetuate the disparity between the developed and the developing states.

In attempting to deal with environmental problems the international system of states is, therefore, faced with very difficult problems of how to arrest the growth trends without simply freezing the status quo. At the same time, unless the exponential growth rates in population, pollution, industriali-

zation, and food shortages are arrested, the peoples in all states will be eliminated as the entire system collapses or be reduced to a bare-survival status.

OTHER ALTERNATIVES

Finding solutions will not be an easy task. Two developments in the last quarter of 1973 amply demonstrate the intermesh of political and economic factors in approaching the complexity of the interrelationships in the ecosystem. One development was the decision of the Arab oil-producing states to withhold oil from states differing with Arab political policies vis-à-vis Israel. The other development was the beginning of the Third United Nations Conference on the Law of the Sea, which was concerned with drafting a multilateral treaty creating an international sea bed authority. The first development illustrates the intertwining of political and economic reactions that flow from a decision to take advantage of the control of sources of energy in the ecosystem. The second development illustrates the complexity of political and economic questions that must be decided in trying to manage or control a major portion of the ecosystem. Neither of these two situations are sudden developments. Both are the result of an "evolution" of political and economic factors interplaying with the environmental factors of continual population growth, increasing industrialization, and the absolute limits on the amount of certain nonrenewable resources.

OIL EMBARGO

The Arab oil-producing states' decision in October 1973 to curtail oil sales to oil-dependent industrial states is the culmination of a number of factors prevalent in the international system. First there has been the continual concern of the Arab states with the existence of Israel. The area of Israel and especially Jerusalem have a historic and important place in Moslem religious tradition. Seeking first their independence from the Ottoman Empire and then from colonial domination of France and Britain, the Arab states have felt that the area of present-day Israel is rightfully theirs. Historically, they argue, they assisted the Allies in World War I on the promise that they would have the territory. They resented the immigration of the Jews into a primarily Arab-populated area. The British withdrawal from Palestine in May 1948 and the establishment of the state of Israel with the accompanying flight of the Arab inhabitants was seen as a betrayal of the legitimate Arab claims to Palestine. The defeat of efforts to prevent the establishment of Israel in 1948 and subsequent armed conflicts with her in 1956 and 1967 became psychological blows to the prestige of the Arab states. But Israel's existence, on the other hand, provided a psychological unity for the Arab states that had not previously existed, as well as an external threat that relieved internal pressures and demands. For some Arabs it provided an incentive for fundamental internal changes.

To all of the Arab states the frustrations created by the existence of the state of Israel were also symbolic evidence of the plight of less-developed states. In 1956 and 1967 the more-industrialized Israel with her technologically skilled population of about 2 million was capable of decisively defeating Egypt, a country having 36 million people. This symbolic demonstration of the inability of less-developed states to exert their influence created an identification between the plight of the Arab states and the frustrations of the other less-developed states throughout the world, who also seemed mere pawns at the hands of the more-developed states.

At the same time that these frustrations were being felt, the development of earlier oil discoveries meant an enriching of national treasuries for certain Arab states. In the period from the beginning of the state of Israel to the 1970s, governments of states that were fortunate enough to have oil gradually began to wrest majority control of their rich industry from foreign domination. In addition, the number of Arab states with oil increased. In 1948 Iraq and Saudi Arabia were the principal Arab oil states, but by the early 1970s Kuwait, Bahrain, Qatar, Libya, and the United Arab Emirates (Abu Dhabi, Dubai, etc.) were coming into their own as oil producers.

These three elements—frustrations over the existence of Israel, the impotence of underdeveloped states, and increasing awareness and nationalist control over Arab oil resources—began to coalesce in the 1970s. First, there was increasing discussion among the less-developed states over ways in which they could force the developed states to seriously assist the developing states. Such awareness was evidenced at the Third Non-Aligned Summit Conference in Lusaka, Zambia, in September 1970. Conference resolutions pointed to the fact that the primary products of less-developed states, especially nonrenewable resources, were of vital concern to the developed states. This point was further discussed at the meeting of the foreign ministers of the nonaligned states in Georgetown, Guyana, in September 1972. Finally, at the Fourth Non-Aligned Summit Conference in September 1973 in Algiers, the less-developed states were urged to use their resources as a bargaining tool.

Second, by the 1970s, it was apparent that the combination of increasing population and accelerating rate of economic development in developed states was resulting in an "international energy crisis." In April 1973 President Nixon, in a special energy message to the United States Congress, pointed out that the United States with 6 percent of the world's population was consuming almost a third of all the energy used in the world, and that if American use of energy continued at the same rate, energy needs would double between 1970 and 1982. In fact, the 24 states in the Organisation for Economic Co-operation and Development (the OECD consists of Australia, Austria, Belgium, Canada, Denmark, Finland, France, West Germany, Greece, Iceland, Ireland, Italy, Japan, Luxembourg, the Netherlands, New Zealand, Norway, Portugal, Spain, Sweden, Switzerland, Turkey, the United King-

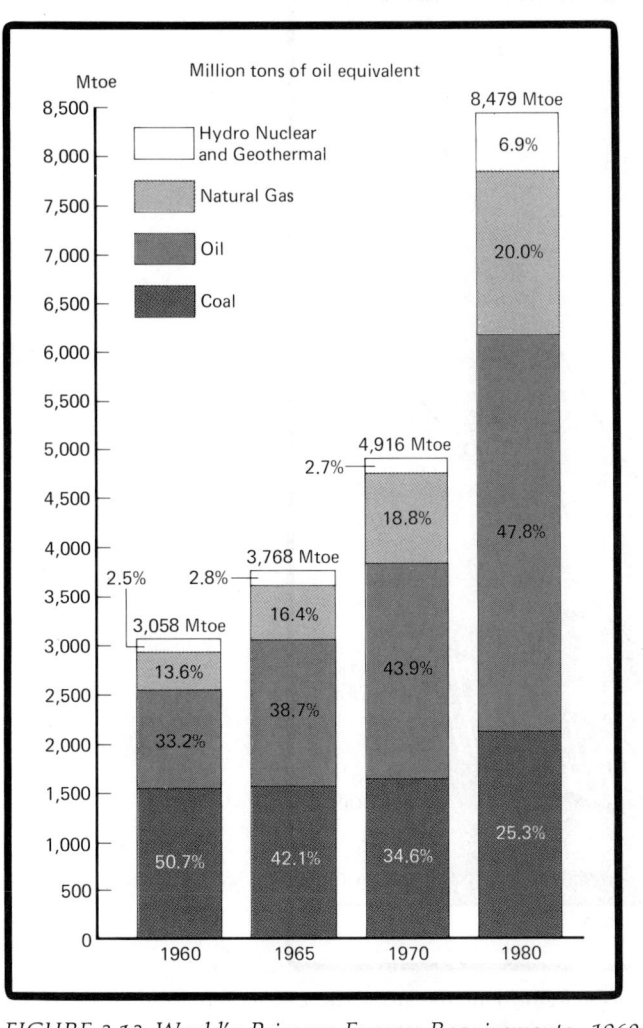

FIGURE 3.13 World's Primary Energy Requirements, 1960–1980

Source: Organisation for Economic Cooperation and Development, Information Service, *OECD at Work for Industry and Energy*, Paris: OECD, 1973, p. 24.

dom, and the United States), with only 20 percent of the world's population, consume nearly two-thirds of the total use of energy in the world. At the current rate of increase of the use of energy, it is estimated, as shown in Figure 3.13, that between 1970 and 1980 the world's primary energy requirements will increase by about 75 percent, with the largest increase being among OECD states, as shown in Figure 3.14. In addition, the largest source of these energy requirements is anticipated to be oil and natural gas. Although

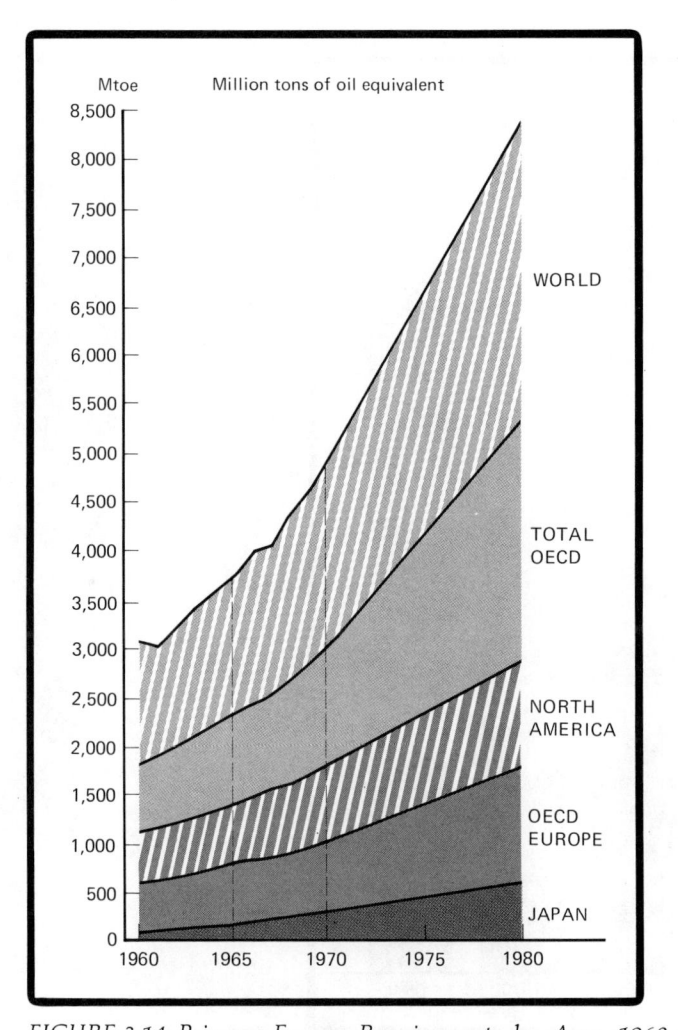

FIGURE 3.14 Primary Energy Requirements by Area, 1960–1980

Source: Organisation for Economic Cooperation and Development, Information Service, OECD at Work for Industry and Energy, Paris: OECD, 1973, p. 25.

the United States was the largest single consumer of energy in 1970, it has been the one OECD state that has been relatively self-sufficient. Yet its 1980 and 1990 projected needs indicate that the United States will increasingly have to rely on external rather than domestic sources. Table 3.5 and Figure 3.15 indicate American gas requirements, but a similar trend also occurs in oil needs.

Most OECD states, however, are already dependent upon the importa-

TABLE 3.5 U.S. INDIGENOUS GAS SUPPLY VERSUS DEMAND
(VOLUMES IN TRILLIONS OF CUBIC FEET)

Year	Demand	Domestic Production	Domestic Supply Deficit
1972	26.1	23.8	2.3
1973	27.7	24.7	3.0
1974	28.8	24.8	4.0
1975	29.8	24.7	5.1
1980	34.5	20.4	14.1
1985	39.8	18.5	21.3
1990	46.4	17.8	28.6

Note: This gap between the projected demand for gas and a somewhat optimistic projection of domestic supply cannot be avoided, even at assumed annual rates of reserve additions of 20, 25, and 30 trillion cubic feet, with a domestic supply deficit developing by the mid-seventies and worsening over the time span considered by the staff. [Figure 3.15] shows the developing supply-demand imbalance.

Source: U.S. House of Representatives, Committee on Interior and Insular Affairs, *Fuel and Energy Resources, 1972, Part II*, Hearings held in Washington, D.C., April 14, 17, 18 and 19, 1972, 92d Cong., 2d sess., 1972, p. 771.

tion of oil and gas from the Middle East. The Middle East, according to recent estimates (1969), has the largest amount of known oil reserves— nearly 62 percent of the known reserves of the world, as Table 3.6 illustrates. France, Italy, the Netherlands, Spain, and Belgium get 100 percent of their oil from Arab states (including Iran, a Moslem state) in the Middle East and North Africa, while Great Britain is dependent upon these sources for about 89 percent of her needs. Eighty percent of Japan's oil needs are met from the Middle East and Africa, while from the same sources Portugal obtains 82 percent, West Germany 70 percent, Ireland about 60 percent, Norway 57 percent, and Australia about 53 percent of basic needs.

With these developed states needing oil resources to sustain their continual growth, and with their high degree of dependence upon the Arab states in the Middle East and North Africa, it was apparent to the Fourth Conference of Non-Aligned States in Algiers in September 1973 that oil-rich states had an economic collective bargaining tool to be applied at any time they desired. The immediate catalyst to such recognition was the fourth round of conflict that broke out between the Arab states and Israel in October 1973. The initial advances of Egypt and Syria and the inability of Israel to achieve a rapid and decisive victory gave psychological support to a view in Arab states that the time was near when the Arabs could exert their influence and force Israel to pull back from the Arab lands she had occupied in the 1967

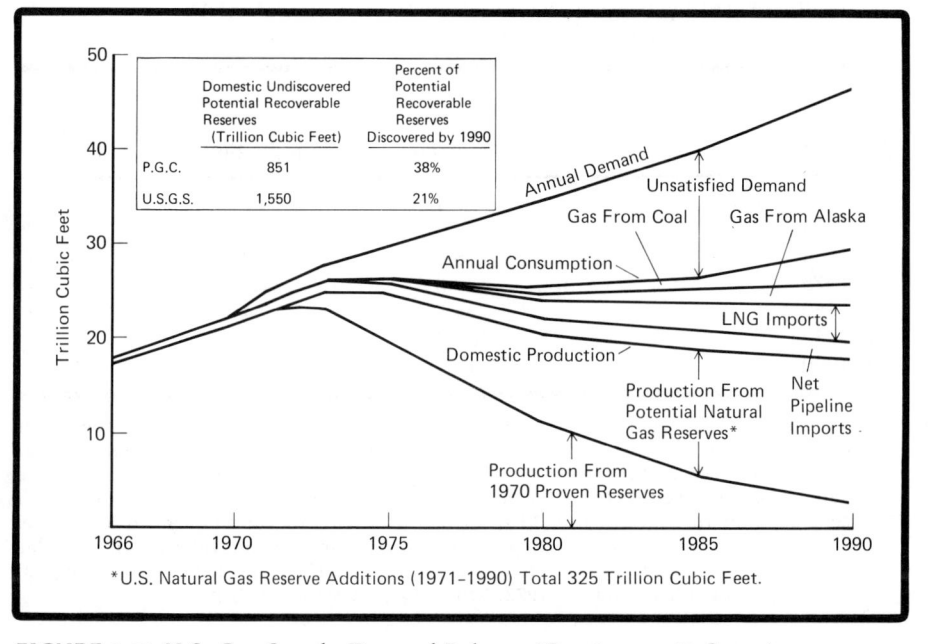

FIGURE 3.15 U.S. Gas Supply-Demand Balance (Contiguous 48 States)

Note: The attainment of a balance between domestic supply and anticipated demand would require the development of approximately 34 trillion cubic feet of new gas reserves each year which represents a sustained development rate 38 percent higher than the historical peak of 24.7 trillion cubic feet of new reserves added in 1956. The probability of reaching this level of annual additions to reserves is remote.

Source: U.S. House of Representatives, Committee on Interior and Insular Affairs, *Fuel and Energy Resources, 1972, Part II,* Hearings held in Washington, D.C., April 14, 17, 18 and 19, 1972, 92d Cong., 2d sess., 1972, p. 771.

war (i.e., from the Sinai Peninsula of Egypt, from the west bank of the Jordan River of Jordan, and from the Golan Heights of Syria). Thus the Arab oil states announced late in October an initial cutback of 25 percent in oil sales to the (primarily OECD) states unless they ceased support of Israel. In the case of the Netherlands, which had allowed its facilities to be used by the United States in rushing additional military supplies to Israel, the Arab states cut off all oil. In addition, the Arab states announced that cutbacks in sales would continue to escalate unless the developed states put pressure on Israel to return Arab lands (not only the areas occupied in 1967 but other portions of Israel, including Jerusalem). To make their point Arab states increased the barrel prices of oil almost 300 percent by October 1973.

By taking advantage of their major world oil reserves, the Arab states were able to use an economic fact of the world ecosystem to achieve their

TABLE 3.6 OIL PRODUCTION AND RESERVES—MIDDLE EAST 1969/1970

Middle East Oil Production—1970 (Thousands barrels daily)	
Abu Dhabi	691
Iran	3,848
Iraq	1,558
Kuwait	2,989
Qatar	361
Saudi Arabia	3,798
Others	496
Total	13,741

Known Oil Reserves—End of 1969	
Middle East	61.6%
Western Hemisphere	14.3%
Eastern Hemisphere and Communist China	11.1%
Africa	10.1%
Other	2.9%

Source: *United States Foreign Policy 1969–1970—A Report of Secretary of State*, Washington, D.C.: GPO, 1971, p. 84.

own political goals. Within days one state after another began to shift its policy from either neutral or pro-Israel in the Arab-Israeli dispute, to become "pro-Arab," and to condemn the actions of Israel. Only the Netherlands and the United States did not appreciably shift their policies. However, the U.S. Secretary of State extended good offices and pragmatic pressure to force Israel to begin to negotiate with the Arab states.

The very fact that certain nonrenewable resources such as oil are in limited supply in the ecosystem was clearly demonstrated by this episode. But beyond this use or misuse of a much needed and limited resource, the events set in motion by the Arab decision to cut oil sales gives an insight into the rapidity with which the unavailability of such an essential non-renewable resource might cause a whole variety of sudden political, economic, and social changes in the international system. The ripple ramifications of the oil embargo touched on a multitude of relationships in the international system. The ramifications were accentuated by the inherent limitations in the ecosystem. Some of the more apparent and immediate consequences of these events were:

1. Economic growth in many of the most industrial countries was threatened. Japan's growth, which has been phenomenal, was sud-

denly threatened with disaster—as was the case of all the states dependent on Arab oil for 75 percent or more of their needs. Great Britain, also in the throes of a coal strike, was forced to lay off thousands and to reduce the workweek to three days. Even the United States, which reportedly relies on the Arab world for only about 7 to 10 percent of oil needs, faced a possibility of a major recession as the scarcity of petroleum aided the price rise and encouraged individual consumers to buy foreign cars (with greater gas mileage). With one out of every ten Americans employed directly or indirectly in the automobile industry, any threat to this American enterprise shakes the entire economy.

2. Major military alliances such as the North Atlantic Treaty Organization were shown to be rather fragile political alliances. The United States, which saw the Arab-Israeli conflict within the context of American-Soviet rivalries, was faced with the fact that its NATO allies were not supporting its Middle Eastern policies. The steps taken with the Soviet Union toward détente were threatened by the divisions among American allies.

3. Even the possibility of new "power" groupings in the international system was suggested by these developments. One could conjecture that there might be major political groupings organized around states who possessed such smiliar economic threats. The "oil threat," compared to the nuclear-weapons threat, could forge coalitions of dependency but in this case to less-developed, oil-producing states. Such dependent states might then be called Arab "satellites."

4. The rapidity of the consequences of the partial cutback of oil supplies indicated that many of the projections of the Club of Rome study were close and realizable. The immediate talk of energy substitutes for oil that *might* increase environmental pollution is an example of the interrelationship among industrial needs, population needs, resource availability, and so on. If nothing else, this slight shift in the availability of a limited resource indicated that subsequent developments would bring about immediate changes in the whole interrelated system.

5. The plight of the less-developed states was made immediately more acute. Not only the increase in prices imposed by the producing states but also the competition among all states has resulted in driving up the oil prices and therefore the creation of a greater imbalance of payments for the less-developed states. In fact, the balance of payments of all states was threatened and affected by the oil cutoff.

6. Finally, one clear consequence of these developments was a new kind of nationalism in which each developed state was trying to "go it alone" and find its survival at the price of other states. For example,

France would seek her own oil deals in exchange for arms; and President Nixon announced "project independence," a program to eliminate American dependence on any other state within a decade. Thus instead of seeking efforts to work together, states underwent an almost panic reaction and each state sought only its own survival. This could constitute a new "jungle atmosphere" in international politics.

In one sense the energy crisis may be regarded as only temporary because over a period of years states may develop alternative energy sources. The hardships immediately felt by the average person may, therefore, seem only temporary. Such wishful thinking perhaps illustrates a lack of awareness of the consequences predicted by the Club of Rome, particularly the fragile balance between resources and economic needs. The Arab oil cutoff does indicate that political decisions affecting uses of the environment do have serious consequences. It is in this context that the developments directed toward management of untapped resources must be carefully considered if maximum benefits are to be reaped.

DECLARATION ON THE SEA BED

The efforts made by states since 1970 to assure the nonexploitation of the ocean floor and the sea bed indicate the difficult times ahead in negotiations by states to manage the environment. Accepting the fact that the sea bed and the ocean floor represent a major untapped source of nonrenewable resources in the future—the states of the world in the 25th session of the U.N. General Assembly in 1970, adopted a declaration of principles governing this area. This declaration, which was unanimously accepted by the states, stated in concept that:

1. The sea bed and the ocean floor, and the subsoil thereof, including the resources of the area are the common heritage of mankind;
2. That no state or persons can claim or exercise jurisdiction over the area;
3. That no state or persons shall acquire rights to the resources of the area that is incompatible with the principles of the declaration;
4. That all activities to explore and exploit the resources of the area will be governed by an international regime;
5. That the area shall be open for use for peaceful purposes only by all states, whether they are coastal or land-locked states;
6. That states shall act in the area in accord with international law;
7. That exploration of the area and exploitation of its resources "shall be carried out for the benefit of mankind as a whole, irrespective of the geographical location of states, whether land-locked or coastal,

and taking into particular consideration the interests and needs of the developing countries";

8. That states shall cooperate in scientific research in the area;
9. That steps will be taken to prevent the pollution and contamination and other hazards to the marine environment, so as not to interfere with the marine environment; and that states will protect and conserve the natural resources of the area and prevent damage to the flora and fauna of the marine environment.[32]

This declaration, therefore, has established the goals of preserving and maximizing the resources of this vast area for the benefit of all peoples. Since its adoption in 1970, states have been intensively involved in attempting to implement these goals. Their prime task has been the negotiation of an ocean-space treaty that would establish an international regime to administer the principles of the declaration on the sea bed, ocean floor, and the subsoil thereof. The complexities of this task can be visualized by a very brief examination of *just one* of the many draft treaties submitted to the U.N. Committee on the Peaceful Uses of the Sea-Bed and the Ocean Floor Beyond the Limits of National Jurisdiction—the draft treaty submitted by Malta.[33]

Over 70 states submitted various proposals for the implementation of the 1970 declaration, but the proposal of Malta was the most comprehensive. It was entitled:

> *Draft Treaty concerning the establishment of an international regime, including international machinery, for the sea-bed and ocean floor and the subsoil thereof and for its resources beyond the limits of national jurisdiction, including a precise definition of the area and also concerning a broad range of related issues, including those of the regimes of the high seas, the continental shelf, the territorial sea (including the question of international straits) and contiguous zone, fishing and conservation of living resources of the high seas (including the question of the preferential rights of the coastal State), the preservation of the marine environment including* inter alia *the question of pollution) and scientific research.*

This draft treaty included 250 articles organized into five parts. Part I covered concepts of ocean space under international law, defining the area in general and the elements of international law dealing with jurisdiction regarding navigation, slavery, piracy, and narcotic drugs, hot pursuit, submarine cables and pipelines, overflight, and scientific research. Part II dealt with questions under international law regarding coastal state jurisdiction in the ocean space. Part III dealt with international law principles on national ocean space. Part IV then laid out in detail international law principles for

the international ocean space, defining it as beyond national jurisdiction and as a common heritage of mankind—in accord with the principles of the 1970 declaration. The last part—Part V (Articles 86 to 250)—detailed the International Ocean Space Institutions. It provided for an Assembly, a Council, an International Maritime Court, a Secretariat, an Ocean Management Commission, a Scientific and Technological Commission, and a Legal Commission. This part was

> based on the postulate that, in modern circumstances, unregulated
> freedom in ocean space beyond national jurisdiction is not in the
> interests of coastal States or of the international community as a whole;
> beneficial use of ocean space is restricted and many contemporary
> problems are insoluble unless the new international legal order, which
> must replace existing regimes of the seas, makes provision for strong
> and equitably balanced international institutions with powers to
> administer ocean space beyond national jurisdiction and to manage its
> living and non-living resources on behalf of the international
> community. Basic prerequisites to an orderly economic development
> of ocean space beyond national jurisdiction and hence to the equitable
> sharing of all states in the benefits derived from the exploitations
> of its natural resources are (a) a credible mechanism for the maintenance
> of international law and order in ocean space, including the territorial,
> jurisdictional and ecological integrity of ocean space beyond national
> jurisdiction and (b) certainty in international law and mechanisms for
> the peaceful and certain settlement of disputes. This latter requirement
> necessarily involves the creation of an international court with binding
> powers of adjudication.[34]

In complex detail this section of the Malta draft treaty laid down binding obligations for states to ensure the principles of the Declaration on the Sea-Bed and the Ocean Floor. It created an international government—a long-range policy-directing body, the Assembly; a short-range policy body, the Council; a management commission that actually operates the granting of exploration and exploitation leases for portions of the ocean floor for specific purposes; a scientific commission to assure that these bodies act in accord with the latest scientific knowledge; and an international court to handle disputes that might arise. Voting in the Assembly and the Council would follow a very complex formula to assure that the rights of each state are considered and balanced with the rights of the community of states as a whole.

This Malta draft treaty, as well as the draft treaties submitted by all the other states, was full of problems that needed to be resolved if there is to be adequate management of these nonrenewable resources for the maximum benefit for all the peoples of the earth. It is not an easy task, but it constitutes the most fundamental and detailed negotiations that must be imple-

mented if the goals laid out in the 1970 declaration are to be realized. The work on combining the Malta draft with the drafts of the other states commenced at the Third U.N. Conference on the Law of the Sea. The intricate negotiations are expected to continue in several separate meetings so that individual states can carefully consider the steps to be undertaken. It is anticipated that by 1975 all the details of this environmental management treaty will have been worked out.

CONCLUSION

The Limits of Growth study, as well as some of its preliminary releases of the study, has provoked intense reactions. Critics have called it "scare tactics," "pretentious nonsense," and more "gloomy prophecies." It has been characterized as oversimplified, too pessimistic, too computerized, without adequate compensation for the adaptability of humans to cope with such crucial dilemmas.[35] The most comprehensive examination of the *Limits of Growth* has been the study carried out as a project of the Science Policy Research Unit of the University of Sussex and entitled *Models of Doom: A Critique of the Limits of Growth*.[36] The Sussex group systematically examines the assumptions, values, and the degree to which these assumptions correspond to the facts about the real world. They are highly critical in great detail on many, if not most, of the assumptions in building the computer model. Probably their strongest criticism is this:

> *The major weaknesses of the world dynamics models is that they illustrate the pessimistic consequences of exponential growth in a finite world without taking account of politics, social structure, and human needs and wants. The introduction of an extra variable—man—into thinking about the world and its future may entirely change the structure of the debate which these models have so far limited to physical properties.*[37]

However the Sussex critique does acknowledge that *The Limits of Growth* models do represent the "most ambitious" attempt so far to bring together these elements affecting the future of the world. Further they express "complete agreement" with the M.I.T.-Club of Rome study on the urgency of these problems. Despite the many detailed and devastating criticisms, the Sussex group did not suggest a substitute model of the ecosystem.

The Club of Rome study does for the first time attempt to interrelate many of the interconnecting facets of the ecosystem and some of the apparent trends for the future. This study and the U.N. analyses do suggest that these are vital variables affecting the environment in the future and cannot be ignored. They do suggest, despite the critics, that there are environmental forces already at work that are real and possibly quite immediate. And the

Sussex criticism that the one variable not projected into the future is the human reaction to these developments seems very valid. How that human variable will react to the exponential developments may well be the key to whether the dire predictions of the *Limits of Growth* are realized.

That states acknowledge the problems delineated in *The Limits of Growth* is increasingly evident. The Stockholm Conference on the Environment in 1972 and the attempts to deal with the resources of the sea in the 3rd U.N. Conference on the Law of the Sea are not the only efforts. The August 1974 World Population Conference in Bucharest adopted a "Plan of Action," and the 6th Special Session of the U.N. General Assembly (April–May 1974) called for the "establishment of a new international economic order" to deal with the disparity of resources. The World Food Conference in Rome in November 1974 focused on the problems of establishing a world food reserve against hunger and starvation. Whether these steps, and many others, do more than just acknowledge the problems depend upon the degree to which states and individuals perceive a mutual concern in their solution.

NOTES

[1]See John Prebble, *The Darien Disaster*, London: Becker and Warburg, 1968.

[2]U.S. Department of State, *Participation of the United States Government in International Conference*, July 1, 1947–June 30, 1948 Washington, D.C.: GPO, pp. 319–321.

[3]Paul R. Ehrlich and Anne H. Ehrlich, *Population—Resources—Environment; Issues in Human Ecology*, San Francisco: Freeman, 1970, p. 52. For one of the more recent proposals on colonizing outer space see: Herbert N. Woodward, *The Human Dilemma*, New York: Brookdale Press, 1972.

[4]World Bank, *Address to the Board of Governors by Robert S. McNamara, President, World Bank Group*, Copenhagen, World Bank, 1970, pp. 9–10.

[5]Information on the halibut problem is based on the *Annual Reports* of the International Fisheries Commission (as the halibut commission was originally titled), 1930–1953, and on *Annual Reports* of the International Pacific Halibut Commission, 1954–1972. Occasionally, these annual reports have been titled "Regulation and Investigation of the Pacific Halibut Fishery . . ." for a given year. Ironically, as Soviet and Japanese fishing vessels moved into this North Pacific halibut area in the late 1960s, the "false" issue of territorial jurisdiction was raised. It is uncertain as to what impact on the fishery has been. The United States-Canadian catch dropped to 31.7 million pounds by 1973, but what the catch has been by the Soviets and Japanese is uncertain.

[6]For a detailed consideration of this see Norman Moss, *Men Who Play God—The Story of the Hydrogen Bomb*, Baltimore, Md.: Penguin, 1970, pp. 90–121.

[7]United Nations, *The United Nations and Disarmament, 1945–1970*, New York: United Nations, 1970, pp. 192–193.

[8]*Ibid.*

[9]See John W. Spanier and Joseph L. Nogee, *The Politics of Disarmament—A Study in Soviet-American Gamemanship*, New York: M. Praeger, 1962, p. 120.

[10]See the annual reports of this committee to the General Assembly of the United Nations, especially the 1969 report which has an updated summary of the impacts of the radioactive contamination of the environment by nuclear tests, United Nations General Assembly, Official Records, XXIV Session Supplement No. 13, *Report of the United Nations Scientific Committee on Atomic Radiation*, especially pp. 13–68.

[11]See articles on these three developments and their possible ecological damage in *Environment*, November 1971, pp. 2–15.

[12]See Thomas Whiteside, *Defoliation*, New York: Ballantine, 1970.

[13]"Officials Confirm S.E. Asia Target of Cloud-Seeding," (from *The New York Times* News Service), *The Oregonian*, July 3, 1971.

[14]Sheldon Novick, *The Careless Atom*, Boston, Mass.: Houghton Mifflin, 1969, as quoted in Ehrlich and Ehrlich, *op. cit.*, p. 136.

[15]Max Savelle, *The Origins of American Diplomacy: The International History of Angloamerica 1492–1793*, New York: Macmillan, 1967, p. 5.

[16]See, for example, Peree Jalee, *The Pillage of the Third World*, New York: Monthly Review Press, 1968.

[17]Andrew Hill Clark, *The Invasion of New Zealand by Peoples, Plants and Animals*, New Burnswick, N.J.: Rutgers University Press, 1949, pp. 39–42.

[18]Peter H. Buck, *Vikings of the Sunrise*, Philadelphia: Lippincott, 1958, pp. 269–276.

[19]Fred Cottrell, *Energy and Society: The Relation Between Energy, Social Change, and Economic Development*, New York: McGraw-Hill, 1955.

[20]See Barbara Ward and Rene Dubos, *Only One Earth—The Care and Maintenance of a Small Planet* (an Unofficial Report Commisisoned by the Secretary-General of the United Nations Conference on the Human Environment, Prepared with the Assistance of a 152-member Committee of Corresponding Consultants in 58 countries), New York: Norton, 1972, especially pp. 14–17.

[21]U.N. Department of Economic and Social Affairs (Population Studies, No. 48), *A Concise Summary of the World Population Situation in 1970*, New York: United Nations, 1971, p. 6.

[22]Donella H. Meadows, Dennis L. Meadows, Jorgen Randers, and William W. Behrens III, *The Limits of Growth*, New York: Universe Books, 1972, pp. 55–60.

[23]Committee on Resources of Man, of the Division of Earth Sciences, National Academy of Sciences–National Research Council, *Resources and Man: A Study and Recommendations*, San Francisco: Freeman, 1969, p. 119.

[24]See, for example, Barbara Ward and Rene Dubos, *Only One Earth*, New York: Norton, 1972, pp. 122–126; and John Maddox, *The Doomsday Syndrome*, New York: McGraw-Hill, 1972.

[25]Meadows et al., *op. cit.*; see also Jay W. Forrester, *World Dynamics*, Cambridge, Mass.: Wright-Allen Press, 1971.

[26]U.N. Economic and Social Council, *Problems of the Human Environment—Report of the Secretary-General*, Document E/4667, May, 26, 1969, p. 4.

[27]*Ibid.*, p. 5.

[28]*Ibid.*, p. 6.

[29]One hundred and ten states attended the conference; the USSR and the Eastern European states were invited but at the last minute did not attend. They were protesting the fact that the (East) German Democratic Republic was not invited. In addition to states, representatives of a wide variety of nongovernmental organizations participated in one way or another in the deliberations of the conference.

[30]U.N. Document E/4667, *op. cit.*, p. 9.

[31]*U.N. Monthly Chronicle*, 9, no. 7 (July 1972), 89.

[32]U.N. General Assembly Resolution 2749 (XXV).

[33]U.N. General Assembly, Official Records: Twenty-Sixth Session, Supplement No. 21 (A/8421)—*Report of the Committee on the Peaceful Uses of the Sea-Bed and the Ocean Floor Beyond the Limits of National Jurisdiction*, pp. 105–193.

[34]*Ibid.*

[35]See, for example, Burnham P. Beckwith, "The Predicament of Man? A Reply," *The Futurist*, 6, no. 2 (April 1972), 62–66, which includes a response by Dennis Meadows of the *Limits of Growth* group; and Maddox, *op. cit.*, pp. 282–287, which is a postscript devoted to an attack on the *Limits of Growth*.

[36]H. S. D. Cole, Christopher Freeman, Marie Jahoda, and K. L. R. Pavitt (eds.), *Models of Doom: A Critique of the Limits of Growth*, New York: Universe Books, 1973. Included at the end of the book is a commentary by Meadows et al. (*The Limits of Growth*), answering the critique.

[37]*Ibid.*, p. 209.

4

MAN
AND
HIS
HUNGER

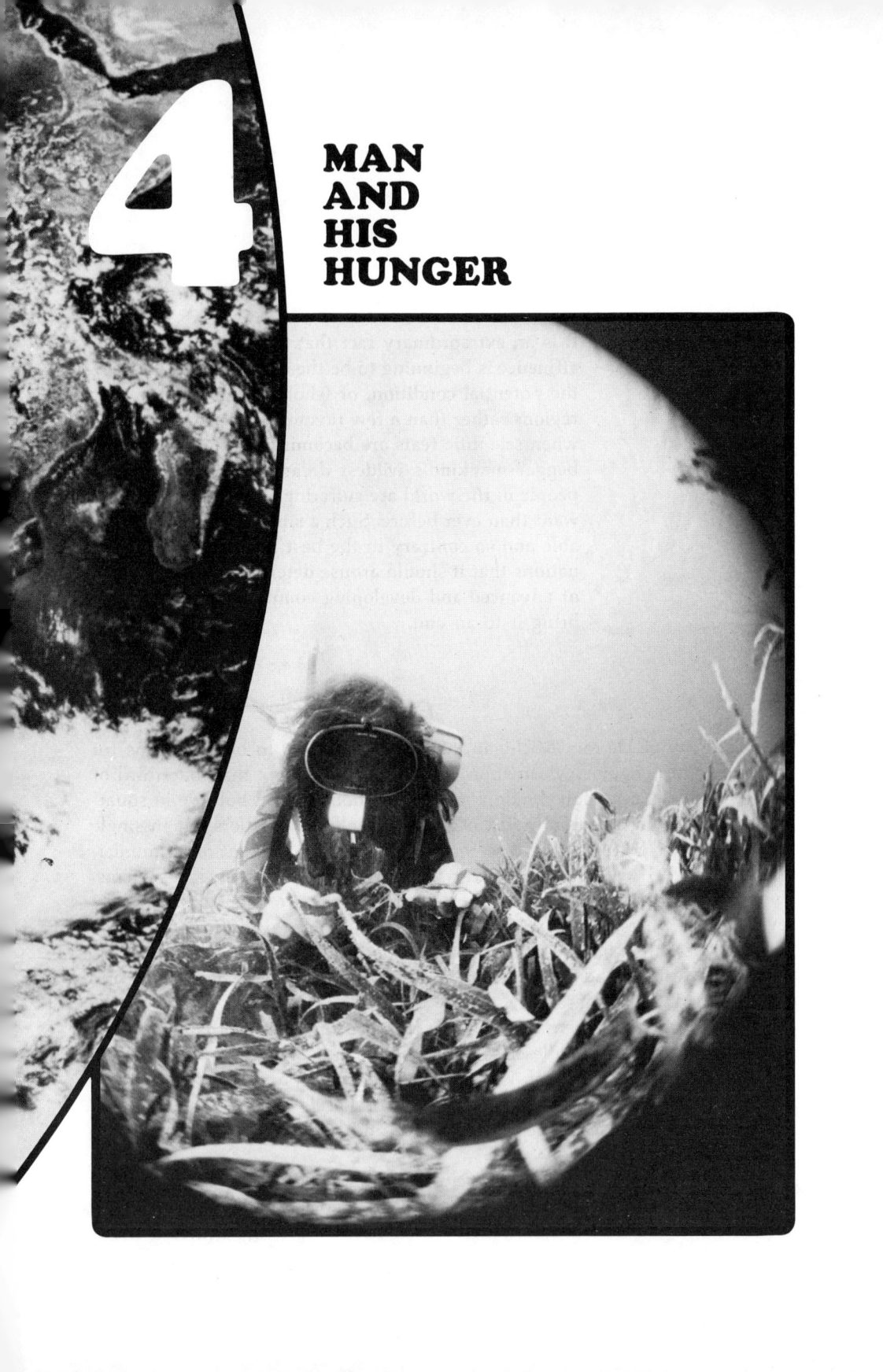

It is an extraordinary fact that at a time when affluence is beginning to be the condition, or at least the potential condition, of whole countries and regions rather than a few favoured individuals, and when scientific feats are becoming possible which beggar mankind's wildest dreams of the past, more people in the world are suffering from hunger and want than ever before. Such a situation is so intolerable and so contrary to the best interests of all nations that it should arouse determination, on part of advanced and developing countries alike, to bring it to an end.

U Thant
1962

The City of Detroit, Michigan, has spent $750,000 to build a home for five species of penguins. Meanwhile, in Mexico City, more than one-third of the population, 1.5 million people, have no real homes at all but live in squatter settlements. In Calcutta, India, 58 percent of all city dwellers live in single rooms inhabited by more than five persons. In Brazil 45 percent of all municipalities have no water supply. Sixty-six percent have no sewage systems.

If you happen to be Swedish, you can expect to live approximately seventy-three years. But if you are Togolese, your life expectancy is thirty-five years, less than half of what it is in Sweden.

New Zealand had 405 telephones per thousand people in 1967–1968. Tanzania had 2 per thousand.

Our international environment is full of contrasts: Jordan's refugee camps and America's middle-class suburbs; the peasant economy of Burma and the staggering wealth of Wall Street and Madison Avenue; the international jet set and the starving inhabitants of Peru's barriados; budgets of $80 billion for defense in the United States and under $275 million for the United Nations.

However much we regret or rejoice in these disparities, the stratification of wealth and power and, increasingly, the polarization between haves and have-nots are facts of international existence. Despite the United Nations

principle of one state, one vote, no two states are equal, politically or economically. And since most of man's conflicts have arisen out of competition for political and economic resources, our purpose in this chapter is to consider what the vast disparities in wealth and resources mean for the future relations among nations and the continued existence of our planet.

ECONOMIC DISPARITIES

When we speak of developed and less-developed nations, we are merely using academic shorthand to refer to the rich, industrialized nations on the one hand, and on the other, the poverty-stricken Third World, composed of most of Latin America, Africa, Asia, and the Middle East. The dichotomy of developed and less-developed is an oversimplification ignoring the vast diversity in both categories—a diversity that needs to be kept in mind particularly as we generalize about less-developed countries as a whole in the following pages.[1] It is common to classify nations as developed or less-developed according to a relatively simple indicator such as per capita income or per capita gross national product. What is important, however, are the conditions that account for disparities in income and national productivity.

Nations are distinguished by the relationships among their levels of technology, population, and resources, as Figure 4.1 shows. The more advanced the technology and the economy, the greater the nation's ability to support a larger population at a higher standard of living and to utilize effectively resources to improve the quality of life. Iron ore, for example, is of little value except as an export if there is no industrial plant to refine it and to produce goods. And an industrial plant without skilled workers is inefficient and unproductive.

The United States is a nation with comparatively advanced technology, low population density, and abundant resources. Like most wealthy, industrialized nations, we have developed our economy over generations of time. Bangladesh, on the other hand, has little technological know-how, high population density, and few resources. More than one-half the world's people live in such technology-deficient nations with large populations and inadequate natural resources. Most of these nations of the Third World are just emerging from traditional subsistence economies. They have only recently begun the process of creating "modern" nation-states and improving the material well-being of their citizens, and they are trying to telescope their modernization into a few decades. In most developing nations, however, at least three-fourths of the population is still engaged in agriculture, often on tiny, undercapitalized plots of land farmed with crude methods. The middle-class is small, illiteracy common, and education seldom goes beyond primary

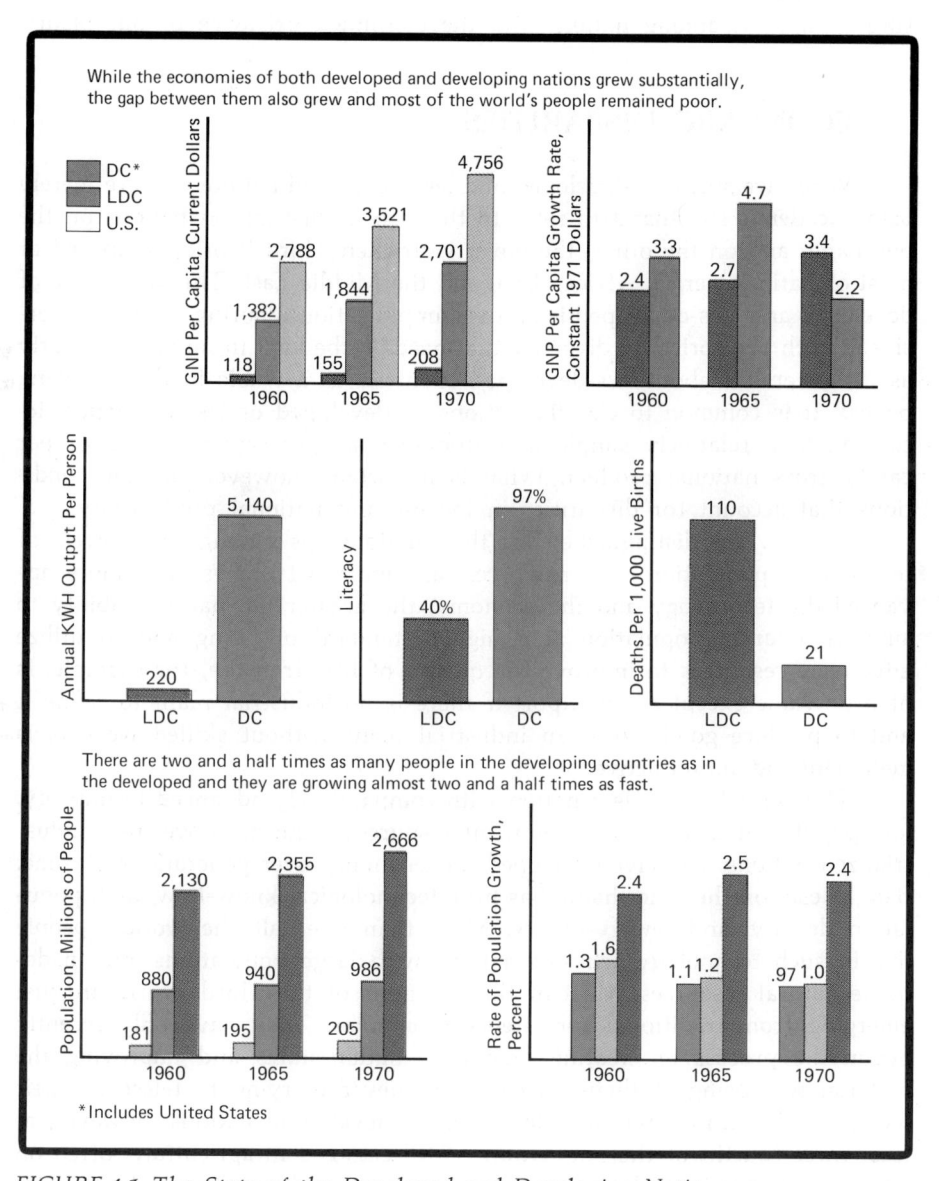

FIGURE 4.1 The State of the Developed and Developing Nations

Source: U.S. Department of State, *United States Foreign Policy 1972: A Report of the Secretary of State*, Department of State Publication 8699 (1973), p. xxi.

school, except for a restricted group of elites. Widespread and increasing unemployment is one of the most serious economic and social problems: Estimates suggest that some 20 percent of the male labor force is unemployed. Since private personal savings and capital for investment are scarce, these economies are greatly dependent on trade, foreign aid, and external capital for economic development. Consequently, external indebtedness is high.

The small West African republic of Ghana is more or less typical of many Third World nations. Only 7.7 percent of the 8.8 million population lives in urban areas, yet urban unemployment is rife. Cocoa is the main export commodity, and the nation is heavily in debt, a condition that contributed to coups d'état in 1966 and 1972. For every 1000 persons in Ghana there are approximately 70 radios, less than 1 television set, 5 telephones, 7 automobiles, and 1 hospital bed. Per capita income is about $250 a year. Seventy-five percent of the population is illiterate, and life expectancy is thirty-nine years. Although the country has the potential for being nearly self-sufficient in food supply and has some mineral and fuel resources, the path to modernization will not be easy.

Economic development implies growth in the total output of goods and services, growth in per capita productivity, and a reasonably equitable distribution of these benefits throughout the society. Yet these basic indicators do not adequately reflect the complexities of the development process in which the political, social, economic, and culutral life of a nation are closely interrelated. The proposals for the Second United Nations Development Decade emphatically point this out:

> It cannot be over-emphasized that what development implies for the developing countries is not simply an increase in productive capactiy but major transformations in their social and economic structures. Their economies are characterized by dualism which has often the effect of making technological and economic advances sharpen the contrast between their modern and backward sectors and widen social and economic disparities. There are inequalities and rigidities in their social structures emanating from systems of land tenure, administrative hierarchies, educational systems and inadequate educational opportunities, external forces, and various traditional practices and customs. Within this framework, an increase in output or income only represents one of the indicators of development. . . . [T]he process of development has itself to be viewed in terms of fundamental structural changes and as much with reference to concepts and methods appropriate to planned social transformation as those customary to economic analysis and policy-making. Indeed, for this reason, the distinction often made between economic and social objectives is not a very meaningful one to draw.[2]

To further their economic development, nations of the Third World must:

1. Accumulate sufficient capital for investment;
2. Build a national economic infrastructure (i.e., roads, transportation and communications systems);
3. Diversify the economy;
4. Increase productivity of the labor force through education, training, and mechanization;
5. Expand employment opportunities;
6. Manage natural resources to avoid depletion;
7. Expand export trade and obtain favorable trade terms for primary and manufactured products;
8. Check population growth;
9. Reform internal socioeconomic processes impeding development;
10. Maintain political stability.

Obviously, the priority assigned to each will vary from nation to nation as circumstances demand, even though the overall list is applicable to the Third World generally. Table 4.1 illustrates economic and demographic conditions in the *least-developed* countries where problems are most severe. In much of Indochina the first priority for development is to end the wars that have ravaged countries such as Vietnam, Cambodia, and Laos for many years. Immediate issues in Indonesia are enormous problems of overpopulation, unemployment, and fundamental deficiencies in education and administrative structure. Burundi in East Africa has suffered from chronic political instability largely due to "tribal" conflicts. Nigeria has yet to achieve national unity and heal the scars of the Biafran revolt despite her relatively good economic situation based upon oil resources. Ghana must reduce a huge debt and diversify her economy so that earnings are not heavily dependent upon cocoa. Senegal and Mali, among others, face the immediate problem of overcoming the effects of a six-year drought. Bangladesh's first priority must be to establish itself as a nation with an effective government and economic system. Setting national priorities necessarily involves the weighing of related values, such as deciding how to balance civil liberties against the need for law and order. As events in Brazil, Chile, and Greece demonstrate, repressive regimes may mean economic gains but at a cost to democratic values.

As if internal development were not a big enough task, the new nations must accomplish all this within a highly stratified and largely inhospitable and unsympathetic international system. They must attempt to find a place in a world dominated by the huge conglomerations of economic and political power represented by the industrialized nations and their ubiquitous multinational corporations. The new nations meet head-on an international econ-

omy dedicated to profit making, unwilling to grant more than token trade concessions to underdeveloped economies, suspicious of schemes to redistribute wealth or resources, and miserly in its financial and technical assistance to the noncompetitive. In addition, some nations are still struggling to throw off the last vestiges of colonialism; others no sooner rid themselves of the colonial yoke than they found themselves unwillingly embroiled in the political and ideological rivalries of the great powers and more subtle forms of imperialism. Finally, following the example of the developed world, the new nations have allowed national distrust and rivalry to interfere with their relations with one another. And there is no international court of social, economic, and political justice to which the Third World may appeal for redress of grievances.

Table 4.2 contrasts economic growth in developed and less-developed nations between 1961 and 1971. While gross domestic product in less-developed nations has increased, the growth of population and an estimated average price increase of 3 percent means that real growth was less than 5 percent, the development target in the 1960s.[3] Such statistics do not point out the compounding problems of unemployment, inflation, and political instability in most developing nations. For example, the per capita income of oil-rich Kuwait was $3460 in 1968, compared with $3580 for the United States. By no stretch of the imagination, however, are economic conditions comparable in the two countries. Useful as aggregate figures and percentage rates of growth may be, they cannot accurately portray the quality of life, the human dimensions of underdevelopment. Perhaps we need to see the daily collection of bodies from the streets of Calcutta or the malnourished children of what was once Biafra (Eastern Nigeria) to appreciate the meaning of poverty.

The overall record of development in the past twenty years is mixed. Many Third World nations, such as Israel, Mexico, Taiwan, and Yugoslavia, have shown remarkable progress in agricultural productivity, industrialization, education, social services, and in economic management and the effective use of capital. Others, such as Ghana, Bolivia, and Syria, remain mired in instability, inefficiency, and corruption. In a few such as Haiti during the last years of "Papa Doc" Duvalier's dictatorial reign, per capita income fell, exports diminished, roads crumbled into total disrepair, and once fertile farmlands became wastelands. Between 1950 and 1967 developing nations as a whole increased their total production of goods and services at an annual average rate of 4.8 percent, with export earnings financing over two-thirds of total investments.

Meanwhile, of course, the rich nations of the world have become richer still, and at an ever faster rate, so that the gap between rich and poor has actually increased. Between 1960 and 1965 the per capita gross domestic product of the developed countries increased $59 a year to $1725, while in

TABLE 4.1 ECONOMIC AND DEMOGRAPHIC CHARACTERISTICS OF LEAST-DEVELOPED COUNTRIES

Countries	Land-Locked	Population (Million) 1969	CDP Criteria				
			Gross Domestic Product per Capita $ (1968)	Manufacturing Share in Total Production % 1968	Literate Adults as % of Adult Population 1968	Annual Rate of Growth GNP or GDP 1960–1968 %	Annual Rate of Growth Food Production per Capita 1961–1969 %
Afghanistan	*	16.5	91	11	8	1.9	0
Bhutan	*	0.8	n.a.	n.a.	n.a.	1.9	n.a.
Botswana	*	0.6	106	8	20	3.7	n.a.
Burundi	*	3.5	53	4	10	2.4	1.2
Chad	*	3.6	73	4	7	−0.1	−6.6
Dahomey		2.6	91	5	10	⌠ 2.9 ⌡ 4.0	0
Ethiopia		24.8	64	9	5	4.6	0
Guinea		3.8	89	6	5	5.4	−0.3
Haiti		4.8	83	12	11	1.5	−5.3
Laos	*	2.9	72	n.a.	15	2.6	2.3
Lesotho	*	0.9	87	1	40	4.2	−11.2
Malawi	*	4.4	69	8	15	3.8	5.1
Maldives		0.1	n.a.	n.a.	n.a.	2.9	
Mali	*	4.9	92	8	2	3.4	−0.9
Nepal	*	10.8	82	11	9	2.8	0
Niger	*	3.9	89	6	1	−2.1	0.5
Rwanda	*	3.5	43	n.a.	10	4.6	2.7
Sikkim	*	0.2	n.a.	n.a.	n.a.	1.7	
Somalia		2.7	60	n.a.	5	4.2	1.1
Sudan		15.3	115	7	12	3.7	−1.0
Tanzania		12.9	71	6	17	3.9	0
Uganda	*	9.5	95	8	25	4.0	0.7
Upper Volta	*	5.3	51	6	7	2.3	−0.9
Western Samoa		0.1	n.a.	n.a.	n.a.	n.a.	n.a.
Yemen (Arab Republic)		5.6	110	n.a.	10	4.8	0.8
For comparison:							
India		523.9	85	14	28	3.5	0.5
Kenya		10.2	125	11	22	4.8	2.8
Philippines		37.2	170	18	72	3.4	−0.3
Bolivia	*	4.9	200	15	40	6.9	−0.1

n.a. = not available.
Source: Organization for Economic Co-operation and Development, *Development Co-operation*, Paris: OECD, 1972, pp. 104–105.

developing countries it rose only $3 to $157. A per capita growth rate of 3 percent in a country such as India produces an increase in annual income of only $3 per capita, while in the United States it produces $120. In our age of intensive international communication through news media, diplomatic contact, and international organization, this ever-widening gulf between the

TABLE 4.1 (*Continued*)

Annual Growth Rate of Exports % 1960–1968	Annual Exports per Capita $ 1968	Share of Agriculture in Total Labour Force %	Railway Lines (Miles)	Improved Roads (Miles) per 1,000 Sq. Miles	Expectation of Life at Birth (Years)	Thousands of Inhabitants per Physician	Adjusted Enrolment Ratios: 1st & 2nd Levels
3.8	4	80	0	29	n.a.	21.4	11
n.a.	n.a.	n.a.	0	n.a.	n.a.	n.a.	6
n.a.	27	91	410	6	n.a.	27.6	44
10.7	5	95	0	90	33–38	61.8	18
6.6	11	90	0	1	29–35	90.8	20
6.8	16	84	359	53	37	31.3	20
5.1	7	88	485	8	35	64.6	8
0.0	15	80	611	32	26–28	46.9	19
0.5	11	79	187	64	45	14.0	27
n.a.	0.5	81	0	30	52	24.6	32
n.a.	18	85	0	58	45	19.1	76
9.8	16	81	353	89	n.a.	46.9	31
n.a.	n.a.	n.a.	0	n.a.	n.a.	n.a.	n.a.
3.6	5	81	398	10	35	51.1	14
n.a.	n.a.	94	64	85	33	41.2	19
9.1	14	97	0	4	37	57.2	6
18.4	4	95	0	280	n.a.	76.3	44
n.a.	n.a.	n.a.	0	n.a.	n.a.	n.a.	n.a.
2.4	10	89	0	10	n.a.	30.0	6
3.4	19	78	3,380	1	40	24.6	14
4.8	23	95	1,460	28	40–41	17.3	23
7.1	29	89	620	41	n.a.	8.9	32
20.3	4	86	290	28	32	76.2	8
−4.1	n.a.	74	0	n.a.	n.a.	2.2	83
n.a.	2	90	0	13	35	62.5	5
3.0	4	73	37,004	285	41	6.8	44
10.0	40	88	650	47	43	10.6	45
7.0	30	53	710	350	55	1.3	84
14.0	34	58	2,209	3	53	3.1	49

n.a. = not available.
Source: Organisation for Economic Co-operation and Development, *Development Co-operation*, Paris: OECD, 1972, pp. 104–105.

have and have-not nations is keenly felt in the Third World. K. B. Asante of Ghana expressed it clearly when he said:

Our world is polarized into the have and have-nots. It would be wonderful if Neil Armstrong spoke for all mankind when he said on

TABLE 4.2 ECONOMIC INDICATORS FOR DEVELOPING AND DEVELOPED COUNTRIES (PERCENTAGES)

	1961–1965	1966	1967	1968	1969	1970	1971
Developing Countries Average Annual Rate of Growth							
Total Gross Domestic Product	5.1	4.8	5.2	5.9	6.3	6.5	6.0
Agricultural Production	2.3	1.8	4.6	3.0	4.0	2.5	1.8
Manufacturing Production	8.4	7.0	5.2	9.2	9.8	7.6	8.2
Population	2.6	2.6	2.6	2.5	2.6	2.5	2.4
GDP per capita	2.5	2.2	2.6	3.3	3.6	3.9	3.5
Developed Countries Average Annual Rate of Growth							
Total Gross Domestic Product	5.1	5.5	3.4	4.9	4.5	3.7	3.9
Agricultural Production	1.8	2.0	6.1	2.5	1.1	1.5	2.4
Manufacturing Production	6.0	7.5	2.3	6.2	5.8	3.9	2.9
Population	1.3	1.1	1.0	1.0	1.0	1.0	1.0
GDP per capita	3.8	4.4	2.4	3.8	3.5	2.7	3.0

Source: World Bank, *Annual Report, 1971*, Washington: World Bank, 1971, pp. 58–59; *Annual Report, 1972*, Washington: World Bank, 1972, pp. 76–77; *Annual Report, 1973*, Washington: World Bank, 1973, pp. 82–83.

landing on the moon "one small step for man; one giant step for mankind." Though I was excited and sat with my eyes glued to tele-vision until the early hours of the morning, I did not feel he spoke for me. I do not belong to that part of mankind. But I and countless others want to belong to one mankind.[4]

Indonesia's President Suharto voiced a similar reaction to President Nixon after the Apollo 11 moon landing. "A great leap for whom?" queried President Suharto.

Modern science and technology have given us the knowledge to bridge the gap between what is possible and what is desirable, between what is and what ought to be. The revolution of rising expectations is a result. We have means available to us to increase agricultural production, to limit population,

to virtually eradicate diseases such as smallpox, malaria, tuberculosis, polio, and measles, to decrease infant mortality, to build inexpensive, sanitary housing, to provide uncontaminated water, to increase the rate of economic development, to train skilled workers, and so on. The developed world has the knowledge and the wealth to do these things and could, if it chose, share to a far greater degree the benefits of wealth and knowledge with the Third World. But such a sharing flows from a sense of world community and mutual interest, and this is in very short supply. Yet we believe that the vast inequities between the haves and the have-nots threaten to turn them into two hostile, warring camps, whose enmity may jeopardize us all, rich and poor alike.

"Who can now ask where his country will be in a few decades," queried the Commission on International Development, also known as the Pearson Commission, "without asking where the world will be."[5] Perhaps nowhere is this question better illustrated than in how we face the challenge of meeting one of man's basic needs—food.

HUNGER

The Food and Agriculture Organization (FAO) of the United Nations estimates that between one-third and one-half of the world's population, mostly in developing nations, suffers from hunger or malnutrition. In India it is estimated that 4 million people are totally blind, and possibly three times as many are partly blind, owing largely to Vitamin A deficiencies. Whereas the average daily caloric intake in the United States is 3000, in Somalia, Saudi Arabia, and Bolivia it is only 1800.

FOOD PRODUCTION

Agricultural production at the present world level is sufficient to provide a daily diet of 3000 calories per day (including 100 grams of protein) for a world population of slightly over 2 billion persons—2 billion *fewer* people than the present world population. Assuming that the earth's population will reach 6 or 7 billion by the year 2000, annual food production will have to increase by 3 to 3.5 percent per year in order to provide a standard diet for everyone. But the problem of providing the world's population with adequate food is made much more complex by the fact that over half the world's population is confined to less than one-seventh of the world's agricultural land, while one-sixth of the population occupies more than half of the productive soil. Even if total production were adequate, a vast redistribution system would be necessary to ensure that everyone received an adequate diet.

TABLE 4.3 DEVELOPING COUNTRIES: GROWTH OF AGRICULTURAL PRODUCTION, 1960–1970

Region	Percentage Increase from Preceding Year		
	1960–1968 Average	1969	1970[a]
Developing Countries Total	2.5	4.4	2.5
Western Hemisphere	3.2	1.8	3.5
Central American Common Market	5.4	—	3.3
Other Central American and Caribbean	3.9	−4.6	8.9
Andean Group[b]	2.3	1.0	3.3
Other South America	3.1	4.9	1.2
Africa	1.9	4.6	—
North Africa	1.8	−0.4	2.3
West Africa	1.3	7.6	−4.0
East Africa	3.0	1.9	3.5
Other Africa	1.5	7.4	−0.3
West Asia	5.5	−2.4	−1.6
Southern and South-Eastern Asia	2.5	6.1	3.3
Asia Group[c]	3.2	4.9	4.5
Southern Asia[d]	2.1	5.7	4.4
East Asia[e]	3.4	8.0	0.5

[a]Preliminary.
[b]Bolivia, Chile, Colombia, Ecuador, and Peru.
[c]Indonesia, Malaysia, Philippines, and Singapore.
[d]Ceylon, India, and Pakistan.
[e]Burma, China (Taiwan), Khmer Republic, Republic of Korea, Republic of Vietnam, and Thailand.
Source: U.N. Economic and Social Council, Report of the Secretary General, *Review of Salient Features of the World Economy 1970–1971*, E/5036/Add. 3, 8 June 1971, p. 5.

Developing countries as a whole have increased agricultural output 2.8 percent per year during the past two decades, which is comparable to the increase in the industrialized nations but only slightly in excess of the annual population growth of 2.5 percent, as shown in Table 4.3. As a result, *per capita* food production in developing nations today is only slightly higher than in 1955, as Figure 4.2 indicates. Output per farm worker has increased less than 1 percent a year and output per hectare only 1.5 percent. Estimates suggest that every increase of 100 million in population requires an additional 13 million tons of cereals and more than 14 million tons of meat, milk, eggs, and fish. Although the population in most developing countries may need

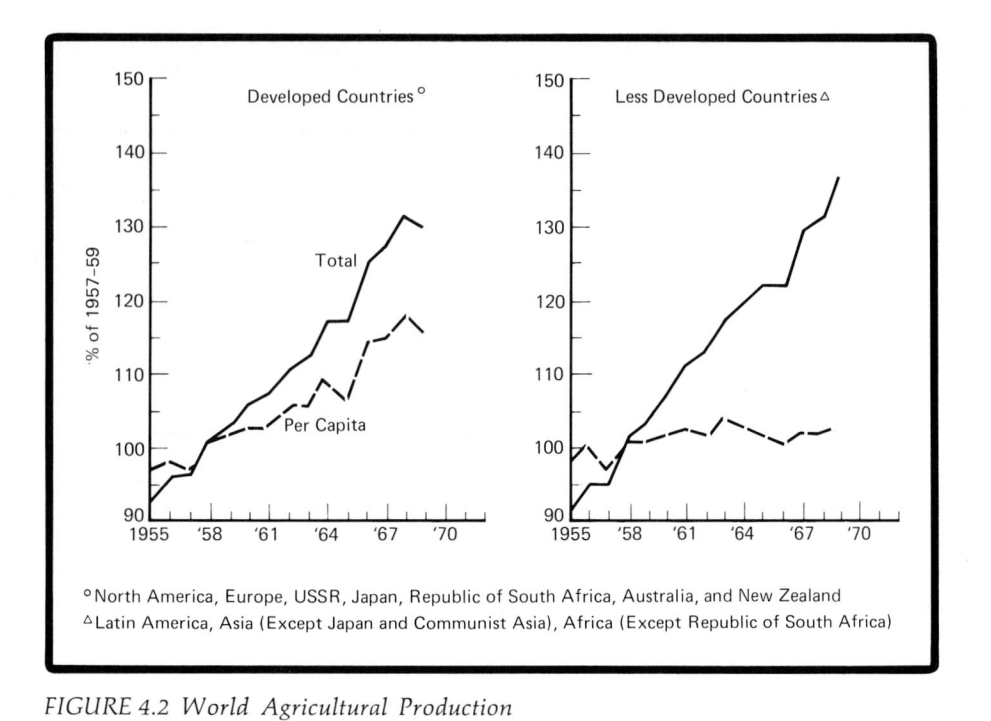

FIGURE 4.2 *World Agricultural Production*

Source: U.S. Department of Agriculture, *Economic Progress of Agriculture in Developing Nations, 1950–1968,* Foreign Agriculture Economic Report No. 59, Washington: GPO, 1970, p. 8.

only a 20 or 30 percent increase in per capita caloric intake, they require a 40 to 50 percent increase in per capita protein supply to reach Western European standards of 1960. Such an improvement in diet would require a 200 to 300 percent increase in the production of protein foods. For the developing nations to end hunger and improve the quality of diet, the total food supplies of 1960 according to Table 4.4 would have had to be increased 43 percent by 1970, 102 percent by 1980, and 261 percent by the year 2000.

Unfortunately there is no clear-cut answer to the question "What are the prospects for increasing food production in the future?" Experts differ in their opinion of our ultimate ability to appropriate enough fruits of the land for our minimal needs. Certain increases in food production can be expected through enlarging areas under cultivation and improving crop yields through intensive planting of better varieties of cereals and through the use of irrigation, fertilizers, and mechanization. Since seven-tenths of the earth's surface is under the sea, and since we now draw from it only one one-hundredth of our food, we might also turn our attention to the sea as a

TABLE 4.4 INDEX OF NEEDS IN TOTAL AND ANIMAL FOOD SUPPLIES FOR
THE DEVELOPING REGIONS, FOR THE DEVELOPING COUNTRIES,
AND FOR THE WORLD AS A WHOLE (1960 = 100)

Region	Total Food			Animal Food		
	1970	1980	2000	1970	1980	2000
Far East	143	210	386	163	296	621
Near East	146	185	295	184	232	370
Latin America[a]	145	195	345	169	225	396
Africa	133	163	272	166	203	398
Developing Countries	143	202	361	166	274	532
World	129	168	267	133	181	299

[a]Excluding the River Plate countries.
Source: U.N., *World Population Conference, 1965*, vol. III, New York: United
Nations, 1967, p. 421.

largely undeveloped source of food. The production and utilization of new
foods such as algae and synthetics are further possibilities for meeting future
demands for food as is hydroponics (soilless cultivation). In addition, improved methods of preservation, storage, and transport will surely make
much more food available to people everywhere.

THE GREEN REVOLUTION

Some experts believe that we have already embarked upon a "Green
Revolution," a period of agricultural expansion resulting from the introduction of recently developed high-yield cereal varieties. The new seeds have
been hailed as a bright hope for eliminating hunger, and in many instances
they have already increased production notably. In 1943 Mexico averaged
wheat yields of 11.5 bushels per acre. Half of the wheat needed was imported. By 1964 the average yield of the new varieties was 37 bushels per
acre, and the country had wheat available for export, despite the doubling
of the population. As a result of the new rice varieties, the Philippines has
become, for the first time in recent history, self-sufficient in rice. Also as a
result of the new grains, India's 1967–1968 food harvest was 12 to 15 percent higher than her previous best harvest.

These are remarkable improvements, but the new agricultural technology is costly and carries with it many unclear consequences. It is estimated,
for example, that with the new varietals, farmers' use of fertilizers in India
has risen more than sixfold in seven years—from 600,000 tons in 1963–1964
to 4 million tons in 1970–1971. From 1960 to 1967 the percentage of India's
total export earnings required to finance fertilizer imports alone rose from

2.5 percent to 20 percent. The high-yielding wheat costs about 60 percent more per acre to grow than the varieties it replaced, and this estimate does not include any calculation of the short- or long-term effects of increased amounts of fertilizers and pesticides on the ecological balance. But we know from our own experience what some of the effects may be. For example, water runoffs from fertilized lands carry particles of the chemicals with them, and along with pollution from industrial, municipal, and other sources befouled 29 percent of America's stream miles by 1971. Almost two-thirds of the polluted stream miles are east of the Mississippi, where population density is high and where there is greater difficulty in providing an adequate supply of safe drinking water. The *estimated* cost of cleaning up the streams is staggering; and we do not know the *real* costs of pollution abatement or the impact that efforts to cleanse the environment will have on the national economy.

Another effect of the Green Revolution—the decrease in infant mortality and the mortality of mothers resulting from better nutrition—will mean population growth. William C. Paddock has pointed out some dreadful Malthusian-like consequences of such a situation: "If the only check on population is starving and misery and you introduce another improvement in technology which increases the food supply, then the ultimate effect is to increase the amount of misery because you increase the number of people." Historically agricultural advances have touched off baby booms that have in turn cancelled out the increased supply of food. Ireland, as Paddock documents, is a perfect example.

> *The Irish population in the 17th century had more or less come into balance with the land. There were 2 million Irishmen there, living in misery. Then along came a Green Revolution with the introduction of the Irish potato from this hemisphere. Because of the potato, output per acre grew spectacularly, as did the number of Irishmen in response. The population grew to 8 million people by 1835. Then a new disease arrived in Ireland, the potato blight, which caused a series of crop losses. Two million Irishmen died; 2 million Irishmen immigrated to the United States; leaving 4 million Irishmen living in Ireland in a degree of misery and poverty as severe as in the 17th century; that is, before the whole thing started.*[6]

Of course, the modern world may avoid such dire consequences by checking population growth and by committing itself to a large-scale program of equitable distribution of increased agricultural yields. But these measures require revolutionary changes in national policies and in international relationships.

We believe, therefore, that the fundamental question concerning food production is not whether increases are possible, for they certainly are, but whether nations will organize to produce the investment funds and establish the necessary priorities to alleviate hunger. Adequate food supplies in developing nations depend upon high investment of resources and competent economic management. Victor Herer states that,

> *To attain a 3.5 percent growth of agricultural production, agricultural investment would have to equal 22 percent, and to attain a 4.5 percent increase, 29 percent of net agricultural product. This means that a 3.5 percent–4.5 percent growth of agricultural production places a heavy burden upon the agricultural income of a developing country.*[7]

Since 70 to 80 percent of the national income of most developing nations comes from the agricultural sector, plowing more investment back into agriculture is at the partial expense of industrialization, social services, and education. Such investment is crucial, however, for the importing of food— in tropical Africa, for example—where it is not absolutely necessary, is expensive and counter productive to long-range development. Developing nations will have to be largely self-sufficient in producing their own food if they are ever to reduce their balance-of-payments deficits to manageable proportions. Few new nations are as fortunate as Kuwait, whose oil income provides almost unlimited capital for imports.

It is possible to conceive of a sustained increase of 3.5 percent per year in food production against the current average increase in population of 2.5 percent. Maintained during the next fifteen years, the rate of growth in the agricultural sector would avoid a serious breakdown in the precarious balance between population and food. Yet it appears that few governments are willing to commit themselves to such a goal. Indeed in the Far East and Latin America, per capita food production in 1965 was less than before World War II. The Pearson Commission points out that the "less developed countries, which had been net exporters of 14 million tons of cereal grains each year in the 1930s became net importers of 10 million tons each year in the 1960s."[8] This is partly a result of population growth, but it is also a reflection of the social and economic values held by the political leadership in those areas. Fulgencio Batista of Cuba and Perez Jimenez in Venezuela spent millions of dollars on show projects, armaments, and conspicuous consumption while the economies of their countries stagnated and the poor became poorer.

In Latin America as a whole, only between 10 and 20 cents per farmer is spent on agricultural research, compared with 17 cents in Japan, about $5 in Western Europe, and $46 in the United States. It is equally low in most of Asia.

Furthermore, developing nations, like the world as a whole, have their internal divisions between the haves and have-nots. FAO and U.N. statistics on Latin America show that at the beginning of the 1960s, the agricultural sector was comprised of 7.5 million land holdings. No more than 1.5 percent of the population controlled 65 percent of the land. Of the 32 million people employed in agriculture, a full 30 million either had no land or had only the very smallest plot. Two million were classified as small holders, and 100,000 had almost two-thirds of the agricultural land. The differential access to land resources is one of the main reasons for rural underemployment, low incomes, and the resulting crushing migration to the cities.

The prospects for the future have been succinctly laid out by Dr. R. S. Sen, past director general of FAO. In a statement to the United Nations Population Commission on March 24, 1965, he said:

> *If a solid foundation can be laid for increasing food supplies to the tune of about double the actual rate of annual increment and this enhanced rate can be sustained over a long period; if family planning is accepted and practiced on a wide scale in the rural communities of the developing countries; if the food producing capacity of the developed nations can be fully utilized and surpluses distributed to the advantage of all and detriment of none; and if international cooperation is further strengthened to this end—the general picture of hunger and malnutrition in the world should show a distinct improvement. . . . Whether all these "if's" will be answered in the positive is another matter. But the alternative is clear.*[9]

THE THREAT OF FAMINE

In some heavily populated areas of the world the outbreak of famine and starvation is a distinct possibility in the future. In portions of Asia it is already a fact. Early in 1973, 13 million people in the Indian state of Rajashan, for example, were officially declared to be affected by drought and famine. Figure 4.3 depicts a five-year average for India. For the past six years the sub-Saharan states of Mauritania, Senegal, Mali, Niger, Chad, and Upper Volta have suffered from drought—too little rain to produce a normal harvest—resulting in widespread famine, loss of livestock, and increases in rural and urban unemployment. The erratic rainfall has been at least 10 to 15 percent less than normal years. In 1973 the River Niger was at its lowest level in about forty years, and Lake Chad had less water than any time since 1943. Livestock losses in Senegal have been approximately 40 percent of the total. Upper Volta has lost some 35 percent and Mauritania about 60 percent of their livestock. In early 1973 United Nations officials predicted that without adequate relief supplies to the affected areas some 6 million people (out of an estimated population of 25 million) might perish.

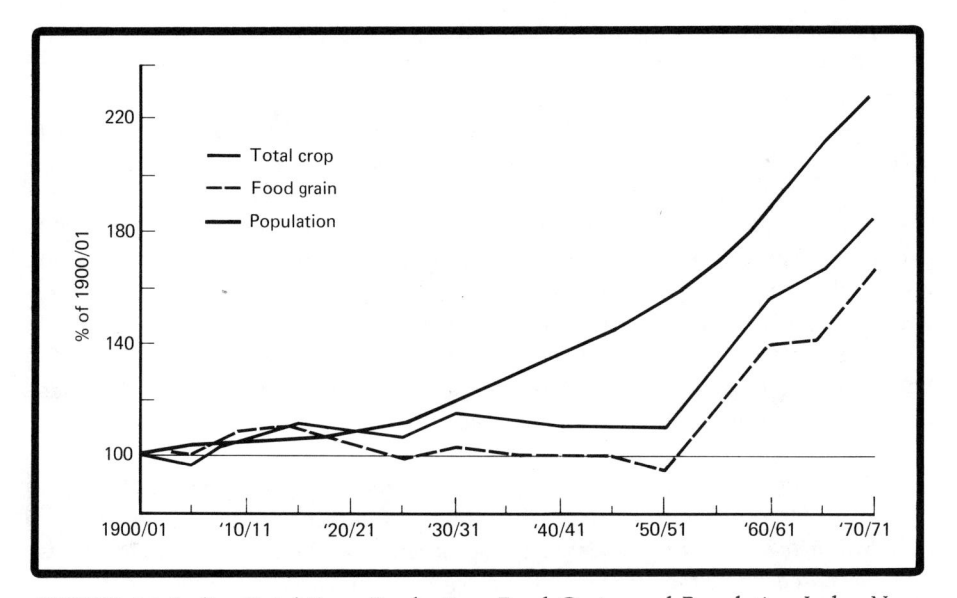

FIGURE 4.3 *India: Total Crop Production, Food Grain, and Population-Index Numbers, 5-Year Average*

Source: U.S. Department of Agriculture, *Economic Progress of Agriculture in Developing Nations, 1950–1968*, Foreign Agricultural Economic Report No. 59, Washington: GPO, 1970, p. 141.

Elsewhere in Africa similar conditions exist. In Ethiopia, for example, some 50,000 to 100,000 people died in 1973 as a result of drought—yet pleas for international famine relief were largely ignored for months. To the extent that such conditions are a result of changing weather patterns in the world as a whole, drought and famine may well continue. Although famine relief can provide a temporary palliative, it is an expensive and inadequate short-range solution. The West African nations have the grim task of developing their economies while using precious earnings just to stave off starvation. Such fragile economies will need massive assistance to recover from these setbacks, let alone to facilitate long-range development. Available national and international reserves tells us that if food production just keeps pace with population growth, the number of people suffering from nutritional deprivation and hunger will double by the end of this century. Proposals for the creation of a World Food Bank are a well-meaning and humanitarian gesture which may ease the conscience of the rich. However, such agencies would not, ipso facto, solve world problems of food supply and demand. Thus the challenge to the United Nations World Food Conference meeting in Rome during November of 1974 was immense.

FINANCING DEVELOPMENT

The financial costs of development in the Third World are met through three major sources: export earnings (about 75 percent); public loans and grants (about 15 percent); and private capital (about 10 percent). In considering these under headings of Trade and Development Assistance a qualification is necessary: They are aspects of economic growth, which is an essential but not the sole prerequisite of development.

TRADE

Since international trade is an important source of national revenue, all nations seek to expand their trade with other nations and to increase their trade advantages by selling more abroad than they buy. The major difference between domestic and international trade arises from the fact that virtually every country manages its own monetary system. Thus trade between two nations involves two national currencies and the transfer of payments from one monetary system to another. This poses little problem if the currencies are freely convertible into each other or into gold. However, most nations of the Third World have inconvertible currencies, that is, currency that is not usable in the international market because its value is maintained through strict currency control. The Ghanaian cedi, for example, is valued at one U.S. dollar within Ghana, but it is practically worthless outside the country. This means that countries with inconvertible currency must earn internationally accepted currency (e.g., dollars, pounds, sterling, francs, marks) through export in order to purchase what they need abroad.

International trade expands a nation's consumer choices by providing food and manufactured goods not produced at home. If the trade balance is favorable (that is, if exports exceed imports), international trade provides capital for domestic economic development. The export of tin from Bolivia, for example, can finance the building of schools, hospitals, irrigation systems, and so on. Yet the developing countries rarely achieve a favorable balance of trade. First, the process of creating a modern industrialized economy requires the importing of enormous quantities of costly fuels, machinery, and equipment. Second, since many new nations are not agriculturally self-sufficient, they must import considerable amounts of food as well as materials to transform traditional agriculture. Third, many new nations have difficulty resisting the temptation to import luxury consumer goods or using scarce capital on prestige items such as airlines. Finally, and most important, developing nations import more than they export mainly because they do not have many products to export.

On the whole, developing nations must rely upon one or two commodities to earn foreign exchange. Bolivia's primary export is tin, Brazil's is

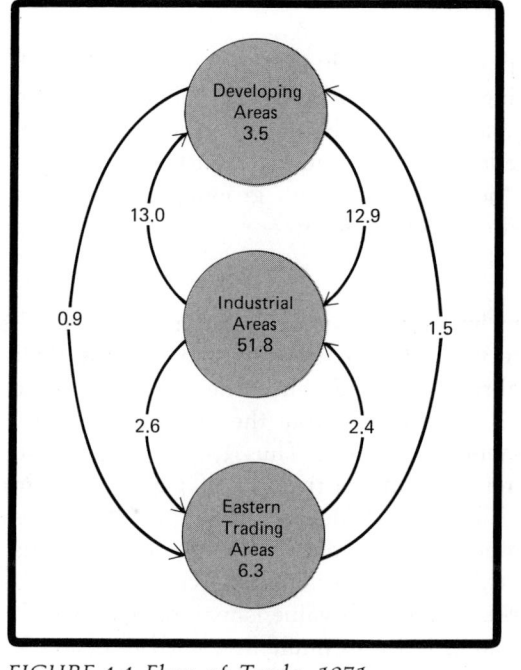

FIGURE 4.4 Flow of Trade, 1971

    Source: G.A.T.T., *International Trade, 1971*, Geneva: G.A.T.T., 1972, p. 3.

coffee, Cuba's is sugar; Burma depends upon rice, Ghana upon cocoa, and Egypt upon cotton. Exporters of one commodity are at the mercy of wide price fluctuations that are the result of variations in international supply and demand. Nations that rely upon agricultural exports are also greatly affected by variations in production. For example, world-wide demand for cocoa and market speculation in cocoa futures resulted in the following prices for cocoa on the international market: $985 per ton in 1958, $245 in 1965, and $580 in 1966. As a result, many nations that rely upon one primary export commodity have established marketing boards to regulate sales on the international market and thereby achieve some degree of price stability.

    While marketing schemes can help level out fluctuations in export earnings, they cannot alter the fact that their lack of economic diversification puts developing nations at a disadvantage in world trade.

    Figure 4.4 illustrates the relative *proportion* of international trade accounted for by the developing nations, the industrial economies of Western Europe, North America, and Japan, and the Eastern trading areas (USSR, East Europe, and China). The percentage of total world exports are calculated within and among the three trading areas. The trade flow of the devel-

oping nations has been increasingly directed toward developed countries, with the new nations importing more than they export. In fact, the proportion of exports among developing nations is gradually shrinking. Meanwhile, the developed nations of both East and West continue to be one another's best trading partners.

While international trade as a whole is expanding, the share of the developing nations has declined. The value of world exports in 1820 was approximately $567 million, in 1962 some $140 billion, in 1968 $238 billion, and in 1971 $346 billion. In 1969 the share of the developing countries in world exports amounted to $48 billion of a total $270 billion, or 17.7 percent, which was less than their 21.4-percent share of the 1960 world total. The new nations accounted for somewhat more than 40 percent of all exports of primary products and 6 percent of all manufactured goods. As some see it, they accounted for most of the hewing of wood and the drawing of water.

A U.N. Conference on Trade and Development. Recognizing that the unequal patterns of international trade will not change quickly of their own accord, the United Nations sponsored a Conference on Trade and Development (UNCTAD) in Geneva in 1964, the specific purpose of which was to consider the trade requirements of the less-developed nations. Spokesmen for the new nations argued that prices of the primary goods they exported were notoriously low in comparison with what they were required to pay for the manufactured goods they imported. To help redress the balance they asked the developed nations for special tariff preferences for their exports, as well as for international stabilization of prices. As would be expected, however, the delegates to the conference found themselves deeply split between the haves and the have-nots. Although the conference created a permanent Trade and Development Board as a forum for trade negotiations, and second and third meetings of UNCTAD were held in 1968 and 1972, little effective action has been taken toward equalizing the fortunes of the have and have-not nations in international trade.

Nevertheless, the voices of the Third World are becoming more strident. In the 1972 UNCTAD conference in Santiago, Chile, the developing nations demanded greater representation in organizations such as the International Monetary Fund, now studying monetary reforms, and in trade negotiations associated with the General Agreement on Tariffs and Trade. Likewise, developing countries called for commodity consultation and special assistance for the least-developed countries. Tensions between developed and developing countries increased when multinational corporations came under special scrutiny and attack. At the Fourth Non-Aligned Summit Conference in Algiers in 1973 and the sixth special session of the U.N. General Assembly in 1974, these economic demands were voiced along with criticisms of the developed nations' political policies (U.S. overseas bases and Indochina policy, the status

of Israel, the racist governments of South Africa and Rhodesia). The non-aligned states are slowly hammering out policies for a new era of international politics in which they are determined to make their voices heard.

Discriminatory conditions persist. A World Bank study pointed out, for example, that tariffs are higher on manufactures imported from developing countries as compared to developed countries. Tariffs also rise with the degree of fabrication—cocoa beans compared with cocoa products—and effectively impede the development of income-producing processing enterprises.[10] This condition is made particularly serious by the fact that the prospects for primary product exports are limited and only through semi- and finished manufactures can developing nations expand their trade earnings rapidly and significantly. Nontariff barriers also exist such as quotas on imports of agricultural products to protect, for example, European farmers, and constitute a formidable obstacle to increasing exports for the less-developed nations.

Without reform in the international economic system, the Third World's balance-of-payments deficit (based on 1960 prices), may amount to between $17 and $26 billion in 1975. Thus unless values change or other alternatives are found, their need for external capital in the form of loans, grants, lines of credit, and technical assistance from developed nations becomes ever greater and—at the same time—ever less certain.

DEVELOPMENT ASSISTANCE

Foreign aid—loans, grants, lines of credit, guarantees, technical assistance, food, and other goods and services—make additional resources available to less-developed nations to supplement national earnings and savings. Economic aid from one government to another and from an international body to a government originated among the Allies during and immediately following World War II. President Franklin D. Roosevelt devised the Lend-Lease scheme to allow the United States to provide supplies to countries fighting Germany (and later Japan), deferring questions of reimbursement until after the war. In 1947, when it appeared that Western Europe was on the verge of total economic collapse, which, the United States feared, would strengthen the European communist parties, President Harry S. Truman announced his government's willingness to finance the reconstruction of Europe under the European Recovery Program, popularly known as the Marshall Plan. And even before the end of World War II, in 1943, the embryonic United Nations created the United Nations Relief and Rehabilitation Administration (UNRRA) to assist with war relief and postwar rebuilding.

Since those early years, both bilateral and multinational aid programs have become a permanent feature of international relations, and they have served many diverse purposes: to assist relief and rebuilding after wars, to transfer

military and other supplies, to meet international emergencies and natural disasters, and to provide technical assistance and economic aid for economic development of the Third World. Developed countries have used aid and investment unashamedly to maintain and penetrate markets for their goods and services, to help their own businesses compete against businesses from other countries, and to protect and find new sources of materials of strategic importance. Since the late 1950s, when the winds of freedom began to blow in the colonies of Asia and Africa, the United States and the Soviet Union both have used foreign-aid programs to woo the political allegiance of the newly emerging nations. Foreign-aid programs have often been cold war battlegrounds.

Because development assistance is a recent phenomenon in international affairs, neither donors nor recipients have been able to rely upon past experience in administering the new programs, which were often ill-planned, hit-and-miss attempts to apply patchwork solutions to extensive and deep-rooted economic weaknesses. In this chapter we are concerned with the extent and ways in which foreign aid has been used to promote economic development in the Third World. The following pages present a brief description of the major lending bodies together with some examples of both the failures and successes of development assistance.[11]

U.N. DEVELOPMENT SYSTEM

Since the establishment of UNRRA, the United Nations has been involved in economic development, first assisting the war-torn nations of Europe, later through resolutions adopted by the Economic and Social Council providing expert technical assistance to member states, and finally through expansion into more general programs of assistance to developing nations. Although development efforts were sometimes overshadowed by the security objectives of the United Nations, the rapid decolonization that took place after World War II dramatically pointed up the need for development assistance in the newly emerging nations. Many argued that international assistance was far preferable to bilateral aid, as the latter was considerably more vulnerable to political jealousy and competition among both the donor and recipient nations. Yet the U.N. assistance programs have also been hindered by national rivalries, the cold war, and the split between the developed and underdeveloped nations. The U.N. financial crisis of the 1960s is a case in point, although it is not directly concerned with problems of development assistance. States such as France and the Soviet Union, among others, refused to pay assessments for peace-keeping operations in the Congo and the Middle East; others were in arrears and defaulting on payments.

In its early years, especially, the United Nations found itself short of funds for development assistance. Until 1949 the regular budgets of the

U.N. agencies were the only sources for financing development. In that year, however, an Expanded Program of Technical Assistance was approved by the General Assembly to be financed by voluntary contributions. During the next five years the annual average expenditures were about $25 million. To supplement the program, a U.N. Special Fund began operation in 1959, emphasizing surveys and feasibility studies. In addition, the development effort of the United Nations is carried out through its specialized agencies (the Food and Agricultural Organization, the World Health Organization, UNESCO, and the International Labor Organization). This collection of decentralized, semiautonomous organizations has become a highly complex system, as R. G. A. Jackson describes:

> *In theory, it is under the control of about thirty separate governing bodies; in the past, much of their work in dealing with administrative problems has been self-defeating. At the headquarters level, there is no real "Headpiece"—no central coordinating organization—which could exercise effective control. Below headquarters, the administrative tentacles thrust downward into an extraordinary complex of regional and sub-regional offices, and finally extend into field offices in over ninety developing countries. This "Machine" now has a marked identity of its own and its power is so great that the question must be asked "Who controls this 'Machine'?" So far, the evidence suggests that governments do not, and also that the machine is incapable of intelligently controlling itself.*[12]

As a whole, the assistance programs of the United Nations have achieved a great deal. By 1965 the annual budget for technical assistance had grown to $50 million and was divided among four major activities: agricultural production, 21 percent; basic resource surveys and developing administrative services, 18 percent; health services, 17 percent; and education, 11 percent. During the first fifteen years the technical assistance program alone awarded 26,600 fellowships and sent 13,000 representatives to nations around the world. Moreover, the United Nations has worked in some areas, such as assisting refugees in developing nations, that have been virtually ignored by the developed countries. Table 4.5 shows the flow of U.N. resources to developing countries between 1964 and 1968. Perhaps equal in importance with financial aid and technical assistance, however, has been the world-wide attention the United Nations has brought to bear upon global interdependence and the need for international efforts to aid developing nations.

WORLD BANK GROUP

The World Bank Group consists of the World Bank itself (formerly known as the International Bank for Reconstruction and Development) and

TABLE 4.5 NET FLOW OF RESOURCES FROM UNITED NATIONS TO THE DEVELOPING REGIONS, 1964–1968[a] (MILLIONS OF U.S. DOLLARS)

Region and Agency Group	1964	1965	1966	1967	1968[b]
United Nations	199	197	244	259	314
U.N. Technical Assistance (regular)[c]	25	29	27	32	31
U.N. Development Program	89	94	121	121	155
U.N. Children's Fund	28	18	24	27	32
World Food Program	9	14	32	33	42
Other[d]	47	41	40	46	54

[a]Grants and loans less subscriptions, contributions, participations, and repayments. In the case of technical assistance of the regular programs of United Nations agencies, contributions are imputed on the basis of scales of assessment.

[b]Preliminary, partly established.

[c]Technical assistance under the regular programs of the United Nations agencies.

[d]United Nations Fund for the Congo, Office of the United Nations High Commissioner for Refugees, United Nations Korean Reconstruction Agency, United Nations Temporary Executive Authority (West Iran).

Source: United Nations, Report of the Secretary-General, *The External Financing of Economic Development: International Flow of Long-Term Capital and Official Donations, 1964–1968*, New York: United Nations, 1970, p. 55.

two affiliates, the International Development Association (IDA) and the International Finance Corporation (IFC). Each has its special functions, but all are aimed at the same objective: the promotion of economic development. Unlike many other lending agencies, which consider political, social, and cultural factors in their decisions to finance development projects, the group's funding depends almost exclusively upon economic and financial considerations.

The World Bank makes loans and credits available to its member governments at conventional rates of interest for high-priority projects designed to increase the production of goods and services and to raise standards of living. Examples include a loan of $21.3 million to Venezuela to increase the water supply to the Caracas metropolitan area and a $46-million loan to Morocco for the development of irrigation and dry farming in the Sebou basin.

The International Development Association finances similar types of projects but on easier terms. IDA loans and credits tend to be issued to countries whose per capita income is exceptionally low (below $250 a year) and who cannot meet their needs for capital through conventional borrowing. Examples of IDA projects include a $2.5-million credit to Sri Lanka (Ceylon) for drainage and flood control, a $26-million credit to the United Arab Republic for the draining of nearly a million acres of land in the Nile Delta, and various loans and credits to 16 countries that will result in an expansion

TABLE 4.6 WORLD BANK, IDA RECORD—1962–1973 (EXPRESSED IN MILLIONS OF UNITED STATES DOLLARS)

	Fiscal Year			
	1962	1963	1964	1965
World Bank				
Loans: Number	29	28	37	38
Loans: Amount	$ 882	$ 449	$ 810	$1,023
Countries	19	19	28	27
Disbursements	$ 485	$ 620	$ 559	$ 606
Repayments to Bank	104	113	117	137
Member Countries	75	85	102	102
IDA				
Credits: Number	18	17	18	20
Credits: Amount	$ 134	$ 260	$ 283	$ 309
Countries	8	9	8	11
Disbursements	$ 12	$ 56	$ 124	$ 222
Usable Resources, Cumulative	758	767	1,451	1,593
Member Countries	62	76	93	94

and/or equipping of some 627 secondary schools and specialized training schools, 52 teacher-training colleges, and 8 agricultural universities.

The International Finance Corporation supplements the activities of the World Bank by concentrating on investments in private enterprise in development member countries on commercial terms and without government guarantees. In the Philippines, for example, the IFC made a $4.5 million purchase of an $11-million debenture issue made by the Philippine Long Distance Telephone Company.

Although, as Table 4.6 indicates, the World Bank Group has gradually increased its part in the financing of development, it has a reputation for being a conservative lending institution, particularly in determining what makes a project economically and technically sound.[13]

EUROPEAN ECONOMIC COMMUNITY

Under the auspices of the European Economic Community are the European Development Fund and the European Investment Bank, both of which provide capital and technical assistance to two groups of recipients: (1) 18 independent African and Malagasy states associated with the EEC and (2)

TABLE 4.6 (*Continued*)

			Fiscal Year				
1966	1967	1968	1969	1970	1971	1972	1973
37	46	44	82	69	78	72	73
$ 839	$ 887	$ 847	$1,399	$1,580	$1,921	$1,966	$2,051
29	35	31	44	39	42	40	42
$ 668	$ 790	$ 772	$ 762	$ 754	$ 915	$1,182	$1,180
166	188	237	298	329	319	—	—
103	106	107	110	113	116	117	122
12	20	18	38	56	53	—	—
$ 284	$ 354	$ 107	$ 385	$ 606	$ 584	$1,000	$1,357
8	13	14	28	33	34	38	43
$ 267	$ 342	$ 319	$ 256	$ 143	$ 235	$ 261	$ 493
1,682	1,767	1,807	2,176	3,182	3,343	4,204	7,019
96	97	98	102	105	107	108	112

Source: World Bank, *Annual Report, 1970*, Washington: World Bank, 1971, p. 3, *Annual Report, 1973*, Washington: World Bank, 1973, p. 3.

the overseas countries, territories, and departments attached to France and the Netherlands. With the entry of the United Kingdom into the EEC, the list of recipient nations will no doubt increase significantly. The fund and the bank are supplemented by special preferential trade agreements.

The amount of assistance given annually by the EEC steadily increased since its inception in 1959, until it reached $263 million in 1971, as shown in Table 4.7. The cumulative EEC commitments, mainly in the form of grants, totaled $1444 million in 1971. Assistance has gone into infrastructure schemes (e.g., transport and communications) and into the financing of capital projects especially in agriculture. In the future the level of technical cooperation is expected to be expanded and diversified.

NON-COMMUNIST DEVELOPED NATIONS

The primary sources of development assistance are the developed nations, who not only contribute to multilateral agencies such as the United Nations but operate their own programs for aid as well. During the decade of the 1960s the economies of the Western industrialized nations grew at an annual rate of 5 percent. Barring unusual circumstances they are expected to

TABLE 4.7 NET EEC FLOWS 1960–1971 (MILLIONS U.S. DOLLARS)

	1960	1961	1962	1963	1964	1965	1966	1967	1968	1969	1970	1971
European Development Fund	4	16	53	65	84	103	111	104	108	114	145	153
European Investment Bank	—	—	—	—	6	12	28	39	40	45	37	31
Other	—	1	1	2	1	1	1	1	1	21	40	79
Total	4	17	54	67	91	116	140	144	149	180	223	263

Source: Organisation for Economic Co-operation and Development, *Resources for the Developing World, Paris,* OECD, 1970, p. 226. *Ibid.,* 1973, p. 370.

continue growing by about 5.3 percent a year during the 1970s. These nations clearly have the capacity to assist others while they themselves enjoy ever greater prosperity.

Bilateral assistance has greatly outweighed multilateral programs, and the total amount of aid from the developed nations as a whole increased each year in the 1960s—Tables 4.8 and 4.9 illustrate. At the same time, however, the *proportion* of their gross national products devoted to foreign aid actually *declined* between 1961 and 1971. The percentage of official and private resources combined dropped from .95 percent to .83 percent—Table 4.10 illustrates. Government-sponsored aid totaled .53 percent of GNP in 1961, but only .35 percent in 1971. Thus even though more money in absolute terms is being provided for the less-developed nations, it does not match economic growth in the developed nations. As the rich are getting richer, they offer proportionately less assistance to those who need it.

Table 4.11 gives some perspective on the relative priority of development assistance programs within the context of national expenditures and compares defense costs and development assistance among members of the Development Assistance Committee of the Organisation for Economic Co-operation and Development. As the table indicates, we live in a world in which defensive shields are a paramount concern. If defenses were lowered and even a small proportion of the reclaimed resources were funneled into programs enhancing social justice, the potential for social peace would most likely increase. Few developed nations are against this notion *in principle,* but the matter usually ends there.

THE UNITED STATES

Since large-scale development assistance began in the 1940s with the European recovery programs, more than 130 countries have received U.S. aid, with the prepondenance going to treaty allies. Between 1948 and 1971, American economic and military aid totaled approximately $150 billion. Even

TABLE 4.8 NET FLOW[a] OF FINANCIAL RESOURCES FROM DAC COUNTRIES, 1961–1971 (NET DISBURSEMENTS, 3 MILLION)

	1961	1962	1963	1964	1965	1966	1967	1968	1969	1970	1971
I. Official Development Assistance	5,197	5,442	5,770	5,957	5,916	6,003	6,552	6,316	6,622	6,840	7,718
1. Bilateral grants and grant-like flows	3,991	4,020	3,940	3,806	3,714	3,701	3,578	3,344	3,250	3,323	3,646
of which:											
Technical Assistance	(778)	747	871	954	1,063	1,233	1,314	1,467	1,528	1,532	1,690
2. Bilateral loans at concessional terms	685	911	1,463	1,746	1,854	1,966	2,238	2,289	2,324	2,393	2,785
3. Contributions to multilateral institutions	521	511	367	405	348	336	736	683	1,047	1,124	1,287
II. Other Official Flows	946	542	245	−41	283	428	508	731	570	1,144	1,279
1. Bilateral	716	527	248	−33	278	375	488	741	585	871	1,012
2. Multilateral	230	15	−3	−7	5	53	20	−10	−15	273	267
III. Private Flows	3,106	2,453	2,557	3,729	4,121	3,959	4,381	6,377	6,587	7,019	8,399
1. Direct investment	1,829	1,495	1,603	1,572	2,468	2,179	2,105	3,043	2,910	3,557	4,087
2. Bilateral portfolio and other	614	147	327	837	655	480	800	971	1,211	777	804
3. Multilateral portfolio[b]	90	239	−33	461	247	175	469	767	419	474	706
4. Export credits[c]	573	572	660	859	751	1,124	1,007	1,596	2,047	2,211	2,802
IV. Grants by Private Voluntary Agencies										855	890
Total Net Flow	9,249	8,437	8,572	9,645	10,320	10,390	11,441	13,425	13,779	15,858[d]	18,285[d]

[a] Gross disbursements minus amortization receipts on earlier lending.
[b] Though these funds are of private origin, they are used by multilateral financial institutions together with those provided under I.3 and II.2 and other funds from non-DAC sources, in programmes governed by criteria similar to those applied in bilateral official development assistance programmes.
[c] Measured by some countries as change in outstanding amounts guaranteed, by others as change in outstanding amounts due on disbursed credits. Interest is included in the sums recorded as outstanding, so that the net flow tends to be overstated if gross new guarantees are arising, and vice versa.
[d] Including grants by private voluntary agencies.

TABLE 4.9 TOTAL FLOWS: THE NET FLOW OF TOTAL OFFICIAL AND PRIVATE
FINANCIAL RESOURCES TO LESS-DEVELOPED COUNTRIES AND MULTI-
LATERAL AGENCIES, 1961–1971
(DISBURSEMENTS, MILLION U.S. DOLLARS)

Countries	1961	1962	1963	1964	1965
Australia	70.9	73.8	96.9	118.8	144.5
Austria	20.2	31.0	5.9	21.3	47.3
Belgium	163.9	118.2	174.7	164.3	220.9
Canada	87.0	109.6	130.5	141.8	169.3
Denmark	33.3	14.7	10.5	31.8	15.2
France	1,406.3	1,395.2	1,242.0	1,360.4	1,299.4
Germany	847.1	609.4	620.7	706.4	734.6
Italy	257.5	390.4	321.1	236.8	265.5
Japan	381.4	286.2	267.4	289.8	485.5
Netherlands	200.3	114.2	134.4	118.4	238.8
Norway	26.9	6.8	21.5	23.0	38.4
Portugal	43.8	40.8	51.1	61.9	30.5
Sweden	51.9	37.3	53.4	67.2	72.7
Switzerland	210.6	161.1	202.8	110.1	191.9
United Kingdom	899.0	743.9	720.8	918.8	1,032.0
United States	4.549.1	4,304.5	4,518.6	5,274.4	5,333.2
Total DAC countries	9,249.2	8,437.1	8,572.3	9,645.2	10,319.7

though bilateral outweighs multilateral assistance by a 10-to-1 ratio, the
United States has always been the largest single contributor to multinational
agencies working for development. American funds account for almost one-
half of all development assistance available to developing countries. Yet
official American aid in 1971 still amounted to less than four-tenths of 1
percent of the gross national product and less than 1 percent of the governmental budget.

Since 1961 American aid programs have been administered by three
agencies: The Agency for International Development (AID), the Peace Corps,
and the Export-Import Bank. A fourth channel—interagency in character—
is the Food for Peace program, and food aid accounted for nearly one-third
of official flows between 1963 and 1968. American aid has ranged around
the world, although in the past few years AID has concentrated on a more
limited number of recipient countries. Aid to Asia has increased partly as a
result of the Vietnam War; aid to Europe and Africa has diminished.

In the past about 90 percent of all capital assistance granted by the
United States was tied to purchases in America, and although this has

TABLE 4.9 (*Continued*)

1966	1967	1968	1969	1970[a]	1970[b]	1971[b]
150.5	193.7	205.5	232.1	404.6	420.3	493.2
49.2	47.9	73.7	80.7	92.5	96.1	93.1
178.0	164.4	243.0	257.3	293.8	308.6	317.4
266.7	271.9	307.6	364.1	578.5	626.4	758.3
21.3	24.8	83.2	151.0	82.6	85.6	138.3
1,319.7	1,341.3	1,720.3	1,710.0	1,828.3	1,834.6	1,636.1
788.5	1,145.4	1,663.4	2,028.3	1,409.3	1,487.1	1,915.2
631.6	287.3	550.4	847.7	676.9	681.9	870.8
625.1	797.5	1,049.3	1,263.1	1,821.0	1,823.9	2,140.5
254.1	228.2	275.5	369.2	451.4	456.6	590.2
17.1	30.2	58.8	75.2	62.8	66.7	64.6
39.7	79.4	48.1	97.6	70.0	70.8	147.0
108.0	120.7	128.8	212.1	204.1	229.3	243.5
109.5	135.5	238.8	119.0	126.3	137.2	245.4
911.0	803.0	760.9	1,146.2	1,245.0	1,278.6	1,586.8
4,920.1	5,769.5	6,017.5	4,825.0	5,656.0	6,254.0	7,045.0
10,390.1	11,440.7	13,424.8	13,778.6	15,003.1	15,857.7	18,285.4

[a]Excluding grants by voluntary agencies.
[b]Including grants by voluntary agencies.
Source: Organisation for economic Co-operation and Development, *Development Co-operation*, Paris: OECD, 1972, p. 214.

changed, the terms of assistance have hardened—loans have replaced grants, and repayment in dollars rather than in local currencies has become the general rule. Local currency loans were discontinued at the end of 1971, allegedly as a result of America's growing balance-of-payment difficulties. (However, to the extent that aid-financed goods are purchased in the United States, foreign aid results in increased exports, and the balance-of-payment drain is reduced.)

American loans to developing countries carry with them numerous statutory requirements, some based on common sense, some on friend-foe principles. There must be formal assessments of the impact of the loan on the recipient country's economy, the viability and profitability of the project or program, the likelihood of repayment, and the attitude of the country toward private investment. Loans generally require the recipient country to

TABLE 4.10 TOTAL FLOWS AND NATIONAL PRODUCT: THE NET FLOW OF TOTAL OFFICIAL AND PRIVATE FINANCIAL RESOURCES IN RELATION TO GROSS NATIONAL PRODUCT,[a] 1961–1971 (PERCENTAGES)

Countries	1961	1962	1963	1964	1965	1966	1967	1968	1969	1970[b]	1970[c]	1971[c]
Australia	0.44	0.43	0.51	0.57	0.64	0.63	0.74	0.73	0.74	1.18	1.22	1.27
Austria	0.30	0.43	0.08	0.25	0.51	0.49	0.44	0.65	0.63	0.65	0.67	0.56
Belgium	1.35	0.91	1.24	1.04	1.29	0.97	0.84	1.17	1.12	1.17	1.23	1.09
Canada	0.23	0.28	0.31	0.31	0.33	0.47	0.45	0.46	0.50	0.70	0.76	0.82
Denmark	0.50	0.20	0.13	0.35	0.15	0.19	0.20	0.67	1.08	0.53	0.55	0.80
France	2.10	1.86	1.48	1.46	1.30	1.22	1.15	1.35	1.22	1.24	1.24	1.00
Germany	1.02	0.68	0.65	0.67	0.64	0.64	0.92	1.23	1.32	0.76	0.80	0.88
Italy	0.66	0.89	0.64	0.43	0.45	0.99	0.41	0.73	1.03	0.73	0.73	0.86
Japan	0.71	0.49	0.40	0.36	0.55	0.62	0.67	0.74	0.76	0.93	0.93	0.96
Netherlands	1.61	0.85	0.92	0.69	1.24	1.22	0.99	1.09	1.31	1.44	1.46	1.63
Norway	0.55	0.13	0.37	0.36	0.55	0.22	0.36	0.65	0.77	0.55	0.59	0.51
Portugal	1.63	1.41	1.65	1.83	0.81	0.97	1.74	0.96	1.71	1.10	1.11	2.12
Sweden	0.36	0.24	0.32	0.36	0.35	0.48	0.50	0.50	0.75	0.63	0.70	0.69
Switzerland	2.19	1.51	1.74	0.86	1.38	0.73	0.85	1.39	0.64	0.60	0.66	1.00
United Kingdom	1.17	0.92	0.84	0.99	1.03	0.85	0.73	0.74	1.04	1.03	1.06	1.15
United States	0.86	0.76	0.75	0.82	0.77	0.65	0.71	0.68	0.52	0.58	0.64	0.67
Total DAC countries	0.95	0.80	0.76	0.79	0.77	0.71	0.74	0.80	0.75	0.75	0.80	0.83

[a]At market prices.
[b]Excluding grants by voluntary agencies.
[c]Including grants by voluntary agencies.
Source: Organisation for Economic Co-operation and Development, *Development Co-operation*, Paris: OECD, 1972, p. 224.

meet certain mutually agreed upon conditions, such as shared costs and local financing. A 1966 loan to South Korea required that nation to meet five objectives in foreign exchange budgeting processes, credit restrictions, revenue collections, and domestic savings. Since the enactment of the Foreign Assistance Act in 1966, popular participation in the development process has been stressed—a new emphasis upon social and political considerations in American programs.[14]

A number of American aid programs have been highly successful. The Marshall Plan was largely responsible for the European recovery after World War II, and millions of dollars recently poured into disaster relief in Peru, Nicaragua, Bangladesh, and elsewhere have helped alleviate critical conditions. At the same time, some observers point out great deficiencies in American aid. For example, estimates suggest that as little as 2 to 3 percent of American bilateral assistance to developing countries has benefited small farmers—those persons who comprise some 75 percent of the recipient population. The number of scandals associated with aid programs are few com-

TABLE 4.11 DEFENSE COSTS AND DEVELOPMENT ASSISTANCE

Country	Defense Costs (1970)		Developmental Assistance (1970)	
	(Millions of Dollars)	Percent of GNP[a]	(Millions of Dollars)	Percent of GNP[b]
United States	77,827	8.0	3,050	0.31
Portugal	400[c]	6.3	28	.45
United Kingdom	5,767	4.9	447	.37
France	5,900[c]	4.0	951	.65
Sweden	1,129	3.6	117	.37
Netherlands	1,096	3.5	196	.63
Australia	1,127	3.4	203	.59
Norway	375[c]	3.4	37	.33
West Germany	6,103	3.3	599	.32
Belgium	695	2.8	120	.48
Italy	2,499	2.7	147	.16
Canada	1,906	2.4	346	.43
Denmark	368	2.3	59	.38
Switzerland	413	2.0	39	.14
Austria	165[c]	1.2	19	.13
Japan	1,582	.8	458	.23

[a]*Source:* Economic Data Book for Countries of Europe, Statistics and Report Division, Agency for International Development, September 1971.

[b]*Source:* Organisation for Economic Cooperation and Development as of June 28, 1971.

[c]Indicates estimate.

Staff note: Information not available as to how much foreign assistance rendered by France, Portugal, United Kingdom, the Netherlands, and Belgium is prior to colonies.

Source: U.S. Senate, Appropriations Committee, *Foreign Assistance and Related Program Appropriations Bill, 1973,* Report No. 92-1231, 92d Cong., 2d sess. September 27, 1972, p. 5.

pared with cases of administrative ignorance and bungling. For example, AID spent some $20 million to generate rupees to assist the Indian family-planning program—a very worthy cause. But by 1971 the United States had already acquired over many years a reserve of some $824 million in rupees available for nonrestricted use.

Assessing American foreign aid is a difficult process—first, because it requires compiling accurate statistics and, second, because it is not self-evident what should be included in the category of assistance. Concerning the

TABLE 4.12 TRANSFER OF U.S. RESOURCES TO FOREIGN NATIONS

| | | Fiscal Year | |
	1971	1972	1973
Security assistance	5,705,380,000	6,236,805,000	5,932,976,000
Development and humanitarian assistance	3,017,073,000	3,479,462,000	4,191,265,000
Grand total, foreign assistance	8,722,453,000	9,716,267,000	10,124,241,000

Source: U.S. Senate, Committee on Appropriations, *Foreign Assistance and Related Programs Appropriation Bill, 1973*, Report No. 92-1231, 92d Cong., 2d sess., September 27, 1972, p. 5.

amount of aid ($150 billion) already mentioned, Senator Daniel Inouye stated: ". . . these figures represent only a fraction of total resource transfers and . . . the true cost has been at least $100 billion more than has been reflected in appropriations for new obligational authority." He points out that military expenditures outweigh developmental and humanitarian expenditures by about a 3-to-2 margin, as Table 4.12 suggests. According to the senator, what is at issue is not American generosity, but the *kind* of foreign assistance we provide.

> *As long as our foreign policy is preoccupied with military objectives we will be unable to respond as fully as we might desire for foreign development and humanitarian purposes. The choice is clear. Once we disengage ourselves from the shortsighted policy of maintaining excessive worldwide military establishments, then, and only then, can we devote more money to benevolent enterprises. . . . Too often we arm friends to fight friends, and their battles are more lethal as a consequence of our military assistance.*[15]

Since these allegations could appropriately be made regarding the "assistance" programs of most developed nations, we do not wish to suggest that the United States alone is responsible for deficiencies in international aid. American aid programs have great impact, of course, for the United States is still the most important source of international aid. We believe, nevertheless, that the context and objectives of all international assistance should be reexamined.

COMMUNIST COUNTRIES

In the absence of official statistics, evaluation of communist aid to less-developed nations is difficult and imprecise. The U.S. Department of

TABLE 4.13 ECONOMIC AID COMMITMENTS TO NONCOMMUNIST LESS-DE-VELOPED COUNTRIES (MILLIONS OF DOLLARS)[a]

	1954–1963	1964	1965	1966	1967	1968	1969	1970	1971
U.S.S.R.	3,346	698	432	1,244	269	307	462	194	862
Eastern Europe	1,023	240	534	228	88	161	430	188	421
China	414	290	109	31	49	166	110	1,079	541
Total	4,783	1,228	1,075	1,503	406	634	1,002	1,461	1,824

[a]Based on Department of State statistics.
Source: Organisation for Economic Co-operation and Development, *Resources for the Developing World,* Paris: OECD, 1970, p. 294. Ibid., 1973, pp. 398, 408.

State estimates the socialist countries' total economic aid commitments between 1954 and 1971, shown in Table 4.13, to have been $15 billion. In addition, some $5510 million was allocated for military aid between 1954 and 1967, with the Soviet Union contributing 90 percent. Grants account for only a small proportion of communist aid; the bulk consists of medium and long-term credits. Although a lag between commitments and disbursements seems typical of all aid programs, communist pledges have at times been exceptionally slow in materializing.

Concentrated in Asia and the Near East, Soviet programs are almost exclusively bilateral. India is the Soviet Union's most important trading partner in the Third World and has been the recipient of aid and assistance on some 40 projects in basic sectors such as iron and steel, precision instruments and oil, as well as in the coal, chemicals, and pharmaceutical industries, and the like. Projects include the Bhilai and Bokaro steelmaking complexes and a number of hydropower stations. The Arab Republic of Egypt is the second-ranking recipient of Soviet aid in the Third World. The most well-known project is the Aswan Dam program featuring a 111-meter high, 2-kilometer wide embankment, power stations, high-voltage transmission lines to Cairo, and an irrigation system that will permit reclamation of 840,-000 hectares of land. Soviet aid programs like those of other countries, have also been characterized by a number of mistakes such as sending snow plows to tropical Guinea in West Africa as road-building equipment.

The Soviet Union has also supplied considerable aid to the less-developed nations of the communist bloc. It is estimated that cumulative flows to Cuba, Mongolia, North Vietnam, and China amounted to nearly $10 billion between 1947 and 1968.[16] In 1971 North Vietnam alone received over $300 million in economic aid from the Soviet Union.

Economic aid from the People's Republic of China to developing nations has shown a dramatic increase since 1970. One report indicates that over half of China's estimated $5.6 billion of assistance between 1953 and 1972

TABLE 4.14 FOREIGN ASSISTANCE ACT APPROPRIATIONS, 1961–1970

Fiscal Year	Administration Request	Congressional Appropriation	Percentage Reduction
1961	2,875	2,631	8
1962	2,883	2,314	20
1963	3,281	2,574	22
1964	3,125	2,000	36
1965	2,462	2,195	11
1966	2,704	2,463	9
1967	2,469	2,143	13
1968	2,630	1,895	28
1969	2,499	1,381	45
1970	2,210	1,425	36
1971	2,008	1,734	17
1972	2,355	1,718	27

Source: Organisation for Economic Co-operation and Development, *Resources for the Developing World*, Paris: OECD, 1973, p. 330.

was granted after 1970.[17] Up to 1971, 28 noncommunist and 6 communist nations had received aid from China, with North Vietnam being the primary beneficiary. Manpower has been a major component of China's aid; for instance, about 12,000 Chinese were reported to be working on the construction of the Tanzania-Zambia railroad in the early 1970s.

AID: THE CONTINUING DEBATE

The overall flow of resources to less-developed nations appears to have reached a plateau in the late 1960s. The tables presented in the previous sections indicate the flow of resources during the 1960s. Since the totals are not adjusted for the effects of inflation, the increases are more illusory than real. The bulk of assistance came from industrialized Western nations, with the communist bloc contributing approximately 5 percent. It is interesting to note that by 1971 the amount garnered from private sources approached 45 percent of the total aid available to the Third World.

The World Bank Group contends that the developing nations could easily and profitably absorb about $3 to $4 billion more in aid annually than they are now receiving, and the World Bank is known to be conservative in such estimates. While there may be limits on the amount of aid and assistance any one country could profitably and effectively utilize, few countries have had to worry about too much money being available. Yet attitudes toward foreign aid have hardened in recent years, especially in the United States where spokesmen for both the right and left have urged the curtailment of aid programs. The right has charged that foreign aid is a "give-

away" to people who will not help themselves; the left sees aid programs as little more than a highly sophisticated form of imperialism. Both presidential requests for foreign-aid funds and actual congressional appropriations have fluctuated, as Table 4.14 indicates.

Perhaps the disillusionment with foreign assistance—on the part of donors and recipients alike—was inevitable. The great expectations of the fifties and sixties seldom took into account the amount of aid or the length of time the new nations would require to modernize. They often overlooked the cultural forces that would hinder change and the effects non-Western values would have upon essentially Western goals. At the same time, much valid criticism can be made of the assistance efforts of the past two decades.[18] Lack of program goals, bureaucratic inefficiency, corruption, and waste were prevalent features of many programs, and too often the aid by-passed the poor completely and lined the pockets of the already well-to-do elites. Furthermore, much of the so-called aid offered by the United States, including portions of the Food for Peace program and much of the billions spent in Southeast Asia, were earmarked not for economic development but for nonproductive military purposes.[19]

DEBTS

Foreign aid is not a panacea for economic development. Yet the fact remains that the Third World must continue to borrow, to receive grants, and to lure private investment if economic growth is to be realized. Even with the aid they have already received, the indebtedness of the less-developed nations has grown at an average compound rate of 14 percent a year. Their outstanding debt has doubled every five years since 1955. The public debt outstanding at the end of 1971—see Table 4.15—amounted to over $79 billion.

Loans, of course, carry with them interest and other service charges. Table 4.16 compares the interest charges of various lending bodies. Debt service, which includes both amortization of principal and payment of interest, rose to $5.8 billion in 1970 as Table 4.17 indicates. Over the past decade the rate of growth of both debt outstanding and debt service has been almost twice the rate of growth of export earnings and almost three times that of gross domestic product.

The nations of Latin America account for by far the largest share of debt outstanding, more than 31 percent of the world total. The major debtors are a relatively few countries, some of which are included in Table 4.18. Nineteen nations accounted for three-fourths of the debt outstanding at the end of 1968.

Of the public debts in 1971, 49 percent was owed to official bilateral

TABLE 4.15 EIGHTY-ONE DEVELOPING COUNTRIES—EXTERNAL PUBLIC DEBT OUTSTANDING BY AREA, 1965–1971 (U.S. $ MILLIONS)

	Africa	East Asia[a]	Middle East[b]
Total Debt Outstanding			
End of Year			
1965	6,698.4	3,891.7	2,496.5
1966	7,476.6	4,380.6	3,083.9
1967	8,085.3	5,261.7	3,983.9
1968	8,853.1	6,293.4	4,683.5
1969	9,395.7	7,762.7	5,449.1
1970	10,865.0	9,217.6	7,022.1
1971	11,922.3	11,217.0	8,899.6
1971—at December 31, 1971,			
Exchange Rates			
Disbursed	8,355.5	7,900.5	5,582.9
Undisbursed	3,566.8	3,316.5	3,316.7
Total	11,922.3	11,217.0	8,899.6
1971—at March 31, 1973,			
Exchange Rates			
Disbursed	8,690.0	8,264.1	5,693.4
Undisbursed	3,691.3	3,401.3	3,329.4
Total	12,381.3	11,665.5	9,022.7

	Africa	East Asia	South Asia	Middle East
(At March 1973 Exchange Rates)				
Bilateral official	7,313.2	6,344.4	12,025.3	3,388.4
Multilateral	2,439.9	2,238.4	3,276.3	782.7
Private				
Suppliers	1,236.7	2,047.8	819.3	1,595.5
Banks	562.8	600.0	169.1	1,051.9
Others	828.7	434.8	8.9	2,294.2
Total at exchange rates of:				
December 1971	12,381.3	11,665.5	16,298.8	9,022.7
March 1973	11,922.3	11,217.0	15,929.9	8,899.6
Increase due to				
exchange rate changes (%)	3.8	4.0	2.3	1.4

Note: Items may not add to totals due to rounding. Includes the countries listed below:

Africa—Botswana, Burundi, Cameron, Central African Republic, Chad, Congo (People's Republic of), Dahoumey, Egypt (Arab Republic of), Ethiopia, Cabon, Ghana, Ivory Coast, Kenya, Lesotho, Liberia, Malagasy Republic, Malawi, Mali, Mauritania, Mauritius, Morocco, Niger, Nigeria, Rwanda, Senegal, Sierra Leone, Somalia, Southern Rhodesia, Sudan, Swaziland, Tanzania, Togo, Tunisia, Uganda, Upper Volta, Zaire, Zambia, plus East African Community.
East Asia—China (Republic of), Indonesia, Korea (Republic of), Malaysia, Philippines, Singapore, Thailand.
Middle East—Iran, Iraq, Israel, Jordan, Syrian Arab Republic.
South Asia—Afghanistan, Bangladesh, India, Pakistan, Sri Lanka.
Southern Europe—Cyprus, Greece, Malta, Spain, Turkey, Yugoslavia.
Western Hemisphere—Argentina, Bolivia, Brazil, Chile, Colombia, Costa Rica, Dominican Republic, Ecuador, El Salvador, Guatemala, Guyana, Honduras, Jamaica, Mexico, Nicar-

TABLE 4.15 (*Continued*)

South Asia	Southern Europe[c]	Western Hemisphere[d]	Total
8,625.8	4,051.8	11,701.4	37,465.6
10,286.4	4,282.8	13,033.8	42,544.0
11,082.3	5,098.8	14,851.8	48,363.8
12,453.8	5,621.4	16,924.9	54,830.0
13,419.2	6,329.0	18,525.7	60,881.5
14,942.2	6,965.8	20,297.6	69,310.2
15,929.9	8,196.8	23,052.5	79,218.0
13,203.2	5,914.7	17,388.8	58,345.6
2,726.6	2,282.1	5,663.7	20,872.5
15,929.9	8,196.8	23,052.5	79,218.0[e]
13,559.3	6,241.9	18,010.1	60,458.8
2,739.6	2,361.8	5,723.0	21,246.3
16,298.8	8,603.7	23,733.1	81,705.2[e]

Southern Europe	Western Hemisphere	Total at Exchange Rates of:		Increase Due to Exchange Rate Changes (%)
		March 1973	Dec. 1974	
4,342.8	6,811.6	40,225.5	39,080.5	2.9
1,779.2	6,338.8	16,855.3	16,142.1	4.4
542.2	4,783.8	10,935.3	10,565.2	3.5
1,254.4	2,800.9	6,529.1	6,311.1	3.4
685.2	2,908.1	7,160.0	7,119.2	0.6
8,193.7	23,733.4	81,705.2	—	3.1
8,606.8	23,052.5	—	79,218.0	—
5.0	3.0	3.1	—	—

agua, Panama, Paraguay, Peru, Trinidad and Tobago, Uruguay, Venezuela.

[a]Does not include publicly-guaranteed private debt of the Philippines estimated at $439 million in 1971.

[b]Does not include undisbursed portion of the debt of Israel for the years 1965–1970.

[c]Does not include non-guaranteed debt of the "social sector" of Yugoslavia contracted after March 31, 1966.

[d]Debt outstanding of Brazil includes some non-guaranteed debt of the private sector to suppliers, excludes the undisbursed portio nof suppliers' credits and of bilateral official loans except for those owed to the U.S. Government.

[e]Includes $5,134 million of loans payable in multiple currencies, and $4,197 million undisbursed on IBRD loans which are shown at book value. For both of these, information on the currencies to be repaid is not available.

Source: World Bank, *Annual Report 1973*, Washington: World Bank, 1973, pp. 12–13, 87.

TABLE 4.16 AVERAGE TERMS OF EXTERNAL FINANCING RECEIVED BY DEVELOPING COUNTRIES, 1967–1969 (GROSS DISBURSEMENTS)

	Interest Rate (%)	Maturity (Years)	Grace Period (Years)	Grant Element (%)[a]
Private Financial Credits	6.8	6	2	13.9
Bonds and Other Private	7.0	10	4	14.6
Private Suppliers' Credits	6.0	9	2	16.1
DAC "Other Official"	6.0	12	3	20.1
Multilateral Loans	5.6	25	5	32.0
Sino-Soviet Bilateral	2.0	16	3	46.0
DAC "Official Development"	2.0	34	8	66.6
Grants	—	—	—	100.0

[a]Discounted at 10%. The 10% discount rate, though arbitrary, has become customary in comparisons of terms of aid by DAC. The "grant" concept is not intended to imply that private capital flows on commercial terms involve a concessionary element. Moreover, when comparing terms of lending from various sources, the interest rate differential is not the only criterion, and other aspects, such as aid tying and price differences, should be taken into consideration.

Source: World Bank, *Annual Report, 1971,* New York: World Bank, 1971, p. 48.

creditors such as the United States and France, 20 percent to multilateral lending agencies such as the World Bank Group and regional development banks, and some 30 percent to private creditors. Between 1967 and 1971 debts to official bilateral and multilateral sources increased 63 percent, and debts to private sources increased 80 percent. In a word, the poor owe the rich. And the rich profit from interest payments and from the economic influence their capital represents abroad. The Third World believes that the size of its debts and the interest charges it pays are exorbitant and it has repeatedly called for a rescheduling of payments, a renegotiation of terms, and the establishment of more liberal lending policies for the future. Less-developed states have also argued for the creation of international funding agencies to finance development on easier terms than the World Bank Group. The net effect of their efforts has not been dramatic, although the World Bank Group has eased its requirements to some degree.

The international economic system is at a point of crisis. If the total amount of foreign aid decreases and the terms remain the same or tighten and if debts and debt service payments continue to increase as rapidly in the future as they have in the past, the entire process of economic development is in serious jeopardy. What is at stake is ever greater economic

TABLE 4.17 DEBT SERVICE PAYMENTS ON EXTERNAL PUBLIC DEBTS OF 80 DEVELOPING NATIONS, 1965–1970 (MILLIONS OF U.S. DOLLARS)

Debt Service Payments During	
1965	3,477.1
1966	3,831.2
1967	4,011.7
1968	4,525.1
1969	4,997.4
1970	5,889.5

Source: World Bank, *Annual Report, 1972,* New York: World Bank, 1972, p. 86.

polarization between rich and poor, with all the bitterness and envy and distrust such incredible disparities generate.

Establishing Priorities. What is at issue is the will of the rich to assist the poor; not their ability to do so. The foreign-aid contributions of both the United States and the Soviet Union total less than 0.1 percent of their respective gross national products. The Pearson Commission as well as various U.N. agencies have recommended the establishemnt of world-wide foreign-aid targets for the next decade. They suggest that the developed countries expand the net flow of financial assistance—see Figures 4.5 and 4.6 —to 1 percent of their own gross national products, of which three-fourths should be in the form of public, or governmental, funds.

Many experts believe that amount of assistance, together with more liberal trade terms and serious Third World efforts to limit the birth rate, would make it possible for developing nations to attain an annual growth rate of 6 percent. "A growth rate of 6 percent per year," according to the Pearson Commission, "would transform the economic outlook in developing countries."[20] More than that, it would hasten growth on a self-sustaining and long-term basis and eventually liquidate the need for much of the aid. Estimates suggest that a 1-percent increase in exports would equal a 7-percent increase in foreign assistance.

Looked at another way, total world aid in 1968 was approximately $13.4 billion compared with the $35 billion the developed nations spent on liquor alone,[21] or with the $80 billion the United States spent on defense. The 1-percent goal could fit into national priorities without hardship and would raise the flow of resources from $13.4 billion to at least $23 billion in 1975.[22] In order for even such a slight adjustment in priorities to take place, however, nations must come to believe, in the words of the Pearson Com-

TABLE 4.18 EXTERNAL DEBT OUTSTANDING (BILLIONS OF U.S. DOLLARS)

	1963	1965	1968	1970	1971
India	4.60	6.25	7.73	9.23	9.95
Brazil	2.22	3.04	4.31	3.80	5.23
Pakistan	1.23	2.07	3.26	4.30	4.61
Mexico	1.63	2.05	3.04	3.79	4.24
Argentina	2.26	1.96	2.22	2.45	2.90
Turkey	1.04	1.32	1.96	2.62	2.98
Chile	0.99	1.22	1.84	2.50	2.63
Nigeria	0.25	0.61	0.58	0.68	0.85

Source: World Bank, *Annual Report*, New York: World Bank, various years.

mission, that "concern with improvement of the human condition is no longer divisible."[23]

INTERNAL ASPECTS OF DEVELOPMENT

There is an internal as well as an international context to economic and social development. Decisions made within the nations of the Third World will largely determine what impact, if any, foreign assistance will have upon the well-being of these states. The Pearson Commission has noted:

> *Stable development would seem to require a more equitable distribution of wealth and a greater degree of participation in political and economic life than has so far been characteristic of many developing countries. Without popular commitment and participation, the sacrifices that will be necessary for development will not be easily borne.*[24]

The rising expectations among citizens of many new nations place an onerous burden upon their leaders. Inevitably, there is conflict between those segments of the population wedded to tradition and those representing change, and the result is often political instability. Since in many new nations the rules of political life are still undefined or vague, power often belongs to those who grab it. Among the states of sub-Saharan Africa, over two-thirds have experienced military coups d'état since independence. In December 1972 the tiny Latin American state of Honduras witnessed its 137th coup d'état in 151 years.

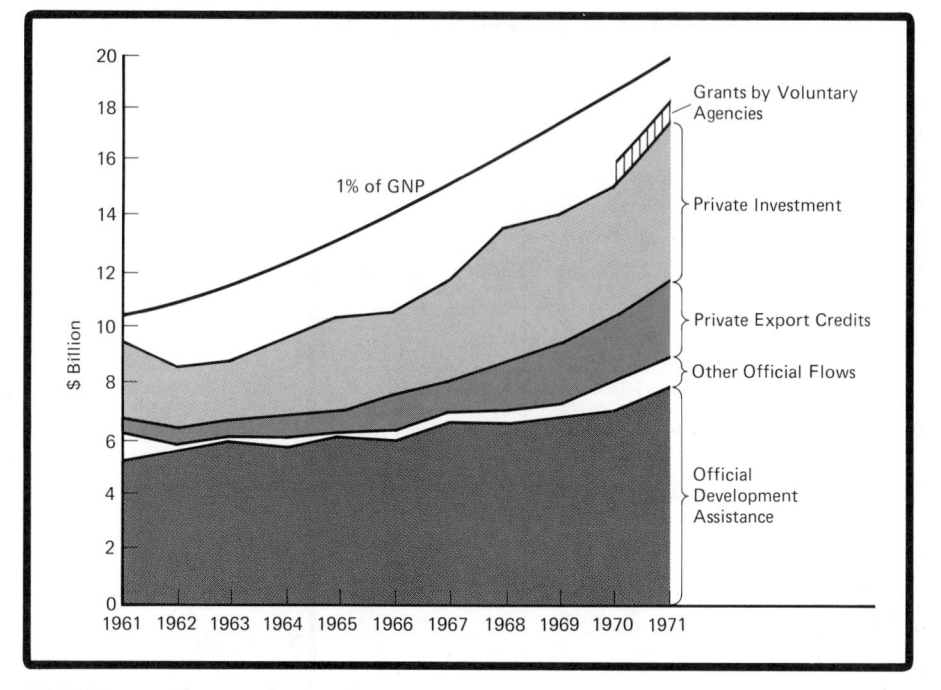

FIGURE 4.5 *The Total Net Flow of Financial Resources from DAC Countries to Developing Countries and Multilateral Agencies, 1961–1971*

Source: Organisation for Economic Co-operation and Development, *Development Co-operation,* Paris: OECD, 1972, p. 44.

Scholars document a positive correlation between low socioeconomic development and political instability and low socioeconomic development and violence.[25] When development moves hand in hand with expectations, instability may be minimized. But when expectations are high and achievements low, any society is ripe for political violence and revolution. As James C. Davies points out:

> *Revolutions are most likely to occur when a prolonged period of objective economic and social development is followed by a short period of sharp reversal. The all-important effect on the minds of people in a particular society is to produce, during the former period, an expectation of continued ability to satisfy needs—which continue to rise—and, during the latter, a mental state of anxiety and frustration when manifest reality breaks away from anticipated reality. The actual state of socioeconomic development is less significant*

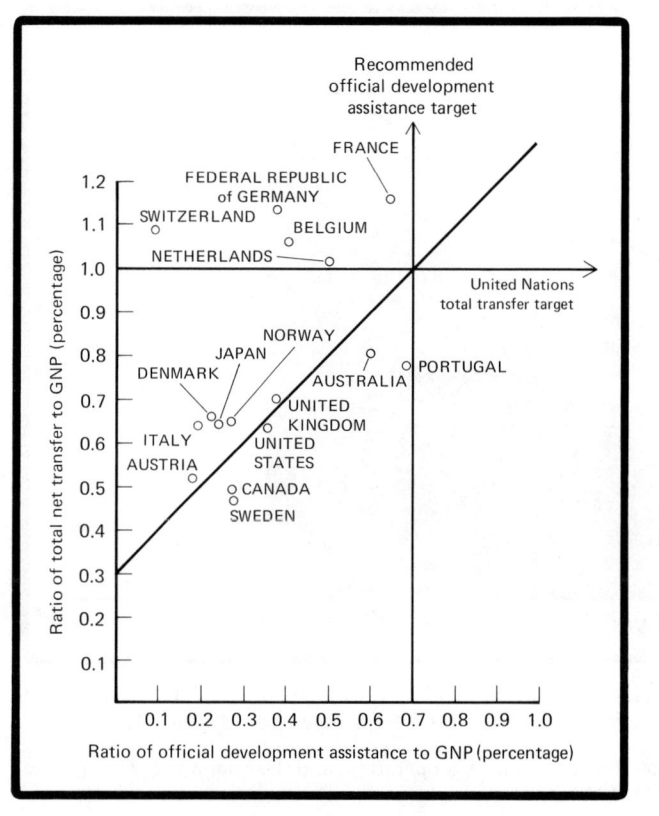

FIGURE 4.6 *Developed Market Economies: Ratios to Gross National Product of Total Net Transfers and Official Development Assistance, 1968*

Source: U.N. Department of Economic and Social Affairs, *The External Financing of Economic Development*, New York, United Nations, 1970, p. 21.

than the expectation that past progress, now blocked, can and must continue in the future. Political stability and instability are ultimately dependent on a state of mind, a mood, in a society.[26]

Leaders of the developing nations have important choices to make. They must decide along which of several possible routes to development they will lead their people. They may follow the path of least resistance and strive to build commodity-ridden cultures following the Western example. Or they may embrace the Soviet or Chinese models and institute a forced march toward modernization, channeling resources into heavy industry at the expense of consumer goods. Fidel Castro chose such a program for Cuba. Development imposed from the top is costly in terms of maximiz-

ing individual freedom, but it is appealing to nations in a hurry to modernize, for more "democratic" methods are undoubtedly slower and sometimes less efficient. Or leaders of less-developed nations may choose, as many Latin American leaders have chosen, to build elitist regimes in which a few enjoy the fruits of modernization and industrialization while the masses are relegated to lives of bare subsistence. One study calculated that if the richest 5 percent of Latin Americans were to reduce their per capita consumption from its present level of *15 times above* the average to a level of only 9 times higher, the increase in investment thus made possible could raise the annual growth rate for the continent as a whole from 1 percent to 4 percent.[27]

There is little consensus among experts—politicians or social scientists —on the best strategy for fostering development.[28] Some favor a gradualist approach, a natural development of society and economy to productive power over time. Others argue that more vigorous activity must be engaged if capital is to be accumulated in sufficient quantities to overcome corresponding increases in population and expectations. Marxists and neo-Marxists contend that socialist planning is the best means to eradicate poverty and avoid capitalist exploitation. As yet, no panacea has been found, but decisions still have to be made.

In order to explore in more detail some of the choices open to developing nations we will consider three hypothetical situations. We assume that nothing has occurred to change the present international environment. The economic and political relationships between the rich and poor nations remain as we have described them, and the gap between rich and poor continues to widen.

SCENARIO I
As the expectations of the population rise, the leaders of underdeveloped country "X" use increasingly harsh measures to counteract discontent. Punitive laws are passed allowing "preventive detention" and the conscription of labor. An underground opposition develops. Civil strife appears imminent. National leaders seek aid and military assistance from a world power. The developed nation responds by sending military and police equipment and advisers to restore order, technicians to build the economy, experts to advise the civil administrators, teachers, doctors, and trained workers to provide needed skills. Private firms are encouraged to invest in the new nation, their investments being guaranteed by the patron state. Trade increases between the two nations, and "X" finds its balance-of-payments deficit growing.

Slowly but effectively, the local leaders lose the power of decision over the internal affairs of "X." Their economic dependence forces them to follow the "advice" of the external power. A modest program of development

siphons off major discontent, however, and those who speak out against the government's policies are imprisoned or driven underground. The elite enjoy some benefits of modernization while the masses receive whatever benefits happen to trickle down to them. The once independent nation has become a client of the great power that came to its aid.

Aspects of Scenario I are already recognizable in some nations of the Third World, such as Gabon and Liberia. In all such nations some degree of national independence has been sacrificed to great powers in exchange for assistance in maintaining a measure of economic and political stability. Unfortunately for the client states in such relationships, however, the dominant nation uses its influence to further its own economic and political interests while the long-term welfare of the new nation is given short shrift.

SCENARIO II

Expectations are also rising among the people of nation "Y." The leaders here are well aware that their nation is torn by internal differences and is in danger of becoming a neo-colonial state. In the face of opposition from critics abroad and from a small group of elites who have benefited from colonial ties in the past, the government embarks upon a system of economic planning designed to foster economic growth and social reform—but not at the cost of political independence.

They nationalize the major firms owned and controlled by external interests, including banks, but this policy makes it difficult for "Y" to obtain external loans and credits. They place strict controls upon imports, and nothing may be imported except items absolutely essential to the growth of the country and the physical well-being of the people. An absolute ban is placed on electric toothbrushes, hair straightener, skin lighteners, perfume, after-shave lotion, weight-reducing pills, electric can openers—and even the importation of whiskey is prohibited, which makes some government ministers grumble.

A new system of agricultural cooperatives and collectives improves upon traditional methods of farming, and the nation soon becomes self-sufficient in food, albeit without Chivas Regal. The savings resulting from adequate food production are plowed into developing more efficient and productive agricultural units so that agricultural products may also be exported.

The government invests heavily in building up the weak infrastructure, tapping new resources and diversifying the economy. A modest program of light industry is started, and the government requires that most large manufactured goods imported from abroad (e.g., automobiles) be at least partially assembled within the country by the local labor force. All timber exported from the country must be cut and dried in local plants. Outside firms are

invited to start industries in "Y" provided the government or local cooperatives own 51 percent of the stock and the entire plant is turned over to the
national government at the end of ten years. In the meantime, the government guarantees to cover any losses incurred by the foreign firm.

"Y's" stringent developmental policies keep it somewhat isolated from
the international economic community. Modernization is slow and difficult
and requires some sacrifice from all segments of the population, but the new
nation maintains its independence.

Nations such as Tanzania and Chile (during the Allende government)
that have chosen paths closely resembling Scenario II have maintained their
independence at the cost of a slow rate of development and some political and
economic isolation. Their policies of central planning, nationalization, and
strict control over the economic sector have made them slightly suspect to the
United States, their biggest potential source of aid, since such measures are
not believed to be entirely compatible with capitalist and free-trade theories.
The aid available to these nations is limited, and trade terms are harsh. In the
present international system, the road to development is long and hard for
nations that choose to "go it alone."

SCENARIO III

A third possibility for the new nations is described in Scenario III. At
present it is still entirely fantasy, based upon the notion that the undeveloped
nation's economic frustrations will eventually cause them to band together in
an aggressive posture toward the developed world. Military warfare between
the developed and undeveloped nations is unlikely, for it would pit mice
against tigers. But of course mice have been known to fight tigers in Vietnam
and in wars of national liberation from colonialism. They may do so again,
perhaps eventually with suitcase-size atomic bombs obtained through the
international black market in arms. Short of actual war, however, we find
ourselves in an international situation similar to Scenario III.

The international economic structure remains constant while the relative position of the Third World deteriorates. The developed nations depend
less and less upon imports from the underdeveloped nations and show no
signs of increasing trade with the Third World except for their own advantage. Terms of assistance become more stringent, and inflation means that
the available aid accomplishes less.

Leaders of the developing nations find themselves beleagured by discontent at home and take punitive measures against their own people. Political upheavals replace "moderates" with "radicals." The developed nations
make some attempt to subvert the most strident regimes, but for the most
part they adopt a "wait-and-see" attitude. Although the new governments
appeal to the United Nations for assistance, U.N. resources are simply in-

adequate to meet the demands placed upon them. Finally, the new nations call a Third World People's Conference out of which is born a program of economic aggression toward the developed world. As far as possible, the Third World trades only among its member states. Expatriate firms are expropriated without compensation, and aliens are summarily deported. The developed nations retaliate, and the international community rushes head-long into an economic and racial cold war.

The three scenarios represent three different prospects for the Third World—*dependency, autonomy, or mobilization.* A comparative analysis of trends and alternatives may be a prescientific exercise in conjecture, to be approached with caution, but it does alert us to possibilities. Author Helio Jaguaribe has assessed dependency and autonomy in Latin American development in an instructive way in Table 4.19. His list of "probable results" makes the point that future developments in Latin America will have an impact on the United States and international politics *and vice versa.* National models of development must include the *interactive* influences of national and international politics.

PROSPECTUS

If there are to be other more positive possibilities for the future of the new nations and the international community as well, they will have to be built upon an entirely new appreciation for the benefits to all nations of global planning, economic cooperation, and a more equitable distribution of the world's resources and wealth. The current international crisis arises more out of a failure to realize potentialities than out of any failures of our former efforts to change the international order.

Checking the procreative process, balancing population and resources (particularly food), utilizing technology, increasing productivity, creating problem-solving economic and political organizations—all are necessary to check the threats of population growth and resource depletion, to attack the conditions that account for a world polarization of have and have-nots, and to improve the quality of life for all persons regardless of national boundaries. "There are really no material obstacles to a sane, manageable, and progressive response to the world's development needs. The obstacles lie in the minds of men."[29]

Political rhetoric aside there has never been a global strategy for world development. Development is always tackled nation by nation, or occasionally by regions. As the first biennial review and appraisal of the International Development Strategy for the Second United Nations Development Decade

TABLE 4.19 DEPENDENCE AND AUTONOMY IN LATIN AMERICA: FORCES, MODELS, CONDITIONS, AND PROBABLE RESULTS

Alternatives / Factors and Conditions	Dependence (Based on Present Regime of Participation. Strategic Decisions and Factors are U.S.-Controlled or Oriented.)	Autonomy (Strategic Decisions and Factors Are Latin American-Controlled or Oriented.)	
		Reformist Way	Revolutionary Way
Leading forces	Consular and foreign bourgeoisies plus conservative armed forces plus conservative civil middle class	Nationalist military (or progressive parties) plus intelligentsia, national bourgeoisie, progressive middle class, and masses	Revolutionary intelligentsia plus radical military groups and popular forces
a. Economic model	a. Technocratic neoliberalism	a. National developmentalism with regional integration	a. Developmental socialism
b. Key instrument	b. U.S.-controlled multinational corporations	b. Public enterprise, national and regional	b. Public corporation
Sociopolitical conditions	Alliance of business and military, supported by conservative middle class; repression of intelligentsia and masses; reasonable economic growth	Prevalence of nationalists in armed forces (or electoral prevalence of progressives), supported by leading forces listed above	Precondition: general Latin American social disruption caused by continuous aggravation of present status quo for more than ten years
Political model	Colonial fascism	Varying combinations of national capitalism and state capitalism	Developmental socialism
Probable results	a. Satellite and provincial development or b. Disruptive aggravation caused by dualism; tendency toward revolution	a. National and regional autonomous development or b. Disruptions caused by conflicting parochialism and tendency toward dependence	a. No U.S. intervention: neutral socialism or b. U.S. intervention: Chinese-like revolution or multiple Vietnams constituting popular liberation wars

Source: Helio Jaguaribe, *Political Development: A General Theory and a Latin American Case Study*, New York: Harper & Row, 1973, p. 536.

stated," . . . International Development Strategy remains more a wish than a policy. It has not yet taken hold with anything like the force needed."[30] Meanwhile, the U.N. General Assembly passes resolutions calling for establishment of a new international economic order, for measures favoring the least-developed countries, for convening a special session of the General Assembly to discuss development and economic cooperation, and so on. If development were nurtured by verbiage, the entire world would be exorbitantly rich.

The Third World, in Frantz Fanon's cryptic words, consists of the "wretched of the earth" because of their poverty, their exploitation, their subjugation, and their psychological bondage to the developed nations.[31] At present the nations of the Third World seem to have no constructive alternative but to look to their own development, define for themselves what values they wish to maximize, and then do what they can to realize them without much assistance from the developed powers. Yet we believe that such a course contains considerably more threat than promise for the future. In our opinion the chance to build a peaceful world will come only when a common concern for the welfare of all people takes priority on the agenda of international politics. And that, we believe, is the critical challenge to human values in the next several decades.

NOTES

[1]Less-developed countries include the following:

Africa: Algeria, Angola, Botswana, Burundi, Cameroon, Central African Republic, Chad, Democratic Republic of Congo, Dahomey, Ethiopia, Gabon, Ghana, Guinea, Ivory Coast, Kenya, Lesotho, Liberia, Malagasy Republic, Malawi, Mali, Mauritania, Mauritius, Morocco, Niger, Nigeria, Rhodesia, Rwanda, Senegal, Sierra Leone, Somalia, Sudan, Swaziland, Tanzania, Togo, Tunisia, Uganda, United Arab Republic, Upper Volta, Zaire, Zambia.

East Asia: China, Indonesia, Hong Kong, Korea, Malaysia, Philippines, Singapore, Thailand, North and South Vietnam.

Middle East: Iran, Iraq, Israel, Jordan, Lebanon, Syria.

South Asia: Bangladesh, Burma, Afghanistan, Ceylon, India, Pakistan.

Southern Europe: Cyprus, Greece, Malta, Portugal, Spain, Turkey, Yugoslavia.

Western Hemisphere: Argentina, Bolivia, Brazil, Chile, Colombia, Costa Rica, Dominican Republic, Ecuador, El Salvador, Guatemala, Guyana, Honduras, Jamaica, Mexico, Nicaragua, Panama, Paraguay, Peru, Trinidad and Tobago, Uruguay, Venezuela.

[2]U.N. Department of Economic and Social Affairs, Report on the Committee for Development Planning, *Towards Accelerated Development: Proposals for the Second United Nations Development Decade*, New York: United Nations, 1970, p. 5.

[3]Gross domestic product is the same as gross national product except for the exclusion of net factor payments on foreign investments.

[4]Quoted in U.N., *A Study of the Capacity of the United Nations Development System*, vol. 1, New York: United Nations, 1970, p. 55.

[5]Commission on International Development, *Partners in Development*, New York: Praeger, 1969, p. 9 (hereafter cited as *Pearson Commission*).

[6]U.S., House of Representatives, Committee on Foreign Affairs, Proceedings Before

the Sub-Committee on National Security Policy and Scientific Developments, *The Green Revolution,* 91st Cong., 1st sess., December 5, 1969, p. 75.

[7]U.N., *World Population Conference, 1965,* vol. 1, New York: United Nations, 1967, p. 378.

[8]*Pearson Commission, op. cit.,* p. 32.

[9]U.N., *World Population Conference, 1965,* vol. 1, New York: United Nations, 1967, p. 284.

[10]Robert S. McNamara, "Effects of Trade Policy on Economic Development," in U.S. Commission on International Trade and Investment Policy, *United States International Economic Policy in an Interdependent World, Compendium of Papers: Volume II* (1971), pp. 315–316.

[11]The reader should be alerted to the fact that foreign-aid statistics vary considerably for many reasons including different reporting systems (e.g., allocations rather than disbursements). The tables used in the following section are for illustration of trends. For an analysis of "The Foreign Aid Number Game" see Willard L. Thorp, *The Reality of Foreign Aid,* New York: Praeger Publishers, for the Council on Foreign Relations, 1971.

[12]U.N., *A Study of the Capacity of the United Nations Development System,* vol 1, Geneva: United Nations, 1969, p. iii.

[13]Furthermore, in the minds of some the World Bank Group is dominated by the United States. Thus the governor of the Fund and Bank from Chile, Alfonso Inostroza, charged that:

> In the 22 months of the present Administration, our country has received not one
> new loan from the World Bank, in spite of having submitted elaborate projects for
> its consideration. . . . The origin of this behavior is the situation resulting from
> the decision of the Government of Chile to nationalize five private U.S. enterprises
> which were exploiting our principal copper deposits, as senior representatives of the
> Bank have informed the authorities of my country, including myself. . . . In the
> case of Chile, the Bank's management acted in a manifestly precipitate and
> prejudiced manner, long before the Chilean copper nationalization process was the
> subject of a final decision in regard to compensation. . . . In acting as it did, the
> World Bank acted not as an independent multinational body at the service of the
> economic development of all its members, but in fact as a spokesman or instrument
> of private interests of one of its member countries.

Quoted from World Bank, 1972 Annual Meetings of the Board of Governors, *Summary Proceedings,* Washington, D.C.: World Bank, 1972, pp. 55–57.

[14]The United States government also offers private investors investment guaranties on the principals and interest of loans as well as political risk insurance covering U.S. investments against currency inconvertibility, expropriation, and war damage (including revolution and insurrection). These links between government and private industry tie the latter directly to U.S. foreign policy.

[15]U.S. Senate, Committee on Appropriations, *Foreign Assistance and Related Programs Appropriation Bill, 1973,* Report No. 92-1231, 92d Cong., 2d sess., September 27, 1972, p. 7.

[16]See W. Raymond Duncan (ed.), *Soviet Policy in Developing Countries,* Waltham, Mass.: Ginn/Blaisdell, 1970; Vassil Vassilev, *Policy in the Soviet Bloc on Aid to Developing Countries,* Paris: Development Centre of the Organisation for Economic Co-operation and Development, 1969.

[17]Paul Bernetel, "The Chinese Connection," *Africa,* no. 22 (June 1973).

[18]See Albert O. Hirschman, *Development Projects Observed,* Washington, D.C.: The Brookings Institution, 1967; Denis Goulet, *The Cruel Choice: A New Concept in the Theory of Development,* New York: Atheneum, 1971.

[19]Willard W. Cochrane has written:

> In my view the causes of the ineffectiveness of U.S. assistance programs in the
> developing countries are basically three in number: (1) continued and petty
> interference on the part of Congress which has focused attention in successive
> aid-giving agencies on contractual details, accounting and reporting rather than on

program goals; (2) emphasis on combatting communism which has directed attention away from the requirements of economic development, and (3) a preoccupation with short-run crash programs which has diverted attention away from the long-run *basic development needs of the countries involved.*
"Agricultural Aspects of U.S. Economic Relations with Developing Countries," in U.S. Commission on International Trade and Investment Policy, *United States International Economic Policy in an Interdependent World, Compendium of Papers: Volume II* (1971), p. 277.

[20]*Pearson Commission, op. cit.,* p. 125.

[21]*Ibid.,* p. 140.

[22]*Ibid.,* p. 147.

[23]*Ibid.,* p. 8.

[24]*Ibid.,* p. 54.

[25]See, I. R. Feierabend, R. L. Feierabend, and B. Nesvold, "Social Change and Political Violence: Cross National Patterns," in H. D. Graham and T. R. Gurr (eds.), *Violence in America*, New York: New American Library, 1969, pp. 606–668.

[26]James C. Davies, "Toward a Theory of Revolution," *American Sociological Review*, 27, no. 1 (February 1962), 6.

[27]Raul Prebisch, "Hacia una Dimamica del Desarrollo Latino Americano," *Supplemento de Comercio Exterior, Mexico, Banco Nacional de Comercio Exteriör, S. A.* (April 1963), pp. 5–6, quoted in U.N. Department of Economic and Social Affairs, *Progress in Land Reform*, 4th Report, New York: United Nations, 1966, p. 158.

In a study of the income disparities of 39 developing countries, in which the income of the wealthiest 5 percent is measured as a multiple of the bottom 40 percent, there is a wide range of differences among countries. There are eight countries in which the per capita income of the top 5 percent is more than 30 times greater than that of the lowest 40 percent. There are 16 countries in which the ratio is less than 15 to one. [In the United States, the ratio is 5 to 1.]
World Bank, 1972 Annual Meetings of the Board of Governors, "Annual Address by Robert S. McNamara, President of the Bank and Its Affiliates," *Summary Proceedings*, Washington, D.C.: World Bank, 1972, p. 25.

[28]Among recent studies on the topic see:

Agency for International Development. *Development Assistance in the New Administration.* Report of the President's General Advisory Committee on Foreign Assistance Programs (1968).

Assisting Development in Low-Income Countries: Priorities for U.S. Government Policy. A statement on National Policy by the Research and Policy Committee for Economic Development. New York: Committee for Economic Development, 1969.

A New Conception of U.S. Foreign Aid. Washington, D.C.: National Planning Association, 1969.

Development Assistance: Efforts and Policies of the Members of the Development Assistance Committee. Paris: Organization for Economic Co-operation and Development, annual.

Partners in Development. Report of the Commission on International Development. New York: Praeger, 1969.

The Rockefeller Report on the Americas. Chicago: Quadrangle Books, 1969.

[29]World Bank, *Address to the Board of Governors by Robert S. McNamara, President, World Bank Group*, Copenhagen: World Bank, 1970, p. 23.

[30]United Nations, Press Release GA/4940, *Resolutions of the General Assembly at Its Twenty-Eight Regular Session, 18 September–18 December 1973*, December 19, 1973, p. 138.

[31]Frantz Fanon, *Wretched of the Earth*, New York: Grove, 1965.

5 MAN AND HIS WEAPONS

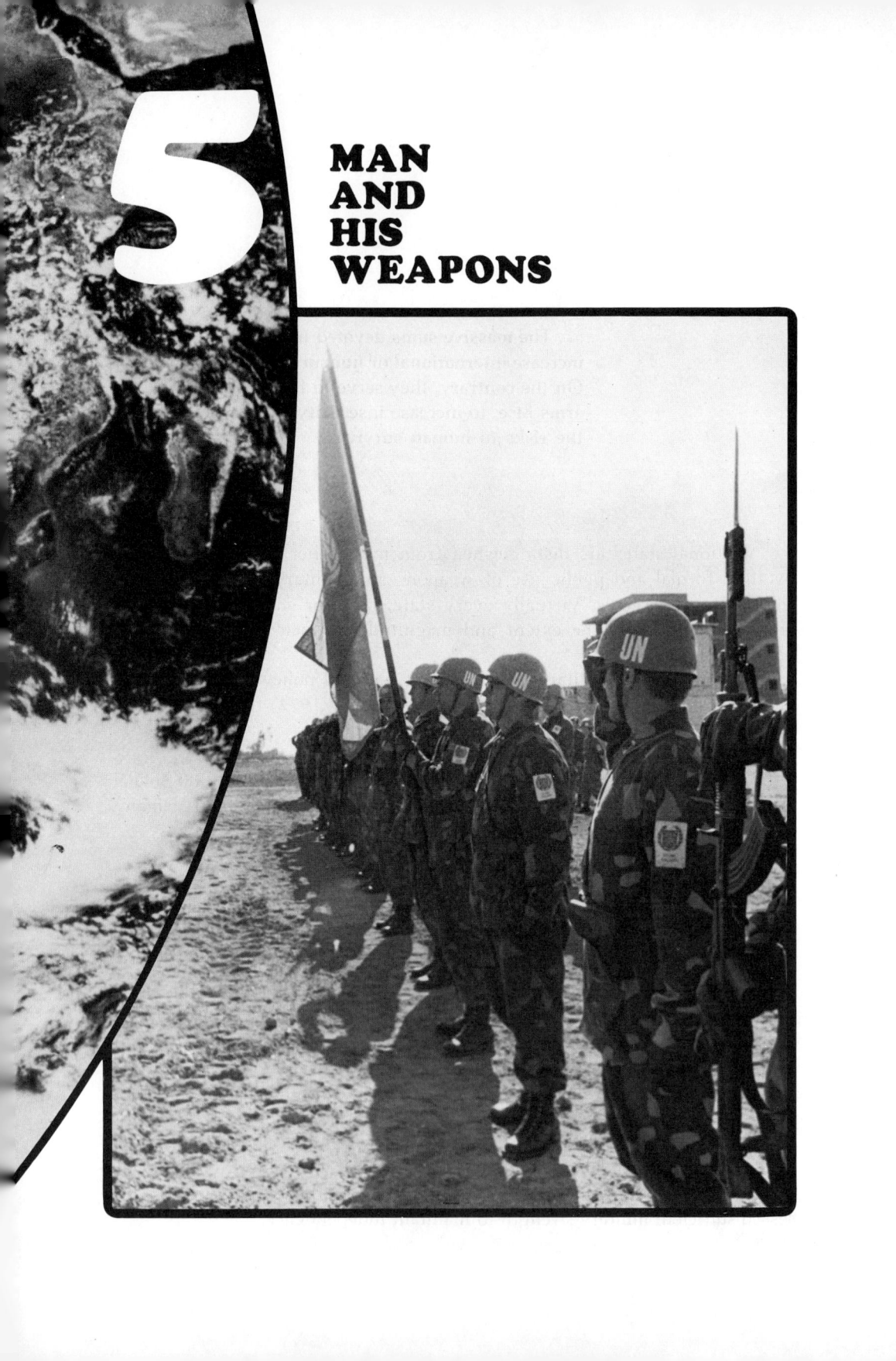

> ... The massive sums devoted to armaments do not
> increase international or human security or happiness.
> On the contrary, they serve to feed the escalating
> arms race, to increase insecurity, and to multiply
> the risks to human survival.
>
> U Thant
> 1971

National states are distinguished from most other social organizations by their formal and public use of weapons and military means to achieve and secure their goals. Virtually every state, large or small, has a military establishment.[1] Only the extent and magnitude of their military machines vary.

The role of the military as a means of national policy is self-evident in daily newspaper headlines. One day in September 1972, for example, *The New York Times* carried the following news headlines:

Uganda Reports a Tanzania Invasion; 3 Towns Said to Fall to 1,000 Soldiers
Israelis Report 60 Arabs Killed as Raids Ended; Heavy Fighting in Lebanon
    Delays Pullback by 12 Hours
British Soldier Kills a Gunman in Londonderry Catholic Area
U.S. Reports Jets Bomb Targets Near Hanoi
Arab Guerillas Are Reported to Get Direct Shipments of Soviet Weapons

On this same day, the extent of necessary military support was being debated in the election campaigns in two very different countries. In the United States there were deep divisions between President Richard Nixon and the presidential aspirant Senator George McGovern on the extent of military budget support necessary to ensure the security of the country. In the Bahamas an election was taking place in which the incumbent political party in the then internally self-governing British colony was committed to a program leading to independence of the Bahamas within a year. The opposition argued that independence could not be achieved so rapidly. The principal debate focused on the question of whether or not the island territory possessed sufficient military strength to maintain independence.

In virtually every state, large or small, independent or on the verge of achieving independence, a major issue is not a question of whether to have a military machine at all, but rather how much of the resources of the state must be committed to maintain an "adequate" military posture for security. The reality of the international system is that while food and shelter are essential for the survival of individuals, almost every state gives the highest priority to military means as essential for its survival.

THE PRESENT COMMITMENT TO WEAPONS IN THE INTERNATIONAL SYSTEM

The extent to which weapons and military establishments are a significant feature of the present international system in the 1970s is clearly evidenced by a few facts.

By 1970 the nations of the world were spending over $200 billion on military expenditures, *yearly*. The yearly amount spent on military expenditures by 1970 was "equivalent in dollar value of a year's income produced by the 1,800,000,000 people in the poorer half of the world's population."[2] By 1970, 23,819,000 individuals, yearly were serving in the armed forces of the various states at an average cost of $8,008 per person. Over 7 percent of the world's gross national product was devoted yearly to military expenditures by 1970. By the early 1970s the amount of the gross national products devoted annually to military expenditures in about half the countries of the world equaled or exceeded the annual growth increases in gross national products. As Table 5.1 shows, regardless of development level, the majority of states of the world commit a significant portion of their gross national products to military expenditures.

The military burden increases to staggering proportions during a period of increased tension or actual conflict. The October 1973 conflict between Israel and the Arab states is an example. Prior to the outbreak of the 1973 conflict, Israeli military expenditures constituted 25.1 percent of the country's gross national product. Israeli economists have estimated that the cost of the eighteen-days of conflict (October 6 to 24, 1973) cost Israel $10 million per hour or $240 million a day. The total cost for the eighteen-day conflict for Israel was $4,320 million or 78.5 percent of her $5,500,000 gross national product.[3] In addition after the cease-fire on October 24th, the tension continued, and Israel was unable to demobilize the bulk of her armed forces. From October 24, 1973, until January 25, 1974, when the Israeli forces moved back on the Sinai front to the pullback line agreed on the week before, the cost of maintaining Israeli forces was estimated at $1 million per hour. Thus from the period of October 24, 1973, to January 25, 1974,

TABLE 5.1 RELATIVE BURDEN OF MILITARY EXPENDITURES, 1970

Military Expenditures as % of GNP	Gross National Product per Capita			
	Under $100	$100–$199	$200–$299	$300–$499
Over 10%	Laos Vietnam, North	Cambodia Vietnam Republic of	Iraq Jordan Syrian Arab Republic	Albania Korea, North
5–10%	Burma Somali Republic	China, People's Republic of Egypt Sudan		China (Taiwan) Iran Malaysia
2–4.9%	Chad Ethiopia Guinea India Indonesia	Central African Republic Mauritania Nigeria Pakistan Senegal Thailand Yemen Zaire	Congo (Brazzaville) Ghana Korea, Republic of Morocco Turkey	Algeria Brazil Dominican Republic Peru
1–1.9%	Afghanistan Dahomey Haiti Niger Upper Volta	Cameroon Kenya Malagasy Republic Mali Tanzania Togo Uganda	Bolivia Ecuador El Salvador Honduras Paraguay Philippines Rhodesia, Southern Tunisia	Colombia Guatemala Guyana Ivory Coast Nicaragua Zambia
Below 1%	Malawi Nepal	Sri Lanka Sierra Leone	Liberia	

simply maintaining the strength of the Israeli forces cost $2,256 million or about 41 percent of Israel's gross national product. Israel avoided bankruptcy through the decision of the United States to grant her $2,200 million to help pay for the costs of the war, and Jews outside of Israel pledged the

TABLE 5.1 (*Continued*)

$500–$999	$1,000–$1,999	$2,000–$2,999	Over $3,000
Saudi Arabia	Israel		
Cuba	Germany, East	Czechoslovakia	United States
Portugal	Greece	Soviet Union	
	Poland	United Kingdom	
Argentina	Bulgaria	Australia	Canada
Chile	Hungary	Belgium	Denmark
Lebanon	Italy	France	Germany,
Mongolia	New Zealand	Netherlands	West
South Africa,	Romania	Norway	Kuwait
Republic of			Sweden
Spain			Switzerland
Uruguay			
Venezuela			
Yugoslavia			
Cyprus	Austria	Finland	
Gabon	Libya		
Trinidad			
& Tobago			
Costa Rica	Ireland	Iceland	
Jamaica	Japan		Luxembourg
Mexico			
Panama			

Source: U.S. Arms Control and Disarmament Agency, *World Military Expenditures 1971*, Washington, D.C.: GPO, 1972, p. 6.

state an additional $2 billion. For a state of approximately 2.9 million people these sums represent a fantastic burden for military security.

But the military burden in a conflict situation is not simply financial; it is also a human burden in terms of the lives lost and the individuals

captured. In the 1973 eighteen-day conflict 2,335 Israeli soldiers were killed. Compared to Israel's population of approximately 2.9 million people, the proportionate loss of life for the United States would have been about 168,000.[4] In other words, in eighteen days Israel lost three times the number of Americans killed over a ten-year period in the Vietnam conflict. The dimensions of a military burden such as this indicate a great disproportion when viewed in light of other social priorities.

The present commitment of the superpowers—the United States and the Soviet Union—to military expenditures is staggering. With military expenditures averaging between $75 and $80 billion for each year since 1968, the American military budget yearly exceeded the gross national products of every other country in the world—see Figure 5.1—except the Soviet Union, the People's Republic of China, the United Kingdom, France, West Germany, Japan, and Italy. The average yearly United States military budget in the beginning of the 1970s was nearly 4 times the total yearly amount of the expenditures of its NATO partners in Western Europe (i.e., Belgium, Denmark, France, West Germany, Greece, Iceland, Italy, Luxembourg, the Netherlands, Norway, Portugal, Turkey, and the United Kingdom, who together have a military budget of about $20 billion).

The military budget of the Soviet Union, averaging $45 to $55 billion per year in the same period, yearly exceeded the gross national product of every country in the world but the United States, the People's Republic of China, the United Kingdom, France, West Germany, Japan, Italy, and India. The yearly military budget of the Soviet Union at the beginning of the 1970s was greater than the total gross national product of all the independent states in Africa.

The yearly amount of money spent simply on research and development of new weapons in the United States by 1970 (about $7,800 million) exceeded the total military expenditure of France by more than $1 billion. By 1970 the yearly military budgets of the United States and Soviet Union together totaled more than the yearly combined gross national products of India and the People's Republic of China with their combined populations of 1.3 billion people.

While the developed states yearly expend nearly eight times as much for military expenditures as do the developing states, the priority commitment of the developing states to build up military power is greater, as shown in Figure 5.2. If one compares public expenditures for public health and education versus public expenditures for the military, this fact is clearly demonstrated. All the developing states of the world together spend $21.9 billion on military, about 16 percent more than they spend on public education and public health. Thirty of the developing states, however, commit more for the military than for public health and education: Spain, Portugal,

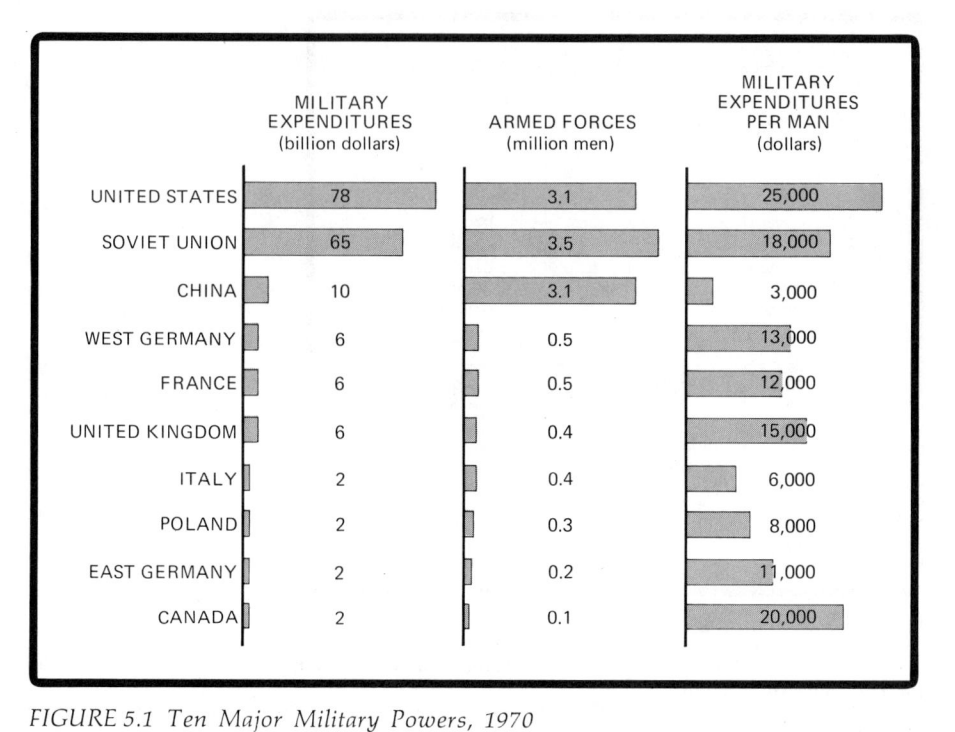

FIGURE 5.1 Ten Major Military Powers, 1970

Source: U.S. Arms Control and Disarmament Agency, *World Military Expenditures 1971*, Washington, D.C.: GPO, 1972, p. 51.

Turkey, Haiti, Brazil, Cambodia, the People's Republic of China, Taiwan, North Korea, South Korea, Laos, North Vietnam, South Vietnam, Burma, Afghanistan, India, Pakistan, Iran, Iraq, Israel, Jordan, Lebanon, Saudi Arabia, Syria, Yemen, Arab Republic of Egypt, Ethiopia, Mauritania, and the Somali Republic.

In 1970 the developed states committed more for public education and public health ($178 billion) than for military expenditures ($168 billion). Excluding the United States and the Soviet Union, the remaining developed states spent about $43 billion on the military contrasted with $52 billion for public education and public health. Of the developed states, only the United States, the Soviet Union, and France commit more resources to the military than to public education and health.

The trend of increase in arms in developing states has meant that between 1961 and 1970 the size of armed forces and military expenditures in developing states has grown three or four times as fast as in the developed states. Table 5.2 and Figures 5.3 and 5.4 show that, at the same time, the

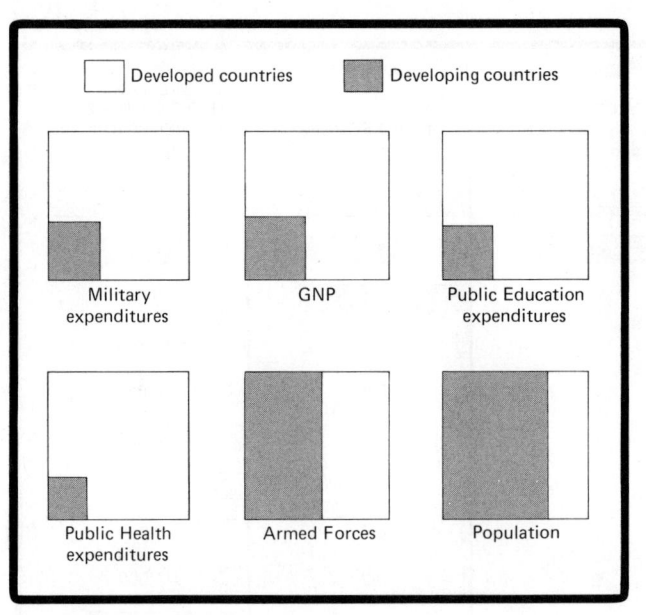

FIGURE 5.2 *Shares of World Total, 1970*

Note: Each box represents world total. Shaded portion shows percent of world total in developing countries.

Source: U.S. Arms Control and Disarmament Agency, *World Military Expenditures 1971*, Washington, D.C.: GPO, 1972, p. 5.

growth in expenditures for education and public health in both developed and developing countries has lagged.

It is difficult if not impossible to estimate what proportion of the resources of the world are consumed in military expenditures. It is apparent that about 9.7 percent of the gross national products of the states of the world are devoted to weapons systems. Weapons systems *are* a very integral element of political states.

THE WEAPONS GAME

Once a state decides to use weapons and a military system to maintain or achieve its goals, it becomes involved in an almost inevitable game with other states. A state determines the necessary amount of weapons by assessing its strength with respect to the strength of those states that it feels threaten its security. Security means having sufficient military strength to prevent one or more states from limiting another state's freedom of action.

TABLE 5.2 PER CAPITA MILITARY EXPENDITURES AND RELATED
DATA: 1970 (CURRENT DOLLARS PER CAPITA)

	Military Expenditures	Gross National Product	Public Education Expenditures	Public Health Expenditures	Foreign Economic Aid Given
Summary					
World Total	57	881	46	22	3
Developed	183	2,701	150	75	10
Developing	10	208	9	2	—
North America*	352	4,670	270	131	19
Europe	136	1,947	108	60	6
Developed	157	2,179	124	69	7
Developing	30	731	22	14	1
Latin America	10	510	15	5	—
Far East	12	290	12	1	1
Developed	15	1,907	75	4	14
Developing	12	148	7	1	—
South Asia**	3	103	2	1	—
Near East**	44	366	16	5	—
Africa	4	202	8	3	—
Developed	18	830	2	11	—
Developing	3	155	21	2	—
Oceania*	95	2,504	108	72	14
By Country					
World Total	57	881	46	22	3
North America	352	4,670	270	131	19
United States*	379	4,758	264	130	19
Canada*	89	3,651	325	133	21
Europe	136	1,947	108	60	6
NATO, European	70	2,144	93	63	12
Belgium*	72	2,640	129	67	14
Denmark*	74	3,120	178	170	13
France*	118	2,904	120	7	25
Germany, West*	100	3,019	120	156	17
Greece	53	1,067	21	12	—
Iceland*	—	2,500	100	25	—
Italy*	47	1,739	74	16	6
Luxembourg*	27	3,303	173	80	—
Netherlands*	84	2,400	158	93	17

TABLE 5.2 (*Continued*)

	Military Expenditures	Gross National Product	Public Education Expenditures	Public Health Expenditures	Foreign Economic Aid Given
		By Country			
Norway*	99	3,436	180	57	9
Portugal	45	639	9	10	7
Turkey	12	255	11	3	—
United Kingdom*	105	2,168	101	97	9
NATO total	195	3,215	168	92	—
Warsaw Pact	210	1,867	128	61	1
Bulgaria	36	1,153	43	21	—
Czechoslovakia*	114	2,103	75	68	—
Germany, East*	129	1,889	82	48	6
Hungary*	54	1,388	50	28	—
Poland*	69	1,212	52	47	—
Romania*	30	1,099	34	23	—
Soviet Union*	270	2,047	159	69	2
Other European	45	1,567	79	49	2
Albania	43	364	54	14	—
Austria*	22	1,932	89	93	5
Finland*	30	2,170	146	93	—
Ireland*	12	1,414	62	50	—
Spain	35	970	25	16	—
Sweden*	139	4,025	351	157	14
Switzerland*	67	3,254	133	81	5
Yugoslavia	33	927	29	27	—
Latin America	10	510	15	5	—
Argentina	21	989	30	1	—
Bolivia	4	208	7	2	—
Brazil	11	372	3	2	—
Chile	18	717	42	20	—
Colombia	5	335	11	6	—
Costa Rica	—	532	28	15	—
Cuba	34	612	50	7	—
Dominican Republic	7	357	10	4	—
Ecuador	4	295	13	1	—
El Salvador	3	293	11	5	—
Guatemala	5	337	6	4	—
Guyana	4	313	15	8	—
Haiti	1	73	1	1	—
Honduras	3	254	8	2	—

TABLE 5.2 (*Continued*)

	Military Expenditures	Gross National Product	Public Education Expenditures	Public Health Expenditures	Foreign Economic Aid Given
		By Country			
Jamaica	3	578	26	11	—
Mexico	4	651	16	8	—
Nicaragua	6	406	12	4	—
Panama	1	726	36	14	—
Paraguay	5	250	6	2	—
Peru	14	353	15	5	—
Trinidad and Tobago	14	773	29	15	—
Uruguay	15	740	35	6	—
Venezuela	20	990	44	43	—
Far East	12	290	12	1	1
Burma	1	75	2	1	—
Cambodia	18	110	5	1	—
China, People's Republic of	12	144	7	—	—
China (Taiwan)	33	374	14	1	—
Indonesia	2	64	—	—	—
Japan*	45	1,907	75	4	14
Korea, North	49	317	10	1	—
Korea, Republic of	11	258	11	1	—
Laos	13	72	3	1	—
Malaysia	17	352	19	6	—
Mongolia —	19	569	57	2	—
Philippines	3	266	7	2	—
Thailand	6	174	6	1	—
Vietnam, North	15	75	5	1	—
Vietnam, Republic of	59	175	3	1	—
South Asia**	3	103	2	1	—
Afghanistan	1	89	1	1	—
Ceylon	1	169	7	4	—
India	3	96	2	1	—
Nepal	1	80	1	—	—
Pakistan	5	134	2	1	—
Near East**	44	366	16	5	—
Cyprus	13	900	27	10	—
Egypt	27	198	11	3	—
Iran	29	355	11	6	—
Iraq	31	278	18	3	—
Israel	477	1,897	99	24	—

TABLE 5.2 (*Continued*)

	Military Expendi- tures	Gross National Product	Public Education Expendi- tures	Public Health Expendi- tures	Foreign Economic Aid Given
By Country					
Jordan	51	250	10	3	—
Kuwait	104	3,929	141	69	—
Lebanon	18	526	14	2	—
Saudi Arabia	77	581	24	7	—
Syrian Arab Republic	36	261	9	1	—
Yemen	3	120	1	2	—
Africa	4	202	8	3	—
Algeria	7	303	20	5	—
Cameroon	3	171	7	2	—
Central African Republic	4	133	5	2	—
Chad	2	72	3	1	—
Congo (Brazzaville)	7	259	26	8	—
Dahomey	2	94	4	2	—
Ethiopia	2	69	1	1	—
Gabon	6	618	36	16	—
Ghana	5	249	− 8	3	—
Guinea	4	81	11	1	—
Ivory Coast	5	339	27	6	—
Kenya	2	141	1	2	—
Liberia	2	235	5	3	—
Libya	24	1,653	79	24	—
Malagasy Republic	2	120	12	1	—
Malawi	—	71	3	2	—
Mali	1	100	3	2	—
Mauritania	7	150	4	2	—
Morocco	6	210	9	3	—
Niger	1	79	2	1	—
Nigeria	3	105	2	1	—
Rhodesia, Southern	5	269	6	3	—
Senegal	4	179	4	3	—
Sierra Leone	1	157	1	1	—
Somali Republic	3	65	198	1	—
South Africa, Republic of*	18	830	2	11	—
Sudan	7	120	6	1	—
Tanzania	1	100	3	1	—
Togo	2	141	4	1	—
Tunisia	4	236	19	8	—
Uganda	2	134	—	2	—

TABLE 5.2 (*Continued*)

	Military Expenditures	Gross National Product	Public Education Expenditures	Public Health Expenditures	Foreign Economic Aid Given
By Country					
Upper Volta	1	60	2	1	—
Zaire	3	109	5	2	—
Zambia	5	400	12	10	—
Oceania	95	2,504	108	72	14
Australia*	106	2,639	112	69	17
New Zealand*	38	1,903	88	87	—

*Developed country or region. (Country without asterisk is developing.)
**All countries in region are developing.
—None or negligible.
Source: U.S. Arms Control and Disarmament Agency, *World Military Expenditures 1971*, Washington, D.C.: GPO, 1972, pp. 14–17.

Sufficient military strength means having enough weapons either to prevent interference by other states or to deter other states from acting against the state. Deterrence means to deny another any chance of success by inflicting punishment or creating a loss great enough to outweigh any possible gain. (The implications of deterrence strategy will be discussed in more detail later in this chapter.) Because each state operates on a similar rationale, the weapons game is inevitable.

For example, two states, X and Y, are at political odds, and X has 100 bombers. For Y to feel secure it must have an equal number of bombers or other defenses to counter X's 100 bombers. To feel really safe Y can easily rationalize that it needs more than 100 bombers plus defense systems to counter X's weapons. Thus an escalation of weapons systems becomes an inherent part of the weapons game. The escalation is not simply quantitative, however, but qualitative—an escalation takes place in both the types and the sophistication of defensive and offensive weapons. With few exceptions the weapons game becomes even more complex than this simplistic example. There are few situations in which only two states play in the weapons game. States have a multiplicity of relationships. Each state reacts to the weapons developments in a number of other states. States are constantly shifting their perceptions of which other states are their friends or enemies. The smaller states may never have the capacity to play the weapons game alone. They may have to rely on political alliances, or they may be forced into

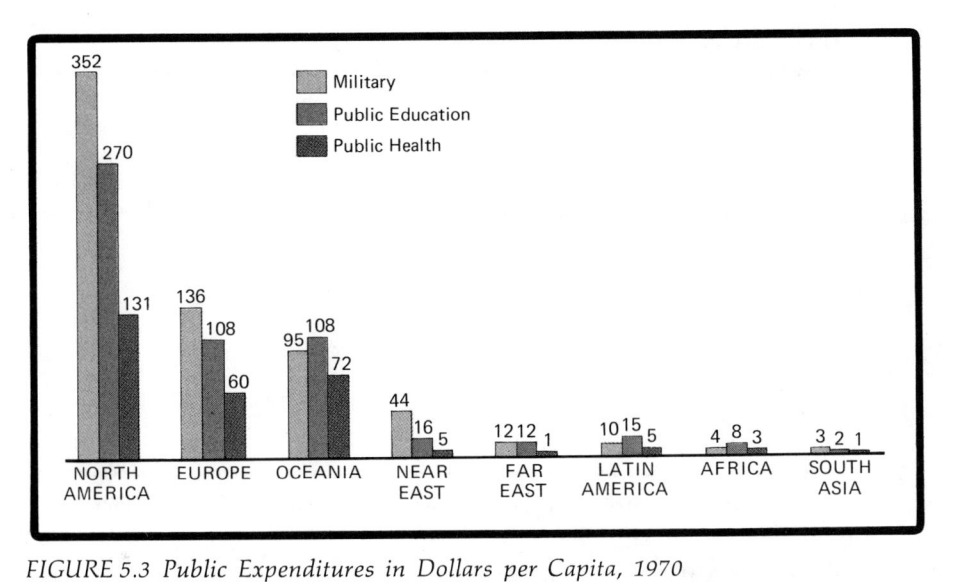

FIGURE 5.3 *Public Expenditures in Dollars per Capita, 1970*

Source: U.S. Arms Control and Disarmament Agency, *World Military Expenditures 1971*, Washington, D.C.: GPO, 1972, p. 17.

military alliances with other states that will give them some degree of latitude in achieving or maintaining their goals.

Weapons systems, for the small as well as the large states, are attempts at visual display, a demonstration of the ability to pursue goals independently without interference from other states. However, the dependence not only on the weapons systems but on the necessity of continually countering the weapons systems of other states means that states have become so dependent upon moves and countermoves in the weapons game that they really are not independent. The commitment to the weapons game is rationalized as a means of securing independence of action; but the irony is that states that continue to play the game actually cannot act independently at all. The weapons commitment of states forces them to make their policy priority decisions largely in response to the weapons commitment decisions of other states, rather than in terms of what may be in their own best interests.

By a frightening paradox the weapons system commitment of states establishes an interdependence of states based upon military systems. The chief difference between the role played by the small and large states in the weapons game is one of magnitude. The breadth of the interests of the largest states—the superpowers (i.e. the U.S. and the U.S.S.R.)—in many respects allows them a lesser degree of independent action than is available to the small states. The superpowers, for instance, are continually reacting to the moves of each other in the weapons game. They are involved more

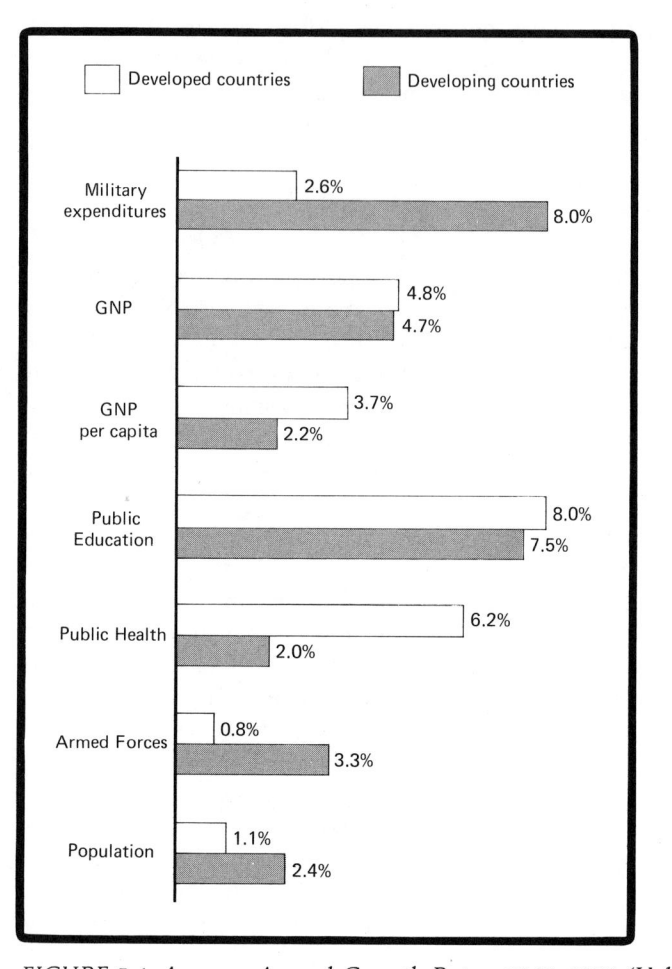

FIGURE 5.4 Average Annual Growth Rates, 1961–1970 (Values in Constant Prices)

Source: U.S. Arms Control and Disarmament Agency, *World Military Expenditures 1971*, Washington, D.C.: GPO, 1972, p. 4.

often and more intensely in attempting to deter each other's military strength. Their moves, instead of being independent, are largely determined by the moves of the other superpower.

The second paradox of the weapons game is that instead of creating security it increasingly creates insecurity. As a state plays the weapons game and steadily escalates its weapons systems, it creates insecurity among its potential enemies and even poses threats to its friends. Its military escalation own weapons commitments. Escalation then moves to more and more des- causes insecurity in other states, which in turn respond by increasing their

tructive weapons—a fact that does not enhance global security but that results instead in a nuclear arms situation with the ultimate possibility of global destruction. Instead of increased security, there is increased insecurity in an absolute sense.

THE ESCALATION OF WEAPONS SYSTEMS

The decade of the 1970s represents a high point in the evolution of the weapons game in terms of the escalation of weapons systems. Not only has the rate of producing weapons increased but also the kinds of destructive weapons available. In fact, the sophistication and the destructiveness of contemporary weapons systems surpasses the comprehension of most people. The escalation of the weapons systems has resulted in a shift from stockpiling weapons to wage war to stockpiling weapons argued essential for survival in peace.

Historically, the development of different kinds of weapons has been slow. By the middle of the twentieth century, however, with the accelerated changes in technology, the momentum of weapons developments has reached an incredible pace. The shift from the use of clubs to the bow and arrow occurred in a longer historical period than the shift from bows and arrows to swords and knights in armor. The development of firearms, first in the form of hand guns, for a long time resulted in developments in tactics to maximize their effectiveness. This was followed by developments in a wider variety of firearms and the mobility of their use.

The development of cannons for use on land and ships, and the development of automatic weapons like the machine gun began a new series of weapons escalations. Machine guns were countered on the land by tanks, then tanks by heavier automatic weapons. Heavier tanks were countered by bazookas and eventually the recoilless rifles. Balloons and the first airplanes added a new dimension, first as observers for artillery and then as fighting units themselves. From fighter and strafing planes to bombers and to the countering antiaircraft batteries the dimensions of war in the air as well as on land and sea have evolved relentlessly. From cannon-equipped wooden sailing ships to steel steamships with fast-firing multiple batteries of large guns to the countering weapon of submarines and aircraft carriers the development of weapons on the sea has expanded with ever-increasing rapidity. The exponential rate of growth of different kinds of weapons since World War II to the present weapons systems of the superpowers is an era in which multiple nuclear warhead intercontinental ballistic missiles delivered from underground silos or nuclear-powered submarines make the development of jet-powered planes and supersonic bombers seem almost primitive, let alone the weapons systems of World War II.

Even more significant than the escalations in the types and diversity of weapons systems has been the escalation in the destructive capability of weapons sytems. It is a long way from muskets and rifle balls, to dumdum exploding bullets, to the Big Bertha cannon of World War I, to massive bomber attacks, V-2 rockets, and the two atom bombs used in World War II. British Prime Minister Winston Churchill, after reading the American report on the successful testing of the first atomic weapon in New Mexico in July 1945, said: "What is gunpowder? Trivial. What is electricity? Meaningless. This atomic bomb is the Second Coming in wrath."[5] At that moment in 1945 a single weapon with the destructive equivalent of 20,000 tons of T.N.T. was a startling escalation in destructiveness. But in reality the "Second Coming in wrath" was the rapidity of the destructive capability that followed in the subsequent shifts not simply from conventional to atomic weapons, but from atomic to thermonuclear weapons. By the early 1960s the Soviet Union, in the largest nuclear weapon test to date, tested a nuclear bomb with a force equivalent to 57 million tons of T.N.T. (i.e., 57 megatons). It is not only the destructive capability of nuclear weapons that is overwhelming but also the delivery systems that have been developed. For example, the missiles on just one U.S. Trident-type submarine have the capacity to destroy 167 cities in the Soviet Union.

Even more destructive of human life than nuclear weapons are chemical and bacteriological weapons. While poison gas was used in World War I, the horror of its effects and the problem of controlling its dissemination tactically has resulted in an informal moratorium on its use. Despite this moratorium, the potential of chemical and bacteriological weapons is not only real, but the stockpiles of these weapons are also a part of the escalating weapons game. A U.N. study by experts from 14 states has indicated that the payload of a single strategic bomber with a bacteriological weapon could affect life in an area of up to 100,000 square kilometers. By contrast, a 1-megaton nuclear weapon, also a single payload, would affect only up to 300 square kilometers, as Table 5.3 shows.

FACTS AND FIGURES

A clear indication of the escalation of military priorities can be seen by examining military expenditures at the outset of the 1970s. Between 1961 and 1970 military expenditures world-wide increased by 75 percent, from $119.1 billion to $208.5 billion. Military expenditures in the United States increased from $1.5 billion in 1940 to $47.8 billion in 1961, from $77.8 billion in 1970 to $84.2 billion for the fiscal year 1973–1974 (with the projected request for fiscal 1974–1975 reaching a high of $92.6 billion).[6]

Between 1961 and 1970 military expenditures for the United States increased 62.8 percent. During the same period they increased in Greece by 182.1 percent, in Denmark by 116.5 percent, in Portugal by 154.4 per-

TABLE 5.3 COMPARATIVE ESTIMATES OF DISABLING EFFECTS OF HYPO-
THETICAL ATTACKS ON TOTALLY UNPROTECTED POPULATIONS
USING A NUCLEAR CHEMICAL OR BACTERIOLOGICAL (BIO-
LOGICAL) WEAPON THAT COULD BE CARRIED BY A SINGLE
STRATEGIC BOMBER

Criterion for Estimate	Types of Weapon		
	Nuclear (one megaton)	Chemical (15 tons of nerve agent)	Bacteriological (biological)[a] (10 tons)
Area affected	Up to 300 km^2	Up to 60 km^2	Up to 100,000 km^2
Time delay before onset of effect	Seconds	Minutes	Days
Damage to structures	Destruction over an area of 100 km^2	None	None
Other effects	Radioactive contamination in an area of 2,500 km^2 for 3–6 months	Contamination by persistence of agent from a few days to weeks	Possible epidemic or establishment of new endemic foci or disease
Possibility of later normal use of affected area after attack	3–6 months after attack	Limited during period of contamination	After end of incubation period or subsidence of epidemic
Maximum effort on man	90 per cent deaths	50 per cent deaths	50 per cent morbidity; 25 per cent deaths if no medical intervention
Multiyear investment in substantial research and development production capability[b]	$5,000–10,000 million	$1,000–5,000 million	$1,000–5,000 million

[a]It is assumed that mortality from the disease caused by the agent would be 50 per cent if no medical treatment were available.

[b]It is assumed that indicated cumulative investments in research and development and production plants have been made to achieve a substantial independent capability. Individual weapons could be fabricated without making this total investment.

Source: U.N. *Basic Problems of Disarmament*, New York: United Nations, 1970, p. 209 (i.e., section of Report on "Chemical and Bacteriological [Biological] Weapons and the Effects of Their Possible Use").

cent, in East Germany by 685.7 percent, in Finland by 42.9 percent, in Brazil by 338.4 percent, in Laos by 387.5 percent, and in Israel by 542.8 percent.

Between 1961 and 1970, only four states had an absolute decrease in military expenditures—the Dominican Republic decreased by 6.3 percent, Indonesia by 21.7 percent, Mali by 37.5 percent, and New Zealand by 29.1 percent. Five states—Haiti, Sri Lanka, Liberia, Malawi, and Sierra Leone—show no dollar change in military expenditures between 1961 and 1970. If one assumes that 40 percent of the increased military expenditures in the period between 1961 and 1970 is due to inflation costs, then in addition to these 9 states that had either no change or a decrease in military expenditures, there were 14 other states having no increase in military expenditures.[7] On the other hand, there were 43 states that had military expenditures increases of 200 percent or more.[8] For the overall trends from 1964 to 1970 see Figure 5.5. From 1961 to 1970 the greatest increases were in the Middle East, Africa, and the developed states in the Far East.

Since 1967 there is a difference in the rate of increase in military expenditures when developed and developing states are compared, as Figure 5.6 shows. In the developed countries the *rate of growth* in military expenditures is declining, whereas in developing states it continues to grow. Thus while the commitment in the developed states since 1967 appears to be leveling off, in the developing states the arms race is increasing. There are a number of factors contributing to this situation, chief of which is that there has been a major arms race among the major powers since 1945, the same period during which many colonial areas achieved independence and sought international prestige.

In 1946 when the United Nations came into being, there were 50 member states, but by 1974 there were 138 member states. At least 73 of these new members of the United Nations are former colonial territories that achieved independence during this period. While many of these new states achieved independence peacefully, some achieved independence by military actions. Even those states that achieved independence peacefully have either been faced with internal security problems or with external conflicts that required arms. The period is one that is replete with violence. The FLN fight for Algerian independence over seven years, the unsuccessful Ibo independence attempt in the Biafran conflict within Nigeria, the fight between the Dutch and the Indonesians, first over Indonesian independence and later over West Irian, and the hot and cold conflict between India and Pakistan, first in Kashmir in 1947, along the West Pakistan border in 1965, and then later in 1971 leading to the independence of Bangladesh, are but a few illustrations of conflicts among or within the excolonial states. The withdrawal of Britain from Palestine in 1948 not only resulted in the creation of

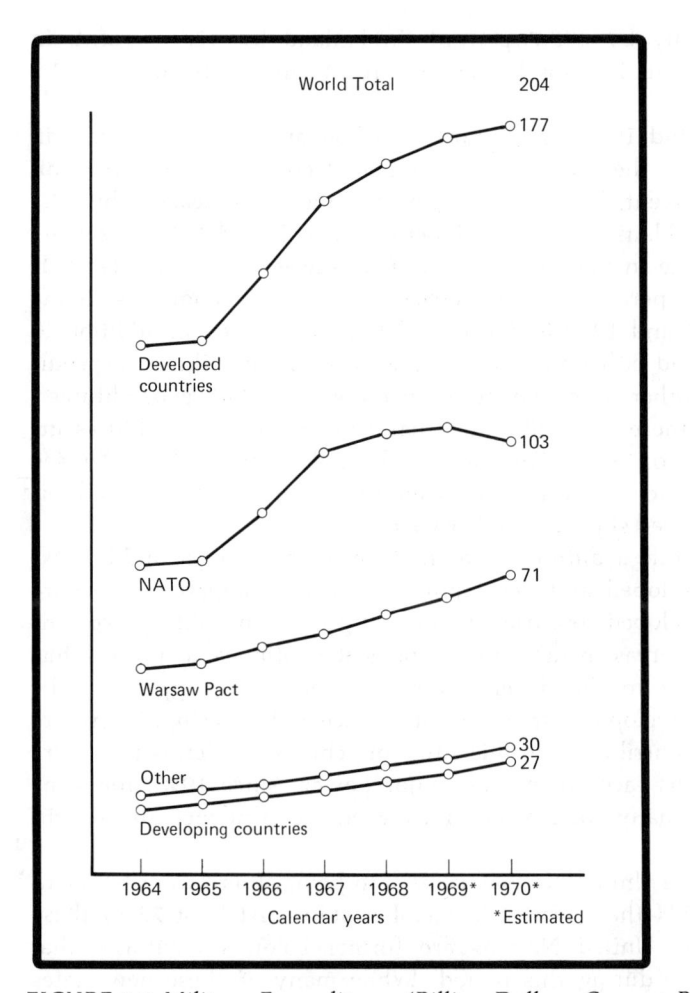

FIGURE 5.5 *Military Expenditures (Billion Dollars–Current Prices)*

Source: U.S. Arms Control and Disarmament Agency, *World Military Expenditures 1970*, Washington, D.C.: GPO, 1971, p. 1.

Israel but was followed by the Israeli-Arab wars of 1948, 1956, 1967, and 1973. And in-between 1948 and the present, as was mentioned before, tensions between Israel and her Arab neighbors have resulted in military engagements virtually every month, if not every week. The unresolved divisions of Korea, the former Japanese colony, and the former French-controlled Indochina have resulted in major conflicts.[9] Internally, many of the newly independent states have been subjected to internal violence. In Syria, for example, between 1945 and 1972 there have been at least six successful mili-

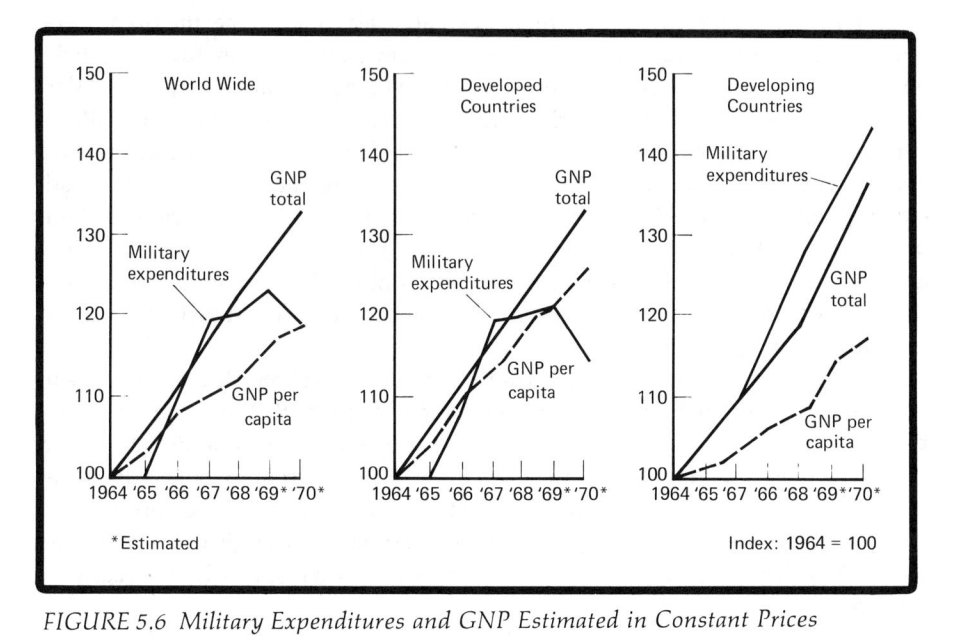

FIGURE 5.6 Military Expenditures and GNP Estimated in Constant Prices

> *Source: United States Foreign Policy 1971—A Report of the Secretary of State,* Washington, D.C.: GPO, 1972, p. 257.

tary coups and several unsuccessful attempts. Similar situations of internal unrest can be cited in a wide variety of former colonial areas, all of which really involve a continuation of the decolonialization process, as these states attempt to establish their own nationalistic identities.

SURPLUS ARMS

Whether in land warfare or warfare on and under the sea, the transformation of military systems hardware has been more rapid in this period than any previous time in history. This situation is such that by the time weapons are developed from the drawing board to effective production, they have often become obsolete. Before they can be utilized, each new development by one side immediately results in efforts by the other side to produce countermeasures. All of these accelerated developments in addition to increasing the enormity of current arsenals have also created the greatest continuous supply of obsolete weapons ever available in history.

Partly to balance the costs of their own weapons developments, and partly to support their potential allies and friendly regimes, the major powers have engaged in a massive selling of their own obsolete arms. This surplus of obsolete arms has been made available at just the time that the decolonization developments have created a demand for arms.

The two superpowers sell their obsolete weapons to the major powers who use them to upgrade their weapons systems, and they in turn sell their obsolete weapons to lesser powers. George Thayer, in his study *The War Business*, estimates that the yearly volume in arms trade is around $5 billion —more money than was spent by all states for military expenditures in 1930.[10] Between 1945 and 1969 he estimated that the United States had either given or sold $59 billion in arms. During the same period Britain provided about $5 billion in arms, France $7 billion, and the Soviet Union and its allies and the People's Republic of China delivered about $7 billion in arms to other states. By comparison the weapons sales of private dealers is estimated at only $30 million per year.

To date, at least, weapons traffic has not involved trade in nuclear devices. The United States, the Soviet Union, France, Britain, and the People's Republic of China have not sold or given nuclear weapons to other states. If it is a saving grace, the fact is that the current business in arms is a business in conventional weapons. However, it must be recognized that these major powers have stimulated the escalation in arms in other states to as much a degree, or a greater degree, than the other states have created a demand.

One of the key elements in the escalating weapons game since 1945 has been the concerted policy of the Soviet Union and the United States during the cold war either to provide or to sell weapons systems to strengthen their allies. During the period from 1945 to 1955, the United States tended to give away its obsolete arms, but as the weapons game costs escalated, the United States officially began selling them, often below their actual cost, but nonetheless as a device to offset military expenditures. Two billion dollars a year in surplus arms sales by the United States reduces American defense budget requirements by $2 billion.

The use of gifts, or the sale of arms by these major states, results in a constant feed into the escalating arms race in the developing states. For example, during the height of U.S. containment policy toward the Soviet Union, the United States was a chief provider of arms to Pakistan in an attempt to ring the Soviets with a string of armed American allies. India's greatest security threat, however, was Pakistan. So as Pakistan's military strength escalated with U.S. surplus, India began to broach the Soviet Union for assistance. To offset possible Soviet influences in India then, the United States provided arms sales to India. Pakistan then felt the threat of growing Indian military strength and made overtures to the People's Republic of China. Thus by the time of the India-Pakistan war of 1965 and the Bangladesh conflict in 1971 both India and Pakistan were using American military equipment.

One wonders if there had been no build-up of arms in these two coun-

tries whether either of these two conflicts would have taken place. The paradoxes created by such behavior are many. It is probably best illustrated by the fact that in a few weeks in late October and early November 1972 the U.S. transfer of weapons to the Republic of South Vietnam gave that country, in material at least, the third largest air force in the world.

THE BALANCE OF TERROR

The net effect of this type of behavior by the super powers and the major powers has been to create such an insecurity in the developing states that they have been induced or required to divert priorities from capital development of their economies to the acquisition of weapons. Few of the developing states have been able to escape the ever-escalating weapons game. Thus in developing states between 1961 and 1970 there has been an increase of 164 percent in military expenditures compared to an increase of 66 percent in developed countries. During this period Belgium increased her military expenditures by 78 percent, while Zaire (the former Belgian colony) increased its military expenditures by 500 percent. France increased her military expenditures by 47 percent, but her former colony, Guinea, has had an increase of 275 percent. United Kingdom military expenditures from 1961 to 1970 increased by 56 percent, but the military expenditures in its former colony of Nigeria increased by 508 percent.

Although the escalation in budgetary commitments for weapons in the developed states has begun to stabilize, at least in growth rates, the upward rate of increase in the developing states is almost exponential. Once the escalation in the developing states has been initiated, a self-generation of ever-increasing escalations appears to be strongly enhanced.

In addition to the escalations in the destructiveness and costs of weapons systems, there has also been an incredible escalation in the sophistication of weapons—dehumanized to a degree that one wonders whether man is able to control them. Herbert F. York, who served for a number of years as the Director of Research and Engineering in the U.S. Department of Defense, in 1970 published a book entitled *Race to Oblivion.* It pointed out in considerable detail the complexities involved in establishing the missile weapons systems.[11] In developing the war game with missiles with nuclear warheads, the superpowers engaged in a series of "ifs"—because there has never been a nuclear war as yet! It is recognized that the United States and the Soviet Union each have sufficient missiles with nuclear warheads to more than destroy the other state. This has resulted in *deterrence* strategies through which both sides attempt to establish their military systems in such a way as to assure that if one state embarks on a "first-strike" attack, the other state will have the capacity to retaliate with sufficient strength to make the effects of the retaliation so great that the first strike would never succeed.

The deterrence concept has resulted in various types of escalation games. First, there have been weapon systems developments such as the antiballistic missiles (ABMs) designed to intercept the first-strike missiles. This has in turn been countered by the Multiple Independently Targeted Reentry Vehicle (MIRV) systems, which in essence are missiles with multiple warheads; once in flight they release a number of warheads all directed to different targets, as Figure 5.7 illustrates. The MIRV systems assure that retaliatory attacks will have enough success to deter a first-strike strategy. Second, in all these developments it is apparent that if either side embarks on a nuclear strike, the time for a reaction by the other side (taking into account all the immediate operating technological developments in warning systems) may be only a matter of minutes.

This has meant that the development of missles has involved a complex of electronic control systems to which decisions can be conveyed almost instantaneously. Scientists and technicians have computed reactions to attempt to cover every possible contingency. However, the essential point that York and others make is that the moment for decision is so brief and the steps to be taken to mobilize the retaliation missiles so complex, that the introduction of a human factor into the decision-making process creates an inefficiency that time will not tolerate.

Missile systems are further complicated by the necessity of introducing controls to prevent unplanned accidents and to assure, at least in the case of the United States, that the President can "press the button," sending off a retaliatory strike before a first strike makes retaliation impossible. Such systems have created a "balance of terror." They have added a complexity to military weapons systems almost beyond the capacity of any individual, except a few military scientists and technologists, to comprehend fully.

Each new weapons system in the escalating weapons game involves a new sophistication and complexity. The weapons game played by the nuclear powers is very different from that played by powers using conventional weapons. The 1967 war between Israel and the Arab states started with a massive air raid by Israeli forces that virtually destroyed the air force of the United Arab Republic. The U.A.R. immediately alleged that it was not simply Israeli planes that were involved in the strikes but also U.S. planes from aircraft carriers nearby in the Mediterranean Sea. The U.A.R. obviously hoped that this assertion of American support of Israel would lead to Soviet involvement in behalf of the U.A.R. This did not happen. The Egyptian military leaders apparently had no understanding of the fact that the warning systems for possible missile attacks between the United States and the Soviet Union were so sophisticated that they involved tracking systems that virtually identify every object in the air. Because the Soviets were fully aware that no U.S. planes were involved in the Israeli attack, they were also aware

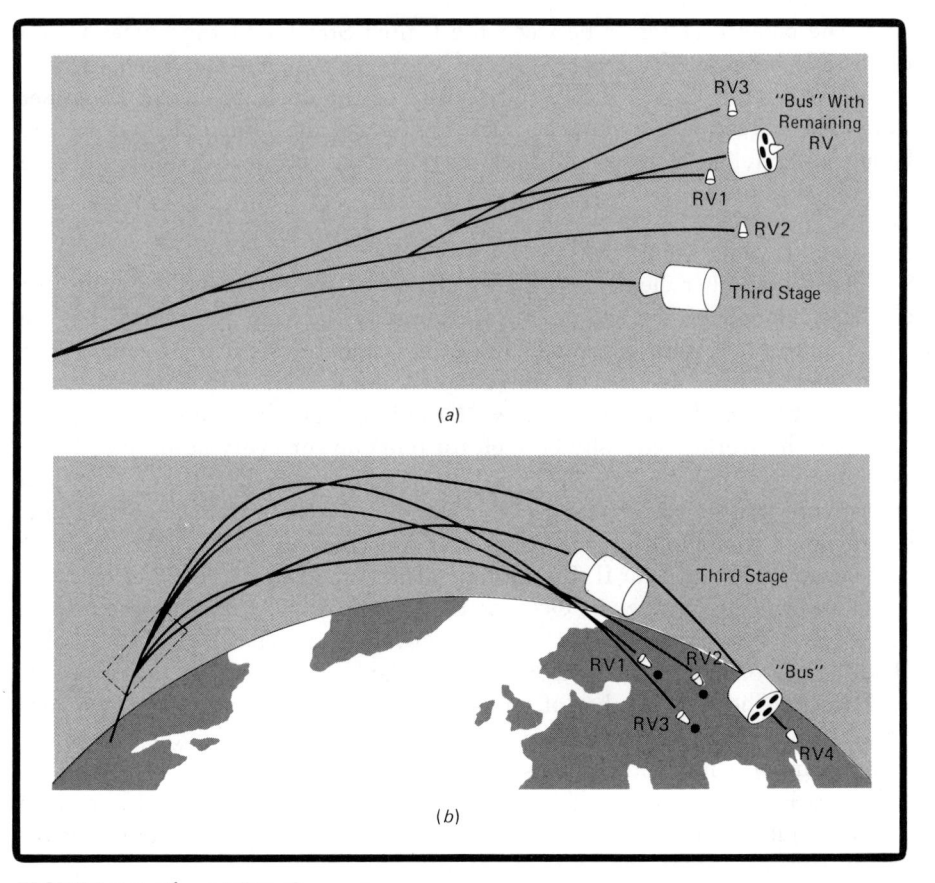

FIGURE 5.7 The MIRV Concept

Note: [The] MIRV concept on which the current U.S. Minuteman III and Poseidon programs are based is illustrated by the idealized drawings in the two figures. Each offensive missile will carry aloft a "bus," containing a number of individual reentry vehicles, or RV's (in this example four are shown). A single guidance and propulsion system will control the orientation and velocity of the bus, from which the reentry vehicles will be released sequentially [*a*]. After each release there will be a further adjustment in the velocity and the direction of the bus. Thus each reentry vehicle can be directed to a separate target [*b*]. The actual separation of the targets depends on how much energy (and therefore weight) one is willing to expend in the post-boost maneuvers of the bus. Besides being a potentially attractive means of penetrating an adversary's ABM defenses, MIRV, with sufficient accuracy, is well suited to being a "counterforce" weapon, that is, a system capable of destroying the adversary's strategic offensive forces.

Source: U.S. House of Representatives, Committee on Foreign Affairs, Subcommittee on National Security Policy and Scientific Developments (Hearings on) *Diplomatic and Strategic Impact of Multiple Warhead Missiles,* July 8, 9, 15, 17, 22, 24, 30, and August 5, 1969, 92d Cong., 1st sess. (1969), p. 300.

that any intervention by Soviet planes would be almost instantaneously detected by American tracking systems.

The balance of terror between the United States and the Soviet Union is possible because of the sophisticated weapons systems that keep each of these two nuclear powers fairly fully aware of the deployments of the other state. The other nuclear powers, such as France, the United Kingdom, the People's Republic of China, and India have not, as yet, developed this degree of sophistication.

MORE AND MORE ARMS

Lastly, another element in the escalation of weapons is the simple fact of the escalation of the amount of weapons available in the world. By the 1970s more arms were present in the international system than ever before in history. This is as true of conventional arms as it is of nuclear arms. Thayer estimates that there are now 750 million operable military rifles and pistols in the world—virtually enough for one gun for every adult male.[12] He also points out that in the 1967 Six-Day War between Israel and the Arab states more tanks were involved in the battle in the Sinai than the total number of tanks committed by the Allies and Axis powers in the 1942 battle of El-Alamein in World War II. By the time of the eighteen-day conflict between Israel and the Arab states in October 1973 there was a further escalation of forces. The Israeli and Syrian tanks involved in the battle for the Golan Heights approximated the total number of tanks involved in the battle for El-Alamein. The total number of tanks involved on the Israeli and Arab sides on all fronts equaled those of the 1944 Battle of the Bulge in the Ardennes. The continual conflict in East Asia also had led to a massive escalation of forces, as Figure 5.8 shows. The tonnage of conventional bombs dropped on Vietnam during that conflict surpassed by several times the bomb tonnage dropped by the Allies during all of World War II. The weapons in the nuclear arsenals of the United States and the Soviet Union are now equivalent to fifteen to twenty tons of T.N.T. for every person in the world. The magnitude of the arms stockpile and the magnitude to which arms have been committed in international conflicts in the past twenty-five years are the ultimate facts in the escalation of weapons.

CONSEQUENCES OF THE WEAPONS GAME

Government leaders in the current weapons game are constantly arguing that security depends upon the "maintenance" of a current weapons system. For example, U.S. Secretary of Defense Melvin Laird argued before the Senate Armed Services Committee on March 15, 1971, that national security planning for the 1970s must involve three criteria:

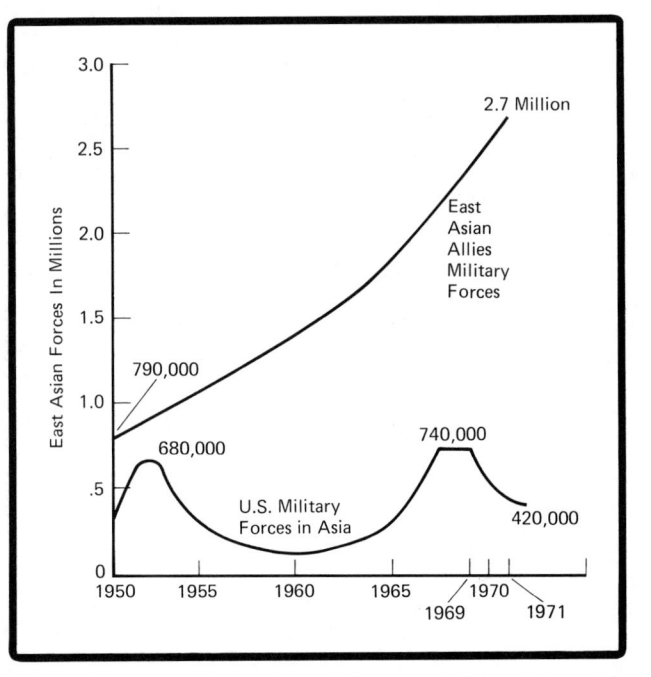

FIGURE 5.8 *Growth in Armed Forces of East Asian Allies of the U.S. (i.e., South Vietnam, South Korea, Thailand, Japan, and Philippines)*

Source: *United States Foreign Policy 1969–1970—A Report of the Secretary of State,* Washington, D.C.: GPO, 1971, p. 38.

1. *Preservation by the United States of a sufficient strategic nuclear capability as the cornerstone of the Free World's nuclear deterrent.*
2. *Development and/or continued maintenance of Free World forces that are effective, and minimize the likelihood of requiring the employment of strategic nuclear forces should deterrence fail.*
3. *An International Security Assistance Program that will enhance effective self-defense capabilities throughout the Free World, and, when coupled with diplomatic and other actions, will encourage regional security agreements among our friends and allies.*[13]

His further testimony explained the necessary improvements (i.e., escalations) in weapons systems necessary to maintain the strategic nuclear capability, as well as the programs necessary to "enhance the self-defense capabilities" of U.S. allies. In other words, security is not accomplished by the maintenance of weapons *per se* but only by the continued escalation of weapons systems. Figure 5.9 is an illustration of this. One of the chief consequences of the weapons game, therefore, has been a fundamental shift in

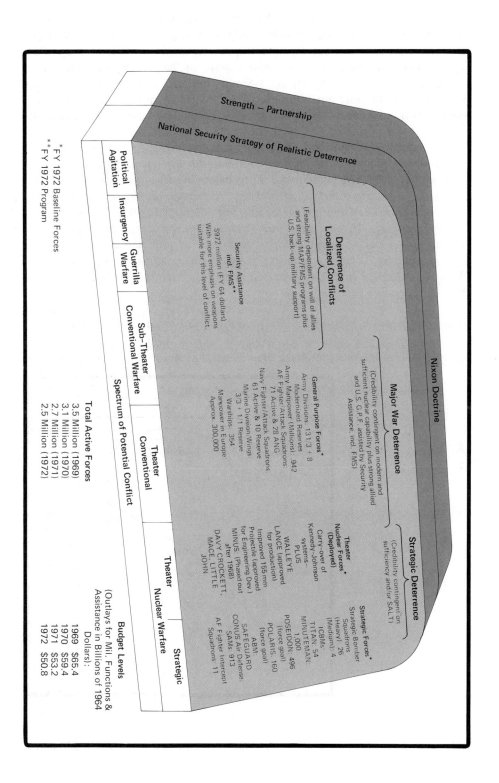

the concept of the military role in the international system. It is characterized, too, by the shift in title of the military element of the U.S. government. Up to and for a short period after World War II the military establishment in the United States was called the War Department; but since 1949 it has been called the Defense Department. This may be symbolic in the case of the United States, but the reality of the symbolism has been characteristic of the role of the military in most states since World War II, even in those states in which the title of the military establishment remains the same.

A SHIFT IN PREPAREDNESS FOR WAR

Prior to 1945 the military role in states during peacetime was minimal, but adequate military strength that could be expanded to defend the state in case of war. At the end of a war it would again recede in importance and size. For example, at the time of U.S. entry into World War I, in April 1917, the U.S. War Department employed 2,816 civilians in Washington, D.C. During 1918 this number rose to 37,400, but by 1922, after the war, it contracted to 4,900 civilian employees. Similarly, the actual military forces, which were small in number before the war, expanded to enormous size during the war, and then after the war contracted almost to their prewar size. Comparable examples could be cited for most other nation-states.

Thus prior to the late 1940s it was typical in the international system for military forces to be small during peacetime and to be rapidly expanded in anticipation of, or during, a period of conflict. Since the late 1940s, however, the concept has changed. Military forces are no longer conceptualized as being developed to defend a state in an emergency. Rather they are viewed as a necessity for security in peacetime as well as during a period of conflict in the international system. In part, this is a consequence of the technological complexity of the current weapons systems. It is no longer possible for most states, in this rapid era of communications, to find the time to mobilize forces and manufacture the arms necessary to support such forces.

The net effect of this conceptual shift in the use of military forces and weapons has been to establish the military element as a much more permanent establishment. Security no longer depends upon the ability of a state to mobilize its military resources in response to a crisis in the international system. Security now is dependent upon a continual maintenance of a commitment to the weapons game.

FIGURE 5.9 Nixon Strategy for Peace (Strength–Partnership–Negotiations)

Source: U.S. Department of Defense, Statement of Secretary of Defense Melvin R. Laird on the *Fiscal Year 1972–1976 Defense Program and the 1972 Defense Budget* before the Senate Armed Services Committee, March 15, 1971, p. 161.

This shift from transitory military establishments to permanent military establishments has had important consequences for the international system. Within both the developed and the developing states the military establishment has not only acquired a more permanent character, but its size and its ties with elements in the domestic political and economic systems have made it a pervasive influence in the whole foreign policy decision process. For the international system this has not simply resulted in an increase in the weapons game, but it means that the weapons game is enmeshed with domestic political and economic choices. Any attempts, therefore, to unwind the weapons game becomes increasingly difficult because they involve not simply creating trust relationships among states—which could lead to de-escalation of the weapons game—but extrication of the military system from its enmeshed ties with the domestic political and economic systems.

In developing states the more permanent military system has resulted in a proliferation of the military bureaucracy and its influence, as well as a permanent involvement of those sectors of the economy that support and sustain military influence. The effect of these developments is manifested in a number of ways on the foreign policy decision process, which contributes to sustaining the weapons game as an essential element of national policy.

In the United States, for example, the growth of the military bureaucracy is evidenced in a number of ways. In the 1920s and 1930s the civilian employment in the then War and Navy Departments combined averaged about 100,000 individuals. Since the mid-1950s the civilian employees of the Defense Department has averaged about 1 to 1.1 million individuals. In the 1920s and 1930s the civilian employees of the defense agencies constituted only about one-sixth of the total employees in the federal government. In the 1950s, 1960s, and into the 1970s the civilian employees of the Defense Department constituted nearly one-half of all the civilian employees of the federal government. The fact that virtually one out of every two members of the bureaucracy of the U.S. government has a personal stake in the maintenance of the weapons game implies that this bureaucratic element has a significant, if not overwhelming, influence on policy choices.

THE ROLE OF THE MILITARY IN FOREIGN POLICY DECISIONS

In the United States the shift to a more permanent military system has not only meant an increase in the bureaucracy and its incumbent influence, but the concerns of the military by virtue of the weapons race have become more enmeshed in foreign policy decisions. In the 1920s and 1930s with few minor exceptions the whole of the U.S. military establishment was located in the continental United States or its territories. By 1970, however, the United States military establishment was involved directly in a number of other countries in the international system. By 1970 the United States had 366 major military bases located in 29 other states.[14] In addition, by

1972 military assistance programs were extended by the United States to some 62 different countries. The programs in 18 of these 62 countries were of such magnitude that they were headed by either generals or admirals. All of these programs involved the Department of the Defense in direct negotiations with foreign states. The total military assistance programs in 1972 amounted to $6,236,805,000—over two-thirds of all types of assistance extended by the United States to other countries.[15] The decision as to which states receive military assistance, therefore, are not simply decisions of the Department of State and the President. They are decisions involving the Department of Defense. The size of the programs in comparison to other foreign-aid programs, as well as the magnitude and extent of direct negotiating contact with other states, has meant a deep involvement of the military establishment in the direct formulation and conduct of foreign policy.

This direct involvement of the military in American relations with other states is a natural result of the escalations in the weapons game. By virtue of multilateral military security treaties such as the Rio Pact of 1947, the North Atlantic Treaty of 1949, the ANZUS Treaty of 1951, and the SEATO Treaty of 1954, bilateral mutual defense treaties with the Philippines, South Korea, Taiwan, and Japan, executive agreements of defense with Denmark, Iceland, Spain, Canada, Liberia, Iran, Turkey, Pakistan, and the Philippines, and 34 other general executive policy declarations, the United States had involved itself, by the 1970s, in military defense arrangements with 47 states. These commitments provided the basis for the military establishment of the United States to become directly involved in American foreign relations.

The magnitude of the military bureaucracy, in which the civilian component by 1972 was 1,118,742 individuals, is overwhelming in comparison with the size of the U.S. State Department. By 1972 the State Department employed 36,886 individuals, including the 13,033 employed in nonmilitary foreign assistance programs under the Agency for International Development. Therefore, the *civilian* employees of the U.S. Defense Department were 31 times greater in number than those of the State Department. The ability of the military bureaucracy to mobilize itself as an influence on foreign policy decisions can be suggested by these size comparisons. It is even more evident when one argues that the military bureaucracy is essentially concerned with the security of the United States, particularly when military security is argued as the topmost priority in foreign policy decision making.

The military leaders in other states, dependent upon U.S. arms aid or supplies, are more prone to deal with the U.S. military missions than with the diplomatic missions from the Department of State. In developing states dominated by military regimes the State Department's embassies play a minor role in comparison to the Defense Department's military-aid missions in the day-to-day relations between the United States and these military

regime states (this has been especially true in South Vietnam and Laos). Even in those developing and developed states not dominated by military regimes their military establishments deal directly with the U.S. military establishment, thus often supplanting or by-passing the more traditional foreign policy units of government. A major question then in the 1970s is not whether the *needs* for military security are dominating the policies of the nation-states, but rather whether the permanent *military establishment themselves* are dominating the major policy decisions affecting the international system.

In the United States, for example, Congress by the power of the purse, theoretically at least, has the final decision as to the allocation of funds that determine the general policy alternatives of the government. Yet in dealing with the permanent military establishment Congress is virtually overwhelmed. The small bodies of the appropriations committees in the Senate and House of Representatives are given the task of reviewing the validity of the policy proposals (and therefore budget appropriations) of the Department of Defense. Within the Department of Defense some 30,000 individuals are concerned with the preparation of the budget (i.e., policy proposals). In contrast, less than 50 individuals in the Congress, via hearings, must attempt to ferret out the validity and necessity of the policy requirements demanded by the Department of Defense. In the midst of the continuing technological advancement of weaponry it becomes particularly difficult for these few members of Congress to weigh clearly the alternatives purposed by the military establishment, which is able to mobilize experts testifying on all manner of questions.

THE MILITARY ECONOMY

As if this were not alarming enough, the fact of the permanence of the military establishment means that large sectors of the domestic economy in the United States are permanently involved in the production of the weapons systems requested by the Defense Department. In 1971, $32,444 million in defense procurement contracts were awarded private enterprises in the United States. These defense contracting firms directly employed some 10,778,000 American workers. With some 86,929,000 individuals in the employed work force in the United States this means that one out of every eight employed Americans is directly supported by military procurement contracts. Obviously, many more Americans are indirectly employed as a consequence of these military contracts.[16]

Military Logrolling. The interests of these workers therefore constitute a significant informal lobby in support of the budget (policy requests) of the Department of Defense. They become a meaningful influence upon the members of Congress in several ways. Many states in the United States that

have military procurement as a major base of their industries make their influence especially felt by their elected representatives in Congress. In California, New York, and Texas—three states with large congressional delegations—the maintenance of military contracts is a key economic welfare issue. The reelection of a member of Congress may hinge on his or her continued support of the military and procurement contracts. In these three heavily populated states the defense contracts in 1971 totaled nearly $12 billion.

One way for members of Congress to endear themselves to their constituencies is to bring economic benefits, such as retaining or extending military contracts, to their districts. An analysis by the *Congressional Quarterly* in 1972 shows a high correlation between those congressional leaders who sat in the Senate and House Armed Services Committee and those who supported defense contracts and Department requests.[17]

In addition to support from certain members of the Congress whose districts benefit from military contracts, and support from the millions of persons employed in the military weapons industries, the military establishment has the additional pressure on congressional policy decisions exerted by the industrial leadership. The seven top military contractors in the United States each received over $1 billion in contracts in 1972 including $1,705,-434,000 to Grumman Aerospace Corporation and $1,719,760,000 to Lockheed Aircraft.[18] The economic state of these industrial companies is such that they also have a major supportive role to assure that the Defense Department priorities dominate. It is the combination of these economic elements of influence that President Eisenhower warned of in his farewell address when he expressed concern about the possibility of the "acquisition of unwarranted influence, whether sought or unsought, by the military-industrial complex."

Secrecy. The ability of the legislative arm of the U.S. government to assert policy control over the weapons establishment is also hindered by the necessity for secrecy in the considerations of military policy requests. On the one hand, secrecy is argued as essential to prevent the details of sophisticated weaponry from being made available to potential enemies. On the other hand, secrecy in the form of intelligence-gathering agencies is argued as an essential aspect of the maintenance of a weapons system. The ability of congressmen to evaluate the military establishment's proposals is often hindered by the inability to explore fully and publicly the pros and cons of proposed weapons systems.

Congress is also unaware of the magnitude and scope of the intelligence-gathering agencies. In the name of security, the Central Intelligence Agency (CIA) was given authority to operate in 1949 without the normal annual review of the Congress. Its budget is hidden within the appropria-

tion accounts of other agencies, and while there are joint committees to provide legislative oversight of the agency, none of these discussions are public. One of the more recent glimpses into the implication of this element of secrecy occurred in 1971. Various members of the Senate attempted to find out the degree to which the United States was involved in secret military operations in Laos. A declassified report of the Subcommittee on U.S. Security Agreements and Commitments Abroad indicated that not only was the CIA supporting an army of 30,000 irregulars in Laos but that the U.S. expenditures for 1971 in Laos were more than six times the national budget of the Laotian Government itself.[19] Senator Symington of Missouri, one of the members of the CIA Oversight Committee of the Senate Armed Services Committee, stated publicly that he felt the subcommittee itself did not know the full extent of the American involvement through the CIA in Laos. The ability of the Congress to discuss policy priorities is hindered by the "requirement" for secrecy in the activities of the CIA. Military requirements, it is argued, require secrecy, but the effect of this secrecy is also to deny Congress and the public the ability to weigh alternative policy decisions.[20]

Thus one of the consequences of the permanent military establishments is the increasing inability of the civilian arm of government to assert a control in making of foreign policy decisions. While these illustrations have been drawn from the experience of the United States, comparable examples can be given from many of the other developed states. Even in the Soviet Union one hears of the "collusion" between the military leaders and the technical managers of the industrial plants who are also permanently involved in weapons production.

THE MILITARY IN DEVELOPING STATES

In the developing states there is a dichotomy between those governments that have made major commitments to the weapons game and those that have not. However, increasingly more and more of the developing states have evolved permanent rather than transitory military establishments. In many of the developing states the military have actually taken over the public control of the government. While the majority of the developing states are under the control of civilian governments, more of the developing states are being dominated by military regimes. In some developing states the military establishments are not simply concerned with protecting the states against perceived enemies, but they have become instruments of social change.

The military takeover in Egypt in 1952, for example, was led by Gamal Abdul Nasser and other military officers committed to the elimination of feudalism, the eradication of monopolies, and the establishment of social justice. Nasser and his successor Anwar al-Sadat, as well as the other officers involved in the 1952 ouster of the Egyptian monarchy of King Farouk, were

all members of the 1938 graduating class of the Egyptian military academy, the first class to accept cadets from all social classes (not just the aristocracy). As such, this group of military leaders were committed not only to the elimination of British influence, but the establishment of basic economic and social changes in Egypt. The economic development of Egypt since 1952 testifies to the influence of the military leaders in bringing about basic agrarian reforms that have undermined the political power and economic position of the Egyptian upper class.

ENVIRONMENTAL PRESSURES OF THE INTERNATIONAL WEAPONS GAME

One effect of the weapons game, particularly because of the now fairly permanent involvement of the domestic economic and political systems in the process, is that it continues to contribute to the disparity between the haves and have-nots. The commitment to the weapons game means for the have-not developing states that ever larger proportions of their gross national products are being consumed in military expenditures that are not conducive to developing the domestic economy to offset the basic need of food and other vital needs of their expanding populations.

The superpowers, the United States and the Soviet Union, are committing resources to their military "requirements" but at the same time are also developing the other segments of their own economic needs. Meanwhile, they are increasingly consuming greater and greater proportions of the world's resources.

As the pressure of population increases becomes more evident in the next twenty years, the pressures on the have-nots to acquire more of the world's resources will also increase. States already heavily committed to the weapons game may be tempted to use their weapons systems against their neighbors to seize the resources as the population pressures increase. One inherent danger was implied in the 1968 Report of the Secretary-General of the United Nations *On the Effects of the Possible Use of Nuclear Weapons and the Security and Economic Implications of States of the Acquisition and Further Development of These Weapons.*[21] The danger is that there are from 14 to 17 states, many of them developing states which have the potential, should they decide to give it priority support, to develop their own nuclear weapons systems. Any escalation extension of nuclear weapons systems motivated by a desire to force other states to give them their equal or "just" share of the world's resources poses serious threats to the present international situation.

Assuming the increasing disparity between the developed and developing states, the ultimate limitation of nonrenewable resources, and the in-

creasing consumption of the world's food and other resources by the superpowers with their superior military strength, the temptation of the have-nots
to opt for military devices to get their proportional share increases as the
population pressures continue. Short of a possible decision to go to nuclear
weapons systems, the temptation to venture into biological and chemical
weapons systems may become a reality.[22] These types of weapons are comparatively cheap to obtain and the threat of their use, especially in view of
their extreme destructibility of human life, may be options chosen by states
who feel they have little to lose.

Developing states dominated by military regimes are likely to envision
military means to resolving internal situations. Developed states in which the
economy is deeply involved in the weapons game are unlikely to unilaterally
de-escalate the weapons game and thereby release resources to relieve the
pressures of developing states. These developed states have, through the
weapons game, created a security system dependent upon a continual development of weapons to offset the other developed states. Any stop in the
escalating arms developments immediately creates an insecurity. As if in a
horrible dream, the continual playing of the weapons game has created a
complexity of situations which have tremendous potential for increased conflict in the international society. Any efforts to extricate states in the international system from these dilemmas seem very difficult if not impossible.

EFFORTS TO CONTROL
THE WEAPONS GAME

Since the seventeenth century the states in the international system
have made various attempts to control, eliminate, or stabilize the weapons
game. Three basic approaches have been attempted: efforts toward disarmament, efforts to provide for alternative means of security for states, and
efforts to control the use of existing arms.

DISARMAMENT
Disarmament is a concept that involves the reduction or the elimination
of arms. *Efforts at disarmament* have been made repeatedly for nearly one
hundred and fifty years with few successes. The best capsule illustration of
frustrated efforts at disarmament can be seen in this example. Although the
czar of Russia in 1816 proposed a simultaneous reduction of all armed forces
by states, progress in this area had been so insignificant that in September
1959 Premier Nikita Khrushchev of the Soviet Union renewed this proposal
by calling for "general and complete disarmament." Between 1816 and 1959
many comparable efforts were made. France took the initiative in making

such proposals in 1831, 1863, 1867, and 1869, as did Great Britain in 1870 and Italy in 1877. The question was considered at the Hague peace conferences in 1899 and 1907 and by the League of Nations, which convened the World Disarmament Conference in 1933. In one manner or another the United Nations has, from 1946 to the present, been attempting to bring about agreements on the general reduction of arms, and in 1965 another world conference on disarmament was proposed for the 1970s.

Building Trust Among Disarming States. Most of these efforts at a general reduction of arms have resulted in failure of one form or another. Virtually all of them have ended up in a chicken-and-egg argument: How can we disarm and still feel secure when a basic sense of trust among states is missing? How can we establish trust among states without first reducing the arms that threaten global security?

Various approaches have been tried to solve this essential dilemma. Although agreements on the goal of a reduction of arms have often been made, implementation is comparatively rare. The League of Nations Covenant set out the goal of achieving the maximum reduction possible of arms consistent with the maintenance of national security. Despite several years of preparatory work, the 1933 World Conference on Disarmament convened by the League was a total failure. The records of the conference are full of what now appears to be endless arguments as to the comparability of national armaments. Was the reduction of one Soviet rifle equal to one Japanese rifle? Or did their varying capabilities mean that for every reduction of one Japanese rifle the Soviets would have to eliminate 1.2 rifles? Despite these kinds of discussions, the clear fact emerging from the 1933 conference was that the trust factor among states was not sufficient to arrive at any specific, let alone general, agreements on the reduction or arms.

The U.N. Charter also established a goal for the reduction and regulation or armaments, not complete disarmament, though, which by 1945 was considered unfeasible. The United Nations at its outset was faced with the major weapons escalation toward atomic devices. For five years an attempt was made to separate the consideration of atomic and nuclear weapons from the consideration of conventional weapons. In the atomic weapons area the United States, which in 1946 held a monopoly on this kind of weapons, proposed the so-called Baruch Plan, whereby the production of atomic and nuclear materiel would be subjected to an international inspection system that would assure that such materiel would not be diverted into military production. The Soviet Union was very suspicious of international inspection teams; the Russians saw it merely as a means for the United States to inform themselves of events within the USSR. The Soviet Union was also fearful that the U.S. atomic weapons monopoly might never be destroyed.

Efforts at atomic weapons control were deadlocked by such suspicions until the Soviet Union and other states such as France, Britain, and eventually the People's Republic of China had also obtained nuclear weapons. By then the efforts to break the deadlock and to prevent the escalation of the arms race into this type of weapons systems had become dead issues. As the number of atomic and nuclear powers increased, once again distrust prevented efforts at disarmament.

Multilateral Efforts at Disarmament. No multilateral efforts at disarmament have ever been successful for an extended period of time. The United Nations has tried many varieties of conferences and committees of states to break the deadlock. There have been disarmament committees composed of only nuclear powers, of only the major powers—even a conference of the nonnuclear states. All have been unsuccessful in achieving the goal of disarmament. The most persistent body recently in the international system has been the 18-Nation Committee on Disarmament, which has been meeting in Geneva since 1963. This body is composed of 9 of the major military powers and 9 of the "most neutral" states (although 1 of the major military powers, France, no longer participates in the discussions and the People's Republic of China has never been a member of the committee).[23] Even this body, which has made some progress in the control of arms, has made no progress in the area of disarmament.

A five-power agreement between the United States, Britain, Japan, France, and Italy in the Washington Treaty of 1922 called for a ratio of strength in capital ships. In essence, for every five capital ships for Britain and the United States, Japan could have three, while France and Italy could have 1.67 each. Under this agreement the United States, Britain, and Japan destroyed about 40 percent of their capital ships so that the ratio could be achieved. Tonnage sizes on the types of naval vessels that could be built were also established. In a sense this was a successful disarmament treaty in that it actually led to the destruction of naval ships. However, the treaty was a failure because within a few years distrust set in, and Japan in particular began to violate both the tonnage limitations and the ratio margins. The treaty was already ineffective when Japan formally withdrew from it in 1934. This five-power treaty is the only multilateral disarmament treaty that had even a small degree of success. The failure of multilateral disarmament efforts has not, however, prevented continued efforts to achieve this goal. They still continue. More importantly, the frustrations in these multilateral efforts have led to other methods of trying to control the ever spiraling weapons game.

Bilateral Efforts at Disarmament. The few meager successes in disarmament since the seventeenth century have not been multilateral but bilateral

efforts. The classical treaty in this regard is the nineteenth-century Rush-Bagot Agreement (made in 1817) between the United States and Great Britain (for Canada, which was not then self-governing), in which there was agreement on a limitation in regard to both the number of naval vessels and their total tonnage to be allowed on the Great Lakes. Although it has been revised, this one successful treaty is still in effect. Other minor disarmament successes have been less formal understandings not to militarize joint boundaries.

ALTERNATIVE WAYS OF ENSURING GLOBAL SECURITY

Another major thrust to handle the weapons game has been the effort to seek alternative ways of ensuring the security of states. Two approaches have been attempted. One approach is characterized by the Kellogg-Briand Pact of 1928 which outlawed war as an instrument of national policy. With almost pathetic euphoria most states of the world ratified this treaty in the hopes that the use of military weapons in the achievement of national goals and security would be limited to nonmilitary means. The treaty recognized a goal that was far ahead of the degree of trust that one nation held for the actions of the others. The treaty has been honored more in the breach than in fact. In reality states continued to use military means to achieve their goals. They paid lip service to the treaty by stating that such military ventures were not wars but defensive or preventive actions. While the treaty still remains on the books, it is a record of the dreams and hopes of mankind; in reality the weapons game continues with military ventures being characterized as everything short of war—which is, of course, outlawed!

COLLECTIVE SECURITY SYSTEMS

The League of Nations. The other approach to seek an alternative to the continual development of the weapons game has been the device of collective security systems. The League of Nations and the United Nations both involve multilateral attempts of the international system to provide a collective security system. In theory, at least, the states joined together in the League of Nations were jointly committed to the defense and protection of any member state that felt itself threatened by the military ventures of other states. The League system failed in part because several major states were not members and several other major states withdrew from the organization when its concerns threatened their independent action. The United States never joined, and the Soviet Union was not initially a member of the League. This meant that any efforts of the League to take collective action against military aggressor states might not have the cooperation of nonmembers. In

the military attack of Italy on Ethiopia in 1935 the League tried to adopt a proposal for an oil embargo with the anticipation that the Italian venture would fail for lack of oil to sustain supply lines. This oil embargo proposal was doomed when it became apparent that nonmembers of the League as well as some of the members would not enforce it. The League was also hampered by the necessity of obtaining the concurrence of all states, except the parties to the dispute, in undertaking any actions. In essence each member of the League of Nations was given a veto over collective action to deter aggressor states. This practice led to lengthy and innumerable debates to reduce proposals to the lowest common denominators before a collective agreement on action was possible. Endless arguments on the distinctions between what constituted aggressive as opposed to defensive military actions meant that by the time the League acted the circumstances were so changed the action was mute. As the League debated, discussed, and investigated Japan's actions against China in the 1930s, the Japanese consolidated their control over Manchuria which then proclaimed itself as an independent state seeking its right of self-determination from China. When finally the League acted, military states such as Japan or Nazi Germany countered by withdrawing from the League of Nations.

The United Nations. The U.N. collective security system varies somewhat from that of the League of Nations. It recognizes the reality of the international system in that all states are not equal in military strength. It recognizes that peace is dependent upon the major powers, who in 1945 were identified as the United States, the Soviet Union, France, China, and Great Britain. The collective security system established in the United Nations obligated all members of the organization to defend the other members if and when they were requested to do so by the Security Council. The Security Council could enforce the peace when it arrived at an agreement of 7 of its initial 11 members, including all of the 5 major powers who serve as permanent members of the Security Council.[24] However, the Security Council could only take action after it agreed, by a similar voting arrangement, under Article 39, that the situation or dispute constituted a threat to the peace, a breach of peace, or an act of aggression. In theory, at least, it was recognized that the collective security system would not work unless there was the authority to assure that its decisions were implemented. In theory, therefore, it was recognized that if one or more of the 5 major powers did not agree with a proposed collective support action, there could be no collective action.

In the mood of 1945 there was every hope that the U.N. system would work because of the desire of the major powers to agree to enforce the peace. To avoid the dilemmas that the League of Nations faced in defining

aggression before it could act, the U.N. Charter, in Article 39, states that whenever a majority of the Security Council agrees that there is a threat to the peace, a breach of the peace, or an act of aggression, that body can then decide to take action. The only requirement needed is agreement that one of these three kinds of events has happened. If the major powers can so agree, a variety of actions can be taken: breaking off diplomatic relations, cutting off communications, invoking economic sanctions, and according to the charter, at least in theory, enforcing peace through the creation of an international police force. In theory, too, the charter recognizes that if there is no agreement among the major powers, there will be no collective action. Unless the major powers were willing to commit themselves to such action, no platitudes could promise protection to any state. In theory, therefore, the U.N. collective security system at its inception held out the hope and possibility of multilateral action to protect states threatened by other states.

In practice, of course, the hopes and possibilities of the U.N. collective security system have seldom been realized. On only rare occasions have the major powers been in agreement under Article 39. The level of distrust, especially between the United States and the Soviet Union, has been such that any determination proposed by either party has either failed to get a majority of the Security Council or has been vetoed by one of the major powers.

There have been a few successes, however. In the late 1940s when the newly independent government of Indonesia was attacked by the military forces of its former colonial master, the Netherlands, the Security Council permanent members were in agreement and ordered the withdrawal of the Dutch forces. The Netherlands, in view of the threat from the major powers, backed down and withdrew military forces. Without the use of force the security of Indonesia was protected. In 1966 the Security Council acting under Article 39 agreed on the imposition of limited economic sanctions against the efforts of the white minority regime in Southern Rhodesia to unilaterally assert its independence from Great Britain. These sanctions have not forced down the racist regime, however, because several nonmember states of the United Nations have continued to trade in these selective economic sanctions and because, in 1971, one of the major powers, the United States passed the so-called Byrd Amendment to permit importation of certain "strategic and critical materials," particularly chrome from Rhodesia.

The ability of the U.N. collective security system to provide security for states by international action has failed because the states in the system have not been willing to guarantee that security. The polarization of the international system between the Soviet Union and the United States has meant that any international actions proposed by one side of the conflict is

viewed with suspicion by the other side. To the major states who have sufficient strength militarily to protect themselves, the collective security system of the United Nations serves no reasonable purpose.

One of the more interesting possibilities suggested by the U.N. collective security system was the theoretical possibility of creating an international police force. This concept was the subject of intensive negotiations between 1946 and 1949 in the Military Staff Committee of the Security Council. The major powers disagreed on a number of fundamental issues, and the distrust level between the United States and the Soviet Union was such that it was impossible to arrive at an an agreement to create the force. The concept envisioned in the charter was an international force that could be used to enforce any decisions of the Security Council. Despite the failure to agree on an international force that could be on tap for use in situations requiring a "policeman" to enforce order in the international community, the United Nations in practice has created a number of international forces. As the following list shows, in at least 14 situations the major powers have been able to agree on the creation of some type of a U.N. force, not to enforce the peace or the settlement of the conflict, but as an international force to separate or observe the separation of the conflicting parties.

MILITARY FORCES CREATED BY THE UNITED NATIONS 1947 TO 1973

I. *United Nations Military "Forces" Created Primarily Either to Observe Border Violations or to Observe Violations of Cease-Fire Lines*: These generally number less than about 300 individuals drawn from a number of states that form "military investigating teams" to report on the violations.

   A. Military Observers in Indonesia (August 1947 to April 1951)—concerned with observing Dutch withdrawals from Indonesia.

   B. U.N. Military Observers in Greece (UNMOG) (January 1952 to July 1954)—observed and reported on border violations of Greece with Albania, Yugoslavia, and Bulgaria.

   C. U.N. Truce Supervision Organization for Palestine (UNTSO) (began June 1948 and still in operation at the beginning of 1975)—concerned with observing both temporary and permanent cease-fire lines between Israel and Egypt, Jordan, Syria, and Lebanon.

   D. U.N. Military Observer Group in India and Pakistan (UNMOGIP) (began January 1949 and still in operation at the beginning of 1975)—concerned with observing and reporting on violations of the cease-fire line in Kashmir and Jammau.

   E. U.N. India-Pakistan Observation Mission (UNIPOM) (September 1965 to March 1966)—concerned with observing the withdrawal of forces along the West Pakistan-India border.

    F. U.N. Observation Mission in Lebanon (UNOGIL) (June to December 1958)—concerned with observing and reporting on the infiltration of arms and forces into Lebanon from Syria.

    G. U.N. Military Observer Team for the Cease-Fire in West New Guinea (August to September 1962)—concerned with the withdrawal of Dutch and Indonesian forces.

II. *United Nations Military "Forces" Created Primarily to Interpose Themselves Between the Parties in a Dispute*: These generally number several thousand and are made up of military contingents from a variety of states.

    A. United Nations Emergency Force (UNEF) (October 1956 to May 1967)—concerned with patrolling the Sinai border between Egypt and Israel—at its height involved about 7000 troops.

    B. U.N. Operations in the Congo (OUNUC) (July 1960 to June 1964—concerned with separating the contending Congolese military units, preventing the infiltration of foreign paramilitary and maintaining law and order—at its height involved about 18,000 troops from 34 states plus civilian teams.

    C. U.N. Yemen Observer Mission (UNYOM) (July 1963 to September 1964)—concerned with patrolling the cease-fire lines established between the former government of Yemen supported by Saudi Arabian forces and the revolutionary government supported by Egyptian force—at its height totaled about 400 troops from 3 states.

    D. U.N. Peace-Keeping Forces in Cyprus (UNFICYP) (began March 1964 and still in operation at the beginning of 1975)—concerned with separating Greek and Turkish Cypriots, preventing illegal entry of arms, and stopping military clashes between the two groups—at its height involved about 4000 troops and police detachments from 14 states.

    E. U.N. Emergency Force (UNEF) (began October 1973 and still in operation in January 1975)—concerned with the physical separation of Israeli and Egyptian forces and with patrolling a neutral zone between these forces—at its height numbered about 4000.

    F. U.N. Disengagement Observer Force (UNDOF) (began June 1974 and still in operation in January 1975)—concerned with physically separating of the Israeli and Syrian forces and with patrolling a neutral zone between these forces—at its height it numbered about 1500.

III. *United Nations Military "Force" Involved in Providing Military Security to an Area*

    A. U.N. Security Force in West Iran (or West New Guinea) (UNSF) (September 1962 to April 1963)—following the withdrawal of Dutch forces from the area the UNSF provided military security forces for

the U.N. Temporary Executive Authority, until Indonesian authorities took over governmental control of the area—at its height involved about 1200 troops.

In a technical sense there was a U.N. military command and force in Korea from June 1950 to July 1953. In responding to the outbreak of conflict in Korea in 1950, the Security Council authorized the American President to organize the U.N. forces, and a U.N. command was created. While the vast bulk of the troops were from the United States and South Korea, contingents were provided from 54 other states. At the time of the truce in July 1953 a military armistice commission was created representing the two sides in the conflict. The U.N. military command representatives on the military armistice commission were American military officers.

These have all been rather tenuous actions because the creation of these forces was recommended without a prior decision under Article 39, and there is a legal question as to whether states are therefore obligated to support them. These forces have been created on an ad hoc basis only in disputes in which the major powers agreed that it was essential to separate the conflicting states to avoid escalating the conflict. These so-called peacekeeping forces created by the United Nations have been elements in reducing tensions among states, but they have not provided an alternative for the security provided by the military forces of a state. Their utilization and experience have not as yet had an effect in breaking the distrust levels that have hampered agreement on the possibilities for creating a truly international police force that could provide security to states.

REGIONAL COLLECTIVE SECURITY SYSTEMS

In a tragic sense the efforts at collective security have contributed to an escalation of the weapons game. With the deadlocks and failures in the attempt to provide a universal collective security system for the states in the international system through the League of Nations, and more recently the United Nations, states have resorted to the creation of regional collective security arrangements. Most of these regional collective security arrangements are essentially defense alliances between the Soviet Union and the United States and their allies. The North Atlantic Treaty Organization, which was mentioned earlier, and its Soviet counterpart, the Warsaw Pact Organization, are regional collective security treaties. Each member of these treaties is obliged individually and collectively to defend the other members of the treaty against any threats or attacks on their security. While the arrangements do provide for a collective security, at the same time they pose a greater threat to the potential enemies. The collective threat of the alliance of NATO states inherently necessitates the strengthening of the Warsaw

Pact Organization, and vice versa. In a very real sense this only ups the stakes in the weapons game.

Regional security arrangements can achieve the goal of security only for the states within the arrangement themselves. However, in NATO and the Warsaw Pact security among or within the states in the arrangement may well be defined by the dominant members of the alliance, the United States or the Soviet Union. The United States by means of the Rio Treaty collective security arrangement with Latin American states engaged in the creation of an "international force" to enforce "peace" during a conflict in the Dominican Republic in 1965. And the Soviet Union mobilized an "international force" from the Warsaw Pact states in 1968 to deal with a "conflict" within Czechoslovakia. In both instances the argument was made that these actions were collective actions taken to preserve the security of the other states within the regional arrangement.

There are two regional collective security arrangements in which neither of the superpowers are members: the Arab League and the Organization of African Unity (OAU). In both goals and operations they have attempted to substitute collective security for individual military security efforts. Their success in achieving the goals denied to the League of Nations and the United Nations have not been fully realized. They have had a few minor successes, primarily in preventing the major powers from moving into situations of conflict within the area of these regional arrangements. In 1961, for example, in a dispute between Iraq and Kuwait, where British troops initially went to protect that country's security, the Arab League created an Arab League force (primarily of Tunisian troops), which it sent to Kuwait. They replaced the British troops and provided for the security of Kuwait against Iraq. In several instances in Africa the OAU has attempted by means of committees and commissions to reduce conflict and potential disputes among African states. In a comparable sense the OAU preserved their security, at least from the encroachment of the major powers.

Despite these few successful developments, the efforts to find a security alternative by collective security devices have not as yet evolved as acceptable alternatives to the weapons game. To the medium and small powers the goal of being included in some kind of collective security system is much more important than it is for the major powers, which already have sufficient military strength not to require such protection.

UNILATERAL DETERRENCE
Collective security alliances essentially provide security by threat. They threaten a potential aggressor that an attack on any member of the alliance will be considered an attack on all. Such an alliance raises the cost for the potential aggressor. Classically, collective alliances are designed therefore to

deter aggressive actions because of the preponderance of military strength that will be collectively mobilized. In a comparable manner the United States and the Soviet Union unilaterally, or mutually, pursue such deterrence strategies. By virtue of their nuclear weapons systems each superpower has the capability of destroying the other. Compared to collective security alliances the very extensive nuclear weapons systems of the superpowers are probably more realistic deterrents to blatant aggressive acts against each other. Such mutual deterrence could, of course, be altered by the development of new offensive or defensive nuclear weapons systems that could offset the mutual balance.

The outbreak of conflict in the Middle East in October 1973 raised a number of additional questions on the validity of collective security treaties. The fact that the United States unilaterally placed its armed forces on an alert because of intelligence assumptions concerning possible Soviet intervention in the Arab-Israeli conflict created anxiety among members of the North Atlantic Treaty Organization. The European members of NATO felt that the American action might have committed them without their participation in the decision. Moreover, the decision of the Arab oil-producing states to reduce oil shipments by 25 percent had an immediate impact on the European states in NATO who are largely dependent upon oil from the Arab states in North Africa and the Middle East. One after another, unilaterally, these European states shifted their position to support the Arab side of the conflict, which the Soviet Union was already supporting. Thus the United States and the Netherlands were alone in continuing to support Israel. The 1973 Middle East episode indicated the inherent weaknesses in a collective security alliance in which (1) the dominant member's actions might result in an involvement of commitments without consultation with the others in the alliance and (2) to be viable the alliance has to have an economic integrity or self-sufficiency so that members cannot be weaned away from joint policies by economic or other pressures.

CONTROLLING EXISTING WEAPONS SYSTEMS

The third approach as an alternative to continuing the upward spiral of the weapons game is to seek methods to control the existing weapons systems. Efforts were made in the Hague peace conferences in 1899 and 1907 to outlaw certain types of weapons. Declarations, binding on only the states that signed them, were adopted: outlawing for five years the dropping of projectiles and explosives from balloons; agreeing to abstain from use of projectiles in the diffusion of "asphyxiating or deleterious gases"; and prohibiting the use of expanding (or dumdum) bullets. Amazingly, these weapon developments at the time were considered so horrendous that they should be prohibited.

Gas was used in World War I killing about 100,000 and causing over 1.3 million casualties. The effect of this initial use of poison gas was so devastating and indiscriminate that it resulted in the Geneva Protocol of 1925, which prohibits the use of such chemical and bacteriological weapons as methods of warfare. Not all states have ratified this protocol.[25] However, despite the fact that many states have not as yet ratified the Geneva Protocol, these types of weapons are so difficult to use tactically that there is almost a tacit universal agreement not to employ them. Mustard gas was used by Italy in Ethiopia in 1935–1936, and in World War II, Japan employed poison gas in one engagement on the mainland of China. The prohibition however is simply against the use of these weapons. Most major military powers, however, stockpile such weapons so that they will be available if they are needed.

Prior to the end of World War II, the Hague declarations and the Geneva Protocol were the chief attempts to limit or control the use of arms. In the period since 1946, chiefly through the aegis of the United Nations, the 18-member Disarmament Committee in Geneva, and the Strategic Arms Limitation Talks held in Vienna, Helsinki, and Geneva between the United States and the Soviet Union, a number of agreements have been reached in this area of controlling weapons systems. The chief accomplishments in this approach have been:

1. *The Antarctic Treaty of 1959*—prohibits military use of Antarctica in any way;
2. *The Treaty Banning Nuclear Weapons Tests in the Atmosphere, in Outer Space and Under Water of 1963*—three of the five nuclear powers, the United States, the Soviet Union, and Great Britain, agreed to prohibit any testing of atomic weapons except underground tests;
3. *The Treaty on Principles Governing the Activities of States in the Exploration and Use of Outer Space, Including the Moon and Other Celestial Bodies of 1967*—prohibits any military developments on the moon or other celestial bodies;
4. *The Treaty for the Prohibition of Nuclear Weapons in Latin America of 1967*—states that the use of nuclear energy in Latin America shall be confined to peaceful uses—in essence establishing a military denuclearization of Latin America;
5. *The Treaty on the Non-Proliferation of Nuclear Weapons of 1968*—the nuclear powers that ratified the treaty agreed not to transfer nuclear weapons to any other states; the nonnuclear powers that ratified the treaty agreed not to receive nuclear weapons from any nuclear power.

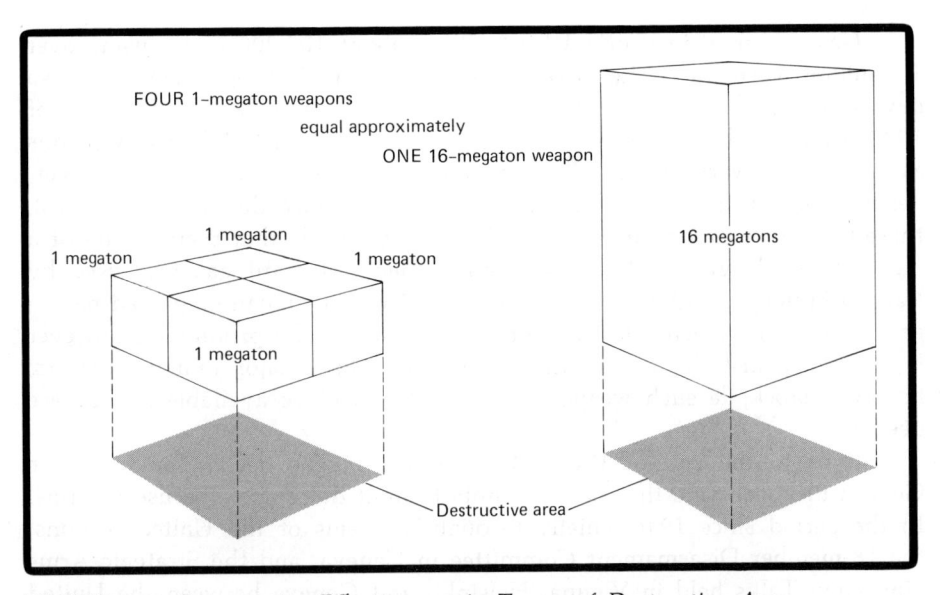

FIGURE 5.10 Comparative Effectiveness in Terms of Destructive Area

    Source: United States Foreign Policy 1973—A Report of the Secretary of State,
Washington, D.C.: GPO, 1973, p. 85.

6. *The Treaty on the Prohibition of the Emplacement of Nuclear Weapons and Other Weapons of Mass Destruction on the Sea-Bed and the Ocean Floor and in the Subsoil Thereof of 1970*—in essence this treaty is intended to prevent the nuclear arms race from extending to the sea bed and the ocean floor.

7. *The Convention on the Prohibition of the Development, Production, and Stockpiling of Bacteriological (Biological) and Toxic Weapons and on their Destruction of 1971*—incurs an obligation for those states that ratify the treaty (which will become effective after 22 states ratify it) to eliminate bacteriological weapons from their arms arsenals;

8. *The Treaty on the Limitation of Anti-Ballistic Missile Systems and the Interim Agreement on Certain Measures with Respect to the Limitation of Strategic Offensive Arms of 1972* between the United States and the Soviet Union—these agreements limit the deployment of antiballistic missiles to two designated areas in each state and limit the number of strategic offensive weapons to those already constructed or deployed when the agreement was signed; also while it limits the number of ground and sea-based missiles, it does not limit the total number of warheads, not does it place any limitation on intercontinental bombers capable of delivering nuclear weapons.

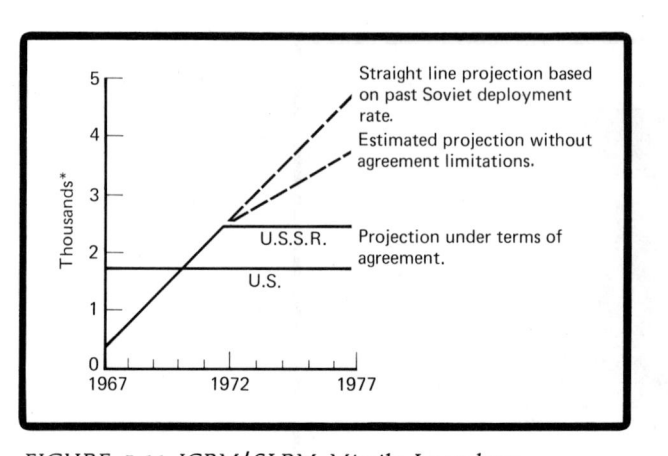

FIGURE 5.11 ICBM/SLBM Missile Launchers

Source: United States Foreign Policy 1972—A Report of the Secretary of State, Washington, D.C.: GPO, 1973, p. 74.

The problems of comparability of weapons systems was an issue in the American consideration of the ABM treaty (see 8 above). In brief, the problem revolved around the fact that the Soviet Union had larger megaton nuclear weapons and a greater number of ICBM/SLBM missile launchers than the United States. On the other hand, the United States had more strategic bombers capable of delivering nuclear weapons. In a word, the agreement had to involve compromises among weapons systems that were not identical. In explaining that the United States got its fair share of the compromise, the U.S. State Department explained that more, smaller megaton weapons were equal to fewer large megaton weapons, as Figure 5.10 shows. According to the State Department and as shown in Figure 5.11, the Soviet Union would end up with more ICBM/SLBM missile launchers, the United States had more strategic bombers that were not limited by the treaty, as shown in Figure 5.12.

The observer can be highly critical of these efforts at the control of the weapons game. It can be argued that they hardly arrest the continued proliferations of the arms race. One can argue that three of the nuclear states, France, India and the People's Republic of China, are not a party to these agreements and that this nullifies the intent of these agreements. One could further argue that many of the nonnuclear weapons states who have the technological and productive ability to produce nuclear weapons systems have not ratified the nonproliferation treaty and thus challenge the validity of its attempt. However, in the whole history of efforts to control the weapons game, these are probably the most significant thrusts.

A number of military experts argue that the best manner to control the weapons game is by the development of deterrent military systems in which

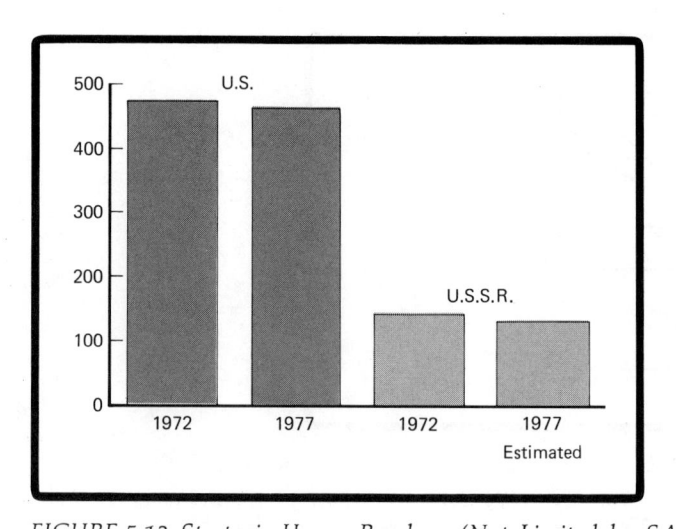

FIGURE 5.12 Strategic Heavy Bombers (Not Limited by SALT)

Source: United States Foreign Policy 1972—A Report of the Secretary of State, Washington, D.C.: GPO, 1973, p. 82.

the destructive costs of the use of the most sophisticated weapons systems serve to control their actual use.[26] This may be the effect of such deterrent systems, but it hardly eliminates the continual problem posed to the international system by the enormity of the military weapons stockpiles.

DE-ESCALATION OF THE WEAPONS GAME AND VALUE TRADE-OFFS

One of the dilemmas in attempts either to control or to unwind the weapons game is uncertainty of the economic and social consequences of any major disarmament efforts. In the more-developed countries the involvement of the industrial complex in the weapons game has, as we have indicated, permanently intertwined armaments with economic well-being. Any potential cut in weapons systems engenders opposition because of the economic consequences and displacements alleged to result from any changes. In the developing states, which tend to purchase rather than produce weapons systems, any disarmament moves would result in the release of masses of manpower. As Figure 5.13 shows, the manpower size of the armed forces in less-developed states exceeds the military manpower of developed states. Therefore the apprehension in the less-developed states concerns the consequences of a release of additional manpower into economies already struggling with unemployment and underemployment problems. However, the

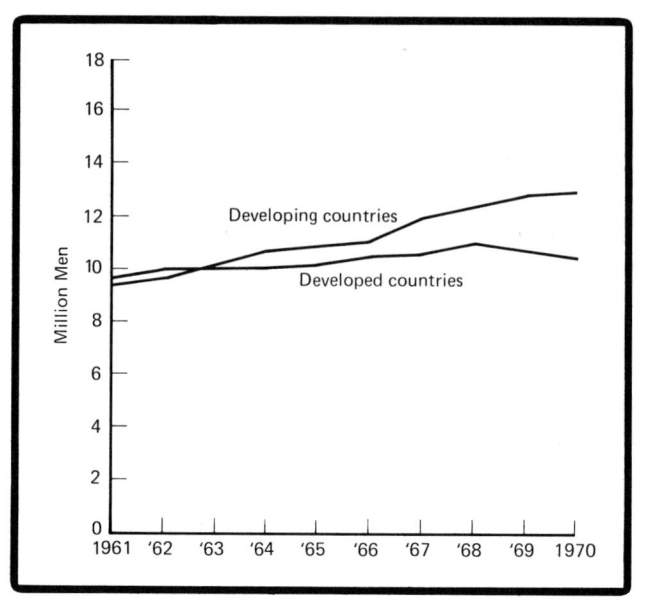

FIGURE 5.13 *Divergent Trends in the Size of Armed Forces in Developed and Developing Countries*

Source: U.S. Arms Control and Disarmament Agency, *World Military Expenditures 1971*, Washington, D.C.: GPO, 1972, p. 7.

release of funds from nonpurchase of military weapons could provide developing states with needed development funds. Nonetheless, the gap between the developing states and the developed states may well widen if the conversion only results in converting industries into nonmilitary production or enhances the rate of economic growth in developed states. Any disarmament efforts that further widen the development gap will not reduce tension and may thereby defeat real efforts at creating a durable peace.

A U.N. STUDY OF THE PROBLEMS OF DISARMAMENT

The states in the United Nations have become increasingly aware of these problems and have had the Secretary-General commission studies by experts on the economic and social consequences of disarmament. Beginning in 1962 several studies have been undertaken.[27] The 25th session of the General Assembly in 1970 requested a study of the problems of disarmament and development and the actions states might undertake to assure that any disarmament efforts close rather than widen the development gap. Such a possibility could be a key factor in building economic and social security for states in a disarmed world.

In 1972 a report by a group of experts on the economic and social conse-

quences of disarmament was issued.[28] The report points out that two of the greatest problems in the international system are the questions of the weapons race and the disparity of development. The experts suggest that these two issues are linked; the vast amount of resources used in the weapons race could be utilized to facilitate development. They felt that if the "blatant contrast" between the *waste of resources* and the *unfilled needs of the less-developed world* were viewed jointly, the result might contribute to arousing public opinion in favor of both "effective" disarmament and "progress" in Third World development. They urged states to consider these two issues together.

For example, they point specifically to consequences that might flow from international agreements involving a comprehensive nuclear test ban, chemical disarmament, the demilitarization of the sea bed and deep-sea environment, the elimination of foreign bases, and the withdrawal of foreign troops.

With respect to a possible treaty on a comprehensive test ban, they suggest that there is some question as to whether peaceful nuclear explosions will be economically attractive within the near future. But if economically viable, they should be made available to nonnuclear states as a means to assist energy development. The resources released by a test treaty would allow for the further development of nuclear energy. Through such a treaty an estimated 20,000 scientists and engineers would be available to assist in the development of *peaceful* nuclear programs. According to the group of experts,

> *If 2,000 tons of fissile material were released for peaceful purposes it would be enough to provide the initial and replacement fuel over their useful life for an installed capacity of about 100,000 electrical megawatts of thermal reactors or an installed capacity of about 500,000 electrical megawatts of fast breeder reactors.[29]*

In essence this would mean a considerable potential increase in plants producing nuclear energy. In terms of the nuclear energy plants already constructed and those on the drawing boards, the total production projected for 1980 is only 300,000 electrical megawatts. Thus this release of fissile nuclear material from the arms race with a test ban treaty might nearly double the production of nuclear energy sources by 1980.

With respect to a potential treaty bringing about chemical disarmament, the group suggests that this would appreciably add resources useful in ecologically acceptable pest control and toxicological research. Laboratory facilities could be converted to civilian uses and would assist in many areas of research and development as well as engendering confidence for further

disarmament steps when the public can see they are no longer being used for military research.

A treaty on the demilitarization of the sea bed and deep-sea environment they feel would open up the full possibilities of the utilization of these areas and their resources for the common benefit of both developed and developing states.

If there were treaties eliminating all foreign bases and providing for the withdrawal of foreign troops, this would have a significant impact on balance-of-payments problems. States withdrawing their forces would enjoy a gain in their balance of payments and, probably, a reduction of funds for military expenditures. In the states from which the troop withdrawals are made, their foreign exchange earning would be reduced, but this might be outweighed by the change in political conditions and their own reduction in military expenditures.

Most importantly the group of experts suggested the benefits from the conversion of military research and development funds to civilian research and development. Studies by the U.N. Secretariat have estimated that the world expenditure on research and development now amounts to $60 billion—about 2 percent of the world gross product—of which about $25 billion is for military purposes, primarily by the more-developed states. The group of experts stated:

> *These research and development resources, when diverted to peaceful uses, might have a great impact on development. A large and imaginative increase in peaceful research and development budgets will be required if all, or even a large part, of the research and development manpower employed on military work is to find peaceful research and development work. It is not possible for us—or probably for anyone —to say what would be the fruits of an expansion in peaceful research and development of the magnitude which disarmament would permit. All we can say with certainty is that there is a vast range of problems in the developing countries and that there are huge sophisticated resources absorbed by military research and development in the developed countries.*[30]

They then suggested a whole list of the possible peaceful uses of military research and development, which appears in Table 5.4.

The group of experts investigated the problem of conversion for developed states. In their 1962 report they had made a detailed study of the conversion of the U.S. economy from the military effort of World War II. The study indicated that the conversion was accomplished with comparatively little dislocation in a rather short time with the end result being a consider-

TABLE 5.4 PEACEFUL USES OF MILITARY RESEARCH AND DEVELOPMENT[a]

Military R and D	Peaceful R and D
1. Chemical and biological warfare	High-yielding varieties of staple food Edible protein Pest and vector control Communicable diseases control (including parasitic diseases)[b] Toxicological research Cancer research

2. Nuclear military programmes	Nuclear energy research and
	    development
	Nuclear explosions for stimulation
	    of gas and oil reservoirs and for
	    fracturing of ore bodies
	Nuclear explosions for large civil
	    engineering projects
	Research on:
	    (i) Small and medium nuclear power
	        reactors for developing countries
	    (ii) Agro-industrial complexes
	    (iii) Desalination

3. Civil engineering institutes for
defence work
	Urban renewal in general
	Research on indigenous building and
	    construction materials for
	    developing countries
	Housing construction methods for
	    quicker, lower cost production of
	    houses for developing countries
	Urban waste disposal, sanitary
	    equipment and pollution
	Highways, railroads, airports for both
	    developed and developing countries

4. Military aerospace research,
engineering, electronics
and telecommunications
	Appropriate aircraft and airport
	    facilities for developing countries
	Artificial organs and limbs
	Recording of human organs' function
	    for diagnostic and monitoring
	    purposes
	Models of vital organs (teaching
	    purposes)
	Observation of various health
	    parameters by means of telemetric
	    technology
	Environmental health monitoring
	Improvement of various laboratory
	    control methods through automated
	    instrumentation (higher precision;

TABLE 5.4 (*Continued*)

Military R and D	Peaceful R and D
	acceleration; design of various portable medical devices etc.)
	Improvement of pharmaceutical control
	Natural resource surveys by remote sensing from aircraft or satellites
	Fuel cells
	Solar energy (with or without use of satellites)
	Geothermal energy
	Natural disasters warning and meteorological research on tropical cyclones
5. Early detection of ICBM by satellite networks Military telecommunications agencies and institutes Military space technology	Natural disasters warning systems Broadcasting, television Communications satellites for education and training Telephones
6. Systems analysis techniques and computer technology used for military, aerospace and nuclear operations, military computerized data banks	Systems analysis techniques and computer technology applied to development problems, including health planning and operations Computer-aided instruction Training programmes on computers, data processing and programming in developing countries Science and technology information systems for developing countries Transfer of technology
7. Naval research institutes	Ocean shipping and ports of developing countries Off-shore oil exploration Mineral resources of the sea; exploration and inventory of water resources of developing countries Tidal power Fish research assessment Aquaculture R and D
8. Military engineering programmes	Human environment: (i) Non-pollutive sources of energy (ii) Recycling of waste (iii) Research on non-pollutive sources of energy (solar satellites, geothermal, fuel cells and other batteries for automobiles, solar cells)

TABLE 5.4 (*Continued*)

Military R and D	Peaceful R and D
9. Armaments industries under contracts by the military	Industrial research and design applied to local materials of developing countries—glass and ceramics Metallurgical processing Industrial chemicals Household chemicals for personal hygienic use Processing of natural fibres Plant and equipment design Appropriate technology Industrial research
10. Military institutes for research on food supplies	Storage and preservation of agricultural products
11. Military institutes for petroleum	Research, exploration and development of petroleum and gas
12. Military vehicles research	Design of automobiles adapted to the needs of developing countries Effects on man of noise and vibration
13. Release of classified information	Advances in peaceful research in any number of areas Transfer of technology Science and technology education
14. Armed forces training programmes	Improvement and strengthening of science teaching in secondary schools of developing countries; building up of scientific and technological capacity·
15. Military research in physiology, pathology and hygiene	Nutritional problems Health hazards of climate Occupational hazards and personal protection Readaptation processes Reanimation Mental health research Health hazards of ultrasonic waves Plastic surgery and burns

[a]Prepared by the United Nations Secretariat in co-operation with the secretariat of the World Health Organization. Many of the subjects listed are elaborated upon in the *World Plan of Action for the Application of Science and Technology to Development* (United Nations publication, Sales No. E.71.II.A.18).

[b]Particularly trypanosomiasis, leprosy, cholera, schistosomiasis.

Source: U.N. Department of Economic and Social Affairs, *Disarmament and Development* (Report of the Group of Experts on the Economic and Social Consequences of Disarmament), New York: United Nations, 1972, Annex III, pp. 33–37.

able growth in the U.S. economy. The 1972 report of the group of experts made an additional analysis of the consequences for the United States if there was to be disarmament and concluded that the impact of moving from a predominantly military to a predominantly civilian economy would have minimum shocks if the conversion simultaneously involved an emphasis on assistance to developing states.[31] Thus their overall conclusion was that a focus by the developed states on assisting the problems of the developing states would ease very appreciably any shifts from a military- to a civilian-oriented economy. The tying together of steps toward a reduction in arms with an increase in assistance to reduce the gap between the developed and developing states would make the achievement of both of these goals not only desirable but possible. Ultimately, they concluded, this would be a major contribution toward peaceful relationships in the world. Conversely, they argue, a separation of these two issues will make it less likely that they will be resolved and less likely that peaceful relations among states can be achieved. Their report suggests that this may be the only way in which states can achieve real security!

QUESTIONS UNANSWERED BY THE WEAPONS GAME

It is apparent that in the 1970s man has allowed weapons to dominate many, maybe even the most significant, policy decisions in the international system. The arms race in the weapons game, with only a few exceptions, is a continual upward spiral. The amount of resources of the finite planet earth that are being consumed for building destructive devices almost outweigh the use of resources for the betterment or even the survival of mankind. Man and his political institutions justify this continual playing of the weapons game as the essential ingredient for survival of the state. The pace of escalation has been such that now in the 1970s many of the economic and political institutions in the nation-states are dependent for their survival on the continuance of the weapons game.

Many key questions remain unanswered in this whole development of man and his weapons. Is stockpiling weapons really the only way for a state to acquire security? Do weapons really bring security for states? Can states survive and continue the weapons game? How can security be achieved without being dependent upon the weapons game? How does mankind extricate itself from the continual upward spiral of the weapons game? Could the amount of expenditures devoted to the research and development of weapons systems for just one year be devoted to seeking other alternatives to provide security for states? Or does the very nature of dividing the world into political states deter the possibility of states ever achieving security without the potential or actual use of force?

NOTES

[1]Costa Rica, Iceland, and three mini-states—Liechtenstein, Monaco, and Nauru—have no military forces. During World War II, Great Britain from 1940 to 1942 and the United States from 1942 to 1945 maintained forces in Iceland. After joining the North Atlantic Treaty Organization in 1949, Iceland in 1951 requested U.S. troops for defensive protection. The presence of these 3000 U.S. troops has since been a constant source of controversy. In 1956 the United States was asked to remove these forces, but this request was later rescinded. It again was an issue in both the 1968 and 1971 presidential elections in Iceland. The conservative coalition elected in 1971 was committed to the withdrawal of the U.S. contingent, but by the end of 1973 a formal request had not been made. (See Don Galenpaul, editor, *Information Please Almanac*, 1974, New York: Dan Galenpaul Associates, 1973, p. 226.) A national army was eliminated in Costa Rica in 1948, and a national police force with side arms only was substituted. It provides ordinary police protection and a small corps of officers for a civilian militia to defend the country in case of invasion. See Alexander T. Edelmann, *Latin American Government and Politics*, rev. ed., Homewood, Ill.: The Dorsey Press, 1969, pp. 183–184.

[2]U.S. Arms Control and Disarmament Agency, *World Military Expenditures, 1970*, p. 1.

[3]"Israel feels economic pinch of its most expensive war" (Associated Press feature story), Eugene *Register–Guard*, November 11, 1973, p. 11B.

[4]"Israelis told war casualty figures higher," Associated Press, the Portland *Oregonian*, December 9, 1973, p. 2.

[5]Quoted in David Bergamini, *Japan's Imperial Conspiracy*, New York: Pocket Books, 1972, p. 84.

[6]This information is derived from the annual reports of the United States Arms Control and Disarmament Agency on *World Military Expenditures* for 1971 and 1972.

[7]Canada, Luxembourg, Turkey, United Kingdom, Bulgaria, Ireland, Argentina, Chile, Honduras, Venezuela, Burma, Philippines, Afghanistan, and Tunisia.

[8]East Germany, Hungary, Spain, Yugoslavia, Bolivia, Brazil, Guatemala, Guyana, Jamaica, Trinidad and Tobago, Cambodia, Japan, North Korea, South Vietnam, Cyprus, Egypt, Iran, Israel, Kuwait, Saudi Arabia, Yemen, Central African Republic, Chad, Congo (Brazzaville), Dahomey, Gabon, Guinea, Ivory Coast, Libya, Mauritania, Southern Rhodesia, Senegal, Somali Republic, Republic of South Africa, Sudan, Tanazia, Togo, Uganda, Upper Volta, and Zaire.

[9]Lincoln P. Bloomfield and Amelia C. Leiss et al., *The Control of Local Conflict*, Cambridge, Mass.: Center for International Studies, 1969, lists at least 52 military conflicts from 1945 to 1967. *Ibid.*, vol. 3, p. 9.

[10]George Thayer, *The War Business: The International Trade in Armaments*, New York: Simon & Schuster, 1969, p. 19.

[11]Herbert F. York, *Race to Oblivion: A Participant's View of the Arms Race*, New York: Simon & Schuster, 1970.

[12]Thayer, *op. cit.*, p. 18.

[13]U.S. Department of Defense, *Toward a National Security Strategy of Realistic Deterrence—Statement of Secretary of Defense, Melvin R. Laird on the Fiscal Year 1972-1973 Defense Program and the 1972 Defense Budget* (before the Senate Armed Services Committee, March 15, 1971), p. 15.

[14]See Defense Department figures quoted in *National Diplomacy, 1965–1970*, Washington, D.C.: Congressional Quarterly, 1970; *Global Defense—U.S. Military Commitments Abroad*, Washington, D.C.: Congressional Quarterly, 1969; and *The Power of the Pentagon*, Washington, D.C.: Congressional Quarterly, 1972.

[15]This data is obtained from U.S. Senate, Committee on Appropriations, *Senate Hearings—Foreign Assistance and Related Programs Appropriations—Fiscal 1973*, 92nd Cong., 2d sess., 1972, 1182 pp.

[16]These figures and many of the others previously cited are taken from *The Statis-*

tical Abstract of the United States, which is prepared annually by the Bureau of Census of the U.S. Department of Commerce.

[17]*The Power of the Pentagon, op. cit.,* p. 3.

[18]The *New York Times,* December 3, 1972, sect. 3, p. 1.

[19]A detailed discussion of these guerrilla operations in Laos can be found in *The Power of the Pentagon, op. cit.,* pp. 68–69.

[20]In July 1973 Congress learned that air force bombing in Cambodia had not only been kept secret from the Congress, but the military had kept it also from the (civilian) Secretary of the Air Force.

[21]United Nations, *Basic Problems of Disarmament—Reports of the Secretary-General,* New York: United Nations, 1970.

[22]*Ibid.,* Report of the Secretary-General on *Chemical and Bacteriological (Biological) Weapons and the Effects of Their Possible Use.*

[23]In July 1969 the membership was enlarged from 18 to 26, and the name changed to the Conference of the Committee on Disarmament.

[24]The U.N. Charter was later amended to increase the membership of Security Council to 15, and decisions could be taken by a majority of 9 of the 15, including the 5 major states.

[25]The United States has not as yet ratified the 1925 Geneva Protocol. In 1969, however, there were hearings in the U.S. House of Representatives on the desirability of ratifying the prohibition. U.S. policy has been to have these weapons available but to use them only in retaliation. President Nixon by executive order has stopped development of new bacteriological weapons.

[26]See, for example, Wesley W. Posvar, "The New Meaning of Arms Control," *Air Force Magazine* (June 1963), 38–45.

[27]U.N. Department of Economic and Social Affairs, *Economic and Social Consequences of Disarmament* (Report of the Secretary-General transmitting the study of his consultative group), New York: United Nations, 1962, 72 pp.

[28]U.N. Department of Economic and Social Affairs, *Disarmament and Development* (Report of the Group on the Economic and Social Consequences of Disarmament), New York: United Nations, 1972, 37 pp.

[29]*Ibid.,* p. 17.

[30]*Ibid.*

[31]Even without assistance to developing nations, conversion to disarmament for the United States is economically feasible. The U.S. Arms Control and Disarmament Agency has studied the problem with the assistance of experts. To quote a recent report:

> Conducted over a period of 2 years by a team of prominent economists and other social scientists from 11 different institutions of higher learning, the study projects the impact of various assumed levels of military spending on national, regional, state, and local levels, as well as their impact on industries and individuals. It includes an analysis of the effects of three different levels of military expenditures on each of the 50 states and the District of Columbia, and on 219 major metropolitan areas. The findings include the following:
>
> — A strong affirmation that the U.S. prosperity is not dependent on military spending.
> — Military spending is not unique. The same effects can be generated by alternative government spending programs or by private spending.
> — In the process of moving from higher to lower levels of defense expenditures, there would be transitional difficulties for some individuals, communities, and industries and a temporary increment to the unemployed rate. It is anticipated that this problem could be eased by advance planning and remedial action by local, state, and national agencies.

U.S. Arms Control and Disarmament Agency, *10th Annual Report to Congress, January 1, 1970–December 31, 1970,* Washington, D.C.: GPO, 1971, p. 26.

6

MAN AND HIS GOVERNMENTAL RELATIONS

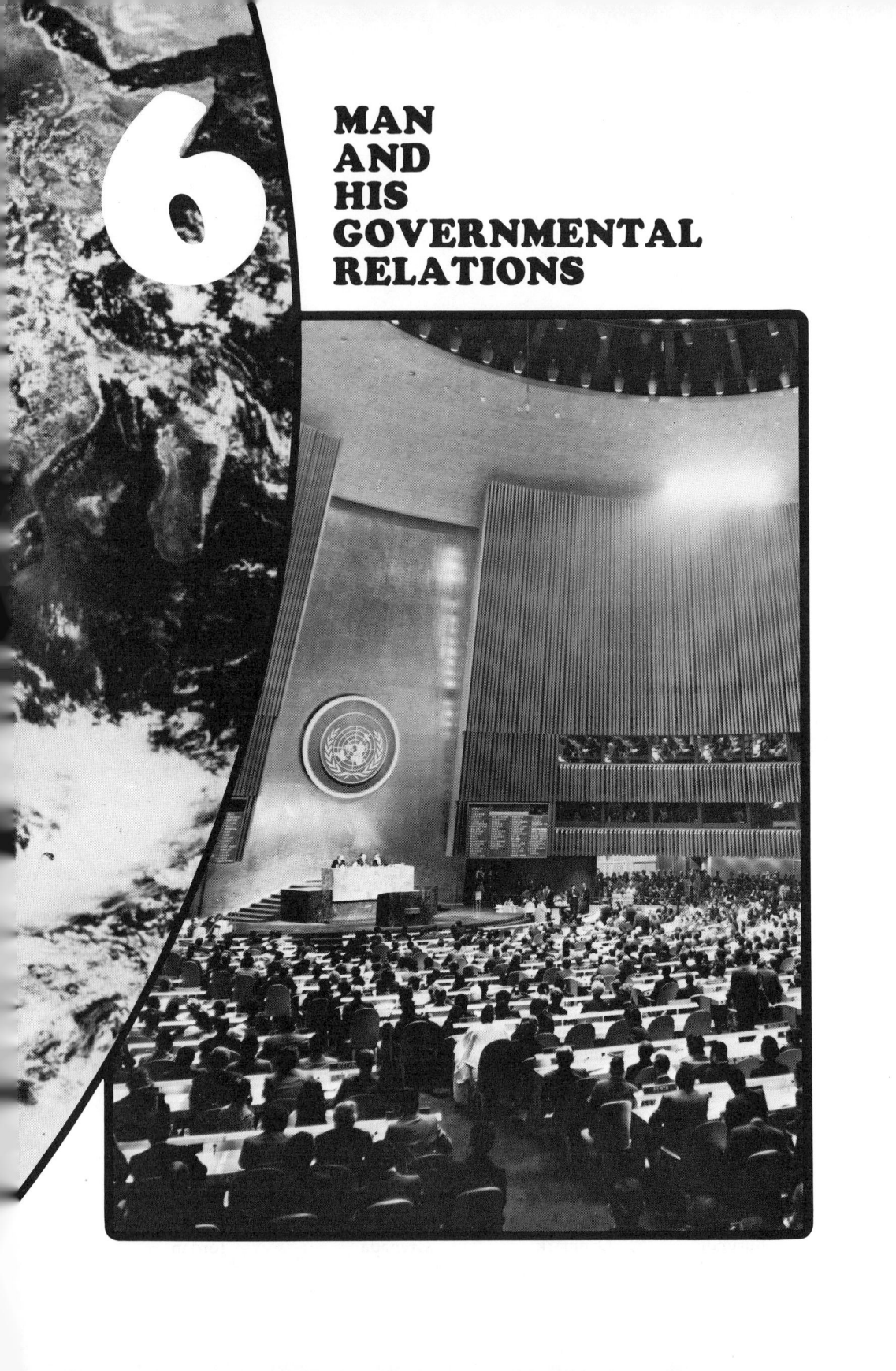

No nation, however powerful and wealthy, is
nowadays sufficient unto itself. Interdependence
is a vital factor in our world and so is the existence
of international machinery to promote an orderly
world development.

U Thant
1968

Since the Peace of Westphalia in 1648 the earth has been organized
politically and juridically into a system of so-called sovereign states. In 1974
there were 150 political states that could be called independent, and some 33
political entities in a dependent political relationship to the independent
states.[1] The following list of independent states does not include Byelorussia
and the Ukraine (both of which are members of the United Nations) nor
Rhodesia, because these three states are not recognized by any other states
as independent.

INDEPENDENT POLITICAL STATES

Afghanistan	Cambodia	Dominican	Guatemala
Albania	Cameroon	Republic	Guinea
Algeria	Canada	Ecuador	Guinea-Bissau
Andorra	Central African	Egypt	Guyana
Argentina	Republic	El Salvador	Haiti
Australia	Chad	Equatorial Guinea	Honduras
Austria	Chile	Ethiopia	Hungary
Bahamas	China, People's	Fiji	Iceland
Bahrain	Republic of	Finland	India
Bangladesh	China,	France	Indonesia
Barbados	Republic of	Gabon	Iran
Belgium	Colombia	Gambia	Iraq
Bhutan	Congo	German Demo-	Ireland
Bolivia	Costa Rica	cratic Republic	Israel
Botswana	Cuba	Germany, Federal	Italy
Brazil	Cyprus	Republic of	Ivory Coast
Bulgaria	Czechoslovakia	Ghana	Jamaica
Burma	Dahomey	Greece	Japan
Burundi	Denmark	Grenada	Jordan

INDEPENDENT POLITICAL STATES (*Continued*)

Kenya	Monaco	San Marino	Turkey
Korea, Democratic	Mongolia	Saudi Arabia	Uganda
People's	Morocco	Senegal	United Arab
Republic of	Nauru	Sierra Leone	Emirates
Korea, Republic of	Nepal	Singapore	United Kingdom
Kuwait	Netherlands	Somalia	U.S.A.
Laos	New Zealand	South Africa	Upper Volta
Lebanon	Nicaragua	Soviet Union	Uruguay
Lesotho	Niger	Spain	Vatican City
Liberia	Nigeria	Sri Lanka	Venezuela
Libya	Norway	Sudan	Vietnam,
Liechtenstein	Oman	Swaziland	Democratic
Luxembourg	Pakistan	Sweden	Republic of
Madagascar	Panama	Switzerland	Vietnam,
Malawi	Paraguay	Syria	Republic of
Malaysia	Peru	Tanzania	Western Samoa
Maldives	Philippines	Thailand	Yemen (Aden)
Mali	Poland	Togo	Yemen (San'ā)
Malta	Portugal	Tonga	Yugoslavia
Mauritania	Qatar	Trinidad and	Zaire
Mauritius	Romania	Tobago	Zambia
Mexico	Rwanda	Tunisia	

The global ecosystem has therefore been compartmentalized into at least 183 different political entities. Legally it can be argued that each of these political entities is sovereign unto itself. In political rhetoric it is argued that each group of peoples has a right to determine its own destiny. Historically, each state jealously attempts to assert its independence from all other states. Historical circumstances or accidents have often determined the boundaries of states with little respect to the ability of the political units to actually exist independent of the other states.

Such a system of political relationships may have been valid in 1648 when the then acknowledged political world was a score of states in Europe. In 1648 most of the people were primarily aware of their immediate neighbors and only vaguely aware of people in more distant parts of the earth. In 1648 there was little industrialization, few trade ties among the states, and little or no communication among peoples at a distance from each other.

In the 1970s the world is still organized politically on the basis of the state-system concept of 1648. True there are many more political entities than in 1648. Yet the legal myth of the sovereign state persists, political rhetoric still advocates rights to self-determination, and each state regardless of the logic of its boundaries attempts to assert to the maximum degree possible its independence from all other states.

If we could be an observer from another world looking at the situation on earth in the 1970s, what would we observe? Apart from a wide variety of short-term problems among states, we could observe that there are three overriding long-range problems that affect everyone on earth. These overriding problems, as we have suggested, are the condition of the environment, the disparity of economic well-being, and the unprecedented magnitude of the arms race. The solution of the first problem is crucial to the ability of mankind to survive. The solution of the second problem is crucial to prevent an outbreak of conflict that could destroy human life on the planet. The elimination of the third problem is essential to prevent mankind from destroying itself. The failure to resolve these problems may appear to the other-world observer as a product of the way in which mankind has politically denied the whole earth.

To the outside observer the political compartmentalization of earth might seem strange. The states are not equal political units. They range from the Republic of Nauru with a population of 6,768 and an area of 8.2 square miles to the People's Republic of China with a population of 800,720,000 and an area of 3,391,502 square miles. They are not wholly self-sufficient. Even a superpower like the Soviet Union had to obtain grain from the United States in 1972. Even an economic power like Japan is so dependent on the importation of oil that she was "forced" to reverse her Middle East policy in the face of the Arab oil boycott in 1973.

It might be easy for the outside observer to suggest that we need to reorganize our planet politically to deal effectively with these fundamental problems. In fact, many idealists have suggested that what we need is a world government. While this may be an obvious solution, not every individual on earth believes in or accepts this solution, and those who do advocate it do not agree on a similar concept of what would be the ideal type of world government.

The facts are these: The world is politically compartmentalized. The nature of the political divisions has developed historically. These political compartments—states—have not been able to exist in complete isolation or separation from each other. They have evolved a wide variety of legal, diplomatic, organizational, and political relationships to enable them to exist in the compartmentalized situation. In addition the people within the states have also evolved a variety of relationships outside the formal ties among states.

The questions that need to be asked are whether these relationships are sufficient or even capable of dealing with the overriding problems upon which human survival depends. Before we can reflect on those questions, we need to acquire a sense of the relationships that do exist among the political compartments on earth.

RELATIONS AMONG
PEOPLES IN A LEGAL SENSE

Prior to 1648 political systems had either been organized in the sense of a universal empire—a single monolithic state—or separate states whose rulers owed ultimate allegiance to God through his representative, the pope. The modern system of states has its origins both in Jean Bodin's concept of sovereignty (i.e., that there is no higher power than the sovereign ruler in a territorial unit) and the Peace of Westphalia. To the evolving society in Europe there was little awareness, acknowledgment, or concern with the fact that there were or had been other universal empires in China, India, the Arab world, or Africa, let alone the Mayan or Incan empires in the Americas. To the Europeans at Westphalia, images of the past were rooted in the Greek city-state system, the Macedonian Empire, and the traditions of the Roman Empire.

The significance of the Peace of Westphalia was to assert that there was an equality among territorial units in that each had no higher authority than their individual sovereign rulers. By such treaties these sovereign rulers recognized each other as equals in that they were equally independent in exercising and asserting control over the territory they ruled. Implicit also was the assumption that such other states as might assert their independence would only achieve this independence, and therefore exist, when they had been recognized as independent by those states that were already accepted as units within the international system.

This recognition principle became embodied in the system of international law evolved by European states. As the developing Industrial Revolution made global ventures possible and necessary, the states asserted their influence and control over Asia, Africa, and the Americas. The legal system that evolved from the Peace of Westphalia meant that *if* Europeans did not recognize other societies as sovereign and organized, they could legally justify occupation and control of these areas. International law in the seventeenth and eighteenth centuries treated non-European areas as "uncivilized" or "unorganized" societies because they were not *recognized* as sovereign states by the existing sovereign states of Europe. This traditional concept of recognition is now under attack because it can result in ridiculous situations. Israel achieved independence in 1948 and despite being involved with the Arab states in four wars, the Arab states do not recognize Israel's juridical existence. Critics of this concept argue that a new state has a right to recognition by the fact of its existence.

The Peace of Westphalia also asserted in fact that states were sovereign and equal in a system of international law—a law among states—not a law

over states. Stress was placed on the sovereign equality of states before the law, even though the law reflected the views of the more politically dominant states. It did not argue that in terms of population or area of resources that states were in fact either equal or equally sovereign and independent. It is a system of law of coordination rather than the more traditional concept of a law of subordination. The law is made by agreement among the states; there is no argument about being subordinate to any universal law authority. The law evolved either from customary practices among states or by virtue of the more formal written agreements—treaties, conventions, executive agreements, and the like—which established a juridical network of obligations among states. Multilateral treaties may involve obligations for most states in the international system, while bilateral treaties bind only two states in the system. The result is that each state has accumulated its own unique combination of multilateral and bilateral treaty obligations.[2] The following list gives the example of New Zealand.

ILLUSTRATION OF THE "TREATY NETWORK"—INTERNATIONAL AGREEMENTS, SIGNED, RATIFIED OR ACCEPTED BY ONE STATE (NEW ZEALAND) IN ONE YEAR (1 APRIL 1971 TO 31 MARCH 1972)

A. *Multilateral Treaties:*
   1969 Vienna Convention on the Law of Treaties
   1962 Amendments to the International Convention for the Prevention of Pollution of the Sea by Oil
   1968 Protocol to the Convention of the International Civil Aviation Organization
   1971 Agreement Establishing a Registry of Scientific and Technical Services for the Asian and Pacific Region
   1970 Convention for the Suppression of Unlawful Seizure of Aircraft
   1970 Amendment to the Statute of the International Atomic Energy Commission
   1969 Acts of the XVIth Congress of the Universal Postal Union
   1971 Agreement relating to the International Telecommunications Satellite Organization Intelsat
   1971 Treaty on the Prohibition of the Emplacement of Nuclear Weapons and Other Weapons of Mass Destruction on the Seabed and the Ocean Floor and in the Subsoil Thereof

B. *Bilateral Treaties:*
   1971 Loan Agreement (Second Railway Project) with the International Bank for Reconstruction and Development
   1971 Exchange of letters with Indonesia providing a New Zealand loan for purchase of New Zealand goods

1971 Exchange of letters with Canada concerning the implementation of a 1970 protocol to the 1932 trade agreement

1971 Exchange of letters with UNESCO with regard to UNESCO assistance in projects in the educational field

1971 Exchange of letters with the United Kingdom concerning the guarantee of the United Kingdom for the maintenance of the minimum sterling proportion by New Zealand

1971 Exchange of letters with the Food and Agriculture Organization relating to New Zealand hosting a FAO seminar on the design and construction of ferro-cement fishing vessels

1971 Exchange of notes with the government of Singapore relating to assistance for the Singapore armed forces and on arrangements for a New Zealand force in Singapore

1971 Exchange of notes with Malaysia for assisting the Malaysian armed forces and on arrangements for a New Zealand force in Malaysia

1972 Agreement with the International Atomic Energy Agency for the application of safeguards in connection with the Treaty on the Non-Proliferation of Nuclear Weapons.[3]

THE UNEVEN DEVELOPMENT OF INTERNATIONAL LAW

As a means of regulating relations among "sovereign and equal" states, such a system of international law in the 1970s has both a significant role and an inadequate role. As a law among states rather than over states, the development of the law has been uneven. It is most sophisticated at points where it is to the mutual self-interest of states to regularize their relationships. In the area of the exchanges of diplomats from one state to another, for example, international law is highly developed in providing for diplomatic privileges and immunities. It is in the mutual interest of all states that their envoys have the maximum degree of freedom from pressure and interference in their roles as representatives of one state in another.

In the area of transportation and commerce the law is also fairly well-developed. It is of mutual interest that there be common landing procedures for international aircraft, for instance, as well as common rules for international ships, if for no other reason than to minimize the occurrence of collisions. Similarly, the transit of goods from one state to another via third states necessitates certain basic agreements so that mutual trade is facilitated.

On the other hand, there are many areas in which the interests of the states vary to a considerable degree, and these are areas in which international law is underdeveloped. For example, how far may a coastal state extend its authority off its coast? For several centuries there was general agreement that the extent of the territorial sea jurisdiction was 3 miles, the distance a state could effectively assert its jurisdiction from land (the distance of a can-

non shot). Even though the possibility of improved artillery might have extended this 3-mile assertion of authority, it remained virtually unchallenged until the twentieth century. As technological developments made it possible for intensive fishing farther and farther from the shore, the question of territorial sea jurisdiction in international law was reopened. Instead of a 3-mile limit many states began to argue 12- and 15-mile limits. An international conference convened by the League of Nations in 1930 was unable to settle the question, though most states by custom held to a 3-mile territorial limit with an additional 9 miles for exclusive fishing rights.

Most coastlines are characterized by a continental shelf that in many cases extends from 15 to 100 miles or so before the depth of the water exceeds 200 meters. By 1945 technological advances made feasible the setting up of offshore rigs to drill for oil on the continental shelf. Several states then advanced, in their self-interest, the doctrine of jurisdiction over the continental shelf as an extension of their land mass. While the continental shelf doctrine was accepted in an international convention in 1958—that is, giving the coastal states rights over exploiting the resources of the continental shelf, disputes have arisen in the North Sea and off the Asian coast as to precisely where continental shelf "boundaries" among states begin and end.

By the early 1970s the question of the extent of the territorial sea was still in dispute. Many states now claim jurisdiction of 200 miles from their shorelines. At the same time, the technical feasibility of the extraction of minerals from the sea bed and ocean floor beyond the continental shelf has raised new questions. While the majority of states have agreed in principle that the sea bed and ocean floor should be under the control of an international authority and that these resources shall be developed for the benefit of all mankind, there is still no agreement on an international treaty settling the issue.

While these are but a few illustrations of the development and inadequacies of international law, it is apparent that as a means of regulating relations among states international law is most developed in the areas in which the mutual self-interests of the several states are comparable or the same. International law is not as "developed," or the "existing" law is subject to challenge, when the self-interests of states diverge.

PRESSURES ON INTERNATIONAL LAW
Since World War II, traditional international law has also been subjected to two other general areas of pressure in its use as a means of regulating relations among states. First proliferation of newly independent states from Asia and Africa and the emergence of the Soviet Union have challenged many concepts of international law as not really reflecting a true *international* law, but rather an international law that has its base, and is biased, in terms

of Roman and Anglo-Saxon traditions of law. Different emphases and different interpretations of the existing international law are being made by the Soviets, the Chinese, other Asians, and Africans in efforts to have it reflect their customs, traditions, standards, and interests.

A second general area of pressure is an increasing awareness that states cannot be entirely sovereign within their territories without causing conflicts in the international system. Increasingly, questions are being raised as to international standards of behavior by states with respect to the fundamental human rights of individuals. Many states are concerned with having international law protect the civil, political, and social rights of individuals. It is argued that individuals as well as states have a status in international law. In Western Europe this has led to the development of a European commission and a European court of human rights concerned with maintaining an international standard to protect the rights of individuals. Prior to the establishment of this European commission and court of human rights, the French-speaking population of Belgium, for instance, in many subtle ways discriminated against the Flemish-speaking Belgiums. The process had been in existence for so long that the discriminatory practices virtually excluded the Flemish-speaking members of the population from certain avenues of work. By virtue of appeal to the European commission (and in some instances the European court) of human rights, the subtle practices of discrimination were brought out in the public eye, and the Belgian parliament responded with an alteration or elimination of the discriminatory laws.

It may be "easy" for the Western European states with their similar cultural heritages to agree among themselves on fundamental human rights, but it becomes a very complex process when cultures and values vary. Yet the need to develop an international law guaranteeing individual rights is real; the contemporary world has experienced many conflict situations stemming from the deprivation of human rights. Controversy existed, for example, over whether there is a legal right of self-determination and the obligations of colonial states such as Portugal to relinquish control of Angola, Mozambique, and Guinea-Bissau (instead of maintaining the legal fiction that these territories have achieved self-determination because they are an "integral" part of Portugal). The policies of apartheid in South Africa are a source of continual tension in the international system because rights of the African majority are denied by an oppressive minority. These laws create different rights for whites, Asians, "Cape Coloreds," and Africans, placing them into separate communities on the basis of race. The Asian and African states protest this as a violation of fundamental human rights. South Africa argues that such international concern violates its right to have internal freedom to adopt its own laws.

While international law in the 1970s faces many challenges posed by

developments in technology and the increasing conflicts among states of varying legal traditions, it still serves to regularize many important relationships
among states. Most of the relationships among states are regularized by accepted principles of international law. Procedures for the exchange of diplomats, trade relationships, responsibilities with respect to foreign nationals
and interests, the passage of ships and airplanes, determinations of national-
ity and citizenship, are all regulated by existing principles of international
law. There is an absolute need to have agreed principles in the interrelationships among states. However, the real challenge to international law in the
future is rooted in its very nature. Law among states develops primarily when
the states have mutual self-interests that are accepted as common legal principles. In those areas in which states have competing or differing self-interests
international law does not command the universal acceptance that would
facilitate resolution of conflicts.

While it would be highly desirable if all state conflicts could be resolved
within the confines of an adjudication body, the fact is that few states in the
international system accept the compulsory jurisdiction of the International
Court of Justice. States are *unwilling*, in the assertion of their sovereign
independence, to subordinate their conflicts to adjudication of the major issues
that divide them. In issues that have only technical legal connotations, they
often agree to adjudication; but political issues are dealt with by other means
in the international system. This does not mean that states do not pay attention to the legal side of the issues. On the contrary, in international disputes
both sides usually explain in great and sometimes exasperating detail the
justification of their acts with reference to their interpretation of what is (or
should be) international law on the subject. The military intervention of one
state against another state is even justified by legal arguments. Self-interest
is a policy of continual self-justification using whatever bona-fide or spurious
material might be available—international law serves one important part of
an argument of being "right." For example, Israel argues under Article 51
of the U.N. Charter that she is exercising an act of individual self-defense
when her armed forces strike into Lebanon and destroy bases of the Palestine
nationalists. Israel argues that such action is a preemptive act of self-defense
to prevent another "terrorist infiltration" of its border. Lebanon argues that
such retaliatory action by Israel is in violation of Article 2, Paragraph 4 of
the U.N. Charter by which all states pledge to refrain from the use of force
against the territorial integrity of any state. The fact of the matter is that
international law at the same time it prohibits the use of force recognizes a
right of individual self-defense. Each side, as in the border problems between
Israel and Lebanon, can claim a right for their actions under international
law. Hence in one sense—perhaps tragic in terms of the magnitude of problems facing individuals on the earth—the Peace of Westphalia and the sub-

sequent development of international law has actually provided legal justification for the division of the earth's surface into separate political entities. They have provided a rationale for the continued separation of states rather than for their unification in facing the issues affecting the survival of mankind.

ACTUAL RELATIONS AMONG UNEQUAL STATES

The sovereign equality concept probably had more validity as a political reality when the states recognized as states in the international system were the states in Western Europe. But as the number of states recognized in the international system has grown, the inequality of states has become more and more evident as a political reality. The right of people to assert their self-determination, which is implicit in the American Declaration of Independence and the French Declaration of the Rights of Man and Citizen, gained momentum in the twentieth century as the absolute monarchies gave way to representative governments. The right of self-determination publically advocated by Woodrow Wilson in 1919, was formalized in the U.N. Charter. While the areas dominated with the outward expansion of European powers into the Americas, Africa, and Asia were not given recognition in the international system, the assertion of the right of self-determination of the peoples in these European colonized territories has now met with acceptance.

The world of the early 1970s is divided into more sovereign independent units than ever before in recent history. Well over seven-eighths of the world population has now achieved independence. Between 1950 and 1973, 64 former colonial areas achieved independence in the international system by acts of self-determination that have been recognized by other states. This contrasts with the situation in 1920, when well over half of the world's population was in colonial regimes dominated by European states.

The diversity among states is greater than ever before, ranging from small island states like Tonga, Nauru, Western Samoa, and Barbados to massive superpowers like the United States and the Soviet Union. States range in population size from less than 7000 people to over 800 million people. States range in the degree of economic development from a gross national product of less than $30 million to over a trillion dollars. The question of whether the states are really equally sovereign is self-evident in their actual inequality. Tables 6.1 and 6.2 show some of the economic and military disparities that exist.

Arguing a legal rationale that states are sovereign and equal is considerably different than the reality of actual independence and obvious inequal-

TABLE 6.1 DISPARITY OF ECONOMIC STRENGTH AMONG STATES, 1971[a]

	Economic Strength				
Rank	Gross National Product (billion dollars)		Population (millions)	GNP per Capita (dollars)	
1	United States	976.8	People's Rep. of China 836.0	United States	4,758
2	Soviet Union	497.0	India 553.8	Kuwait	3,929
3	Japan	197.2	Soviet Union 242.8	Sweden	3,872
4	West Germany	185.5	United States 205.3	Canada	3,651
5	France	145.9	Pakistan 130.2	Switzerland	3,256
6	United Kingdom	121.0	Japan 103.4	Luxembourg	3,237
7	People's Rep. of China	120.0	Brazil 95.2	Denmark	3,146
8	Italy	91.8	West Germany 61.7	West Germany	3,006
9	Canada	78.1	United Kingdom 55.8	France	2,872
10	India	52.9	Nigeria 55.1	Norway	2,864
11	Poland	39.4	Italy 53.6	Australia	2,639
12	Brazil	35.4	France 50.8	Belgium	2,590
13	Mexico	33.0	Mexico 50.7	Iceland	2,435
14	Spain	32.4	Philippines 38.4	Netherlands	2,405
15	East Germany	32.3	Thailand 37.5	United Kingdom	2,168
16	Sweden	31.4	Turkey 35.3	Finland	2,166
17	Netherlands	31.3	Egypt 33.3	Czechoslovakia	2,103
18	Czechoslovakia	30.5	Spain 33.3	Soviet Union	2,047
19	Belgium	25.1	Poland 32.5	Japan	1,907
20	Argentina	23.8	Rep. of Korea 31.8	New Zealand	1,903
21	Romania	22.8	Iran 28.7	Israel	1,897
22	Switzerland	20.5	Burma 27.6	East Germany	1,839
23	Yugoslavia	19.0	Ethiopia 25.3	Austria	1,866
24	Pakistan	17.5	Argentina 24.1	Italy	1,713
25	Rep. of South Africa	16.7	Canada 21.4	Libya	1,653
26	Denmark	15.7	Colombia 21.1	Hungary	1,388
27	Hungary	14.3	Yugoslavia 20.5	Ireland	1,332
28	Austria	13.8	Romania 20.3	Poland	1,212
29	Norway	11.2	North Vietnam 20.1	Bulgaria	1,153
30	Venezuela	10.3	Rep. of South Africa 20.1	Romania	1,099

[a]Includes only the 30 largest of the developed and less-developed states.
Source: U.S. Arms Control and Disarmament Agency, *World Military Expenditures 1971*, Washington, D.C.: GPO, 1972, p. 50.

TABLE 6.2 DISPARITY OF MILITARY STRENGTH AMONG STATES, 1971[a]

Military Strength		
Military Expenditures Rank (billion dollars)	Armed Forces (thousands)	Expenditures per Man (dollars)
1 United States 77.80	Soviet Union 3,535	United States 25,384
2 Soviet Union 65.00	People's Rep. of	
3 People's Rep.	China 3,100	Canada 20,495
of China 10.00	United States 3,066	Soviet Union 18,388
4 West Germany 6.20	India 1,200	Israel 16,259
5 France 6.00	Rep. of Vietnam 1,000	Australia 15,635
6 United King-		
dom 5.90	Rep. of Korea 645	Switzerland 15,071
7 Italy 2.50	China (Taiwan) 522	United Kingdom 15,038
8 Poland 2.20	France 506	Trinidad & Tobago 15,000
9 East Germany 2.20	West Germany 484	Sweden 13,768
10 Canada 1.90	Turkey 477	West Germany 12,742
11 India 1.80	North Vietnam 452	France 11,812
12 Czechoslovakia 1.70	North Korea 438	East Germany 10,891
13 Japan 1.50	Italy 413	Kuwait 10,429
14 Israel 1.40	United Kingdom 390	Norway 9,463
15 Australia 1.30	Indonesia 375	Netherlands 9,058
16 Spain 1.20	Pakistan 340	Rep. of South
17 Sweden 1.10	Egypt 300	Africa 9,000
18 Netherlands 1.10	Poland 287	Denmark 8,178
19 Rep. of Viet-		Czechoslovakia 8,177
nam 1.10	Spain 281	New Zealand 8,077
20 Brazil 1.00	Yugoslavia 257	Chad 8,000
21 Egypt .92	Japan 250	Cyprus 8,000
22 Iran .83	Iran 238	Luxembourg 8,000
23 North Korea .70	Romania 231	Mauritania 8,000
24 Belgium .70	Brazil 225	Poland 7,840
25 Yugoslavia .67	Nigeria 220	Belgium 7,337
26 Pakistan .65	Czechoslovakia 203	Saudi Arabia 6,950
27 Romania .61	East Germany 202	Venezuela 6,581
28 Hungary .56	Cuba 200	Japan 6,088
29 Argentina .51	Portugal 185	Italy 6,051
30 China (Taiwan) .48	Thailand 175	Central African
		Rep. 6,000

[a]Includes only the 30 largest developed and less-developed states.
Source: U.S. Arms Control and Disarmament Agency, *World Military Expenditures 1971*, Washington, D.C.: GPO, 1972, p. 50.

ity. Each state in its public rhetoric asserts its independence from every other state. In reality states are enmeshed in a web of relationships with each other. No state is independent of trade relationships with each other. Not only are states exchanging economic goods, but the private businesses engaged in much of this economic activity carry on their activities despite the political "separation" of states. In an effort to assert or maximize their political independence, most states have established dependent relationships by political or economic alliances with other states. To ensure so-called independent control over their internal communications, states seek and adhere to international mail and telephone rates and agree to international allocation of radio and television frequencies. The full parameter of the interrelationships among states also extends informally in the multitude of individual contacts and ties among their peoples. (For a more detailed discussion see Chapter 7.) This web of relationships plays a crucial role in facilitating or hindering the ability of states to resolve their problems. Real independence and equality are ultimately realized in recognizing that politically the world is *not* compartmentalized.

DIPLOMATIC RELATIONS AMONG STATES

One web in the network of relations between states in the international system is the ties established by formal and regularized exchange of diplomatic representatives, by ad hoc diplomatic missions, and the occasional direct meetings among heads of governments.

VARIATIONS IN EXTENT OF FOREIGN REPRESENTATION

The nature and extent of exchange of diplomatic missions and representatives varies considerably from state to state. Each state that recognizes another state in the international system does not necessarily exchange diplomatic representatives. A major state like the United States has diplomatic representatives in most other states in the international system. In 1970, for example, the United States had diplomatic missions in 122 independent states. In some instances, however, the same ambassador represented the United States in two states as in the Federal Republic of Cameroon and the Republic of Equatorial Guinea. Traditionally, the United States has sent diplomatic missions to both friends and potential enemies in the international system.

The Soviet Union, on the other hand, for a long period of its existence tended to send permanent diplomatic representatives to the other major powers and only to such lesser powers as were either neutralists in the East-West conflict or ideologically in accord with Soviet policy. From 1919 to 1943 the Soviet Union had a kind of dual system of representation with other states.

From its foreign affairs ministry it dispatched diplomatic representation, but through the Communist party it formed an international body known as the Comintern and thereby established direct contacts with the Communist parties in other states—both those in which it had formal diplomatic representation and those in which it did not. To avoid dealing directly with political factions in foreign countries the Comintern was dissolved in 1943 in a gesture to its allies in the anti-Nazi coalition. With Nikita Khrushchev and the pragmatically oriented foreign policy of the Kosygin-Brezhnev regime, the Soviet Union has gradually extended the degree to which it has dispatched permanent diplomatic missions. In 1956 the Soviet Union had diplomatic missions in only four South American states; by 1972 it had missions in every state in South America except Paraguay and Venezuela.

The extent of formal diplomatic relations reflects several factors. Most states have diplomatic exchanges with their immediate neighbors, with the major powers, and with those states with which they have traditional trade, cultural, or historical relationships.[4]

To the middle, small, and mini-power states the possibility of extensive formal diplomatic relations is limited. Their international concerns are not as great as those of the major or superpowers. Thus there is not a vital necessity for widespread diplomatic relations. There are also financial limitations. A small state simply cannot afford, even if it should desire, to have extensive diplomatic missions abroad. For example, while the United States had 122 diplomatic missions to other states, Australia had 76, Tanzania 11, and Malta only 5. This financial impediment is also illustrated in the size of diplomatic missions. The Americans, Soviet, and French missions in London, for example, involve hundreds of individuals, while the mission of many Central American states may be composed of fewer than five or ten individuals.

The significance of this is that the super- and major powers have a greater capacity to utilize regular channels of diplomatic contact but, also, an inclination toward relying upon bilateral diplomacy. The influence of the major powers is felt in most capitals of the world because they have representation directly in them.

The super- and major powers are also able to use their diplomatic missions, not in a covert way, but in an open manner as sources of information and intelligence that provide them with first-hand information in making policy decisions. They are more aware of the subtleties and complexities of issues and are better able to take advantage of every opportunity. In this sense the extent of their diplomatic establishments enhances and enforces their ability to maximize their influence in the international system.

The middle powers and the small states are hampered in their ability to maintain contacts directly with each other and are more likely to use the settings of major international organizations as a meeting ground for their

diplomatic representatives. For example, not one of the African states maintains diplomatic relations with the other 40 odd African states. Ghana and Nigeria, which are probably the most diplomatically active African states, are able to have diplomatic representatives physically present in about half of the other African states. Most small states do have diplomatic missions in the United States, the United Kingdom, France, and the Soviet Union, in addition to the capitals of their immediate neighbors, but many of the smallest states are not able to have even this extent of representation and are hard pressed to represent directly their views on many of the international issues.

THE CONCEPT OF "RECOGNITION"

Any significant or violent change in the political character of a state can, and often does, interrupt this pattern of diplomatic relations. The overthrow of the czarist government of Russia by the Bolsheviks in 1917 resulted in a break in diplomatic relations. The United States did not recognize the Soviet government until 1933, and only then were direct diplomatic relations resumed. The suspicions between the two governments meant that it was not until thirty-five years later that they were able formally to agree on a minimal number of consulates in each other's country. Similarly, the United States did not "recognize" the change of government in China in 1949. Indirect contacts between American and Chinese ambassadors to Poland constituted the only diplomatic relations between the United States and the People's Republic of China in the 1950s and 1960s. President Nixon's visit to Peking in 1972 established the first direct link, and in 1973 special missions were exchanged to explore the possible resumption of regular diplomatic relations.

If the situation involves not a violent change of government but an act that results in the creation of a new state, that new state has to be "recognized" by other states before it can exchange diplomatic representatives. If not, there cannot be direct official relations among the states—a fact that creates innumerable difficulties in dealing with conflicts. As mentioned previously, Israel, which became independent in May 1948, is still not recognized by the Arab states. Even though Israel has fought four wars (1948, 1956, 1967, and 1973) with her Arab neighbors, they officially deny Israel's existence. Consequently, they cannot deal directly with each other and must negotiate through third parties of the United Nations.

It is an accepted practice in international law that states that do not juridically recognize other states may negotiate directly with each other under the auspices of an international organization and this will not constitute an act of recognition. Thus Kissinger in January 1974, when as U.S. Secretary of State he assisted in the finalizing of troop withdrawals along the Sinai-Suez Canal front between Israel and Egypt, could not preside over a direct meeting between these two states. Rather he had to fly back and forth

between the two countries conveying messages from one side to the other. When the withdrawal agreement accepted by both sides was identical, then their military commanders met at the cease-fire line on Kilometer 101, the highway from Cairo to Suez, under the auspices of the United Nations. In a meeting presided over by the general commanding the U.N. Emergency Force representatives of Israel and Egypt then formally signed the withdrawal agreement. This complicated procedure was necessary because Egypt does not "legally" recognize the existence of Israel; it was the only way the two states could directly confront each other without Egypt granting de facto recognition of Israel.

A similar situation prevailed with the creation of the new state of Bangladesh at the end of the India-Pakistan war in December 1971. This new state with 67 million people was not immediately recognized by many states, including Pakistan and the People's Republic of China. Thus Bangladesh, despite its large population, was limited in its ability to carry on diplomatic relations with two important states in its part of the world.

BREAKING DIPLOMATIC RELATIONS

Whether super-, major, middle, or small powers, whether developed or developing, almost all states break diplomatic relations as a first act of reprisal when crucial negotiations fail. This is an incredible practice. At the very stage in which official contacts among states are most essential so that there be no misunderstandings, states that get "mad" at each other in essence say "I won't talk with you directly!"

After the government of Fidel Castro forced out the strong-man rule of Batista in 1959, it was recognized by the United States and diplomatic ties were established. As the Castro regime purged its political opponents and confiscated U.S. banks and investments including seizing American landholdings in Cuba, tension increased between the United States and Cuba. Castro further antagonized the United States by increasing political and economic ties with the Soviet Union and openly avowed his Marxist-Leninist philosophy and goals. As a punitive response, the United States broke diplomatic relations with Cuba on January 3, 1961.

In summary, then, a number of questions can be raised about the traditional practice of permanent diplomatic missions as a facility for mediating relations among states. Can permanent diplomatic missions achieve this goal when not all states have the ability to be represented in every other state? Can states deal with each other when ideological differences prevent them from establishing direct diplomatic relations? How can mediation of differences among states be helped when crisis situations traditionally result in a break in diplomatic relations and the withdrawal of diplomatic missions? Is it possible, or desirable, for states to pool finances according to their ability

to pay to ensure that each is diplomatically represented in every other state? Can states be adequately, and officially informed about the views and attitudes of other states unless they exchange diplomatic missions? What effect does the present system of a less-than-complete web of diplomatic missions have on the outcome of events in the international system? And, lastly, are other diplomatic devices more satisfactory for mediating differences between states?

States are aware of many of the problems and advantages inherent in the exchange of diplomatic missions. They provide continuous official contact among states. They provide a diplomatic "listening" post in each other's state. They are a source of continual information on developments in another state. They are permanently established, which means that the procedural ground rules of negotiations are agreed upon. Any issues that arise between two states exchanging diplomatic missions can be immediately raised without any preliminary negotiations. A normal embassy includes not only the ambassador but specialists in political, economic, cultural, and often military affairs so that contacts and the gathering of information can cover the gamut of relations among states. Lastly, the exchange of permanent diplomatic missions routinizes relationships among states.

CONFERENCE RELATIONS AMONG STATES

States also recognize that not all international issues involve only two states and that all states do not have regularized diplomatic relations by the exchange of permanent diplomatic missions. Historically, states have used the diplomatic device of ad hoc international conferences to meet these two situations. The convening of an international conference normally involves two stages of negotiation, the first on the procedural ground rules and the second (meeting under the agreed procedural rules) on the substantive issues themselves.

SETTING UP PROCEDURES

The procedural negotiations in convening an ad hoc international conference have important consequences for the later consideration of substantive issues. If only two states have a conference, they either agree or disagree with each other. However, if three or more states are involved, the method of agreement may affect the outcome of the ad hoc conference. If unanimity is the agreed rule, then each party to the conference has a veto, and the substantive conclusion is likely to reflect the lowest common level of agreement. If the agreed rule provides for some type of majority decision voting, a higher level of agreement may be possible. But states may be reluctant to be

obligated or bound by decisions to which they were not with the majority. States want the assurance that procedurally they have not lost the ability to achieve their substantive goals.

If an issue is significant enough to require a special international conference, it is highly important that in setting the procedures states do not make concessions affecting substantive issues. This first stage therefore is often prolonged as each party vies for procedural advantages, symbolized, for example, in questions of the shape of the table or seating arrangements.

In the Middle Eastern situation between Israel and the Arab states any attempts to try to meet in an international conference have become virtually deadlocked over whether such a direct confrontation would mean in effect that the Arab states acknowledge the legal existence of Israel. It is a basic tenant of the Arab states to deny the right of Israel to exist. From Israel's viewpoint such an international conference would achieve her goal in that the very meeting would mean the Arab states acknowledged her right to play a part in a Middle East settlement.

In the extended negotiations leading to the Paris Agreements on Vietnam in January 1973, a whole series of procedural issues had to be resolved before the conference could get down to a discussion of the substantive issues. Where should the meeting be held? It took almost nine months to agree that Paris would be a meeting site, as each side did not want to have the meeting place provide a psychological advantage to the other side. Then who should be parties to the conference? North Vietnam, which denied it had troops in South Vietnam, insisted that representatives of the Vietcong in South Vietnam be participants. South Vietnam felt that to include the Vietcong in the discussions gave them an international status that they did not possess. These procedural problems eventually resolved themselves in the "solution of the oval table." The oval table had the North Vietnamese and representatives of the Vietcong on one side with the United States and the South Vietnamese on the other. If a square table had been used, each of the four parties might have been considered to have separate and equal status. With the oval table, however, the four were merged in a sense into two sides, but it was not a clear-cut separation into two sides of two states each. This may sound silly to a rational person, but one of the substantive issues of the Paris conference was the status of the Vietcong. In fact South Vietnam insisted on a complicated procedure in signing of the final agreements of the conference so that it would not acknowledge the equal legal status of the Vietcong. While the reality of their existence may have been apparent, a legal acknowledgment of this fact was unacceptable to South Vietnam.

Apart from these substantive and perhaps unique procedural decisions that need to be made in convening multilateral international conferences, each such conference involves a standard list of procedural arrangements in-

volving decisions on the site and meeting place, the procedural rules to be used in the discussions, arrangements for translators and interpreters, the sharing of costs, and the like. Most major foreign offices have standardized checkoff lists to be considered in arranging a multilateral conference, the length of which constitutes almost a book of details.

SOME PROBLEMS OF INTERNATIONAL CONFERENCES

Despite the problems and dilemmas international conferences have become virtually a routine part of relations among states. At the same time, they constitute, in a sense, an evolutionary stage in the development of more permanent international organizations. Most international conferences are now held under the auspices of international organizations such as the United Nations, which has settled or standardized the procedures involved in international conferences For example, Canada participated in 33 international conferences in 1971; 7 were convened by the United Nations or the U.N. specialized agencies, 9 by commonwealth organizations, 10 by other international organizations, and only 7 were ad hoc international conferences.

Nonetheless, crucial multilateral conferences, such as the Geneva Conference on Vietnam in 1954 and the Paris Conference on Vietnam in January 1973, are not always held under the auspices of the United Nations or other international organizations because the parties to the conference feel it is not in their interests to do so. Most peace conferences at the end of conflicts involve the multiplicity of problems that are inherent in calling such ad hoc conferences.

There is no question that international conferences are a method of trying to regularize relations among states on major issues of conflict. In large multilateral conferences the major powers generally exercise a dominant influence as a condition for their participation. In preparing for the U.N. Conference in San Francisco in 1945 only the major powers met in the preliminary meetings at Dumbarton Oaks in 1944 and Yalta in February 1945 to hammer out a draft of the U.N. Charter. After the Yalta Conference the other allies in World War II were invited to submit amendments to this proposal and to participate in drafting the final version at San Francisco. At the San Francisco Conference the 5 major powers, in what they felt were significant issues, played a game essentially of blackmail with the 45 lesser powers. Repeatedly, the United States and the Soviet Union let it be known that unless their views prevailed, they were not prepared to accept the charter. Obviously, they were recognizing the realistic facts that their mobilization of resources far surpassed those of the smaller states and also that they would bear major responsibilities in trying to make the hopes of the U.N. Charter a reality.

It is very difficult to try to organize a process to build mutual confi-

dence among states with the device of international conferences. International conferences by their nature last only for a very short time and tend to be focused on a momentary issue. Many international conferences, especially the "summit" type conferences of heads of governments are merely general discussions of issues or pompous ceremonies to conclude formally already arrived at agreements, or both, as in the case of the recent trip in 1973 of President Nixon to Moscow.

ORGANIZED RELATIONS AMONG STATES

States have created a wide variety of international (governmental) organizations, partly in response to the problems inherent in ad hoc international conferences, partly because a particular international issue requires a continuing attention by states, partly to provide a continuous diplomatic meeting ground for states, partly to broaden the network of diplomatic contacts, partly as a reflection of a mutual self-interest, as well as for other more specific reasons.

It is difficult to be precise as to just how many international organizations there are among states in the international system. The *Yearbook of International Organizations* indicates that there are at least 229 organizations that have 3 or more states as members.[5] This includes international organizations ranging from the United Nations to the Administrative Center of Social Security for Rhine Boatmen, from the African Postal Union to the Organization of American States, from the International Red Locust Control Service to the North Atlantic Council, and from the Warsaw Treaty Organization to the Cocoa Producers Alliance. In addition to these organizations there are at least another several hundred others that involve only two states. These are organizations such as the International Halibut Commission between the United States and Canada and the mixed claims commissions that exist among many bordering states.

As in Table 6.3, the range of international organizations can be illustrated by categorizing them by the breadth of their functions or concerns and by the number of governments that are members of these organizations.

BROAD AND LIMITED TYPES OF ORGANIZATIONS
The United Nations (and its precursor the League of Nations) is virtually a *universal* organization, including as members most of the states in the international system and encompassing in its concerns almost every possible activity and issue involving interactions among states. Regional organizations, such as the Organization of American States and the Organization of African Unity, are limited in membership, but their concerns cover the widest

TABLE 6.3 ROUGH TYPOLOGY OF EXISTING INTERNATIONAL ORGANIZATIONS AMONG STATES

		Breadth of Functions or Concerns of International Organizations	
		Universal or Very Broad	Limited
Extent of Membership—Number of States Belonging	Virtually Universal or Open to Most States	United Nations	Specialized Agencies such as: World Health Organization UNESCO Universal Postal Union Food and Agriculture Organization Int'l Civil Aviation Organization etc.
	Limited to Certain States	Organization of American States Organization of African Unity Arab League etc.	Regional Security Organizations such as: NATO and Warsaw Treaty Organization Specific Economic, Social, Scientific Organizations such as: Int'l. Whaling Commission Int'l. Sugar Council Danube Commission Inter-American Music Committee Int'l. Bureau of Weights and Measures Pan American Health Organization etc. Bilateral Organizations such as: Int'l. Halibut Commission Joint Brazil-U.S. Defense Commission Int'l. Boundary Commission— U.S. and Canada

possible range of issues relating to the states in the region and, in this sense, are comparable to the United Nations.

The specialized agencies, all affiliated with the United Nations to one degree or another, are generally open to membership to all states, but are focused in one general functional area of international concern such as health, education, food, transportation and communications, financial arrangements, and social justice. Many of these so-called specialized agencies existed before the United Nations was created, while most of the others have been created as a result of conferences called by the United Nations. They represent a decentralized method of dealing with economic and social problems, as not every state is concerned with each of these problems. The Uni-

versal Postal Union, which was established in 1874, is involved in the facilitation of mail across international borders. The International Telecommunications Union is concerned with international cooperation in the rational use of all forms of telecommunications (from providing access to telegraphy lines to determination of radio frequencies so there will be as little overlapping interference as possible). The World Meteorological Organization facilitates interchange of weather information among states. Social justice is promoted by the International Labour Organization, which seeks to improve working and living conditions. The World Bank Group and the International Monetary Fund are concerned with promoting the international flow of capital for productive purposes and particularly by the promotion of private foreign investments and a "balanced growth in international trade." The Food and Agricultural Organization promotes the common welfare by efforts directed toward raising levels of nutrition and standards of living by increasing efficiency in the production and distribution of food and agricultural products. According to the U.N. Educational, Scientific, and Cultural Organization, its purpose is to:

> contribute to peace and security by promoting collaboration among nations through education, science, and culture in order to further universal respect for justice, for the rule of law, and for the human rights and fundamental freedoms which are affirmed for the peoples of the world without distinction of race, sex, language, or religion, by the Charter of the United Nations.

The orderly and safe growth of international civil aviation by the development of standardizing principles and techniques is the focus of the International Civil Aviation Organization. The World Health Organization fosters the highest possible attainment of health of all peoples by a wide variety of activities from exchanges of information on medical techniques and the incident of epidemics, standardization of medical terms and international health immunization certificates, to assistance in preventive medicine programs. Lastly, the Inter-Governmental Maritime Consultative Organization's objective is to facilitate cooperation among states in technical matters affecting shipping in order to achieve the highest practicable standards of maritime safety and efficiency in navigation. In summary, the role of the United Nations is coordinative and catalytic in these economic and social areas of common concern while the role of the specialized agencies is an operative role.

The bulk of the 400 or so international organizations are in the fourth category of limited memberships and limited areas of concern. They may include as members only the cocoa-producing states or the states in a political or military alliance or the states in one region of the world concerned with

a specific problem, or they are organizations between two states for a particular purpose.

MAIN FEATURES OF INTERNATIONAL ORGANIZATIONS

All of the international organizations represent diplomatic means for trying to solve problems facing the international community. The Central Commission for the Navigation of the Rhine was created in 1815 to deal with the mutual problems of use, maintenance, and navigation of the Rhine by the riparian states. The United Nations was created in 1945 as a diplomatic instrument of states to facilitate the peaceful settlement of disputes and conflicts, to attack economic and social causes of conflict, and to build a lasting peace. An international commission on control and supervision was created by the January 1973 Paris Agreement on Ending the War and Restoring Peace in Vietnam as one of several devices to supervise the implementation of the agreement and its protocols.

Despite the different reasons for which states have created international organizations, all international (governmental) organizations have certain features in common:

1. A constituent instrument, generally a treaty or an executive agreement among states;
2. A permanent headquarters;
3. A permanent secretariat or staff;
4. A regular budget, to which states are obligated to make contributions; and
5. Regular or periodic meetings of the organization.

In addition, with a few exceptions that we shall deal with shortly, all these international organizations are organizations that regulate or standardize relations *between* or *among* states. They are not organizations *over* states; they are not international governments. Their authority is generally limited to only those actions that their members desire. They are diplomatic instruments of states. They are not entities apart from states even though they have international secretariats and, often, a sense of permanence.

International organizations sometimes have unreal public images suggesting authority over states. For example, newspapers often have editorials demanding to know why the United Nations is not handling this crisis or another, or demanding that *the* United Nations take action. If the United Nations does not act, the editorials proclaim the ineffectiveness of the organization, or they demand to know why the United Nations refuses to act. Seldom do these editorials state the fact that the United Nations can only do what its member states want it to do. It is the states through the diplomatic device of the United Nations that refuse to act. The United Nations has no

authority independent of the collective decisions or recommendations of its members. It has the potential to take steps to settle a dispute, or enforce the peace, but only if its member states so decide. But, it does not have even this potential if the states disagree on what, or if any, action should be taken in an international dispute or conflict. It was *not* the United Nations through its Security Council that refused to consider the conflict in Vietnam; it *was* the states that were members of the Security Council of the United Nations that informally agreed to not consider the conflict in Vietnam.

Although international organizations are subordinate to their member states, this fact should not be construed to conclude that they do not, or cannot, have a significant impact in building mutual trust and respect and facilitating an understanding among states to settle conflicts through regularized and/or peaceful means. Many international organizations have this potential and, in fact, are performing these roles.

Issues Considered by International Organizations. The range of issues referred to an international organization is illustrated by the wide variety of resolutions that were adopted by the U.N. General Assembly during its 27th session (September to December 1972). Among the resolutions covered were these:

> International action for mitigation of storms
>
> International cooperation in the peaceful uses of outer space
>
> Preparation for an international conference on principles governing the use by states of artificial earth satellites for direct television broadcasting
>
> Preparatory steps toward the convening of a world disarmament conference
>
> Implementation of the results of a Conference of Non-Nuclear-Weapons States
>
> Question of general and complete disarmament
>
> Question of chemical and bacteriological warfare
>
> Urgent need for suspension of nuclear weapons tests
>
> Implementation of the Treaty for the Prohibition of Nuclear Weapons in Latin America
>
> Declaration of the Indian Ocean as a zone of peace
>
> Implementation of a Declaration on the Strengthening of International Security
>
> Reservation of the sea bed and ocean floor under the high seas for peaceful purposes only, and the convening of a conference on the law of the sea
>
> Effects of atomic radiation
>
> The policies of apartheid of the government of South Africa

Relief efforts for Palestine refugees

Review of efforts for peace-keeping operations

Report of a special committee investigating the practices of the Israeli government affecting the human rights of people in the Arab territories occupied by Israel

Support for victims of colonialism and apartheid in Southern Africa

Nonuse of force in international relations and the prohibition of the use of nuclear weapons

Situation in the Middle East

Cooperation among states in the field of the human environment

Special measures related to the particular needs of landlocked developing states

Establishment of a U.N. University

Institutional and financial arrangements for international environmental cooperation

Criteria governing multilateral financing of housing and human settlements

Establishment of an international fund or financial institution for human settlements

Measures for protecting and enhancing the human environment

Problem of economic development and the environment

International prize for the most outstanding contribution in the field of the human environment

Outflow of trained personnel from developing to developed states

Permanent sovereignty over natural resources in developing states

Problem of mass poverty and unemployment in developing countries

Special measures in favor of the least developed of the developing states

Charter on economic rights and duties of states

Dissemination of information and mobilization of public opinion relative to problems of development

External debt servicing by developing countries

Multilateral trade negotiations

Program for the observance of the 25th anniversary of the Universal Declaration of Human Rights

Exploitation of labor through illicit and clandestine trafficking

Draft Convention on the Suppression and Punishment of the Crime of Apartheid

Protection of journalists engaged in dangerous missions in areas of armed conflict

Assistance to Sudanese refugees returning from abroad

Assistance in cases of natural disaster and other disaster situations

International Women's Year

Capital Punishment

Assistance in narcotics control

Narcotic drugs

United Nations Program for Drug Abuse Control

Principles of international cooperation in the detection, arrest, extradition, and punishment of persons guilty of war crimes and crimes against humanity

Crime prevention and control

Channels of communication with youth and youth international organizations

Implementation of the Declaration on the Promotion Among Youth of the Ideals of Peace, Mutual Respect, and Understanding Between Peoples

Increased employment and mobility of young people in the United Nations

Status of the International Covenants on Human Rights

Freedom of information

Human rights and scientific and technological developments

Elimination of all forms of religious intolerance

United Nations conference for an international convention on adoption control

United Nations Conference on Prescription (Limitation) in the International Sale of Goods

International conference of plenipotentiaries on the representation of states in their relations with international organizations

Need to consider suggestions regarding the review of the charter of the United Nations

Respect for human rights in armed conflicts

Review of the role of the International Court of Justice

Measures to prevent international terrorism

Questions with respect to steps being taken to eliminate colonialism in:
    Territories under Portuguese administration
    Southern Rhodesia
    Papua New Guinea
    Spanish Sahara
    America Samoa . . .[6]

Activities or programs of:
    International Atomic Energy Agency
    United Nations Commissioner for Zambia
    U.N. Relief and Works Agency for Palestine Refugees in the Near East
    U.N. Conference on Trade and Development
    U.N. Institute for Training and Research. . . .[7]

As this list indicates, the scope of activities of an organization like the United Nations covers the gamut of issues facing states.

Diplomatic Center. International organizations therefore add to, and supplement, the diplomatic network among states. A large international organization like the United Nations, with many organs and suborgans, committees, and commissions considering the whole range of problems that concern states, thereby becomes a major and perhaps independent center of diplomatic activity. On any given day in the U.N. headquarters in New York City, or the U.N. office in Geneva, numerous U.N. bodies are in session. In order to provide representation most of the 138 members of the United Nations have established permanent diplomatic missions to handle the volume of interstate relations. In addition, many nonmember states of the United Nations as well as representatives from other international organizations such as the Arab League and Organization of African Unity maintain observer missions to follow and keep track of the negotiations in the United Nations. Also present at the U.N. headquarters and at the U.N. Geneva office are representatives of several hundred nongovernmental organizations such as the International Red Cross, the International League for the Rights of Man, the International Chamber of Commerce, and so on. Thus the sites of the United Nations become major centers of diplomatic activity.

In fact, the United Nations headquarters probably has in its immediate environs the representatives from more states than are found anywhere else. None of the African states, for example, exchanges diplomatic missions with every other African state; yet at the U.N. headquarters there are not only representatives from every African state, but there are also representatives from the various nationalist movements in the African colonial territories that have not as yet achieved independence. The setting of the United Nations therefore becomes *the* one place in which diplomats can meet with counterparts from every other African state. These missions in addition to dealing with issues before the United Nations also negotiate on a wide variety of questions that are not on the agenda of the U.N. bodies.

The presence of diplomats in permanent missions at the U.N. sites means that they have the opportunity to negotiate informally on every variety of issue and to develop social contacts and personal ties that over time facilitate relations among states. At ad hoc international conferences diplomats are together for but a brief period. In their interactions they often engage in "vying of egos" as each diplomat establishes rapport with the others. Such a behavior is minimized in the United Nations, where contacts are of a longer duration and involve wide areas of concern and many activities in which the diplomats work together in committee-type sessions to accomplish mutual goals.

DIPLOMATIC DIALOGUE

The U.N. experience contrasts with the situation of diplomats in the capital of a given country. In national settings diplomats vie to achieve their concerns with the host country. Their interests are diverse and their interactions are not always directed toward similar or even comparable issues. In contrast, in the U.N. setting representatives tend to focus on agenda items of the various U.N. organs even though they may not have a direct concern with many of the issues. Nonetheless, involvement with these issues means they become at least more aware, if not more understanding, of the issues and concerns and stances of states other than their own. In ad hoc international conferences states become aware, in the short time available for negotiation, only of the immediate aspects of the particular problem for which the conference was called. In the direct negotiations in foreign capitals, states and their diplomatic representatives primarily focus on issues that are outstanding between their two states.

In this sense of breadth of interactions among states, the United Nations obviously is a unique international organization. Yet in terms of the headquarters of the Organization of American States or the Organization of African Unity or the Arab League the situation is fairly comparable. Even in the case of the specialized agencies, while the focus of concern is on particular problem areas, the headquarter's site plays a comparable role in relations among the states. The FAO headquarters in Rome becomes a center for states in focusing on the world's food problems, and WHO in Geneva becomes a center for the concerns of states with respect to health issues.

Diplomatic dialogue in international organizations is prevalent in a lesser degree in more limited international organizations, although for the most part they are devices to convene diplomats periodically on certain issues. Most of the smaller and more particularized international organizations do not have a sufficient number of subbodies to require that states appoint permanent diplomatic missions to be constantly at their headquarters. Rather they provide an ongoing machinery of procedures and processes to carry out the decisions of states between the periodic meetings of their councils. These procedures and processes vary among international organizations to the extent to which they regularize and facilitate the development of mutual respect and a willingness to settle differences peacefully.

ORGANIZED DISTRUST

Some international organizations are brought into existence during periods of intense mutual distrust so that their procedures become almost ineffective in facilitating mutual trust and respect. This is particularly true of international organizations created solely to observe the implementation of cease-fire arrangements among states following a military conflict. For

example, the Agreement on Ending the War and Restoring Peace in Vietnam signed on January 27, 1973, created an International Commission of Control and Supervision, or the ICCS (composed of Canada, Hungary, Indonesia, and Poland), and a Four-Party Joint Military Commission (composed of military representatives of the United States, Republic of Vietman [South Vietnam], Democratic Republic of Vietnam [North Vietnam], and the Provisional Revolutionary Republic of South Vietnam [Vietcong]. These two international bodies were concerned with the implementation of the military cease-fire, the withdrawal of U.S. forces, the return of prisoners of war, and with other steps as shown in the following list.

STEPS IN THE DECISION PROCESS IN THE INVESTIGATION OF VIOLATIONS WITH RESPECT TO THE CEASE-FIRE, WITHDRAWAL OF FORCES AND RETURN OF PRISONERS UNDER 1973 PARIS AGREEMENT ON ENDING THE WAR AND RESTORING PEACE IN VIETNAM

1. In the case of an alleged violation of the cease-fire, withdrawal of troops, or return of prisoners provisions, either
   (a) the Four-Party Joint Military Commission composed of the United States, South Vietnam, North Vietnam, and Vietcong) by *unanimous* agreement or
   (b) the Two-Party Joint Military Commission (composed of South Vietnam and the Vietcong) by *unanimous* agreement or
   (c) any of these four states
   may request the International Commission of Control and Supervision to investigate the alleged violation.

2. The International Commission of Control and Supervision composed of Canada (replaced by Iran after July 1, 1973), Hungary, Indonesia, and Poland will investigate the alleged violation, but in any question of how to proceed on the investigation they can only take action by *unanimity.*

3. If the International Commission of Control and Supervision investigates an alleged violation, they can only make a *report* on it if they *unanimously* agree, to either the Four-Party Joint Military Commission or the Two-Party Joint Military Commission as required by the Paris Agreement. If the International Commission of Control and Supervision cannot agree unanimously on a report, they will simply transmit the separate views of the commission members.

4. The Four-Party Joint Military Commission or the Two-Party Joint Military Commission will consider a *report* from the International Commission of Control and Supervision and if they can agree *unanimously*, they will take action on the alleged violation.

In the process of their activities the two international bodies were to investigate and observe any violations of the Paris Agreement. However, the agreement provided that these two international bodies in carrying out their roles could only act in unanimity, which is a roundabout way of saying that any of the parties—the United States, North Vietnam, South Vietnam, the Vietcong, Canada/Iran, Hungary, Indonesia, or Poland—could veto observations or investigations of violations of the agreement. The Canadian government,

in reluctantly agreeing to be a member of the ICCS, agreed to participate for only a sixty-day period until it could assess whether such procedures were merely window dressing or had any ability to foster the realistic implementation of the agreement. The agreement further provided for the convening of an international conference, composed of the eight states that were members of these two international organizations, and the People's Republic of China, the Soviet Union, and the United Kingdom. Such a conference was held in Paris late in February 1973 at which time the Canadian foreign minister urged that the conference give some teeth to the ICCS. Instead it adopted platitudinous statements simply confirming the general principles of the January 27 Paris Agreement. These two international organizations, therefore, have virtually no authority unless all members unanimously agree.[8] In protest to these procedures Canada withdrew from the ICCS and was replaced by Iran on July 1, 1973.

The type of procedures and process evidenced in these two international bodies created in the 1973 Paris Agreement on Vietnam probably have a minimum capacity to promote mutual respect and a willingness to settle issues among states peacefully. Such international organizations, while they do have the advantage of continuously bringing contesting parties together, can only act on issues in which all parties agree. In essence each state has the right and ability to prevent any action that it feels is not in its self-interest. Regretfully, such procedures often lead to frustration, bitterness, and an increase in tensions.

ORGANIZED TRUST

In complete contrast is the type of international organization in which the procedures and processes are conducive to a continual building of mutual respect among the states. An example of this is the International Halibut Commission between Canada and the United States. In this international organization the two states appoint commissioners for a specified term. The commission has a scientific staff that assesses the state of the halibut fishery and proposes new regulations for each fishing season. The commission then holds public hearings in each of the significant fishing ports on the west coast of Canada and the United States and gets the reactions of the boat owners, fishermen, unions, canners, and other interested parties to proposed regulations. Then the commission adopts regulations for the next year— regulations that are binding upon individuals from the two countries. These regulations take effect within ninety days unless either government objects —and this rarely, if ever, has happened. Obviously, efforts to maintain a sustained yield of Pacific coast halibut is not as important an issue as is the attempt to maintain a cease-fire and restore peace in Indochina. Before the creation of the Halibut Commission in 1931, however, competition over the fishery did result in considerable conflict between the two states. American

and Canadian fishermen and their boats, prior to 1931, were constantly being seized for violating each state's territorial sea "boundary," and there was considerable bitterness between the parties. The fact that the Halibut Commission now meets in harmony is testimony to the fact that procedures can be established that are conducive to building mutual respect and trust. In fact, as the commission proceeded in its operation, its basic treaty (or constitution) has been modified four times with each modification granting more authority to the international organization. Even though the states retain the ultimate ability to nullify the regulations of the commission, this is a veto after action, not a veto preventing action.

ORGANIZED TO PROMOTE TRUST

Between these two types of international organizations—those concerned with the maintenance of a military cease-fire and those typified by the Halibut Commission—is the United Nations. The United Nations is the type of international organization in which processes and procedures, while protecting the self-interests of states, open up the possibilities of building mutual respect and facilitating a willingness to resolve conflict situations.

This might be best illustrated by looking at both the theory in the U.N. Charter and the practice of the United Nations in handling disputes and situations likely to endanger the maintenance of international peace and security. Theoretically, the U.N. Charter contains several assumptions. First, concerning the management of conflict situations, there was the assumption, that while in a legal sense states are sovereign and equal, it is the major powers that have the ability, *if* they agree, to *enforce* the peaceful settlement of any conflict in the international system. Second, there was a recognition that certain economic and social conditions are root causes of conflict and that small disputes, unless checked, could escalate into conflicts of a more major nature. Third, there was an assumption that one of the effective ways to expose a potential conflict, or "freeze" an open conflict, is by public discussion that would focus the spotlight of public opinion on the situation and the circumstances surrounding it. And while it is the major powers that have the ultimate capacity to determine whether peace is maintained or not, efforts to maintain peaceful relations depend upon the widest possible consensus of the entire community of states that constitute the international system. Finally, there was an assumption that it is more dangerous to promote peaceful relations in platitudes than to recognize clearly the divisions in the international system, especially those differences among the major powers.

Provisions for the Security Council. Based on these assumptions the U.N. Charter provides that the primary responsibility for the maintenance of peace should be placed in a Security Council composed of the five major

powers and ten elected other members of the United Nations.[9] The Security Council was organized to meet momentarily at the request of any state when there is a threat to the peace. It must seek every possible peaceful means of resolving a conflict situation. If peaceful settlement fails and *if* the major powers and four other members of the council agree that a dispute constitutes a threat to peace, a breach of the peace, or an act of aggression, then the charter empowers the Security Council to take any steps its members agree upon to enforce the peace.[10] Under the assumptions in the charter, if these five major powers cannot agree, it is impossible to take any action. In essence, the charter stipulates that if the major powers and four other members of the Security Council agree, they can take any action they feel necessary including the use of military force to facilitate settlement of a conflict. All the other members of the United Nations delegate this right to the Security Council and agree in advance to be obligated by its decisions. Thus if the major powers agree, there will be a peace. But this process also makes it clear that if they disagree, there will not be peace, because there will be no decisions promising action that cannot be enforced. False hopes in the international system are therefore minimized. In a sense the Security Council has become an accurate barometer of the state of tension in the international system.

Actions of the Security Council. In practice, the experience of the Security Council has illustrated both extremes of international realities and as a result has established practices that have helped to prevent the spread of conflict. In the early 1970s it was still clear that the U.N. Security Council was unable, as had been anticipated, to deal with any conflict that *directly* involved the major powers. For example, in February 1966, the Security Council decided to place the issue of Vietnam on its agenda but then informally agreed not to discuss it, recognizing that such a discussion would merely harden the relations among the major powers.[11] In the earlier years of the United Nations, the differences between the permanent members of the Security Council during the period of the cold war, meant that in practice even issues *indirectly* involving these powers could not be acted upon by the Security Council. With a few exceptions, these differences meant that from 1946 to 1956 the Security Council was almost inoperative. This was an accurate reflection of the state of tension existing between the major powers at that time.[12] Of course, there were exceptions as in December 1948 when the Netherlands denounced a truce agreement with the Republic of Indonesia and commenced military operations that ousted the Indonesians from control of their capital. For differing reasons the major powers in this situation were able to agree that there should be a resumption of the truce and that the Dutch forces should withdraw. In the face of great power unanimity the

Netherlands had to withdraw. Similarly, agreement among the major powers resulted in the Security Council forcing cease-fires in the conflicts between the new state of Israel and the Arab states in 1948, 1956, 1967, and 1973 and between India and Pakistan in their conflict over Jammu and Kashmir in 1949. In these instances the Security Council dispatched truce observers so that it could be kept informed as to the degree of implementation of the truce arrangements and could exert further pressure if necessary to ensure that open warfare was not resumed.

By 1956 it was apparent that instead of agreement by the five major powers, peace was really determined by the actions of the two permanent members of the Security Council, the United States and the Soviet Union. When Israel, supported by the United Kingdom and France, took military action against Egypt over the closing of the Suez Canal in 1956, the Security Council was unable to act because France and the United Kingdom were able to veto any possible agreement. The United States and the Soviet Union then agreed to take the issue to the U.N. General Assembly. While theoretically the General Assembly can consider any issue and make recommendations, its power is limited only to recommendations. It does not have the potential ability of the Security Council to compel action. By 1956 the United States and the Soviet Union had acquired sufficient military strength to be able by themselves to enforce a peace (even over the other major powers if necessary). Their support therefore of a General Assembly resolution calling for a withdrawal of forces from Egypt and for a cease-fire had virtually the same impact as if it had been accomplished by a decision of the Security Council.

U.N. Emergency Forces. It was at this stage of events in the perpetual Middle East crisis that the Canadian foreign minister, Lester Pearson, suggested that the way to prevent a further outbreak of hostilities was to separate the contesting parties by the imposition of an international military force between Israel and Egypt. This was an acceptable idea to the United States and the Soviet Union even though they differed as to what would be as a satisfactory settlement. Thus the United Nations established the U.N. Emergency Force (UNEF) in the Middle East, a military unit composed of forces from several states, acceptable as neutrals to the combatant states. It was interposed between Egypt and Israel along their Sinai border to supervise a cease-fire. By 1967 there were deep differences between the two superpowers as to whether the force should continue. This provided opportunities for states that contributed to one side or another of the East-West dispute to seize the opportunity provided by the Egyptian demand (implicitly supported by the Soviet Union) to withdraw the force in May 1967. Shortly thereafter tension in the area escalated, and when the Six-Day War broke out in June 1967, both the United States and the Soviet Union again agreed

that the military conflict must stop. The Security Council then was able to once again impose a temporary cease-fire and reinstall U.N. observer teams along the Suez Canal. While these two superpowers could agree to stop the fighting, they were unable to agree on what the settlement in the Israeli-Arab conflict should be and the Security Council was again unable to take action in the face of major power disagreement.

The precedent of UNEF experience was to evolve a principle to stop fighting despite the inability of the major powers to agree upon a method of enforcing the decision. This precedent has subsequently been applied in a number of other conflict situations in which the major powers have an indirect rather than direct involvement. It was used to separate the Egyptian and Saudi Arabian military units that were supporting opposite sides in a civil war in Yemen in 1963. It was used to bring about a peaceful adjustment between the Dutch and Indonesians over West Irian in 1962. It was used in the Congolese civil war in the 1960s, and it has been used in the conflict between Greek and Turkish Cypriots on Cyprus since 1965. The interposition of an international military force does not resolve a conflict. It prevents the continuance of the military conflict and gradually stabilizes the situation, thereby allowing tension between the contending parties gradually to simmer down, hopefully so that they can settle their dispute peacefully. It did accomplish this in West Irian (West New Guinea), Yemen, and the Congo. And since the October 1973 conflict in the Middle East a new UNEF has been created by the Security Council to separate physically the military forces of Israel and Egypt.

Other U.N. Peace-Keeping Ventures. While these peace-keeping military forces are a very interesting innovation in efforts to maintain peaceful relations, they do not encompass the entire peace-keeping efforts of the United Nations. In activities since 1946 the United Nations have utilized a wide variety of peace-keeping techniques that might be categorized as follows:

1. The dispatch of either a special agent or a commission to investigate conditions on one side or both sides of a frontier;
2. The dispatch of a special representative or a commission to engage in fact finding about outside interference in the internal affairs of a state;
3. The observation of cease-fire lines by observers to investigate each alleged violation and report on their findings;
4. The dispatch of individuals to try to mediate a situation, or a commission to conciliate a situation;
5. The dispatch of a mission to investigate or clarify the facts of a situation;

6. The dispatch of assistance to a state to maintain law and order and thus prevent the internal security from leading to intervention by another state;

7. The dispatch of an international military force to separate contesting factions within a state or the forces of contending states; and

8. The organization and conduct of supervised plebiscites or public-opinion polling to assist in the process of self-determination of peoples.

In any given situation the United Nations may engage in any one, a combination, or all of these peace-keeping techniques. (See Table 6.4). In the Middle East conflict since 1947 the United Nations has had fact-finding committees investigate the problem, mediators attempt to reconcile the parties, truce observers to try to maintain cease-fire lines, conciliation commissions, two peace-keeping military forces to separate the contesting states, and even an international operation to clear and restore the Suez Canal after it was closed by fighting. The majority of these peace-keeping operations have been created by the Security Council, but many have been created by the General Assembly, and on occasion the Secretary-General has on his own initiative sent representatives to help ease a situation.

Preventing the Causes of Conflict. It is political and security problems and the success or failure or peace-keeping efforts that make the bulk of news about an organization like the United Nations. In fact, however, these activities constitute only about 5 percent of U.N. activities. The other 95 percent of this international body's work is concerned with dealing with the economic and social problems that constitute causes of world conflict. The U.N. efforts in dealing with the maintenance of the ecosystem, the crucial problems of the increasing economic and social disparity among states, and the efforts to reduce the weapons race are more indicative of the bulk of the organization's activities. The U.N. Conference on Trade and Development in Geneva in 1964, for example, may have more impact over the long run in the development of peaceful relations among states than the settlement of a specific dispute. At the outset of this conference, it appeared that there was an absolute break between the self-interests of the developed versus the developing states. But, as the lengthy meeting continued from January to June, most states began to realize that their futures depended in the long run upon an eventual resolution of the growing disparity between the developed and developing states. While processes were set in motion in an effort to resolve problems of competition and disparities, confidence among states depends upon a continual mutual exploration of the problems among them.

These activities of the United Nations in grappling with more funda-

TABLE 6.4 UN PEACE-KEEPING AND PEACE-MAKING FIELD OPERATIONS, 1946–1973

Area	Title	Author- izing Body	Appoint- ing Body	Task	Duration
Aden	Special Representative— O.A.H. Adeel	GA	SG	Investigate and recommend "practical steps" for determining wishes of people (United Kingdom NSGT)	June–Aug. 1966
	UN Special Mission to Aden	GA	SG	UN presence in connexion with forth- coming elections.	Mar.–Sept. 1967
Algeria	Personal Representative— Jose Rolz-Bennett	SG	SG	Good offices in seeking release of El Al airliner and occupants held in Algiers	August 1968
Bahrain	Personal Representative— Vittorio Winspeare Guicciardi	SG	SG	Ascertain wishes of people regarding future status (United Kingdom protec- torate)	Mar.–April 1970
Balkans	UN Commission of Investigation Concerning Greek Frontier Incidents	SC	SC	Ascertain facts relating to alleged border violations along the frontier between Greece, Albania, Bulgaria and Yugoslavia; make proposals for averting border viola- tions and disturbances	Jan.–Sept. 1947
	The Subsidiary Group UN Special Committee on the Balkans (UNSCOB)	GA	GA	Good offices; observe compliance with GA resolution calling on the countries concerned not to aid guerrillas in Greece and to cooperate in settling disputes	May–Sept. 1947 Nov. 1947–Dec. 1951
	UN Military Observers in Greece (UNMOG)	GA	GA	Investigate incidents along Greek borders and make periodic reports	Jan. 1952–July 1954
Buraimi Oasis	Special Diplomatic Representative —Herbert de Ribbing	SG	SG	Good offices in dispute between United Kingdom and Saudi Arabia over sovereignty of oasis claimed by Saudi Arabia, and the Sheikh of Abu Dhabi and the Sultan of Muscat and Oman (last two under British protection)	July–Aug. 1960

TABLE 6.4 (Continued)

Area	Title	Authorizing Body	Appointing Body	Task	Duration
Burundi	Personal Representative—I.S. Djermakoye	SG	SG	Assess humanitarian needs	June–July 1972
Cambodia	Special Representative—Johan Beck-Friis	SG	SG	Good offices in dispute with Thailand	Dec. 1958–Feb. 1959
	Personal Representative, later Special Representative—Nils-Goran Gussing	SG	SG	Inquiry and later good offices	Oct. 1962–Dec. 1964
	Three-member Mission	SC	SC	Factfinding concerning complaint of aggressive acts by U.S. and Republic of Viet-Nam	June–July 1964
	Special Representative—Herbert de Ribbing	SG	SG	Good offices in reducing tension with Thailand	Aug. 1966–Feb. 1968
Cameroons under British Administration (Northern)	UN Plebiscite Commissioner Djalal Abdoh	GA	GA	Supervise plebiscite on whether to join Nigeria or postpone decision on future status	Nov.–Dec. 1959
Cameroons under British Administration (Northern and Southern)	UN Plebiscite Commissioner—Djalal Abdoh	GA	GA	Supervise plebiscite on whether to join Nigeria or Republic of Cameroons	Feb.–March 1961
Congo (Leopoldville) (later Zaire)	UN Operation in the Congo (UNOC) Special Representative— Ralph Bunche Andrew Cordier Rajeshwar Dayal Mekki Abbas (Acting) Officer-in-Charge Sture Linner Robert Gardiner Max H. Dorsinville B.F. Osorio-Tafall (Acting)	SC	SG	Military assistance to maintain order and protect Congolese unity; emergency and operational technical assistance	July 1960–June 1964 May 1961–Jan. 1962 Feb. 1962–May 1963 May 1963–April 1964 April–June 1964

Operation / Location	Office and personnel	Authority	Function	Dates
Congo (Leopoldville) (later Zaire)	Commander			
	Lt. Gen. Sean Maceoin			Jan. 1961–Mar. 1962
	Lt. Gen. Kebbede Cuebre			April 1962–July 1963
	Maj. Gen. Christian Kaldager			Aug.–Dec. 1963
	Maj. Gen. Aguiyu Ironsi			Jan.–June 1964
	Civilian Operations			
	Resident Technical Assistance Representative—Sture Linner			July 1960–Sept. 1961
	Chief—Mahmoud Khiari			Sept. 1961–Sept. 1962
	S.H. Ahmed			Oct. 1962–Jan. 1964
	B.F. Osorio-Tafall			Feb.–June 1964
Congo (Leopoldville) (later Zaire)	Representative in Elisabethville			
	Ian Berendsen			Aug. 1960–Mar. 1961
	Georges Dumontet			Mar.–May 1961
	Conor Cruise O'Brien			June–Nov. 1961
	Brian Urquhart			Nov. 1961–Jan. 1962
	George Ivan Smith (Acting)			Dec. 1961
	Georges Dumontet (Acting)			Dec. 1961–Jan. 1962
	Jose Rolz-Bennett			Jan.–June 1962
	Eliud Mathu			June 1962–May 1963
	George L. Sherry (Acting)			Dec. 1962–Feb. 1963
	A. Nashashibi			May 1963–June 1964
		GA	Assist Congolese in seeking a speedy solution by peaceful means of all internal conflicts for the unity and integrity of the Congo	
	Commission of Conciliation in the Congo	GA		Jan.–Mar. 1961
Cook Islands	UN Representative—O.A.H. Adeel	GA SG	Supervise elections (New Zealand NSGT)	Feb.–April 1965
Cyprus	Personal Representative—Lt. Gen. P.S. Gyani	GA SG	Observe progress of peace-making efforts in communal dispute between Greek and Turkish Cypriots	Jan.–March 1964
	UN Peace-keeping Force in Cyprus (UNFICYP)	SC SG	Prevent recurrence of fighting, assist in restoring and maintaining law and order and contribute to normal conditions	March 1964 to present
	Special Representative—			
	Galo Plaza			May–Sept. 1964
	G.A. Bernardes			Sept. 1964–Jan. 1967
	Pier Spinelli			Jan. 1967
	B.F. Osorio-Tafall			Feb. 1967 to present

TABLE 6.4 (Continued)

Area	Title	Authorizing Body	Appointing Body	Task	Duration
	Commander				
	Lt. Gen. P.S. Gyani				March–July 1964
	Gen. K.S. Thimayya				July 1964–Dec. 1965
	Brig. A.J. Wilson (Acting)				Dec. 1965–May 1966
	Lt. Gen. I.A.E. Martola				May 1966–Dec. 1969
	Maj. Gen. D. Prem Chand				Dec. 1969 to present
	UN Mediator—S.S. Tuomioja	SC	SG	Promote peaceful solution and agreed settlement	March–Sept. 1964
	UN Mediator—Galo Plaza	SC	SG		Sept. 1964–Dec. 1965
	Personal Representative—Jose Rolz-Bennett	SC	SG	Good offices	Nov. 1967
Dominican Republic	Mission of the Representative of the Secretary-General in the Dominican Republic (DOMREP), including military observers	SC	SG	Observe and report to Security Council on military, political and economic situation arising from U.S. action and on compliance with cease-fire order	May 1965–Oct. 1966
	Representative—Jose Antonio Mayobre				
Equatorial Guinea	Representative—Marcial Tamayo	SG	SG	Help resolve difficulties with Spain	May 1965–Jan. 1966
Eritrea					March–April 1969
	UN Commission for Eritrea	GA	GA	Investigate popular will regarding future status of former Italian colony	Nov. 1949–June 1950
	UN Commissioner—E.A. Matienzo	GA	GA	Draft constitution in consultation with Ethiopia, inhabitants and local officers of the Administering Authority (United Kingdom)	Feb. 1951–Oct. 1952
	UN Tribunal	GA	GA	Supervise settlement	Sept. 1952–April 1954
Guinea	Special Representative—Adrian Pelt	SG	SG	Liaison with UN and specialized agencies	July–Dec. 1959
	Special Representative—Ansgar Rosenborg	SG	SG	Liaison with UN and specialized agencies	Dec. 1959
	Personal Representative—Jose Rolz-Bennett	SG	SG	Discuss ways and means of settling difficulties with Ivory Coast	July 1967

	Mission	Authority	Purpose	Dates
	Special Mission to the Republic of Guinea	SC	Investigate complaint of armed aggression by Portugal	Nov. 1970
	Special Mission to the Republic of Guinea	SC	Investigate complaint of armed aggression by Portugal	Aug.–Sept. 1971
Indonesia	Consular Commission at Batavia	SC	Watchdog—supervise cease-fire and peaceful settlement between Netherlands and Indonesia (former Netherlands NSGT)	Sept. 1947–April 1951
	Military observers (after 1 Nov. 1947 functioned under direction of Military Executive Board)	SC	Observe	Aug. 1947–April 1951
	Committee of Good Offices	SC	Good offices in bringing about a political settlement	Oct. 1947–Jan. 1949
	UN Commission for Indonesia (formerly Committee of Good Offices)	**SC**	Assist parties in implementing establishment of independent state of Indonesia by July 1950	Jan. 1949–April 1951
India/ Pakistan	UN Commission for India and Pakistan (UNCIP)	SC	Investigate, mediate India/Pakistan dispute over future of the State of Jammu and of Kashmir	June 1948–Mar. 1950
	UN Military Observer Group in India and Pakistan (UNMOGIP) Chief Military Observer— Lt. Gen. R.H. Nimmo Col. J.H.J. Gauthier (Acting) Lt. Gen. Luis Tassara-Gonzalez	SC	Supervise cease-fire	Jan. 1949 to present Nov. 1950–Jan. 1966 Jan.–July 1966 July 1966 to present
	UN Representative— Sir Owen Dixon	SC	Assist in preparation for and supervision of demilitarization, mediate, assume all powers and responsibilities of UNCIP, and arrange for Plebiscite Administrator	April–Sept. 1950
	UN Representative— Frank P. Graham	SC	Effect demilitarization of the State of Jammu and of Kashmir after consultation with the governments of India and Pakistan	April 1951–Feb. 1972
	UN India-Pakistan Observation Mission (UNIPOM)	SC SG	Supervise cease-fire along India-Pakistan border	Sept. 1965–Mar. 1966

TABLE 6.4 (Continued)

Area	Title	Author- izing Body	Appoint- ing Body	Task	Duration
	Chief Officer— Maj. Gen. Bruce F. Macdonald Representative— Brig. Gen. Tullo Marambio	SC	SG	Assist in formulating plan and schedule for withdrawals of armed personnel	Nov. 1965–Mar. 1966
Jordan	UN Presence in Jordan— Special Representative in Amman—Pier Spinelli	GA	SG	Consult with Jordan and Lebanon on promoting peace and security and with- drawing foreign troops; patrol borders, observe and report evidence of foreign intervention	Sept. 1958–Dec. 1967
Korea	UN Temporary Commission on Korea (UNTCUK)	GA	GA	Facilitate the establishment of a National Government for all Korea and provide withdrawal of occupation forces	Nov. 1947–Dec. 1948
	UN Commission on Korea (UNCOK)	GA	GA	Bring about unification of Korea and integration of all Korean forces	Dec. 1948–Oct. 1950
	UN Commission for the Unifica- tion and Rehabilitation of Korea (UNCURK)	GA	GA	Bring about establishment of independent democratic government for all of Korea	Oct. 1950 to present
Laos	Subcommittee to Investigate the Situation in Laos	SC	SC	Investigate complaint of aggression from North Viet-Nam	Sept.–Oct. 1959
	Special Representative— S.S. Tuomioja	SG	SG	Review economic situation	Nov.–Dec. 1959
	Special Representative— Roberto Heurtematte	SG	SG	Discuss implementation of Tuomioja's report	Dec. 1959–
	Special Consultant— Edouard Zellweger	SG	SG	Co-ordinate UN economic activities	March 1960
Lebanon	UN Observation Group in Lebanon (UNOGIL)	SC	SG	Ensure no illegal infiltration of personnel or arms across Lebanese border	June–Dec. 1958
Libya	Commissioner—Adrian Pelt	GA	GA	Prepare former Italian colony for independence	Dec. 1949–Jan. 1952
	Advisory Council	GA	GA	Advise the Commissioner	April 1950–Dec. 1951
	UN Tribunal	GA	GA	Decide disputes	Aug. 1951–Dec. 1955

Middle East

UN Special Committee on Palestine (UNSCOP)	GA	Investigate and report regarding future of Palestine after termination of British League of Nations Mandate	June–Aug. 1947
UN Palestine Commission	GA	Assist implementation of GA resolution regarding future constitution and government	Mar.–May 1948
UN Palestine Truce Commission	SC	Supervise truce between Arab and Jewish communities	April–June 1948
UN Truce Supervision Organization for Palestine (UNTSO)	SG	Observe implementation of truce and report violations to the Security Council	June 1948 to present
Chief of Staff:			
Maj. Gen. Aage Lundstrom			July–Sept. 1948
Maj. Gen. William Riley			Sept. 1948–June 1953
Maj. Gen. Vagn Bennike			June 1953–Sept. 1954
Maj. Gen. E.L.M. Burns			Aug. 1954–March 1958
Col. Byron V. Leary (Acting)			Nov. 1956–March 1958
Maj. Gen. Carl C. von Horn			Mar. 1958–June 1963
Lt. Gen. Odd Bull			June 1963–July 1970
Maj. Gen. Ensio Siilasvuo			Aug. 1970 to present
Mediator— Count Folke Bernadotte	GA	Arrange for essential common services, assure protection of Holy Places, promote a peaceful adjustment of the future situation in Palestine, invite necessary assistance from specialized agencies	May–Sept. 1948
Acting Mediator—Ralph Bunche	SC		Sept. 1948–Aug. 1949
UN Conciliation Commission for Palestine (UNCCP)	GA	Continue activities of mediator as indicated, make proposals for an international regime in Jerusalem and the protection of Holy Places, and facilitate relocation and rehabilitation of refugees	Dec. 1948 to present
UN Emergency Force (UNEF) Chief of Command—	GA	Patrol Gaza and Sinai	Nov. 1956–May 1967
Maj. Gen. E.L.M. Burns			Nov. 1956–Dec. 1959
Lt. Gen. P.S. Gyani			Dec. 1959–Jan. 1964
Col. E.C. Condil (Acting)			Sept.–Nov. 1963
Maj. Gen. Carlos F. Paiva Chaves			Jan. 1964–Jan. 1965
Col. Lazar Musicki (Acting)			Aug. 1964–Jan. 1965
Maj. Gen. Syseno Sarmento			Jan. 1965–Jan. 1966
Maj. Gen. Indar J. Rikhye			Jan. 1966–May 1967

TABLE 6.4 (Continued)

	Suez Canal clearance operation Special Representative—Lt. Gen. R.A. Wheeler	SG	SG	Restore Suez Canal to operating condition	Dec. 1956–April 1957
	Special Representative—Nils-Goran Gussing	SC	SG	Investigate and report on conditions affecting civilian populations and prisoners of war in aftermath of war	July–Sept. 1967
	Personal Representative—Ernesto A. Thalmann	GA	SG	Report on situation arising from measures taken by Israel to change status of the city of Jerusalem	Aug.–Sept. 1967
	UN Middle East Mission (UNMEM)—Gunnar Jarring	SC	SG	Promote agreement among states concerned and assist efforts at peaceful settlement	Nov. 1967 to present
Namibia	Good Offices Committee	GA	GA	Negotiate with South Africa concerning future status of former South African League of Nations Mandate	May–Oct. 1958
	Special Committee for Southwest Africa	GA	GA	Observe conditions in Territory, consult with South Africa on repeal of apartheid laws and on elections and preparation for full independence of Territory	April–Dec. 1962
	Special Representative—A. Escher	SG	SG	Contacts with parties concerning future of Namibia	Oct.–Nov. 1972
Nigeria	Representative on Humanitarian Affairs— Nils-Goran Gussing Erik Jensen Said-Uddin Khan	SG	SG	Assist in relief and humanitarian activities for civilian victims of hostilities, assess relief needs and recommend ways to expedite relief supplies	Aug. 1968–Feb. 1969 Feb.–April 1969 May 1969–May 1970
Oman	Special Representative—Herbert de Ribbing	SG	SG	Fact-finding on such questions as presence of foreign troops, evidence of oppression, instances of sabotage and fighting, existence and scope of "rebel" movement	May–Aug. 1963

	Ad Hoc Committee on Oman	GA	GA	Study and evaluate territorial, historical and political issues involved	Sept. 1964–Jan. 1965
Ruanda-Urundi (later *Rwanda and Burundi*)	Commission for Ruanda-Urundi	GA	GA	Supervise elections in Belgian Trust Territory	Jan.–Nov. 1961
	Special Commission	GA	GA	Implement GA recommendation for full and unconditional amnesty	June 1961
	Five-Member UN Commission for Ruanda-Urundi	GA	GA	Ensure maintenance of law and order, resettlement of refugees, guaranteeing of human rights, and convening of high-level conference to consider union between two countries	Feb.–June 1962
	Special Representative— Taghi Nasr and team of experts	GA	SG	Supervise withdrawal of Belgian forces, help implement Economic Union Agreement, study technical and economic assistance needs, help organize administrative cadres, assist in training internal security forces	June 1962
Sabah/ Sarawak	Special Representative— Max H. Dorsinville	SG	SG	Assess situation arising from deterioration of relations between the two countries; later, advise on further useful steps	Dec. 1963–Feb. 1964
	UN Malaysia Mission— Representative: Lawrence Michelmore	SG	SG	Ascertain whether people of territories wish to join future federation of Malaysia	Aug.–Sept. 1963
Senegal	Special Mission to Senegal	SC	SC	Investigate complaints of Portuguese aggressive military acts	July–Sept. 1971
Somaliland	Advisory Council for the Trust Territory of Italian Somaliland (later called UN Advisory Council for Somaliland under Italian Administration—UNACS)	GA	GA	Advise Administering Authority	Dec. 1950–July 1960
	Independent person— Trygve Lie	GA	King of Norway	Assist Governments of Italy and Ethiopia in agreeing on terms of reference to delimit frontier	July–Oct. 1959
South Asia Subcontinent	Three-member team— Charles, Mace, Head	SG	HCR	Assess nature and magnitude of needs of refugees in India	May 1971
	Personal Representative— B. El-Tawil	SG	SG	Co-ordinate assistance from and through UN agencies and programmes	June–Sept. 1971

TABLE 6.4 (Continued)

Area	Title	Authorizing Body	Appointing Body	Task	Duration
	UN East Pakistan Relief Operation (UNEPRO) Paul-Marc Henry, ASG in Charge William McCall, Acting Chief of Mission in Dacca	SG	SG	Plan, organize and conduct humanitarian relief activities	Aug.-Dec. 1971 Aug. 1971-Mar. 1972 Sept.-Dec. 1971
	UN Relief Operation in Dacca (UNROD) Sir Robert Jackson, USG in Charge Toni Hagen, Chief of Mission, Dacca Victor Umbricht, ASG, Chief of Mission	GA	SG	Co-ordinate relief assistance	Dec. 1971 to present March 1972 to present Dec. 1971-April 1972 March 1972-March 1973
	Special Representative—Vittorio Winspeare Guicciardi	SC	SG	Good offices for the solution of humanitarian problems	Dec. 1971-Feb. 1972
	UN Special Relief Office in Bangladesh (UNROB)—Special Representative and Chief of Mission—Francis Lacoste	GA	SG	Take over certain functions of UNROD	April 1973
South Vietnam	UN Fact-finding Mission to South Viet-Nam	GA	GA	Fact-finding regarding alleged violation of human rights by government	Oct.-Nov. 1963
Togoland under British Administration	Plebescite Commissioner—E.E. Prieto	GA	GA	Determine popular will regarding unification with Gold Coast	May 1956
Togoland under French Administration	Commissioner—Max. H. Dorsinville	GA	GA	Supervise elections	Nov. 1957-June 1958
Uganda	Special Representative—Robert Gardiner	SG	SG	Discuss humanitarian aspects of the problem with President of Uganda	Sept.-Oct. 1972
	Special Representative—F.J. Homann-Herinberg	SG	SG	Help arrange for operation of UN Departure Centres in Kampala	Oct. 1972

Western Samoa	UN Plebiscite Commission Commissioner—Najmuddine Rifai	GA	GA	Supervise plebiscite on approval of constitution and desire for independence on the basis of that constitution (New Zealand Trust Territory)	Dec. 1960–June 1961
West Irian	Representative—Ellsworth Bunker	SG	SG	Negotiate settlement between Indonesia and the Netherlands regarding future status of West Irian	Feb.–Aug. 1962
	UN Military Observer Team for the cease-fire in West New Guinea (West Irian) Commander—Brig. Gen. Indar J. Rikhye	GA	SG	Assist in implementation of cease-fire arrangements	Aug.–Sept. 1962
	UN Temporary Administrator—Jose Rolz-Bennett	GA	SG	Arrange transfer of authority from the Netherlands to UNTEA	Sept.–Nov. 1962
	UN Temporary Executive Authority (UNTEA) Administrator—Djalal Abdoh	GA	SG	Administer the Territory	Oct. 1962–May 1963
	UN Security Force in West Irian (West New Guinea) Commander—Maj. Gen. Said-Uddin Khan	GA	SG	Maintain law and order	Nov. 1962–May 1963; Sept. 1962–April 1963
	Representative—Fernando Ortiz-Sanz	GA	SG	Participate in arrangements for the act of self-determination	Aug. 1968–Oct. 1969
Yemen	UN Representative—Ralph Bunche	SG	SG	Visit Presidents of Yemen and UAR to ascertain views on situation and on what steps might be taken to ease tension and restore conditions to normal	Feb.–March 1963
	Exploratory Mission—Maj. Gen. Carl C. von Horn	SG	SG	Consult with UAR, Yemen and Saudi Arabia officials on nature and functioning of UN observation operation	May 1963
	UN Yemen Observation Mission (UNYOM) Commander—Maj. Gen. Carl C. von Horn; Col. Branko Pavlovic (Acting); Lt. Gen. P.S. Gyani; Chief of Staff—Col. S.C. Sabharwal	SC	SG	Check, certify and report observance of disengagement agreement	July 1963–Sept. 1964; Sept.–Nov. 1963; Aug.–Sept. 1963; July–Aug. 1963
	Special Representative and Head of UNYOM—Pier Spinelli	SG	SG	Good offices in encouraging implementation of disengagement agreement	Nov. 1963–Sept. 1964
Zambia	Special Mission	SC	SC	Assess situation arising from closing of Zambia-Rhodesia border	Feb. 1973

Source: UNITAR News, 5, no. 1 (1973), 13–16.

mental and long-range problems of the international system are comple-
mented by activities in other international organizations such as the specialized
agencies and regional organizations including the Organization of American
States and the Organization of African Unity. And in their very particular
foci of interest the multitude of functional or small international organizations are also dealing with more fundamental dilemmas in the international
system. In a system historically and presently characterized by repeated wars
and military interventions, these international organizations are devoting the
bulk of their effort to trying to understand and deal with elements that under-
pin the system and lead to conflict. If we cannot cope with the environment
and manage our nonrenewable resources effectively, we can only expect conflict to arise over these resources. The efforts of international organizations—
or more properly stated, the efforts of states working through the device of
international organization—foster a sense of community. This sustained focus
on a wide variety of interrelated issues tends to provide the separate states
with common understanding and common experiences even though wars and
battle deaths historically seem the only ways to resolve problems. If this is
true, peace would follow from war, but the history of conflict is repetitious;
conflict follows conflict and interludes of minimal international conflict in the
international system seemingly are shorter and shorter. The usefulness of
international organizations as a device for trying to reverse mankind's commitment to conflict is evidenced by the very fact that states are increasingly
devoting more time to interrelating with each other in international organizations.

DEGREE OF COMMITMENT TO
ORGANIZED RELATIONS AMONG STATES

This is not to imply that states are devoting a major portion of their
efforts to cooperation in international organizations. They are not. More efforts are being made simply to *work* through international organizations in
the 1970s than in the past. Yet the utilization of international organizations
is not very high in state priorities. The regular budget of the United Nations
for 1974 was $270,236,500. By comparison the military budget of Iraq in
1970 was $297 million. States are assessed for the U.N. regular budget by a
formula that calculates their economic development vis-à-vis other states. The
United States, as the most developed state (if assessed according to this criteria), would pay over 55 percent of the U.N. budget. However, to ensure
that the United Nations will not be financially dominated by the United
States, the American share is set at 25 percent of the regular budget total.
For 1974, then, the amount of money the United States contributed as its

share of the U.N. budget is about $64 million. Sixty-four million dollars is one-tenth of the projected cost of the nuclear-powered aircraft carrier *Nimitz* (which costs about $640 million). To push this comparative analysis one step further, the U.S. defense budget proposed for fiscal 1974–1975 is $92.6 billion. Thus the 1974 United States share of the U.N. budget is equivalent to .0007 percent of the U.S. budget for defense!

The regular U.N. budget is not, however, the total funds that states make available to the organization for its various activities. In addition to the regular budget, the United Nations has a series of voluntary budgets to which states are invited, but not obligated, to pay a share. These voluntary budgets cover activities such as the U.N. Development Program (to assist developing states in certain types of preinvestment projects). For the United Nations such voluntary budgets run from about $400 million to $500 million a year. If one includes both regular and voluntary budgets for the specialized agencies, plus the regular and voluntary budgets of the United Nations itself, then the total funds made available by states are about $1 billion. But this $1 billion is only .005 percent of what these same states are spending for military systems. Therefore, although states may be making more use of international organizations than they have in the past, they still are not high on priority scales particularly when compared with the priority given military security budgets. On the other hand, states may be maximizing their dollars in their expenditures *via* international oragnizations. For example, the cost of a year's maintenance of the UNEF separating the armies of Israel and Egypt for 1974 will not exceed $20 million. By comparison, it cost Israel $10 million an hour to wage the eighteen-day conflict in October 1973. Thus the U.N. peace-keeping force for one year will cost the equivalent of two hours of Israeli expenditures on the war. Or, as another example, it is equivalent to a U.N. development program that financed a mineral survey in Gabon in the late 1960s (which discovered an iron range exceeding the rich Mesaba Iron Range in Minnesota).

Contributions of states to international organizations are small in comparison to other expenditures, and international organizations have been in a very precarious financial situation. Controversy over whether states were obligated to pay their financial assessments for the maintenance of peace-keeping forces in the Middle East in 1956–1967 and in the Congo in 1960–1964 resulted in many states refusing to pay their share. Within a few years the accumulated arrears of unpaid assessments exceeded the regular budget of the United Nations and threatened the continued existence of the organization. Some states ignored contributions to the peace-keeping forces because they felt such activities had been illegally created or that the parties to the conflict should pay for costs; others felt that only states that wanted to pay for them should pay. With the creation of the second UNEF in October 1973,

this problem appeared to have been resolved by prior state agreement on an apportioned sharing of the operational costs.

Though we may argue the utility of international organizations and states may recognize their usefulness in minimizing conflict and its underlying economic and social causes, their full usefulness will not be realized until they are high on the priority list of all states, particularly the major powers.

ORGANIZED INTEGRATION AMONG STATES

As we have seen, most international organizations are organizations between or among states. They are not organizations with authority over states. Most international organizations attempt to harmonize relations among states, but they are dependent upon states working together. They do not, however, basically change the relationships among states in the international system.

There are, however, a few international organizations that do change basic state relations. Obviously every international organization has some type of socializing effect on behavior, but some international organizations in concept, if not wholly realized in practice, have been created with a goal of changing the basic relations among their member states. Included in this category of international organizations would be those economic international organizations that are attempts to integrate the economies of their members such as the European Coal and Steel Community, the European Common Market, and the Central American Common Market. The expectation in most of these organizations is that step by step, states can move toward an integration of portions of their economies and, theoretically at least, reach a point where it would be very difficult to reverse the integrative trend.

On the initiative of the French foreign minister, Robert Schuman, Belgium, France, the German Federal Republic, Italy, Luxembourg, and the Netherlands agreed on a treaty establishing the European Coal and Steel Community in April 1951. The agreement to pool their production and marketing facilities in coal and steel was envisaged as a first step toward full economic integration; progress along these lines includes the European Economic Community (Common Market) and the European Atomic Energy Community. There were some hopes for an eventual European *political* community, but by the 1970s this appeared to be a less realizable, perhaps even a less necessary, goal than first fantasized in the 1950s. At any rate, while the individual states do retain a considerable veto power in implementing economic integration, steps taken set in motion basic changes in state ties.

One significant implication of the integration of European coal and steel industries is that it is now much more difficult for these states to "go it alone." Integration, we hypothesize, becomes an important factor in encouraging states to resolve conflicts peacefully, particularly when they cannot separate themselves economically.

Most integrative types of international organizations acquire, as time and integrative steps are taken, an incremental role *over* states by implementing policies that states tacitly agree upon. The High Authority of the European Coal and Steel Community has assumed roles not simply among the states but, in its technical areas, roles over particular economic sectors of the states. For example, it assesses what is essentially a tax over shipments of coal and iron. To this extent it has acquired an ability to exist independent of the states so far as its sources of revenue are concerned.

This is not to argue that these types of organizations are supranational organizations with authority over states. Nor are they international governments. But they are types of international organizations that by their very nature establish a manner of regularizing the relations among states that is different from the more traditional efforts that are almost wholly dependent upon the willingness of the states to approve each and every interrelationship that develops.

ORGANIZED SECURITY ALLIANCES AMONG STATES

The majority of international organizations among states are concerned with trying to resolve or adjust differences among states and thus create a more stable international system. Yet at the same time there are some international organizations that are concerned with mobilizing the military forces of their countries in such a manner as to strengthen their collective capabilities against potential and actual opponents. Prime examples of this type of international organization are the Warsaw Treaty Organization and the North Atlantic Treaty Organization.

These organizations are based upon a pledge to come to the common defense of any of the member states attacked by an external force. Joint mobilization of their military forces may involve working out joint military staffs, plans, and maneuvers. This requires agreement on the allocation of roles for the different military forces, combined efforts at economic mobilization, and if possible standardization of weapons systems.

NATO and the Warsaw Pact Organization are probably the most highly organized security alliance organizations. Nevertheless, the Arab League, the Organization of American States, and the Organization of African Unity also

have provision for commitment to a common defense. In addition there are a number of smaller security alliance organizations such as the ANZUS Council among the United States, Australia, and New Zealand and the Joint U.S.-Brazil Defense Council.

As we saw earlier, most states playing the weapons game enter into these alliance arrangements in order to strengthen military security. The alliances involve formalizing commitments into an organization. They deserve separate mention because they combine elements that bring together member states and, at the same time, institutionalize differences between them and other states and thereby create a divisive element in international politics. They commit their members to a priority for military programs to maintain peace.

Most security communities have one or two dominant members, and many states argue that the communities are in reality an organizational device for the dominant powers to extend their influence into the international system. In the 1965 unrest in the Dominican Republic the United States intervened militarily allegedly to protect American citizens, but the United States had the intervention approved by the Organization of American States as a "peace-keeping" operation to protect the Western Hemisphere from possible subversion. The intervening forces, while almost exclusively comprised of U.S. troops, did include token forces from several pro-American states in keeping with the spirit of the OAS. Similarly, the Soviet Union intervened militarily in Czechoslovakia under the guise of a "peace-keeping" operation of the Warsaw Pact, and token forces from other pro-Soviet Eastern European states contributed troops to the intervention.

On the other hand, in the Arab League and the Organization of African Unity, in which there are no predominant members, the security alliances are essentially defensive mechanisms to try to prevent the intervention of other states from outside their regions. The Arab League in the 1961 dispute between Iraq and Kuwait dispatched a "peace-keeping" force primarily to prevent continued British intervention on the behalf of Kuwait. In this instance the force was made up of military units primarily from Tunisia, which was neutral in the dispute.

Security alliance organizations do provide an international rationale for action or intervention, with justifications that they constitute a collective self-defense against aggression. The United States involvement in Vietnam was justified by the State Department as an act of self-defense under the Southeast Asian Treaty Organization.

Security alliance organizations are a unique breed of international organizations because while they are argued as a security measure, they have an impact in increasing tension in the international system. They are supportive, generally, of efforts of the major powers to dominate the interna-

tional system. While most such security arrangements are sanctioned under Chapter 8 of the U.N. Charter, they actually weaken U.N. efforts to deal with a problem. In the situation in the Dominican Republic in 1965, the United States argued that the United Nations had no right to become involved because the problem was being handled by the Organization of American States.

THE INSECURITY OF SECURITY ALLIANCES

Lastly, the experience of the cutoff of oil by the Arab oil-producing states raises questions as to whether security alliances are true alliances. For example, are they a façade of unity that crumbles under pressure? Certainly the NATO alliance was threatened by the unilateral action of the United States in placing its forces on alert in the October 1973 Middle East crisis. To the NATO "partners" of the United States this action was a blatant demonstration of who was the dominant member of the alliance. Was NATO truly a mutual collective alliance if the strongest partner could take military actions unilaterally without consultation with the other members? To the United States the decision of most of the European members of NATO (except the Netherlands) to submit to Arab oil pressures and shift their Middle Eastern policies to support of the Arab states was a betrayal of the alliance. The further steps of these European states to seek individual oil deals with the Arab states—such as France's "oil for military aircraft" agreement with Saudi Arabia—was providing assistance in opposition to U.S. policies in support of Israel. One might question whether such a security alliance really provides security. If the answer is yes, then one could argue that security alliances, because of their threatening character, increase tensions in the international system and, at the same time, do not provide security for the members of the regional security system.

OUTLINES FOR FUTURE SECURITY

If the states and the people of the earth are to deal effectively with global problems, they must meet them with some sense of community. It is apparent from our review of the international system that a crucial element in attempting to achieve results of maximum benefit to all mankind is how states and peoples relate with one another. Whether the network of relationships involves direct diplomatic contacts, ad hoc international conferences, international organizations among states, or nongovernmental contacts among peoples, experience has suggested that there are hopeful processes and procedures that can be developed. There are also detrimental aspects of these patterns of relationships that need to be minimized. It is probably a false illusion to dream of some universal or world government, yet a greater sense of community is desirable.

With a proliferation of "sovereign and independent" states it is clear

few are really independent; all have dependent relationships. Since all states value their own self-interests, the problem is to build mutual respect, trust, and a willingness to resolve differences through peaceful means. Ultimately, all states have a mutual self-interest that would be served best by regularizing international relations. If one accepts this common goal, then a number of questions remain. How can the diplomatic contacts be extended to include all states with all other states? Certainly trust and mutual self-confidence depend upon the fullest first-hand knowledge of the policies of each other. What processes and procedures in international organizations can be encouraged and/or developed to contribute to a building of mutual trust? Are the experiences of economic integrative organizations a step that should be encouraged in every possible way because of the interlocking ties they develop among states? Is there a greater impact, in the long run, from organized relationships that concentrate on economic and social problems than from those that concentrate on trying to regularize political relationships? Are security alliances as much a detriment to security and trust among states as a boon to providing military support? What alternatives, organizationally, could be substituted for such security alliance organizations? To what degree should nongovernmental developments be encouraged? What areas of concern to states should be the primary focus of interrelationships among states?

We may not be able to provide an exact formula on how to organize relationships among states to provide security and economic welfare for mankind. Even if we could, it might not be acceptable to everyone. But what can be done is to make every effort to see that the existing relationships are improved or altered so that they encourage states to resolve their problems peacefully and to share the limited resources of our environment. We can encourage changes in the diplomatic negotiations among states in favor of those processes and procedures that assist in building mutual trust. We can encourage organizational developments that also foster mutual trust. We can place more focus on the issues of common concern as a means for building trust that will facilitate negotiation on issues on which there are sharp disagreements. We can devise methods of sharing information among states that will build understandings, instead of methods that create suspicion. We need to look on the long-range implications of the methods by which states relate rather than simply on what seems to be an expedient process in the short range.

NOTES

[1]These figures are derived from Steven L. Spiegel, *Dominance and Diversity: The International Hierarchy*, Boston, Mass.: Little, Brown, 1972, pp. 93–96; and from the U.S. Department of State, Bureau of Intelligence and Research, *Status of the World's Nations* (Geographic Bulletin revised) Washington, D.C., G.P.O., 1973, 20pp. Spiegel lists

131 independent states and 52 dependent states as of 1970. In adjusting this list to 1974 a number of dependent states have achieved independence and have become members of the United Nations. Spiegel also lists a number of mini-states in the dependent category. However, the fact that most of the states were extended invitations to attend the Third U.N. Conference on the Law of the Sea means they might be considered as independent. The number of dependent states varies from 33 to 80 depending upon whether they are counted as individual governments or whether they are clustered in administrative units under colonial administrators. However, one might note that the practice of the U.N. Committee of Twenty-Four on Decolonization has argued that each individual unit has the right to assert its eventual independence and does not have to seek independence only in accord with the administrative framework of colonial administrations.

[2]This international web of treaty relationships is laid out in Peter H. Rohn, *World Treaty Index and Treaty Profiles*, 6 vols., Santa Barbara, Calif.: World Treaty Project, American Bibliographic Center, 1974.

[3]New Zealand, Ministry of Foreign Affairs, *Annual Report* for the year ended March 31, 1972, Wellington: Government Printer, 1972.

[4]Steven L. Spiegel, *op. cit.*, develops interesting distinctions among super, major, middle, small, and mini states. The distinction we make is a gradient reflection of population, territorial size, and economic development. The extremes are obvious. The United States and the Soviet Union are *superpowers* because their combinations of these factors are overwhelming in comparison with other states. Equally obvious are the *mini-states*, such as Monaco, San Marino, Andorra, and Tonga. The major, middle, and small powers are gradients between these two extremes. *Major* powers would probably include France, West Germany, Japan, People's Republic of China, and the United Kingdom. Australia, because of its economic development, is an example of a *middle* power, as is India because of her population. *Small* powers might include such states as the Ivory Coast, Iceland, or Paraguay. In essence the distinctions are indicative of the capacity, ability, and desire to be an influence in relationships with other states.

[5]Union of International Associations, *Yearbook of International Organizations*, 12th ed., 1968–1969, Brussels: Union of International Associations, 1969, p. 13. This yearbook does not include international organizations that have less than three members.

[6]Other states earmarked for the elimination of colonialism were: Bahamas, Bermuda, British Virgin Islands, Brunei, Cayman Islands, Cocos (Keeling) Islands, Gilbert and Ellice Islands, Guam, Montserrat, New Hebrides, Pitcairn, St. Helena, Seychelles, Solomon Islands, Turks and Caicos Islands, United States Virgin Islands, Niue and Tokelau Islands, Antigua, Dominica, Grenada, St. Kitts-Nevis-Anguilla, St. Lucia, St. Vincent, Namibia (South-West Africa), French Somaliland, British Honduras, Falkland Islands (Malivinas), and Gibraltar.

[7]The activities or programs of the following were also included: U.N. Industrial Development Organization, U.N. Development Program, U.N. Capital Development Fund, U.N. Conference on the Human Environment, U.N. Conference Exposition on Human Settlements, U.N. Children's Fund, Economic and Social Council, U.N. High Commissioner for Refugees, Committee on Information from Non-Self-Governing Territories, Committee on the implementation of the Declaration on the Granting of Independence to Colonial Countries and Peoples, International Law Commission, U.N. Commission on International Trade Law, Special Committee on the Question of Defining Aggression, Committee on Relations with the Host Country, Problems relating to the financing and administration of the United Nations (including acceptance of the budget, maintenance of the Working Capital Fund, personnel problems, etc.), and Organizational activities such as the election of members to the Security Council, Economic and Social Council, other organs, sub-organs, committees, and commissions of the United Nations.

[8]This is an almost identical situation to the International Control Commission (ICC) created for a similar role in the Geneva Agreements of 1954 on Vietnam. That it failed in its role, for precisely the same reasons suggested by the Canadian government in the 1973 Paris Agreement, is examined in David W. Wainhouse, *International Peace Observation*, Baltimore: The Johns Hopkins Press, 1966, pp. 489–503. Ironically, the Canadians raised

the same questions about this previous ICC, and their prognostications were proved correct as time transpired. Canada withdrew from this control commission in July 1973, and the organization became inoperative until August when the parties agreed to Iran's replacing Canada.

[9]The major powers were defined in the charter as China, France, the United Kingdom, the United States, and the Soviet Union. This may well be a fatal flaw in the charter because it preserves a status quo as to who are the major powers (a status quo of 1945) and the charter cannot be altered without their concurrence.

[10]Before the amendment of the charter only two of the five elected members were required for a majority on essentially substantive questions.

[11]The issue was placed on the Council's agenda because such an action would preclude its being considered in the General Assembly, and while unable to agree on the situation in Vietnam, the United States and the Soviet Union were in informal agreement that any public discussion in any organ of the United Nations would accelerate rather than decrease the difference between them.

[12]This deadlocked situation resulted in 1950, when the General Assembly passed the so-called uniting for peace resolutions, which established procedures for the General Assembly to convene in emergency session to promptly deal with threats to the peace. However, action by the Assembly is only a recommendation unlike an obligatory decision of the Security Council.

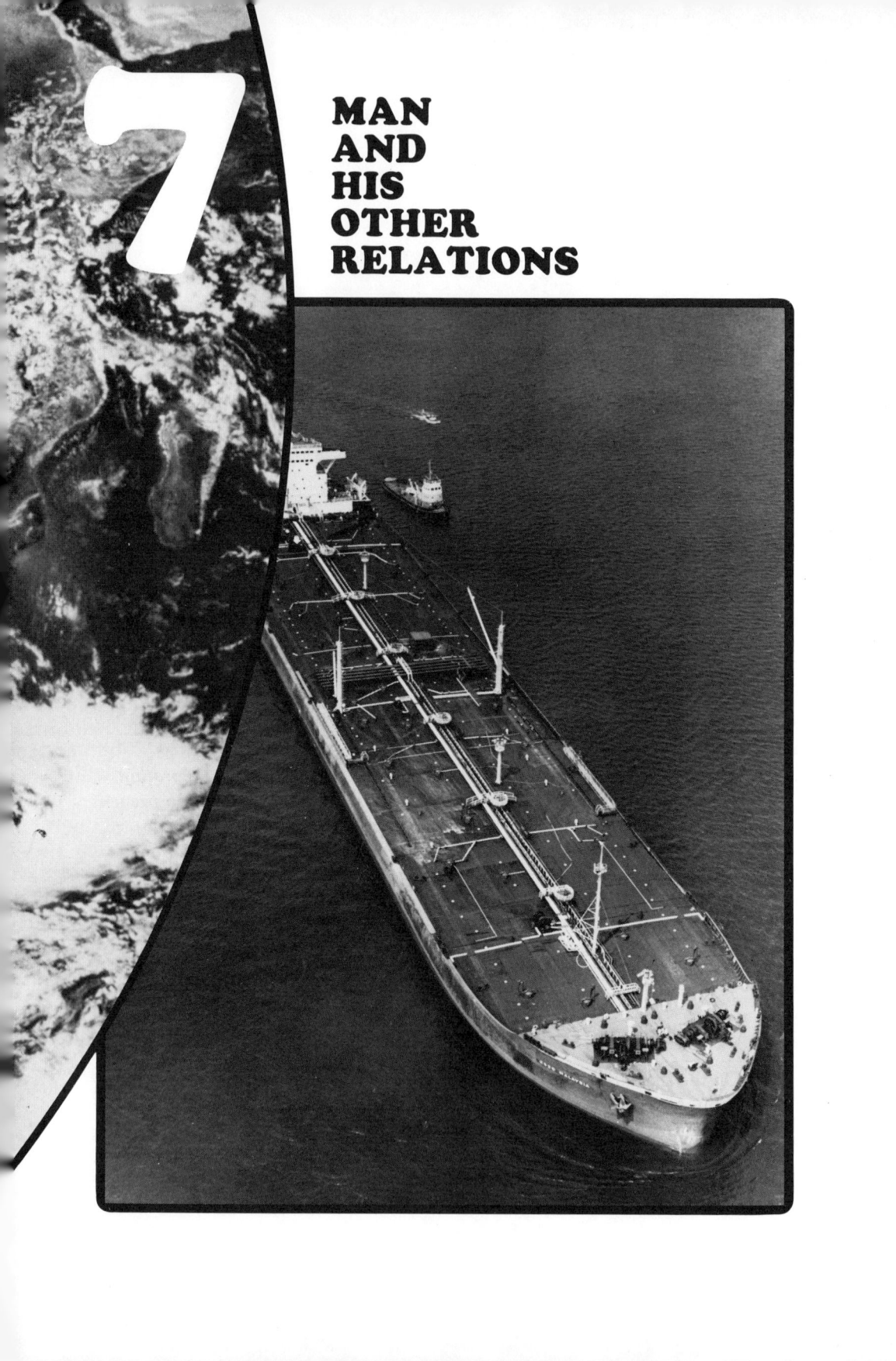

7

MAN
AND
HIS
OTHER
RELATIONS

This accidental
Meeting of possibilities
Call itself I.
I ask: what am I doing here?
And, at once, this I
Becomes unreal.*

Dag Hammarskjold
1959

At 10:05 A.M. on Tuesday, March 20, 1973, Senator Frank Church of Idaho called to order the Subcommittee on Multinational Corporations of the United States Senate in the first of seven sessions to investigate the role of the International Telephone and Telegraph Company (ITT) in Chile in 1970–1971. In his opening statement, Senator Church said:

In this hearing, we shall seek to ascertain whether the ITT corporation and the Central Intelligence Agency cooperated in an attempt to prevent Salvador Allende Grossens from being elected President of Chile in 1970; whether the company sought to induce other U.S. corporations to cooperate with it in bringing pressure upon U.S. Government officials to adopt policies which would make life more difficult for Mr. Allende's government; whether the ITT company proposed to U.S. Government officials policies designed to bring pressure on Mr. Allende's government, and possibly, to lead to Mr. Allende's downfall; whether, as Mr. Allende has alleged, there was a credit embargo imposed on Chile by U.S. banks.[1]

On the second day of these hearings, the subcommittee heard testimony from John A. McCone, a director of ITT who was formerly the Director of the Central Intelligence Agency of the U.S. Government. Under questioning Mr. McCone detailed conversations with Harold S. Geneen, the head of ITT. Geneen proposed to offer up to $1 million of company funds to help finance

a plan (if the United States government had such a plan) to "assist or promote a coalition against Allende" so that he would not be installed as president by the Chilean Congress. McCone transmitted this offer to Richard Helms, then director of the CIA. Then the following dialogue took place:

> **Senator Church:** Mr. McCone, you have testified this morning, and previously, that you believe the actions taken by ITT and the liaison that developed between the ITT and CIA for the purpose of achieving a coalition in the Chilean Congress to prevent Allende's installation as President of Chile, were proper by virtue of the fact that this action was consistent with what had been American national policy and what was at that time national policy. Is this correct?
>
> **Mr. McCone:** That is correct.
>
> **Senator Church:** The policy you have referred to commenced with NATO and the Truman doctrine, and was basically to do everything we could to prevent the spread of communism in the world.
>
> **Mr. McCone:** Yes
>
> **Senator Church:** That was the general objective of our policy at that time; was it not?
>
> **Mr. McCone:** Since World War II and up to recently, international communism has had a very active political action group centered in the KGB Soviet Committee on State Security. Their purpose was to promote the Communist Marxist parties throughout the world in the interests of defeating the Christian Democratic parties and the other parties that stood for the principles of this country. Now, it was the actions taken which you mentioned, and there are a great many more, were basic in their establishment of the policies was to try to frustrate this determined effort of international communism.
>
> **Senator Church:** Do you draw no distinction between the case in Chile and other cases such as Berlin, Korea, or Cuba? The latter were all cases, were they not, where the Communist effort, was a forcible one, that is to say, was an attempt to seize power by force of Arms.
>
> In Chile, Mr. Allende had been elected, had won the popular election and had done so in an open, free, and legal manner. Does that not present a different case from the others, a very different case indeed?
>
> **Mr. McCone:** I am not familiar with the degree to which Allende's Marxist Party was supported by and from the outside, supported financially from the outside by the Communist movement. I do know that many other elections which I am familiar with in various parts of the world, the Communist Party received very substantial support,

financial support, from political action. I have not made an inquiry as to just what the situation in Chile was.

Senator Church: But, Mr. McCone, even if we were to assume that, Mr. Allende had received some financial support—I do not know if he had, but it is a safe assumption based on other patterns—we already have testimony to the effect that a good deal of money was pumped in on the other side from the outside, from the United States. So that does not seem to me to be the relevant question. The question is, is it proper for either the company or the Government to intervene in the internal political affairs of Chile, when a man is chosen by the people in an open and free election? It seems to me that that is a very different question than those which you raise in reference to Communist efforts to seize a government either through insurrection or outright aggression. . . .[2]

From this brief episode it is evident that there are a number of organized relations among states other than those considered in the previous chapter concerning the intergovernmental organization of relations among states. The International Telephone and Telegraph Company is an international corporation involved in activities in over 70 nation-states. Reference is also made in the preceding exchange to organized efforts by Communist political groups. American banks are mentioned as having financial dealings with other states. Two national governmental intelligence agencies, the CIA (United States) and the KGB (Soviet Union) are mentioned as being indirectly involved in the internal affairs of another state. Lastly, the common problems of Christian Democratic parties are mentioned as having mutual relationships. All of these elements—intelligence agencies (even though they are governmental), revolutionary political movements, other political parties, and multinational corporations—are involved in the network of relationships in the international system. Their commonality is that they constitute relationships that penetrate directly or indirectly the sovereignty of states.

The covert activities by states are actions to influence "informally" or to penetrate other states. All states are aware of the existence of these activities, but they are carried out under a veil of secrecy. Such covert activities differ from multinational corporations, political parties, and other nongovernmental organizations (not mentioned in our illustration), in that these latter groups involve organizations that have no formal governmental ties. Nongovernmental international organizations, international corporations, and international political movements are more directly organizations of the relations between the people in one state with the people in another state. However, all of these networks of relations are another and an important ingredient in the organization of the international system.

COVERT RELATIONS AMONG STATES

INTELLIGENCE NETWORKS

Before looking at the nongovernmental network of relations among states we need to briefly look at the intelligence networks. We have noted previously that the official network of direct communications among states is the one provided by the formal diplomatic missions. One role of diplomatic missions is to provide states with up-to-date and first-hand information on the country in which the diplomatic mission resides. However, in addition to this *overt* gathering of information, most states, to some degree, also maintain *covert* contact with developments in other states.

There are two sides to covert relations among states. On the one hand, they involve large intelligence organizations, such as the Defense Intelligence Agency and the CIA in the United States or the KGB in the Soviet Union. These agencies are concerned with the gathering of intelligence and undercover activities in other states. Most of their intelligence gathering is fairly open, but a portion of their activities involves the dispatch of spies, clandestine employment of foreign nationals, as well as other nefarious deeds involving espionage and assassination.

The other type of covert activity involves monitoring of both official and unofficial radio, telegraph, telephone, and often mail communications of states. This generally includes covert interception and decoding of communications between foreign offices and their overseas missions. In the United States this activity is supervised by the National Security Agency. By this process states are able to become privy to the official communications of other states and thus have fuller information than that which might come into their hands in other ways.

Almost all states engage in these covert activities. They "spy" or "listen in" on both friends and enemies in the name of national security. They justify their activities as necessary to prevent being subjected to surprise international developments. In the large states these operations are massive. It is estimated, for example, that the National Security Agency employs over 14,000 individuals in these activities in Washington, D.C., alone. At the same time, it is estimated that the CIA has over 10,000 employees in Washington, D.C.[3] It is estimated the total U.S. intelligence community consumes $6 billion a year and employs 150,000 people.[4]

While states may feel these activities necessary, the existence of these covert networks of contacts among states do not necessarily foster mutual trust. To the contrary, while they provide better insights and better information on interstate relations when their methods are publicly exposed, they often lead to increased tension among states. The shooting down of a U-2 "spy plane" in 1960 over the Soviet Union first resulted in an American

denial that it was an authorized flight. But when the Soviets then produced the captured flyer not only was the denial shown to be a lie, but the whole incident resulted in a "summit" meeting with Premier Khrushchev "walking out" on President Eisenhower.

The dilemma of these kinds of covert activities centers on what is necessary to build trust among states and what is necessary to provide security for each individual state. When Henry L. Stimson became U.S. Secretary of State, he closed down the so-called Black Chamber, the State Department's code-cracking office. When he was later criticized for this action, he explained that he was a gentleman dealing with the gentlemen sent as ambassadors, and that "gentlemen do not read each other's mail." He felt such activities were not conducive to building trust among states. Yet, in 1940, when the United States was approaching World War II, he did not object to the stepping up of such activities when he was Secretary of War. At the time he viewed these covert activities as necessary evils.[5] The unanswered question about this type of interstate relations is whether the information gained is worth the inherent distrust it breeds among states.

Despite the questions that can be raised by this covert means of intelligence gathering, the real questions about intelligence activities are those that go beyond the process of acquiring information. The CIA, for example, is empowered to "perform such other functions and duties related to intelligence as the National Security Council may from time to time direct." Covertly, the CIA has become directly involved in the internal affairs of other states (often through dummy corporations or friendly organizations). A staff report of the U.S. Senate Foreign Relations committee released in August 1971 provided some insight into such covert activities. It reported that the CIA trained mercenaries in Thailand and transported them to Laos by Air America (a private airline sponsored by the CIA). In 1969–1971 the CIA forces in Laos, the so-called *Bataillons Guerriers*, numbered between 30,000 and 39,800 irregulars and constituted the "cutting edge of the Lao Military forces." Because of the secretive nature of the CIA only a few of these "other functions and duties" have come to light. The 1954 overthrow of a pro-Marxist leader in Guatemala (Jacobo Arbenz) was accomplished with CIA assistance, and its exposure caused a lessening of U.S. prestige in Central and South America. The failure of the CIA force of Cuban refugees, trained primarily in Guatemala, to succeed in their anti-Castro invasion of Cuba in the Bay of Pigs incident in April 1961 gave support to other anti-U.S. movements in the Americas. Similarly, the overthrow of the Czechoslovakian government in 1948 was accomplished by covert activities of the Soviet intelligence community.

Covert efforts that involve some kind of direct action in the internal affairs of other states whenever exposed to public attention have always resulted in a hardening of relations among states. *The New York Times* in a

survey of these activities by the CIA has concluded: "Regardless of the acts, the CIA's reputation in the world is so horrendous and its role in events so exaggerated that it is becoming a burden on American policy, rather than the secret weapon it was intended to be."[6]

The increase in other than direct intelligence-gathering covert activities is probably a reflection of the increased tension in international politics. Such a development only increases distrust and may well hinder other efforts to encourage mutual trust among states.

The Necessity for Covert Intelligence Gathering. In another sense intelligence gathering is essential to assure the credibility of deterrence systems of defense. If a state is pursuing its security by the threat of retaliation, it is essential that the potential enemy have sufficient intelligence to be assured that the threat is real. Both the United States and the Soviet Union employ spy-in-the-sky satellites, for example. Both are fully aware of each other's activities in this area, yet neither protests this invasion of its "sovereignty." It has been estimated that a U.S. Satellite Antimissile Observation System (SAMOS) in one ninety-minute orbit of the globe collects more information than 50,000 spies could collect in a year.[7] This satellite system transmits electronic intelligence to ground stations and ejects photo intelligence which is intercepted mid-air over the Pacific Ocean. There are many other technical systems employed, especially by the major powers. And while this spying is a covert activity, it serves to make missile weapons systems credible in calculations of moves by potential enemies. However, to states that are not engaged in the nuclear deterrence weapons game, these spy satellites threaten their security because the nuclear missile state can obviously develop much more intelligence information about them than they in turn can acquire about such major powers. Highly technical intelligence tends to increase the ability of major powers to dominate other states in the system.

The existence of this network of covert activities is a significant element in the relations among states—a divisive element if they are exposed or suspected. Without fuller public knowledge it is difficult to assess whether the successful and unexposed covert activities offset the distrust from the exposed activities. It is a whole area of international relations in which more rumors abound than hard facts simply because of the secret nature of the activities.

ORGANIZED RELATIONS AMONG INDIVIDUALS IN THE INTERNATIONAL SYSTEM

Conceptually, the study of international relations has concentrated on states as the actors in comprising the international system. Idealists often

argue that there would be peace if only the peoples of the world could get together instead of the states, which seem unable to separate themselves from their self-interest assertions. Only recently have scholars and governments begun to look deeper into other aspects of the international system such as the relations among peoples extending across state boundaries.[8] Obviously, there are many such networks of relationships, but three deserve some mention because *they play roles in regularizing relations between or among states.* These are international nongovernmental organizations, the so-called multinational corporations or enterprises, and international political parties or movements.

INTERNATIONAL NONGOVERNMENTAL ORGANIZATIONS

The 1969 *Yearbook of International Organizations* listed the existence of 2188 international nongovernmental organizations (commonly referred to as NGOs). Essentially they are common-interest groups with national affiliates. For example, the International League for the Rights of Man is concerned with promoting and protecting fundamental human rights and has ties with comparable organizations in a number of states such as the American Civil Liberties Union in the United States. Few of these NGOs are wholly universal, but their memberships can be found in a large number of states. The International Chamber of Commerce, for example, has national committees in 41 states and organizational or associate members in 36 other states. Some NGOs are regional in nature, involving only a certain geographical region, such as the European Committee on Rural Law, which has national affiliates in 6 European countries.

Consultative Status of NGOs. NGOs are an organizational means of bringing together peoples in various states with common interests or concern. They are usually nonprofit organizations, although it should be recognized that they are also devices to try to achieve common ends. Those in the area of commerce and industry, for example, often promote national and international policies that mean profits for their members. In a sense they are also international lobbying groups. Often as not their national affiliates are interest groups that lobby with their national government.

Many NGOs have formal relationships with international governmental organizations. In 1970 over 380 NGOs were in what is called "consultative status" to the U.N. Economic and Social Council and its suborgans such as the Population Commission, the Commission on the Status of Women, and the Human Rights Commission. There are various categories in a consultative status. Those NGOs that the United Nations has determined have a fairly universal membership and a universal concern with economic and social problems are given the right to participate in meetings of the U.N. Economic

and Social Council and its suborgans, including the submission of draft resolutions. Other NGOs that focus on one particular problem, such as human rights, have this capacity only when their topic is being considered.

NGOs have also been accorded consultative status with the various specialized agencies. For example, in 1970, 87 were in consultative status with the International Labor Organization in Geneva, 79 with the Food and Agriculture Organization in Rome, and 273 in a relationship with the U.N. Educational, Scientific and Cultural Organization in Paris. The significance of these relationships is that these interest groups do have an opportunity, in the area of economic and social activities, to participate directly in one way or another in the discussions of questions by the states in the United Nations.

In addition to formal consultative ties many NGOs maintain permanent offices in buildings adjacent to the U.N. headquarters. There is considerable interaction between their representatives and diplomats representing states at the United Nations. They often organize meetings, both formally and informally, that bring together diplomats from various countries in a less structured setting for exchanging views.

The Effects of NGOs. In Latin America and in Western Europe there are a number of regional NGOs that pursue lobbying roles. In the European Common Market area there are nearly 400 NGOs pursuing their particular interests. They range from the Common Market Opticians' Group to the EEC Committee for the Cider and Fruit Wine Industry to the Liaison Committee of the Rice-Starch Manufactures of the EEC. Similarly, about 50 NGOs are "accredited" to the Organization of American States and pursue their interests primarily in the area of economic and social questions.

While NGOs are international, involving members from a number of different states, the majority of them are Western. The Soviet Union and its satellite states often views these NGOs with considerable suspicion because such "professional" organizations in the Soviet Union and Eastern European states are government organizations, not private or nongovernmental organizations.

Robert Angell reaches three main conclusions about these international NGOs:

> (1) they are multiplying the number of ties between nations and are therefore probably contributing to a greater sense of belonging to mankind among the participants; (2) they are having some effects, presumably supportive, on the institutions of the United Nations' family; and (3) they indirectly influence governments toward accommodation because their participants have had a positive experience in cooperating with nationals of other countries in their activities.[9]

MULTINATIONAL CORPORATIONS

The second category of international organizations based on groups of peoples rather than on states in the international system are the so-called multinational corporations or enterprises.

> *There is no agreed definition of what constitutes a multinational corporation. Some authorities define it as a company whose foreign sales have reached a ratio of, say 25% (or some other share) of total sales. Some find the definition in organization; i.e., a company that has global product divisions rather than an international division. Others look to the distribution of ownership or to the nationality mix of managers or directors as the determining characteristics. Professor Raymond Vernon of Harvard University, an outstanding authority on the multinational corporation, regards it as a company that attempts to carry out its activities on an international scale, as though there were no national boundaries, on the basis of a common strategy directed from a corporate center. According to Vernon, affiliates are locked together in an integrated process and their policies are determined by the corporate center in terms of decisions relating to production, plant location, product mix, marketing, financing, etc. Mr. Jacques Maisonrouge, President of the IBM World Trade Corporation, characterizes the multinational corporation as one that: (a) operates in many countries; (b) carries out research, development and manufacturing in those countries; (c) has a multinational management; and (d) has multinational stock ownership.[10]*

Depending upon how one defines multinational corporations, the estimates of the number of these enterprises range from 500 to over 3000.

Economic Impact of Multinational Corporations. The significance of these profit-oriented organizations is indicated by the estimate that 300 of the multinational corporations may control 75 percent of the world's productive capacity and employ 20 percent of the labor force on the globe.[11] If (as in Table 7.1) one compares the world sales of multinational corporations with the gross national product of states and compiles a list ranking of the top hundred states and multinational corporations, it will include 51 multinational corporations and 49 states. General Motors, for example, has gross sales that exceed the gross national products of 126 of the 150 independent political states; only 24 states have gross national products exceeding the sales of General Motors. As Table 7.2 illustrates, the growth of multinational corporations has been phenomenal.

TABLE 7.1 COUNTRIES AND COMPANIES 1970

Rank	Country or Company	GNP or sales (billions)	Growth Rate 1965–70 (percent)
1	United States	$974.0	42.98
2	Soviet Union	485.7	60.10
3	Japan	196.7	32.64
4	West Germany	184.8	64.69
5	France	146.3	56.51
6	People's Republic of China	121.0	55.26
7	United Kingdom	116.3	17.23
8	Italy	91.7	61.55
9	Canada	78.0	62.33
10	India	52.5	6.66
11	Poland	46.0	50.52
12	Brazil	40.4	83.85
13	East Germany	39.6	50.57
14	Mexico	33.2	70.79
15	Australia	32.9	44.90
16	Spain	32.5	49.61
17	Czechoslovakia	32.5	47.99
18	Sweden	31.5	62.82
19	Netherlands	31.3	65.03
20	Belgium	25.0	49.72
21	Romania	24.4	64.53
22	Argentina	23.9	49.15
23	Switzerland	20.6	47.73
24	General Motors	18.8	90.44
25	Yugoslavia	18.5	118.16
26	Pakistan	17.9	60.00
27	South Africa	17.8	66.40
28	American Telephone & Telegraph	17.0	53.27
29	Standard Oil (New Jersey)	16.6	44.29
30	Denmark	15.8	57.83
31	Ford Motor	15.0	29.38
32	Indonesia	14.0	34.52
33	Austria	13.7	49.37
34	Bulgaria	11.7	74.36
35	Norway	11.2	60.15
36	Royal Dutch/Shell	10.8	50.35
37	Venezuela	10.3	34.20
38	Finland	10.2	25.64
39	Iran	10.1	70.36
40	Philippines	9.8	89.05
41	Sears Roebuck	9.3	44.94
42	Greece	9.2	65.40
43	Korea, South	8.9	206.51

TABLE 7.1 (*Continued*)

Rank	Country or Company	GNP or sales (billions)	Growth Rate 1965–70 (percent)
44	General Electric	8.72	40.44
45	Turkey	8.68	6.87
46	Chile	8.4	96.59
47	International Business Machines	7.5	110.01
48	Mobil Oil	7.3	47.94
49	Columbia	7.07	38.6
50	Chrysler	6.99	32.07
51	Unilever	6.9	34.96
52	Thailand	6.8	76.18
53	International Telephone & Telegraph	6.4	256.92
54	Texaco	6.3	68.03
55	U.A.R. (Egypt)	6.3	34.04
56	Western Electric	5.9	74.18
57	Great Atlantic & Pacific Tea (New York)	5.7	10.37
58	Peru	5.64	31.95
59	Israel	5.59	64.67
60	China (Taiwan)	5.5	98.40
61	Gulf Oil	5.4	59.40
62	Safeway Stores (Oakland)	4.9	65.36
63	U.S. Steel	4.8	9.40
64	Volkswagenwerk	4.314	86.18
65	Westinghouse Electric	4.313	80.46
66	Standard Oil of California	4.18	71.49
67	Philips' Gloeilampenfabrieken	4.16	99.76
68	J. C. Penney (New York)	4.15	81.34
69	British Petroleum	4.1	68.68
70	Nippon Steel	4.0	
71	Malaysia	3.91	36.53
72	Ireland	3.85	37.25
73	Ling-Temco-Vought	3.8	
74	Kroger (Cincinnati)	3.735	46.22
75	Standard Oil (Indiana)	3.732	51.01
76	Boeing	3.677	81.75
77	E. I. du Pont de Nemours	3.613	19.76
78	Shell Oil	3.589	40.12
79	ICI (Imperial Chemical Industries)	3.509	53.67
80	British Steel	3.495	
81	North Korea	3.5	40.00
82	General Telephone & Electronics	3.4	68.90
83	Hibachi	3.32	
84	Morocco	3.31	27.35
85	RCA	3.29	61.21
86	Siemens	3.196	78.05
87	Goodyear Tire & Rubber	3.194	43.53

TABLE 7.1 (*Continued*)

Rank	Country or Company	GNP or sales (billions)	Growth Rate 1965–70 (percent)
88	Swift	3.1	11.81
89	Farbwerke Hoechst	3.027	
90	Union Carbide	3.026	46.60
91	Daimler-Benz	3.018	
92	Procter & Gamble	2.978	44.63
93	August Thysson-Hutte	2.956	
94	Bethlehem Steel	2.935	13.80
95	BASE	2.874	
96	Montecatini Edison	2.841	
97	Marcor (Chicago)	2.804	
98	Eastman Kodak	2.784	
99	Kraftco	2.751	
100	Greyhound	2.739	

Source: U.S. Senate, Committee on Finance, Subcommittee on International Trade, *Hearings, Multinational Corporations,* 93rd Cong., 1st sess. (1973), pp. 475–476.

For instance, a study of 187 U.S. multinational corporations showed that in 1960 they had 4796 foreign subsidiaries and in 1967 they had 7927, nearly a twofold increase in seven years. Initially, multinational corporations tended to be U.S. based, but in the past decade there has been a steady increase in those based in Europe and Japan.

There is no question that multinational corporations have created a whole network of relations across and through state boundaries. The impact of this development is hard for anyone to assess. Certainly multinational corporations play a very significant role in the transfer of technology and managerial skills, probably more effectively than governments. They are profit motivated, and this goal very clearly defines their perception of achievements. This often means that investment policies of multinational corporations headquartered in a developed state play a significant aspect in any developing state in which the investments are made. They also have a significant impact on the economic development within any state.

These points were aptly illustrated in a 1972 study of the Canadian government on foreign direct investment in Canada. The study pointed out that 60 percent of manufacturing in Canada is controlled by foreign multinational corporations. As Table 7.3 shows, in the manufacturing industries such as petroleum and rubber products, external control exceeded 90 percent,

TABLE 7.2 INCREASE IN WORLD SALES OF THE TWENTY LARGEST MULTI-
NATIONAL CORPORATIONS, 1970 TO 1971

	World Sales[a]	
	1970	1971
1 General Motors	18.8	28.3
2 American Telephone & Telegraph	17.0	18.5
3 Standard Oil of New Jersey (Exxon)	16.6	18.7
4 Ford Motor	15.0	16.4
5 Royal Dutch Shell	10.8	12.7
6 Sears Roebuck	9.3	10.0
7 General Electric	8.7	9.4
8 IBM	7.5	8.3
9 Mobil Oil	7.3	8.2
10 Chrysler	7.0	8.0
11 Unilever	6.9	7.5
12 ITT	6.4	7.3
13 Texaco	6.3	7.5
14 Great Atlantic & Pacific Tea	5.7	5.5
15 Gulf Oil	5.4	5.9
16 Safeway Stores	4.9	5.3
17 U.S. Steel	4.8	4.9
18 Volkswagen	4.3	5.0
19 Westinghouse Electric	4.3	4.6
20 Standard Oil of California	4.2	5.1
Total	171.2	197.1

[a]In billions.
Source: U.S. Senate, Committee on Finance Subcommittee on International
Trade, Hearings, *Multinational Corporations*, 93rd Cong., 1st sess. (1973), pp.
475–476.

while 65 percent of the mining and smelting were controlled from abroad.
The study pointed out that:

> The high and growing degree of foreign control of Canadian business
> activity can affect the balance between the manufacturing and
> resource sectors of the Canadian economy, and between the various
> sectors of manufacturing. The investment decisions of foreign-controlled
> corporations tend to reflect the laws and industrial priorities of foreign
> governments and economies which, in turn influence Canadian industrial
> priorities . . . the anticipated high level of demand for resources by
> foreign economies could lead to undue emphasis on resource develop-

TABLE 7.3 DEGREE TO WHICH CANADIAN INDUSTRY IS CONTROLLED BY MULTINATIONAL CORPORATIONS

Manufacturing Industry	Percentage Majority of Non-Resident Ownership[a] as Measured by			
	Assets	Sales	Profits	Taxable Income
Food and beverages	31.2	27.2	30.1	32.5
Tobacco	84.3	79.9	82.7	83.3
Rubber products	93.1	91.4	90.0	88.4
Leather products	22.0	21.4	25.2	27.3
Textile industries	39.4	28.5	54.4	54.3
Wood	30.7	22.0	23.6	22.9
Furniture	18.9	15.6	20.8	23.2
Printing, publishing and allied	21.0	13.8	22.3	23.2
Paper and allied products	39.4	41.4	40.6	40.2
Primary metals	55.3	51.1	62.4	64.3
Metal fabricating	46.9	45.2	65.0	63.1
Machinery	71.8	72.6	78.9	88.3
Transport equipment	86.6	90.5	89.9	88.5
Electrical products	64.2	62.8	78.2	88.0
Non-metallic mineral products	51.5	42.3	47.0	53.1
Petroleum and coal products	99.5	98.9	98.6	99.4
Chemicals and chemical products	81.5	81.3	89.6	89.4
Miscellaneous manufacturing	53.9	51.2	72.1	72.6
Total—All Manufacturing	58.0	54.7	63.6	62.9

[a]The figures for all the industries in [this table] include information from corporations, except for financial industries, which are exempt from the provisions of CALURA, but which report to the federal government under other federal legislation; it also includes information from government enterprises. The figure for the financial industries may be less reliable owing both to some double counting among reporting firms and the absence of any data from others.

Source: Government of Canada, *Foreign Direct Investment in Canada*, Ottawa: Information Canada, 1972, p. 21. Reproduced by permission of Information Canada.

ment in the coming decades. This, in turn, could impose major limitations on the ability of Canadians in the future to formulate an industrial development policy geared to Canada's own particular growth and employment objectives.[12]

Canada, of course, is a developed state; but if she feels these problems, it is apparent that they are felt even more severely in developing states.

Multinational corporations can have an impact on a state's balance of payments and its ability to achieve a degree of economic stability. On the

other hand, such investments in a developing state may also systematically transform the expectations and desires of the people within the state. It may change basic values within a state. It may therefore have possible fundamental impacts on both the economic and political problems of a state. It may create dependencies for the developing state, dependencies on the multinational corporation that may be directed toward promoting certain types of governments that will maximize their profit goals.

Jonathan F. Galloway has argued, therefore, that multinational corporations have aided the integration of the developed Western nations; and while serving to integrate the less-developed nations into the world economy, they may promote an unbalanced economic "growth" that impedes those states' stable political and social development.[13] He also points out that multinational corporations have bridged some of the separations that have existed between the East and the West. Multinational corporations in Western Europe have participated in joint ventures with Soviet public corporations, as in the case of the agreement between the Soviet Union and Fiat, which has created a new city on the Volga that by 1973 was producing 600,000 cars per year. These joint ventures appear to be increasing.

"Corporate Patriotism." On the other hand, the investment moves of multinational corporations are often publically visualized as a policy of economic penetration of some states by other states. Certainly Canadians and many Western Europeans look with a wary eye on the investment of U.S. based companies in their countries. And as the 1970s proceed, increasing questions are being raised about the investment penetration by Japanese-based multinational corporations. To many in the developing states multinational corporations are seen as a *new economic imperialism* despite the benefits they may give to their economies.

Anthony Sampson, in a study of the International Telephone and Telegraph Corporation, suggests that a large multinational corporation may see itself as above states.[14] He even suggests, after a detailed discussion of its activities, that the activities of ITT may be *beyond* the ability of a state to control. If these activities foster regimes conducive to the business of ITT, the result often creates antagonism among states. Sampson points out that the ITT leadership, for example, sees the integrative development of the European Economic Community as a threat to ITT. His recital of ITT's efforts to overthrow the Allende government of Chile in 1970 included mention of ITT's offering money to the CIA to assist the CIA in their efforts. As we have mentioned, when the Chilean episode became public, the fact that ITT was a U.S.-based corporation resulted in sharp recriminations not only from Chile but from other governments against not only ITT but the United States as well.

In a U.S. Senate hearing on January 23, 1974, Senator Henry Jackson asked officials of the seven largest United States oil companies (all multi-national corporations): "Is there corporate patriotism?" He indicated that there were "reliable" reports that during the October 1973 conflict in the Middle East that some major oil companies cut off petroleum to the United States Sixth Fleet operating in the Mediterranean, allegedly at the request of the government of Saudi Arabia. This necessitated a massive air- and sea-lift of fuel supplies at a time when American forces had been placed on military alert. Senator Jackson called this conduct a "blatant, flagrant example of corporate disloyalty to the United States of America."[15] Whether true or not, this story indicates another dilemma as to the role of multinational corporations. Who are they responsible to? the states in which they operate? the states in which they have their headquarters? Are they sovereign units responsible only to the profit interests of the companies?

Conversely, the increasing number and size of multinational corporations may serve as a stimulus for economic integration among states. Economically separate, an ITT may play one European government against another. Economically integrated, the European Community may exert control over an ITT. In this sense multinational corporations may, against their intentions, serve as a catalyst for economic integration among states.

POLITICAL PARTIES OR MOVEMENTS

The third type of nongovernmental organizations that has created a network of relationships among peoples in states and across state boundaries is what one might call political movements or political parties in the international system.

Parliamentarian Types. There are two patterns of networks evident in the international system that involve political parties or movements. One is reflected in the developments in Western Europe such as in the Council of Europe. While not really a governmental international organization, it is an organization of Western European parliamentarians whose meetings have laid a basis for negotiations among their states leading to developments like the European Economic Community. The Council of Europe has been instrumental in bringing together parliamentarians of various political persuasions such as the Christian Democrats and Social Democrats of various European states; it has established bridges between politicians of comparable political views in the various Common Market countries.

The European Coal and Steel Community, the European Economic Community, and the European Atomic Energy Community are visualized as eventually sharing a common European parliament that would include individuals directly elected by the people in these countries. Until this becomes a

reality, the assembly of the European Economic Community consists of members of the various parliaments apportioned according to the political strength of the various parties in each of the European Common Market states. The experience of their actions has meant that coalitions of political parties crossing state boundaries have been encouraged. While this is still in a formulative stage, the possibility of political party coalitions across state boundaries could have significant ramifications affecting the relations among these states.

In the same sense the Socialist International which has membership from Socialist parties in 47 states has, in its periodic congresses, provided a common meeting ground for socialist politicians irrespective of their separate states. In the early 1950s, for example, such contacts between socialist leaders in Israel and Burma resulted in their negotiating, as heads of their governments, several trade agreements following their meeting in a Socialist International Congress in Rangoon.

Revolutionary Movements. The other type of political party or political movements having an international network are so-called revolutionary movements. Soviet ideological goals up to the death of Stalin in 1953 (which gave additional impetus to achieving consolidation of the state socialist revolution in the Soviet Union), were equally concerned with fostering comparable revolutionary movements in other states. This involved ties between the Communist party in the Soviet Union with Communist parties in other states. Since the death of Stalin and the coexistence policy of Khrushchev and his successors, the Soviet Union has, by comparison, quietly minimized its official policy of actively supporting revolutionary movements in other states, though the ideological and other supportive ties as shown in Figure 7.1, are still retained.

In fact, one of the major elements in the schism between the Soviet Union and the People's Republic of China is that China feels that the coexistence policy is a betrayal of Marxist-Leninist ideology with which China is attempting to maintain active support ties through revolutionary movements in other states. Thus Communist parties in many states have been torn between Soviet and Chinese viewpoints. Nonetheless, there exists a network of relationships between the parties in the Soviet Union and China with political movements in a wide variety of states.[16]

In addition to the Communist party network, there are a number of other revolutionary links such as the links, for example, between Castro in Cuba and revolutionary movements in Colombia, Peru, Bolivia, Brazil, Uruguay, and even the revolutionary movements in Angola. The Algerian government has been linked with revolutionary movements in the Portuguese territories of Africa. More prominent in the public newspapers have been links between Egyptian, Syrian, and Libyan governments and the various factions in the Palestine nationalist movement.[17]

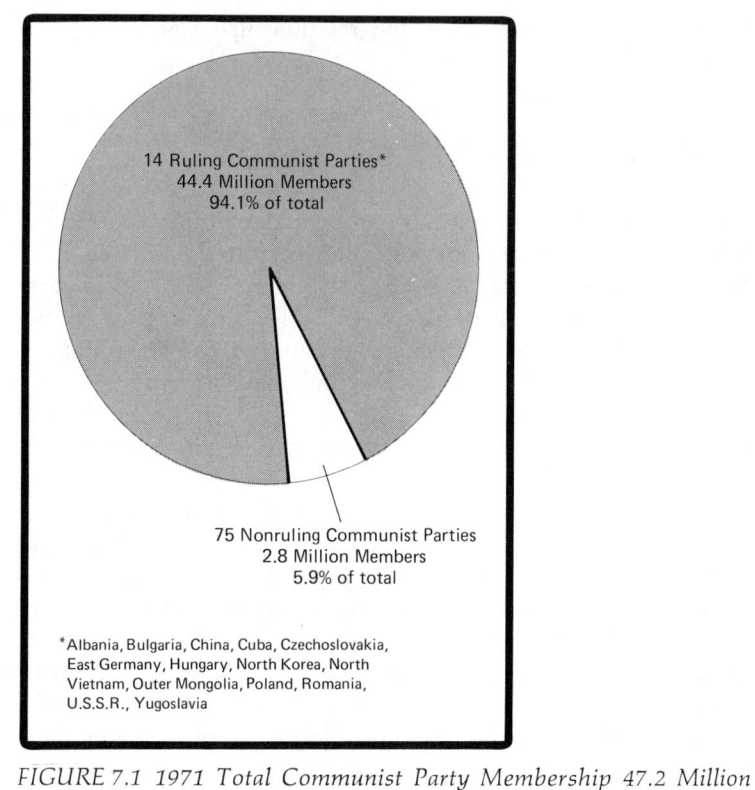

14 Ruling Communist Parties*
44.4 Million Members
94.1% of total

75 Nonruling Communist Parties
2.8 Million Members
5.9% of total

*Albania, Bulgaria, China, Cuba, Czechoslovakia,
East Germany, Hungary, North Korea, North
Vietnam, Outer Mongolia, Poland, Romania,
U.S.S.R., Yugoslavia

FIGURE 7.1 1971 Total Communist Party Membership 47.2 Million

Source: U.S. Department of State, Bureau of Intelligence and Research, World Strength of the Communist Party Organizations, 24th Annual Report, Washington, D.C.: GPO, 1972, pp. vii and viii.

These networks of revolutionary political movements involve nongovernmental ties in a number of states with quasi-governmental ties in other states. One might argue that it is essential that all societies undergo rather basic social changes or revolutions, and many argue that there will not be peaceful relations in the world until this happens. On the other hand, it is also argued that far from creating peaceful relationships, such revolutionary relationships are one of the fundamental disruptive forces within the international system.

However one assesses the role of the international NGOs, multinational corporations and enterprises, or ties of groups within states with external political parties or revolutionary political movements, it is clear that these facts of international contacts are significant. They are part of a network within the international system and are concerned primarily with relationships among peoples rather than among states. They have both positive and

negative effects in the process of regularizing relationships among states in the international system.

PENETRATION OF "SOVEREIGN" STATES

Despite the fact that the world is compartmentalized into separate political units, such compartments are not watertight or totally isolated from one another. Moreover, interrelationships are not limited simply to governmental relations among states. They involve a wide variety of other activities within, between, and among states. People travel between one state and another, they engage in trade, they communicate, and they organize by every conceivable means. To a greater or lesser extent, governments control these interrelationships among peoples. But no state or society is either completely open or closed.

Contacts among states are not limited to official governments. No state is completely cut off from nonofficial contacts with other states. The degree of openness among states varies in degrees and in possibilities. However, it is difficult to assess the full extent to which contact among states is limited by official government relationships or expanded by contacts among individuals. In any case, governments cannot completely prevent, should they desire, penetration of their state.

There are two general categories of penetration of states. One of these is the organized covert intelligence activities by governments, the other, the activities of organized groups of individuals. As additional networks of contacts, we are impelled to question their contributions to the ability of the international system to cope with its fundamental problems. What is the effect of such activities or groups on environmental problems, the problem of economic disparity among states, and problems of the weapons game, and so on? What positive or negative effects do such organizations and activities have on decisions, on the processes of decisions states must undertake to face global and other problems in the international system?

For states to be adequately informed about events and developments in other states, intelligence is essential. No state is a completely open society, and covert intelligence is, unfortunately, viewed as a necessity if states are to be adequately informed about other states. But the very fact that a portion of intelligence gathering is gained by covert and often devious means breeds distrust among states, especially if such activities are publicly exposed as a penetration of another state. To what degree does adequate intelligence help states resolve their basic differences? To what degree does intelligence gathering inflame basic differences among states? States that play the weapons game —and most do in varying degrees—base their security on the potential either to defend themselves or to retaliate if threatened. No state will publicly re-

veal its full military potential to other states. Yet, at the same time, unless other states are adequately informed as to the credibility of another state's military system, such systems cannot provide an absolute or even an adequate deterrent to attack. To what degree is covert intelligence essential to prevent conflict? To what degree does covert intelligence gathering encourage conflict? Covert intelligence activities leading to covert activities by one state in the internal affairs of another state, may bring about changes that prevent conflict. On the other hand, they may result in increasing tension or promoting warfare among states. To what degree should states engage in covert activities to influence events and decisions in other states? How can covert activities in another state be limited to activities that prevent conflict, rather than activities that increase tension and potential conflict? To the extent that these questions continue to be relevant, we believe they are an expression of the troubles or help in creating a new, trustful world.

Another category or organized penetration of states involves a wide range of organizations. It includes international nongovernmental organizations, multinational corporations, and political movements. The proliferation of international nongovernmental organizations reflects the fact that people with common interests or concerns see increasing validity in attempting to influence governmental decisions in areas of their particular concern. Again, it is difficult to assess the usefulness and impact of these activities in influencing decisions concerning international problems. Governments, especially in their international (governmental) organizations, accept and recognize the role of these groups by accrediting them a variety of consultative relationships. The more open societies give greater support to this engagement of international interest groups than do closed societies. To what degree do international NGOs influence decisions in international organizations? To what degree do international NGOs through their national affiliates influence governments to implement recommendations of international (governmental) organizations? To what degree do international NGOs serve as conduits for governments to transmit information to the individuals primarily concerned with particular issues? Or to what degree are international NGOs manipulated by governments? To what degree do they contribute to the independent stance of the secretariats of international organizations? To what degree do they provide a "people's voice" in the international system—a voice separate from governments? However these questions are answered, we must add another: How will the world be changed or improved by any answer?

Multinational corporations, as we have seen, are nongovernmental organized economic units in the international system existing primarily for corporate profits. To what degree do they mobilize economies? To what degree do they foster or impede the transference of technological and managerial skills? To what degree do they bind or loosen the economies of states? To what degree do they foster the interests of the capitalist states in the

international system? To what degree do they foster the dominance of the developed states over the less developed? To what degree are they overpowering influences in the international system? To what degree are they "sovereign" units separate from states? To what degree do they foster or impede economic integration among states? To what degree do they influence or determine choices in states as to economic priorities? To what degree do they bind or create tensions between or among states? These are all questions requiring answers before we can begin to assess the impact of multinational corporations on the ability of the international system to cope with its fundamental problems. In any case, we must ask whether any corporation—private or public—so long as it seeks to maximize its own welfare or profit adequately serves or addresses itself to the *needs* of mankind, whether these needs concern survival or realization of potentialities.

International or transnational political movements whether of an evolutionary or revolutionary character are another network of organized relations of people that penetrate across state boundaries. To what degree do they foster cooperation or lead to tensions among states? To what degree are they used as "informal" agents of states? To what extent are they a socializing influence in the international system? To what degree do they integrate or divide political systems in the international system? Again we need answers, more detailed answers, to these questions to assess fully the influence of international political movements in helping the international system to deal with its basic problems. But, again, even if we had full answers, we need to comprehend what values we seek to maximize in such interdependent activities and relationships.

As we appraise the degree of success states have had in resolving basic problems that affect the entire globe, our general conclusion is that much remains to be done. Perhaps the greatest problem is in the very fact of a state-based and parochial international system. If this view contains a fundamental truth, then it may be very important to look at alternative means of how people in one state may interact with people in other states to meet common problems. We live on a single planet, a single complex interrelated ecosystem, and it seems essential that the fact that people have created separate political units and values should not in and of itself mean that people either through or apart from their governments cannot cope with the fundamental problems that affect us all.

NOTES

*From *Markings*, by Dag Hammarskjold, translated by Leif Sjoberg and W. H. Auden. Copyright © 1964 by Alfred A. Knopf, Inc. and Faber and Faber Ltd. Reprinted by permission of the publishers.

[1]U.S., Senate, Committee on Foreign Relations, Subcommittee on Multinational Corporations, *Hearings . . . Multinational Corporations and United States Foreign Policy* (on The International Telephone and Telegraph Company and Chile, 1970–1971), March 20, 21, 27, 28, 29, and April 2, 1973, 93rd Cong., 1st sess., 1–2.

[2]*Ibid.*, pp. 120–121.

[3]See David Kahn, *The Code-Breakers*, New York: Macmillan, 1967, esp. Ch. 17.

[4]U.S., *Congressional Record*, 93rd Cong., 1st sess., vol. 119, no. 56 (April 10, 1973), 5.6866–68. The U.S. intelligence community includes CIA, NSA, DIA, Army, Navy, Air Force, State Department, FBI, AEC, and the Treasury Department.

[5]Henry L. Stimson and McGeorge Bundy, *On Active Service in Peace and War*, New York, Harper & Row, 1948, p. 188.

[6]*The New York Times*, April 25, 1966, p. 30. © by The New York Times Company. Reprinted by permission.

[7]Patrick J. McGarvey, *C.I.A.—The Myth and the Madness*, Baltimore, Md.: Penguin, 1973, p. 39.

[8]See Robert C. Angell, *Peace on the March—Transnational Participation*, New York: Van Nostrand Reinhold, 1969. © 1969 by Litton Educational Publishing, Inc. Reprinted by permission of Van Nostrand Reinhold Company. Angell looks at the intersocial web of relations that are developing as a result of living abroad by virtue of study, teaching, settlement, participation in assistance programs, service in foreign missions, residence abroad for business reasons or military service, and participation in the activities of international nongovernmental organizations or service in the secretariats of the United Nations and the specialized agencies. He argues that there is thus a broadening stream of influence on national policy makers supporting accommodation among states resulting from such transnational participation.

[9]Angell, *op. cit.*, p. 145.

[10]U.S. Department of Commerce, Bureau of International Commerce, Office of International Investment, *The Multinational Corporation—Studies on U.S. Foreign Investment*, vol. 1 (March 1972), 7.

[11]Werner J. Feld, "The Changing Impact and Incidence of Non-Governmental Organizations: A Quantitative Approach," paper delivered to the Sixty-sixth Annual Meeting of the American Political Science Association, Los Angeles, Calif.: September 8–12, 1970, p. 10.

[12]Government of Canada, *Foreign Direct Investment in Canada*, Ottawa: Information Canada, 1972, pp. 5–7. Reproduced by permission of Information Canada.

[13]Jonathan F. Galloway, "Multinational Enterprises as World-wide Interest Groups," paper presented to the Sixty-sixth Annual Meeting of the American Political Science Association, Los Angeles, Calif.: September 8–12, 1970, pp. 11–15.

[14]Anthony Sampson, *The Sovereign State of ITT*, New York: Stein and Day, 1973. One of the most intriguing aspects of this study is the manner in which I.T.T. and its national affiliates have involved leading political figures in the board and operations of their company—the involvement constitutes almost a Who's Who of the leading political decision makers in foreign policy of many states.

[15]"Oil Firms Accused of Disloyalty for Cutting Supply to Military," Portland *Oregonian*, January 24, 1974, p. 10.

[16]This network of Communist parties can be plotted out. See for example, U.S. Department of State, Bureau of Intelligence and Research, *World Strength of the Communist Party Organizations*, 24th Annual Report, 1972 ed., 159 pp.

[17]See Brian Crozier, "The Study of Conflict," *Conflict Studies* no. 7, London: Institute for the Study of Conflict, 1970, especially the section on "International Links and Strategic Consequences," pp. 11–23.

8

REFLECTIONS

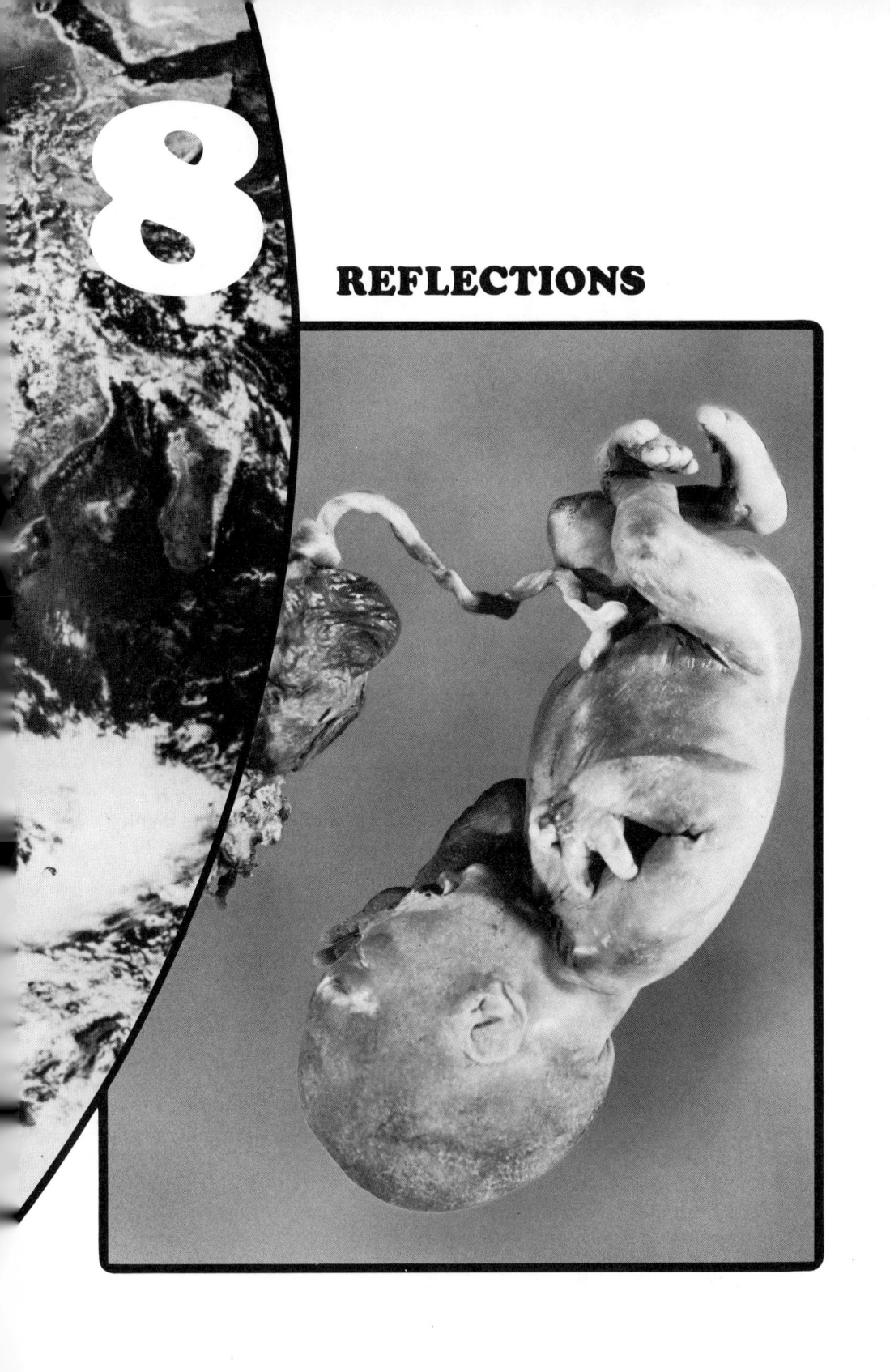

It is hard to imagine a world in which people live together without quarreling, maintaining themselves by producing the food, shelter, and clothing they need, enjoy themselves and contribute to the enjoyment of others in art, music, literature, and games, consume only a reasonable part of the resources of the world and add as little as possible to its pollution, bear no more children than can be raised decently, continue to explore the world around them and discover better ways of dealing with it, and come to know themselves accurately and, therefore manage themselves effectively. Yet all this is possible, and even the slightest sign of progress should bring a kind of change which in traditional terms would be said to assuage wounded vanity, offset a sense of hopelessness or nostalgia, correct the impression that "we neither can nor need to do anything for ourselves," promote a "sense of freedom and dignity" by building "a sense of confidence and worth." In other words, it should abundantly reinforce those who have been induced by their culture to work for its survival.[1]

B. F. SKINNER
1971

In *Ape and Essence* Aldous Huxley offers a biting, satirical view of life in a post–World War III society that worships the devil Belial. According to Belial, lunatic dreams of "progress" and "nationalism" were responsible for bringing about his reign. In one passage Huxley cogently outlines one of our human paradoxes.

Well, what are the facts? The first is a fact of experience and observation —namely that nobody wants to suffer, wants to be degraded, wants to be maimed or killed. The second is a fact of history—the fact that, at

a certain epoch, the overwhelming majority of human beings accepted beliefs and adopted courses of action that could not possibly result in anything but universal suffering, general degradation and wholesale destruction.[2]

That "certain epoch" that Huxley alluded to in *Ape and Essence* appears, in reality, to be dangerously close as world resources become depleted, population grows, pollution increases, weapons proliferate, poverty deepens, and national priorities remain virtually unchanged. International cooperation is stunted by myopic national ideologies of competitive advantage, deterrence, protectionism, racial and religious superiority, and other credos of narrow self-interest and exclusiveness. The conduct of nations guided by such beliefs and instruments ensures that collective decision making remains underdeveloped.

We *hope* that *Ape and Essence* will never be more than a fine piece of fiction. We *fear* that it may be prophetic unless mankind ceases choosing courses of action that, in Huxley's words, cannot possibly result in anything but "universal suffering, general degradation and wholesale destruction." In our gloomiest moments, we imagine four distinct roads to that "certain epoch" that could usher in the likes of Belial: (1) an imperium of the rich and powerful over the poor; (2) war among members of the imperium for total control; (3) an uprising of the Third World; (4) the overwhelming of our capacity to adapt and to cope with world problems until societies disintegrate into something similar to medieval kingdoms.

The tendencies underlying the first two situations are already apparent in the current international system. If the accommodation between the Western nations, led by the United States, and the Soviet Union and its Eastern European allies continues to grow, it may result in a condominium of the rich and powerful that could effectively rule the earth for many years—for this handful of states already controls the major economic and military resources of the world. If accommodation and cooperation should break down, war between the two power blocs would most likely be employed to determine who rules. Alternatively, a nuclear accident could result in warfare between the two blocs. In any case, warfare among members of an imperium is not unusual.

The third possibility represents a major change from current world conditions. If the plight of less-developed states approaches actual, or merely perceived, desperation, they may respond with fanatical attacks on the developed nations, perhaps even using bacteriological and chemical weapons. With nuclear weapons, some nations of the Third World might seek to exercise a "veto" over the actions of the rich and powerful through nuclear blackmail. Desperate people will take desperate and even suicidal action. Thus the

ingenuity with which world economic disparities are managed may, more than any other factor, determine the future of the international political system.

The fourth situation is simply a projection of the current status quo— a somnambulant stumbling into the morass our current behavior is creating. The question of who dominates the international system under these circumstances would be largely irrelevant, and any mythology of universalism would probably be only curdled ideological pap in a hungry, dirty, despoiled world.

Yet we believe that mankind still, at this moment, has the capacity to create an alternative future to these four grim possibilities. It will not be easy or inexpensive, but neither was harnessing nuclear energy or putting men on the moon, accomplished feats that were regarded merely as science fiction a few decades ago. We believe people and nations *can* change, that we can move away from policies of deterrence and coerciveness toward cooperation. In this chapter we discuss a few aspects of new approaches to international politics that require that nations and individuals begin thinking in Alvin Toffler's terms of what is possible, probable, and preferable in our global political life. First we look at the need for the development of international consciousness and a sense of international accountability. Then we consider what constructive role the United States might play in creating a new international environment. Finally we give you our personal thoughts concerning what the individual can do to aid the process of searching out a new design for the future.

INTERNATIONAL ACCOUNTABILITY AND CONSCIOUSNESS

The international community is in desperate need of a new kind of accountability among nations. In the past, we have thought of accountability solely in accounting terms—dollars and cents, profit and loss. Now we must seriously begin to take into consideration the effect of our actions upon the quality of life on earth now and for generations to come. We must view our resources as finite and our human existence as precarious and make decisions accordingly.

The question is whether it is possible in a capitalist economy, or in any modern bureaucratic state, to develop a sense of long-range purpose, to inquire into the meaning of activity, and to calculate priorities with a global view. If so, each nation must consider itself internationally accountable for all unilateral decisions that have global effects (and that means nearly all decisions). More than this, nation-states must turn toward the kind of global cooperation Malta proposed regarding the use of the sea bed. As we pointed

out in Chapter 3, Malta suggested to the United Nations that an international Oceans Space Institution be created to administer the use of the sea bed, which would be considered the heritage of all mankind.[3] As a representative body it would be responsible for overseeing the sharing of resources and the prevention of damage to the ecosystem. National and international use of the sea bed might thus be evaluated according to whether it enhanced or endangered the biological survival of mankind, whether it improved or impaired the flora and fauna of the earth, and whether it provided for the needs of future generations.

One way to increase accountability and to promote the development of international consciousness is to foster the creation of counterorganizations that monitor the actions of established institutions—national, international, governmental, and private.[4] Examples of such counterorganizations at a national level are Nader's Raiders, consumer-advocate groups, and Common Cause. Organs of the United Nations such as the Scientific Committee on the Effects of Atomic Radiation perform some international watchdog functions. We need many more independent assessors of the impacts of public and private activities at every level of polity. Historians and philosophers have always been willing to give us the benefit of such judgments after the fact. Now we need independent courts of social justice that are willing to make evaluations pertaining to the future.

CREATING DIALOGUE

There can be no accountability without dialogue and information sharing. Compared with our technological ability to gather and disseminate data, the willingness of nation-states (and private corporations) to share information is primitive indeed. For example, in 1964 the Secretary-General of the United Nations circulated an inquiry to the 115 member governments asking for their views and policies regarding population. Only 54 states, or less than half the total membership, responded at all, and even fewer provided any specific data on their actual policies.[5] Most governments, whatever their ideological positions, seem to subscribe wholeheartedly to what might be called the DuPont philosophy.

When Ralph Nader's group turned its searchlights on the DuPont corporation, they were informed by president Charles McCoy that DuPont kept secret all information "harmful to the corporation." Like other companies, DuPont enforces the rule by obliging employees to sign a contract that grants the corporation the right to cancel retirement benefits if the former employee "willfully engages in any activity which is harmful to the interest of the company."[6]

Such corporate pettiness and paranoia have clear parallels in government espionage, secrecy, elaborate systems for classifying documents, loyalty checks,

and surveillance of public employees, and so on. Such defensive management by governments stems at least in part from the ancient interpretation of self-interest, which asserts that a nation can secure its own well-being only at the expense of others. Therefore, the less others know about the nation, the greater its security. Today this kind of defensiveness will kill us all. We can approach global realities at the global level only when nations see that their survival depends not upon secrecy and rivalry, but upon openness and cooperation.

A free flow of scientific and human information among nations will help us plan for an adequate world supply of food, help us think about population problems, help us to meet natural disasters, help us to make wiser decisions about nuclear power and the dangers of radiation, help us to learn more about the effects of one natural phenomenon upon others. Information alone, however, is inadequate. We need "early warning systems" for consultation, for harmonizing differing national standards, and for preventative and prescriptive action. The Intergovernmental Maritime Consultative Organization (IMCO) is one such system. IMCO has, for example, developed international conventions on liability of shipowners and the right of nations to destroy or tow away vessels that pose oil-spill hazards. It has set limits on the discharge of oil on the high seas. It is proposing limits on the size of oil tankers, strict specifications on construction of liquified natural gas and liquified petroleum gas tankers, and a code for the construction of ships carrying dangerous cargoes in bulk. Without information sharing and the organization of effective monitoring systems, we cannot make a sustained and coherent approach to identifying global problems and to setting standards and enforcing rules that will mitigate dangerous conditions whenever they occur. The process involves trust and mutuality—the most powerful ingredients of positive reinforcement for international cooperation.

If nations commit themselves to sharing information with one another and find the results to their benefit, they may very likely come to the realization one day that it is also in their best interests to share other resources as well. By redistributing food supplies, mineral wealth, petroleum, transportation facilities, and other forms of wealth as well as knowledge, we could remove many sources of fear, hostility, and insecurity among nations and thus release a great supply of human energy that could be used to enhance life everywhere. The logic behind sharing resources is similar to arguments in favor of a guaranteed annual wage in the United States. But we need to carry the idea beyond the borders of our own country if we do not want to see the world split into two warring camps, the haves and have-nots. We must ask where our country will be in the next few decades in the context of where all the other nations of the world will be. We cannot morally or realistically accept the idea of freedom and survival for some and not for others. Yet this

is exactly what is happening. As we move into the era of a postscarcity economy, the nations of the world with low technology, high population density, and minimal resources—most of the Third World—find their relative condition worsening. Their proportion of world trade is declining while their indebtedness is reaching staggering proportions. Moreover, the amount of technical and developmental assistance that the Third World receives from most industrialized nations (relative to their own growth) has also declined. To achieve greater accountability in international politics we need more than the international sharing of information important as that is. A true sense of accountability comes from the way we view the world. As Robert McNamara commented regarding economic development: "The obstacles lie in the minds of men. We have simply not thought long enough and hard enough about the fundamental problems of the planet. Too many millennia of tribal suspicion and hostility are still at work in our subconscious minds."[7]

EXPANDING GLOBAL CONSCIOUSNESS

A profound revolution in consciousness will depend upon the presence of positive reinforcements for individuals and nations who choose to commit themselves to international survival. It makes more sense to ask individuals and nations to sacrifice what appears to be in their immediate self-interest in favor of promoting international trust and stability and survival when they can see some relatively concrete and immediate advantages to themselves for making such "sacrifices." As we stated in Chapter 2, it is difficult to recognize those reinforcements, obvious as they are, precisely because they are the qualities that, until recently, we have taken entirely for granted or have not valued highly: clean air, clean water, a viable natural environment, sufficient space, sufficient food, healthy bodies, and a peaceful world.

National leaders who choose to pursue internationalist policies must be supported by their respective electorates and legislative bodies or they will be hesitant to take risks inherent in developing international trust. Before national leaders will receive such support, however, each nation must reconsider the time-worn credos of individual freedom and national sovereignty. Some of the freedoms that individuals and nations prize today are dubious and anachronistic. To allow a private firm or government (or the two in collusion) to pollute in the name of freedom calls into question the very concept. The flip side of the freedom to pollute is a form of subjugation in which the individual has no choice. All mankind should have the right to pure air and water, the right to be protected from radiation poisoning, the right to continued enjoyment of the natural environment. It seems clear that we can be guaranteed these universal rights only when controls are placed on every individual, corporation, and governmental body violating these rights. The realities of the twentieth century demand a new balance between control and

freedom. They must become complementary rather than polar opposites. We must begin to think about what characterizes a free man and what constitutes a free society in an endangered, troubled, and interdependent world, rather than focus primarily upon our exclusive individual, corporate, and national needs and desires. Otherwise freedom and dignity ring hollow.[8]

People of the twentieth century have often naïvely assumed that the achievements of science and technology would relieve them of the necessity of wrestling with the hard questions of goals and values and global and human survival. Most, if not all difficulties, we have told ourselves, can be overcome merely by applying and organizing technology efficiently and effectively.[9] Technological optimists assure us, for example, that even if agriculture does fail to meet our food requirements and even if we do use up our scarce resources, science will discover satisfactory substitutes and synthetics. Food can be produced from inorganic materials, solar energy can be harnessed to replace fossil fuels, and new ways can be found to recycle wastes. In effect, they say, we can control our destinies without neo-Malthusian fears. Perhaps. They also predict we will soon be able to control the reproduction of human beings through techniques such as genetic surgery, cloning, and extrauterine gestation. Humans created through such methods can, in essence, be made to order—specially adapted for space travel or undersea life or whatever. Scientists say all this is possible. But such far-reaching decisions must not be left to the specialists who consider only *whether* it can be done. As President Eisenhower warned us, "in holding scientific research and discovery in respect, as we should, we must also be alert to the equal and opposite danger that public policy could itself become the captive of a scientific-technological elite."[10] The scientific enterprise does not make moral decisions. And if *we* equate what is *possible* with what is *desirable*, we abdicate our responsibility and our privilege of deciding what enhances human life and how we wish to bring that about. Moreover, our greatest social problems persist, not because we lack the technology, but because we lack the foresight, concern for others, and dedication to the task of mobilizing our socioeconomic systems to find humane solutions. Technology will never supply this.

THE UNITED STATES
IN INTERNATIONAL POLITICS

The great power and resources of the United States virtually ensure this country a position of international leadership for years to come. But power is not a moral force, and in this sense America is symptomatic of the tensions of the modern age. The United States can choose to use its influence to bring the world closer to the revolution in conscience and consciousness

upon which survival and peace depend. But in order to have such an impact the United States will have to change its notions of leadership, for any special contribution to the future of the international community will have little to do with our status as a military power or with our self-image as defender of freedom *par excellence* or with our commodity-ridden economy. J. W. Fulbright has written:

> *The foremost need for American foreign policy is a renewal of dedication to an "idea that mankind can hold to"—not a missionary idea full of pretensions about being the world's policeman but a Lincolnian idea expressing that powerful strand of decency and humanity which is the true source of America's greatness.*[11]

The problem that America must come to grips with is this: *What kind of a model for a future society does the United States want to represent in a highly interdependent world?*

REDEFINING SELF-INTEREST

If the United States is to be a positive model, it must commit itself to the notion of world interdependence and redefine its self-interest accordingly. The United States will not be secure in a world in which it consumes a disproportionate share of world resources. Americans will not be secure if we continue polluting the world with toxic materials, weapons, and rivalry. We will not be secure if we persist in believing we have the right to make political decisions for other nations. It is in our own self-interest to mitigate these sources of international enmity and tension, and we can do so if we choose. In a report to the Congress in 1971 President Nixon acknowledged the need for a new way of looking at national self-interest.

> *... What is new is the fact that we now face an increasing range of problems which are central to our national well-being, but which are, by definition, global problems, or problems which can only be dealt with effectively on a global scale. . . . [One] is our shared and transcendent interest in the livability of our common home, the earth. To those problems, and the opportunities they present, that interest must be our guide and the guide of others. The nurturing of that interest has now become a prime task of American leadership.*[12]

The Contradictions of Military Policies. Despite President Nixon's eloquent words, it is evident that our nation (along with the other major powers) remains unwilling to include military policy in the realm of global problems and shared interests. Our national security strategy, recently rechristened

"positive deterrence," is in fact an elaborate system of threats toward others.[13] Threat arouses fear. As fear, frustration, and hostility mount, they increase the probability of desperate and irrational behavior.[14] It seems patently contradictory to attempt to solve global problems and experience "shared and transcendent interest" by threatening other nations and by preparing for war. If history can teach us anything, it can teach us that nations do not successfully promote what in this book we have defined as true "peace" through the instruments of war.

A new role for the United States in world politics begins with the recognition that we are responsible for the *consequences* of our actions, not merely for the idealism of our rhetoric. Nowhere has this country been less willing to explore the consequences of our foreign policy than in our defense and military aid programs (the Vietnam debate perhaps will become an exception). In 1964 Secretary of Defense Robert McNamara assessed military assistance as follows:

> *In my considered judgment, this (military assistance) program, and the foreign aid program generally, has now become the most critical element of our overall national security effort. . . . If we are to meet the avowed Communist threat across the entire spectrum of conflict, then we must also be ready to take whatever measures are necessary to counter their efforts to promote guerrilla wars and insurrections. And much of this can be accomplished only by the assistance, both military and economic, we give less prosperous allies. . . .*[15]

Whether military assistance is, in fact, what the Third World needs is highly questionable. What clearly is in process is a competition among the industrial powers, led by the United States, to sell arms to the developing nations of the world. The international record of such sales is long: American F-104 interceptors to Jordan and Pakistan, a squadron of F-4 Phantoms to Iran, 12 F-5s, among the most modern U.S. fighter-interceptors to Morocco, American A-4B tactical attack aircraft to Argentina; British Hawker Hunter jet fighters to Chile and India; Soviet Mig-21s to Iraq and India, French Mirage IVs to South Africa, Czechoslovakian armored cars and bazookas to Cyprus, and on and on.[16] In the Indian subcontinent and in the Middle East, these sales have contributed to intensive arms races that have made political and cultural tensions more explosive than ever.

Whether the consequences of international gunrunning is in the continued interest of the United States, world peace, or freedom is also highly questionable. We must judge whether the billions of dollars we pour into the international traffic in armaments—at least half of which go to developing nations[17]—stabilize or exacerbate world tensions and the likelihood of

war. We believe that the United States is increasing the possibilities of lethal conflicts and giving in to the vested interests of the military and their corporate partners when we unquestioningly aid and abet the diverting of resources from social and economic justice and development into even more ambitious military programs. We must judge and accept responsibility for the domestic and international consequences of our own militarism and military policies.

Our insistence that "if you want peace, prepare for war," becomes counterproductive when others follow our example.[18] And there is ample evidence that other nations *do* wish to follow our example despite international attempts to halt nuclear proliferation (so that nuclear weapons remain the monopoly of the great powers) and to stabilize the levels of these weapons of insanity. A survey of university students in 14 nations in 1968–1969 revealed that in 5 nations more than 40 percent of the students sampled believed their countries should have their own nuclear weapons.[19] If this attitude among future leaders of the Third World remains relatively stable over time, our global future appears precarious indeed. If change is to come, the United States itself must begin to repudiate militarism.

The Contradictions of Economic Policies. The former President's apparent recognition of "our shared and transcendent interest in the livability of our common home, the earth," does not seem yet to have altered our economic thinking any more than our military policies. We know that over one-fifth of the American shellfish beds have been closed because of pollution.[20] One estimate suggests that the annual toll of air pollution on health, vegetation, materials, and property values in this country amounts to $16 billion annually— more than $80 per person.[21] Nevertheless, the President's Commission on International Trade and Investment Policy recently concluded that "even if we had full knowledge of the costs and benefits of environmental control, the United States should not strive for zero pollution levels." The commission warned that "if the United States insists on antipollution standards that are stricter than those of other countries, our export- and import-competing industries may be placed at a competitive disadvantage."[22] This is surely a case of the economic dog wagging the ecological tail! While the President's commission did not make policy, it unfortunately reflects the opinions of corporate and financial leaders who enjoy considerable influence with those who do.

Our policies regarding the use of pesticides have been equally unresponsible. The United States is one of the world's primary producers of pesticides (1133 million pounds in 1969, 409 million of which were exported). During the past decade we have slowly come to realize that many pesticides once considered harmless are acutely toxic to humans and produce adverse effects on the total ecosystem. Residues of pesticides and herbicides, as well as mer-

cury, become concentrated as they pass through the food chain, causing measurable changes in body chemistry and, in a growing number of cases, death. New regulations have banned some pesticides, most notably DDT, and regulated others. Yet the fact that no nationwide figures are collected routinely on the use of pesticide chemicals calls into question our determination to act on our growing awareness of their dangerous side effects.[23]

A MODEL FOR THE FUTURE

Several years ago the State Department conducted a study of official foreign visitors to the country.[24] They were asked what they considered the most significant aspects of their visit. A surprising number mentioned the Tennessee Valley Authority (TVA) project. Although it is now more than three decades old, and replete with problems, TVA did represent a commitment to values of the future: conservation, reforestation, treatment of a geographical region as an ecological unit, the mobilization of people, material, and money to improve upon nature for the benefit of all. The TVA captured our visitors' imaginations. This country will continue to capture individuals' imaginations only to the extent that we use our human and economic resources to preserve the natural environment and search out humane and workable solutions for our own social problems: persistent poverty, racial strains and antagonisms, inadequate medical care for all citizens, neglect of the aged, an inefficient and inequitable judicial system, and so on.

As remarkable as many of our material and technological achievements are, they are achievements in which most of the rest of the world (and many of our own people) can take little comfort. Disneyland in California also attracts many of our foreign visitors, but it is hard to see how sprinkling replicas of Disneyland across the globe can possibly improve the human condition. Julius Nyerere makes it clear that Tanzania, for example, does not need more coke bottles and electric toothbrushes. What it does need is a system of ethics and planning that will improve society.[25]

The United States can offer a model of a just and sane society when we determine our foreign policy, our social programs, our technological achievements according to the extent to which they support or improve a humane existence on earth. If we fail to present such a model for the future, we will have no "special" role in shaping that future (except as we practice the archaic and often disastrous ways of the past). If we succeed, we shall be an "idea mankind can hold to." We, too, need new visions and new choices.

Prescriptive Measures. To develop ourselves as a society modeled for a future interdependent world, we need to ask what prescriptive measures are necessary to solve particular problems and how we can overcome inertia, engage in anticipatory action, and reassess values and institutions not attuned

to present realities. We believe there are basic imperatives facing the United States and the international community. First, the armaments race must be halted and national defense systems gradually lowered through reciprocal agreements. Second, the international community must set and work toward a morally acceptable standard of existence (e.g., daily caloric intake, literacy, etc.) and commit the necessary resources to bring about such conditions. Third, national economic priorities must be recalculated with world proportionality and equity in mind to include assistance to peoples and nations that do not enjoy the basic standards (assuming, of course, that they want them). Finally, superordinate goals and means for resolving differences must be developed as a substitute for the traditional, exclusive goals and alliances of power politics.

We realize that these and other goals we have advocated will require unprecedented change, financial commitment, and mobilization of energy and talent. Merely to keep abreast of our dilemmas seems so difficult that some question the feasibility of striking out in new directions and attempting to develop institutional structures and personnel competent to attack separately or simultaneously the problems we have raised. But politics is not a holding action; it is the art of the possible. As President Nixon has pointed out:

> *We anticipate that the potential for conflict will exist as long as men and nations have different interests, different approaches to life, different ideals.* Therefore we must come to grips with the paradoxes of peace: *As the danger of armed conflict between major powers is reduced, the potential for economic conflict is increased. As the possibility of peace grows stronger, some of the original ties that first bound postwar alliances grow weaker. As the nations around the world gain new economic strength, the points of commercial contact multiply along with the possibilities of disagreement.*[26]

The list of paradoxes and dilemmas is actually much longer. Do we, for example, ban DDT and ignore the problem of controlling malaria? Resources such as money have multiple uses, but the cost of one program may entail the sacrifice of another. The fundamental question, then, is which programs are to be given priority, and to answer this we need a new kind of cost-benefit analysis with a future orientation.

Moral Development. The thrust of the future must be moral development. Human nature and the human condition are not immutable. The world is ripe for a creative politics that will propel us beyond the status quo, combining what is good from the past with what is necessary for the future. Even so talented a body as the National Science Board feels the inadequacies of our current approach to change.

> *Environmental science, today, is unable to match the needs of society for definitive information, predictive capability, and the analysis of environmental systems as systems. Because existing data and current theoretical models are inadequate, environmental science remains unable in virtually all areas of application to offer more than qualitative interpretations or suggestions of environmental change that may occur in response to specific actions.*[27]

The act of creation, according to Arthur Koestler, is the connecting of previously unrelated dimensions of experience.[28] To the extent we can encourage and obtain such creative responses to the difficulties that confront us, we will move beyond the sterility of bureaucratic procedures, worn-out traditions, and circular patterns of behavior and arrive at new ways of linking up means and ends.

THE ROLE OF THE INDIVIDUAL

What does the world-wide need for revolution in conscience and consciousness mean for the individual? Obviously, the impact of a single individual upon the problems we have raised is infinitesimal. Yet the cumulative effects of individual behavior are undeniable. We all know that automobiles produce a large proportion of the smog that blights our cities. At the same time, we know that the contribution of each single automobile to air pollution is minute. Each individual thus decides that the benefits to him of driving his car outweigh the small amount of smog he produces in doing so. When millions of motorists make the same decision, the results are a menace to the health and safety of us all.

LOOKING BACKWARD

While most of us want change for the better, we cling to old ways of thinking and doing. We talk about the need for mass transit systems to reduce our dependency upon air-polluting automobiles, but what we actually construct is not rapid transit systems but more freeways. One reason we choose a backward orientation is because the future is so uncertain. We project onto it many catastrophic expectations: loss of autonomy, anarchy, despotism, forced submission to alien ideologies or to international institutions, and so on.

We also choose the past in an effort to ease our sense of dislocation in the present.[29] Society suffers today from the pervasive conviction that the individual can do very little. We feel cut off from the possibilities of relevant social action. Bombarded by too many demands, too much contradictory in-

formation, too many unclear values from which to choose, often we feel we have no choices at all. Our dislocation destroys our sense of efficacy and weakens our faith in the future, creating anxiety and depression, lowering our interest in achievement, and leaving us vulnerable to chemical and theological fantasies. Many of us long for the past, when it seems that life was slower, simpler, and more manageable. In this sense, "ancestor worship" exists even in highly sophisticated societies. It is still another way of avoiding the realities of both the present and the future.

We also choose the past because change is indeed difficult in modern bureaucratic societies. Bureaucratic institutions do suppress the person rather than facilitate his opportunities and growth.[30] Constituency demands, unorthodox problem solving, individual interests, deviancy from norms—all are threatening to self-perpetuating and self-justifying bureaucrats and bureaucracies, and they vigorously defend themselves against such intrusions.

BECOMING INTERNATIONALISTS

We human beings protect ourselves from paralysis of will by looking at decisions and events from an egocentric and short-range point of view. It is understandable that most of us are concerned only with today and our immediate family. To feel responsible for our neighborhood, our country, and what is more, the world, is an obligation that we do not want and that is often simply beyond the limits of our will and imagination.[31] Little wonder that many refuse to make any commitments whatsoever and instead live out lives of numbness, desperation, or self-gratification.

A new consciousness with conscience begins with awareness. Awareness can be curative when linked with expression beyond privatization. A political culture that does not induce individuals through positive reinforcements to work for its survival is in serious trouble. Somewhere between the dropout and the true believer there must be efficacious individuals who see themselves in relation to others and who are willing to commit a portion of their time and to join with others in common effort. Symbolic protests about national or world conditions will not be enough. The truth of the intention is in the action. We need *sustained* efforts to carry reform movements through to the completion of their outlined goals. Bourgeoning evidence in the area of environmental protection attests that such efforts do have impacts.

> A scientist in a small Maryland suburb worked after hours with schoolchildren to mount a community-wide campaign to pass the first municipal ordinance in the nation banning nonreturnable beer and soft-drink containers.
> Two women talking at a party in Washington, D.C., invited five friends to join them in forming Concern, Incorporated. The organization has

mailed out more than 400,000 copies of ECO-TIPS, a housewife's guide to environmental buying, and has answered more than 90,000 unsolicited letters and inquiries.

A biology teacher in Lewes, Delaware, conducted a door-to-door campaign with his students to save nearby beaches from pollution and development. His efforts brought about major changes. Planned sewage and industrial facilities were relocated. And some of the remaining natural dunes along the Atlantic coast were saved. The state government has adopted the strongest coastal land use legislation in the country.

Two young university professors spent their summer sampling the polluted waters in the Pittsburgh area from a canoe. The evidence they collected was used by a U.S. attorney to prosecute a number of companies for pollution. The first conviction, handed down in June 1971, was the first Refuse Act conviction based on citizen-supplied information.[32]

Common private action, while effective and necessary, will never substitute for systematic administrative and legislative action. But without citizen participation and support, administrators and lawmakers will continue to serve special interests and fail to sense the enormity of their responsibility to the general welfare. Citizen action creates conditions for change, as the District of Columbia Court of Appeals has noted: "A new sensitivity to issues of environmental protection has imposed new responsibilities on the courts, the legislature, and the administrative agencies."[33]

What we have suggested thus far is conventional and familiar: If we take our responsibilities seriously, work hard, join with others, and speak with a concerted and persevering voice, we can make a difference. All of this is true, but it lacks imagination and power. Our aggressive feelings tell us instead to scream our rage at the indifference, bigotry, injustice, cruelty, selfishness, exploitation, and death wishes that surround us. We want to reject the timidity that makes us choose the familiar and insistently demand an answer to the question, "When are we going to create a movement that looks to the future rather than the past?"

The true revolutionaries of the future are internationalists. They are those who, like the astronauts, behold the totality of earth and mankind in awe and reverence, yet unlike our zealous space voyagers, place little value on planting a national flag on the moon. They are not the conditioned robots of a particular society. They are intolerant of the injustice, barbarism, and obscenity that parades as civilization. They reject neat ideological formulas of the past—Marxian or Burkian—and assign themselves the task of answering again these questions: Who are we? Where are we going? They are men

and women who do scream STOP when they see the world careening toward destruction and who dedicate themselves to making the world less alienated, less rigid, less unrealistic. They face the reality of change—precise or illusive as that celebration of life may be.

HARD QUESTIONS

Truth, John Milton tells us in *Areopagitica*, was a virgin who came into the world in perfect shape, glorious to look upon. Deceivers arose and defiled her; they hewed her lovely form into a thousand pieces and scattered them to the four winds, so that ever since her sad friends have been obliged to gather up her pieces, one by one, as they have found them. We are still deprived of her perfection.

We do not have the answers to our global dilemmas, yet it is imperative that we begin and hasten the search, for as we question and perceive and act, we shape the world around us. Relatively slight shifts in our assessment of alternatives and in the choices we make may bring about considerable changes in our behavior. Persistently, insistently, relentlessly, we must, with U Thant, ask the hard questions:

> . . . *Why is there still so much horrid killing going on in this world? Why is there war in Indo-China and why does it last so long? Why is there no peaceful and just settlement in the Middle East? Why does the world spend 200 billion dollars a year on armaments? Why are there still colonized people? Why are there divided countries? Why are not all countries participating in the United Nations? Why is there so much poverty, hunger and illiteracy persisting on the same planet side by side with wealth, abundance and waste? Why is there racism and* apartheid? *Why are there so many violations of human rights? Why are our common heritages, the oceans, the atmosphere, our rivers and the beauty of our world suddenly in danger? Why are there still atomic tests? What will the future of mankind be? Where is materialism going to lead us? And so on. . . . In each hemisphere, on each continent, in each country, these questions are given different weight and urgency. A man dying of hunger or of a bullet in Asia is asking "why" more dramatically than his fellow man who may feel strangled by over-urbanization in Europe or in North America. But each one requests an answer to his interrogations and turns to the institutions and to the leaders of this world who proclaim that they are working for peace, justice and progress. And each year many millions of people die without having received a satisfactory answer to their question. . . .*[34]

A revolution in conscience and consciousness would mean the possibility of a future that does not include the four horsemen of the apocalypse. The choice is ours. "Markets for peace and war are both engineered."[35] What we do in the next ten or twenty years will determine the quality of life, if not the continued existence, of man on earth.

NOTES

[1]B. F. Skinner, *Beyond Freedom and Dignity*, New York: Knopf, 1971, p. 214.

[2]Aldous Huxley, *Ape and Essence*, New York: Bantam, 1958, p. 96; and Harper & Row, 1948, p. 128.

[3]U.N. General Assembly, Official Records, *Report of the Committee for Peaceful Uses of the Seabed and Ocean Floors Beyond the Limits of National Jurisdiction*, 26th sess., Supplement No. 21, pp. 105–193.

[4]For a fuller discussion of this idea see Daniel Goldrich and Joseph A. Kremers, "From the Corporate State Through Vietnam to the Developmental Community," Paper presented at the Annual Meetings of the American Political Science Association, Washington, D.C.: September 5–9, 1972.

[5]The inquiry was circulated as authorized by General Assembly Resolution 1838 (XVII) and the results presented in Document E/3895/Rev. 1.

[6]Thomas DeBaggio, "Corporate Secrecy: Issues for the Seventies," *The Nation*, 214 (February 28, 1972), 269, quoted in Goldrich and Kremers, *op. cit.*, p. 18.

[7]World Bank, *Address to the Board of Governors by Robert S. McNamara, President, World Bank Group*, Copenhagen, Denmark: World Bank, 1970, p. 23.

[8]See Christian Bay, " 'Freedom' as a Tool of Oppression," in C. George Benello and Dimitrios Roussopoulos (eds.), *The Case for Participatory Democracy*, New York: Viking, 1971, pp. 250–270.

[9]See, Herbert F. York, *Race to Oblivion*, New York: Clarion Books, 1971.

[10]Quoted in York, *op. cit.*, p. 9.

[11]J. W. Fulbright, *The Arrogance of Power*, New York: Random House, 1966, p. 247.

[12]Richard M. Nixon, *U.S. Foreign Policy for the 1970s: Building for Peace*, A Report to the Congress, February 25, 1971, p. 208.

[13]U.S. Department of Defense, *Statement of Secretary of Defense Melvin R. Laird before the Senate Armed Service Committee on the FY 1972–1976 Defense Program and the 1972 Defense Budget*, March 15, 1971.

[14]John R. Raser and A. Seixas, "ABM, CBW, and the MAD Strategy," mimeo, Western Behavioral Sciences Institute, n.d., p. 5.

[15]Quoted in Denis Goulet and Michael Hudson, *The Myth of Aid*, New York: Idoc Books, 1971, p. 98. Since 90 percent of American "aid" has been tied to purchases in the United States, we hardly "give" to "our less prosperous allies."

[16]In the fiscal years 1952 to 1961 the U.S. military grant-aid programs and military sales amounted to a total value of $22 billion—$17 billion in grant aid and $5 billion in sales. According to the Defense Department, the comparative amounts were to be radically altered in the 1962–1971 period—that is, $15 billion in military sales and $7 billion in grant aid. U.S. Congress, Joint Economic Committee, Subcommittee on Economy in Government, Hearings, *Economic Issues in Military Assistance*, 92d Cong., 1st sess., January 4, 5, 6, 18, and February 2, 1971, pp. 1–2.

[17]U.S. Arms Control and Disarmament Agency, *10th Annual Report to Congress, January 1, 1970–December 31, 1970* (1971), p. 20.

[18]Such policies can be counterproductive in quite another way—they increase the possibility of accidents. For example, at least two antiaircraft missiles with nuclear warheads have been launched accidentally. Nuclear weapons have been dropped accidentally from

aircraft in this country, in Spain, and elsewhere. Fortunately, in 33 known serious accidents there has not been an unintended nuclear explosion. But we have come close. In 1961 a B-52 bomber jettisoned a 24-megaton bomb over North Carolina. The bomb had 6 interlocking safety mechanisms, all of which had to be triggered in sequence to explode the bomb. Five of the interlocks were set off by the fall. Milton Leitenberg, "So Far, So Good," *Environment*, vol. 12, no. 6 (July–August 1970), 26–35. See also John R. Raser, "The Failure of Fail-Safe," *Trans-Action*, vol. 6, no. 3 (January 1969), 11–19.

[19]"My Country Should Have Its Own Nuclear Weapons"

"MY COUNTRY SHOULD HAVE ITS OWN NUCLEAR WEAPONS"

Nation "n"	Agreement %	Uncertain %	Disagreement %
Australia (140)	30.7	10.0	59.3
Canada (276)	16.6	9.1	74.3
United States (655)	68.2	9.9	21.8
Denmark (303)	2.0	3.0	95.0
Sweden (198)	9.5	4.5	85.9
Netherlands (915)	3.6	3.1	93.3
Finland (269)	10.6	4.1	84.4
Yugoslavia (178)	15.7	15.7	68.6
Brazil (173)	70.0	9.8	20.2
Ceylon (235)	43.4	10.2	47.4
S. Korea (300)	71.4	6.0	22.7
Ghana (296)	38.1	12.2	49.6
India (279)	83.8	5.7	10.4
Nigeria (300)	64.4	8.0	27.6

Data are from the Multi-Nation Student Survey conducted by John R. Raser, Claus Iversen, David Finlay. Characteristics of the study have been reported in Claus Iversen, *Handbook for Multi-National Student Survey*, La Jolla: Western Behavioral Sciences Institute, 1969. See also Claus Nelund (nee Iversen), *From National to Evolutionary Thinking*, Copenhagen: Multivers, 1972.

[20]Before 1935 between 100,000 and 300,000 pounds of soft-shell crabs were commercially harvested annually in San Francisco Bay. The industry is virtually nonexistent today, largely because of pollution. Similarly, the annual harvest of shrimp from coastal areas dropped from over 6.3 million pounds before 1936 to only 10,000 pounds in 1965. U.S. Council on Environmental Quality, *Environmental Quality: Second Annual Report, 1971*, p. 107.

[21]Such estimates would be even higher if they included the impact on aesthetic and other values, if they included the cost of discomfort from illness, or if other damages could be more precisely traced to pollutants. It has been estimated that "total spending required for the major sources of environmental pollution between 1970 and 1975 is . . . about $105 billion—23 percent for air pollution control, 36 percent for water pollution control, and 41 percent for solid waste management." *Environmental Quality: Second Annual Report, 1971, op. cit.*, p. 110.

[22]U.S. Report to the President Submitted by the Commission on International Trade and Investment Policy, *United States International Economic Policy in an Interdependent World* (July 1971), p. 130. The report continues: "We believe that setting the level of acceptable pollution is largely a domestic decision not subject to rigid international standards."

[23]*Environmental Quality: Second Annual Report, 1971, op. cit.*, p. 247.

[24]Bryant M. Wedge, *Visitors to the United States and How They See Us*, Princeton, N.J.: D. Van Nostrand, 1965.

[25]Julius K. Nyerere, *Uhuru na Ujamaa: Freedom and Socialism*, New York: Oxford University Press, 1968.

[26]"Opening Address by the President of the United States Richard M. Nixon," in World Bank, 1972 Annual Meetings of the Boards of Governors, *Summary Proceedings*, Washington: World Bank, 1972, p. 1 (italics added).

[27]National Science Board, *Environmental Science—Challenge for the Seventies* (1971), in *Regional Environmental Systems Analysis*, Oakridge, Tenn.: Oakridge National Laboratory, 1973, p. 3.

[28]Arthur Koestler, *The Act of Creation*, New York: Dell Publishing Company, 1964.

[29]Robert Jay Lifton, *Boundaries: Psychological Man in Revolution*, New York: Vintage Books, 1970.

[30]See Jack R. Gibb, "Fear and Façade: Defensive Management," in Richard R. Farson (ed.), *Science and Human Affairs*, Palo Alto, Calif.: Science and Behavior Books, 1965, pp. 197–214.

[31]"When the conditions for psychic growth are present, the native initiative of infancy is maintained, and the individual becomes conscious that social constructs experienced by the child as absolutes, since he has had no hand in shaping them, may in fact be altered by the impact of his will. For many, however, the attainment of this level of awareness is impossible, because the general conditions for growth are absent through some form of psychic deprivation, or because the social institutions specifically resist the possibility of active roles, especially on the part of the young. Schools encourage passive acquiescence and demand obedience to rules the child has had no hand in shaping. Other social institutions are equally authoritarian." C. George Benello, "Group Organization and Socio-political Structure," in C. George Benello and Dimitrios Roussopoulos (eds.), *The Case for Participatory Democracy*, New York: Viking, 1971, p. 41. Copyright © 1971 by C. George Benello and Dimitri Roussopoulos. Reprinted by permission of Grossman Publishers.

[32]*Environmental Quality: Second Annual Report, 1971, op. cit.*, p. 96.

[33]Welford V. Ruckelshaus, 2 ERC 1123, 1125, 1 FLR 20065, 20067 (1971), quoted in *ibid.*, pp. 176–177.

[34]U. Thant, U.N. *Press Release*, SG/SM/1467, Chicago (May 1971).

[35]Philip S. Haring, *Political Morality*, Cambridge, Mass.: Schenkman, 1970, p. 7.

Index

77 7 6 5 4 3

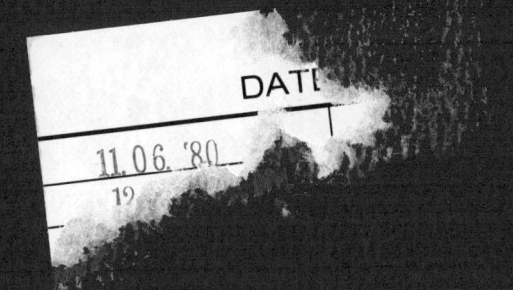